Life oh life! Let it be

🦢 *A FLIGHT OF DELIGHT* 🦢

ANCIENT VEDIC WISDOM FOR THE MODERN WORLD

Jyotikar Pattni

Aum hrim shrim Sri MahaGanadhipattaye namoh namah.

Printed in Victoria, Canada

Note for Librarians: a cataloguing record for this book that includes Dewey Classification and US Library of Congress numbers is available from the National Library of Canada. The complete cataloguing record can be obtained from the National Library's online database at:
www.nlc-bnc.ca/amicus/index-e.html
ISBN 1-4120-2107-3

TRAFFORD

This book was published on-demand in cooperation with Trafford Publishing.
On-demand publishing is a unique process and service of making a book available for retail sale to the public taking advantage of on-demand manufacturing and Internet marketing. On-demand publishing includes promotions, retail sales, manufacturing, order fulfilment, accounting and collecting royalties on behalf of the author.

Suite 6E, 2333 Government St., Victoria, B.C. V8T 4P4, CANADA
Phone 250-383-6864   Toll-free 1-888-232-4444 (Canada & US)
Fax 250-383-6804   E-mail sales@trafford.com   Web site www.trafford.com
TRAFFORD PUBLISHING IS A DIVISION OF TRAFFORD HOLDINGS LTD.
Trafford Catalogue #04-0031   www.trafford.com/robots/04-0031.html

10   9   8   7   6   5   4   3

⚞ River life ⚟

Rivers flow, through mountains, rifts, greenlands, highlands, deserts, valleys, and rough places, in perpetual cycles of water currents. Seaward bound, they eventually merge in oneness with the grand divine ocean.

We are but different rivers flowing with different energies and different forces, in different directions. At last, we merge in oneness with the pathless ocean of 'eternity', the sheer coincidence of which meet the pathless eternal sky in delight of twilight, at the sunrises and at the sunsets. The dawn and the dusk are divine moments of eternal time.

Life perpetuates, rotates, revolves, and evolves in Karma - act or deed or inertia. Every single process of our life is profoundly significant to our Soul. Although our paths may be different in the capering flight of river life, we meet together in destiny.

All things connect by energy and force. All things are inter-related together, somehow, somewhere, in somewhat profound sense. Our paths meet, for a reason and a purpose beyond the intellectual and emotional spectrum.

Our paths may be different, our fates may be different, our personalities may be different in the collective web of karmic threads, but our soul compassion unites us together in the light of delight!

Life oh life let it be what it may be. Let it be, come what may. Face it, accept it, grit it, but grin and shrug it away. Life oh life! Let it be a great shadow across the green pastures, which looses itself to the dusk. Life oh Life! Let it be a flight of the river.

Life oh life! Let it be 'a flight of delight'.

∽ *Light a candle of delight with your smile* ~

Despair not. Do not be depressed. Do not feel lonely. Do not be afraid. Do not quit. Take deep breaths and empty all your burdens, no matter what. Nurture your weathered spirit with love. Heal your wounded heart, gracefully and compassionately with profoundness.

Come oh human child, realise that our human world is wounded and weeping more than we could ever understand. Have fathomless faith in Nature. Trust your "insight", truthfully, gently, and precisely, in seeking help. Learn to listen in profound silence. We all need someone to lean on no matter what. What really does matter is that we lean on Mother Nature whose magnificent charisma and divinity manifests beyond the wholesome reality. Be happy eternally and give happiness to others. You do not need an I.Q. to be happy. Life is full of sorrows and struggles but Divine Bliss is our essential nature and destiny. Life oh life! Let it be a flight of delight.

Waste not your time anymore brooding, moaning, and complaining. Stop living a grey life. Start living a wonderful fuller life with wonderful rainbows. A Life that is filled with spiritual harmony, eternal joy, true compassionate love, healthy laughter's, simple fun, real happiness, and infinite wisdom.

Stop justifying the material matter. You came into this world empty-handed and you shall die empty-handed too. Realise your true spiritual essence and justify your existence.

Why do we have to exercise so much power, force, and aggression when we can obtain, gain, and possess everlasting hope and everlasting faith, with love, compassion, and peace. Take refuge in profound quietness, and merge in oneness with the charioteer of your soul in silence. Commit to your Soul. Anticipate in reaching the distant star of destiny. Life oh life! Let it be a flight of delight.

ᔕ DEDICATION ᕫ

Dedicated to my beloved brother Dr. Bharat Kaku Pattni (a compassionate spirit of life), who passed away into the spiritual world at the age of forty-two, in Knoxville, Tennessee, U.S.A., in August 1999.

A profound silence of prayer without words is better than lyrics of words put together when that profound silence captures the delightful glory of this magnificent eternal nature in a cosmic marriage of 'oneness' with the soul infinite. Words cannot adequately or appropriately express the joy and the delight of that one eternal light of truth, which refracts through the prism of our third eye, a rainbow of seven rays of enlightenment. Silence is the mother of humanity. Profound silence is blissfully divine. Profound silence manifests before life and profound silence manifests after life. Silence is the language of the soul. In profound silence reposes the final beatitude of truth.

The world of spirits is mystically unknown. The nightingale with its glittering stars is mystically beautiful. It is here on the known earth, the inhabitants are torn and numbed. The earth is filled with, distant echoes of 'all this, that and the other' the human ego, an illusion of falsity, and complex web of political power controls. The beautiful human existence is torn, fragmented, differentiated in numbness by all the loud noises, hasty wars, sudden tragedies, and inexplicable hurt.

May we never cease to pray in silence at the dawn and the dusk for all the beautiful spirits in the spiritual world who fill our empty space with most extra ordinary energy, fathomless love, and fathomless hope.

Peace and harmony be with the spiritual world.

Aum Shantih Shantih Shantih.

August 2003

ACKNOWLEDGEMENTS

I am more than grateful to God almighty supreme and my great parents for having given me this life - the human existence. I am more than grateful to be able to benevolently experience, the merging in fusion, of the delight of sacrificial fire of the earth and the delight of the illuminating radiance of the omnipotent sun.

My wife is my best friend. Her support has been profound. I am grateful to her for cherishing my human integrity with her impartial, unbiased, impersonal, and objective friendship.

I am grateful to Suzanne Colomba DiVirgilio for editing the final text of the manuscripts and for her encouragement.

Thanks to my publishing team at Trafford Publishers for their support.

Thanks to Kamlesh Vijay Kotedia for creating a unique cover design.

Guru Mata Shree Rukshmaneeben K Joshi always upheld her faith in my talent and skills, doubtlessly. Guru Mata's faith made me believe in myself.

Without 'Shiva's', spiritual inspiration, I would not have been able to complete, revise and re-update this book.

In happiness, I remain at the feet of God almighty eternal supreme; whereat I surrender in silence as a humble servant of humanity and an imperfect talent of life. Life oh life! Let it be "A flight of delight".

November 2003

⟡ CONTENTS ⟡

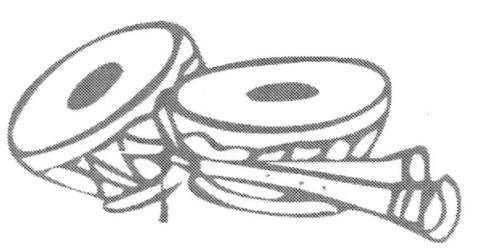

❧ FOREWORD ❧

The problem with the 'life gene' pool is that there is no lifeguard as such. We live and survive with our own risk. We thrive and survive, regardless of the magnitude of our swimming proficiency. We depend on "mind". We rely on "thoughts". We live and survive on memories and the shadows of the memories created in the subconscious mind from our experiences.

Experience is a wisdom that we do not get, until just after we need it, or just after it has happened. Experience is profound in silence. It requires great patience. 'Experience' is paternally associated with the spirit of life. Experience is not academic, nor is it institutional; rather it is the essence of evolution in life. Whether we seek 'experience' or encounter 'experience', we travel through it in the passage of time.

In time, we encounter life's moments. In time, we wonder in our thoughts thinking and convincing ourselves of the most convenient form of survival. Experience is an absolute lifetime process of learning and in this process, we mould in spirit. We face life, we accept it, we grit it, we grin at it, we shrug it off, and we evolve in our essential nature.

'Change' is the very characteristic of transformation from one form into another form. 'Form' is dynamic. Soul is static. Soul is sacred and soul is compassionate. Essentially, we are compassionate human fellows in nature and we have the innate talent to love and to be together in compassionate union. In love, the whole person cherishes the subtleties of the soul.

'Togetherness' is a divine human strength and in togetherness, universal peace transcends from eternity onto Earth. 'Togetherness' is a meeting of earth and heaven in time and space. 'Togetherness' is a moment of prayer. When we pledge allegiance to our inner most spirit of life, and believe in one universal faith – the fathomless faith, we leap into the spiritual planes of the eternal para-existence. We transform progressively from the mundane gross physical earthly survival into the physical existence, when we accept life whole-heartedly and take responsibility of our karma.

When we gracefully study and evaluate our life process retrospectively beyond the wholesome life into an absolute life experience, we evolve onto the meta-physical existence onwards onto the spiritual existence.

Because of karmic evolution, we realise that the present lifetime is a result of the past lifetime and a potential for the future lifetime. The 'lifetime' may be a moment, a phase, an experience, or a daunting survival of impermanence. Compassionate love and integrity of altruism are god given talents to human kind for bringing 'togetherness' in humanity.

'Oneness' is a representative of the divine blissful ocean of eternity, wherein all the rivers merge and loose their names, form, and ego identity. Each of us is a uniquely different river with different form, name, and energy. We are bound to the physical plane of the earth and the green pastures of materiality by 'karma'. There is no 'physical lifeguard', as such, fully responsible in merging us to the divine ocean of eternity. No grand maestro except the everlasting unconditional love and inspiration of the eternal supreme para existing soul infinite, that which is verily the cosmic soul.

The micro cosmic essential individual human soul and the macro cosmic eternal infinite soul, merge in 'oneness', in the ocean of eternity or the fathomless sky in delight of twilight of the dawn and the dusk. This 'oneness' is a pathless eternity whereat truth reposes.

Truth is a formless eternity that transcends onto this earth in time and space to take a form. 'Aum' emanates as the primordial divine word, symbol, form, vibration, prayer-dialogue, devotion, music, hymn, poetry, philosophy, and science of intricate nature. It is a meeting of the light of the Sun and the light of the human sacrifice in the twilight of prayer, devotion, humanity, and profound silence. The purpose of human life is to sacrifice its whole towards realising its true divine higher self, that which is verily the soul. The Vedic delight implies inner fathomless peace, and inner fathomless happiness.

Human sacrifice, in sacred prayer, sacred devotion, sacred compassionate love, and sacred profound silence, is a light of fire, which beholds the flame of the spirit of life. It is essentially the fire of human life.

A flight of delight is an unfolding pilgrimage of the soul in the passage of human lifetime. The imperfect personality faces the two faces of life (the known 'impermanence' and the mystical 'unknown'). The personality then accepts life as it is, in its fullest. The personality wants to become a spirit of life, but grits with fear. In the passage of time, the spirit of life survives gross physical world wherein all that is 'certain' and 'known', bring about, fear, insecurity, inhibitions, habits, hypocrisy, power warfare, hatred, anguish, death, and impermanence, to all that is 'life spirit'. In this impermanence, the spirit of life thrives on to grow more powerful in status, name, prestige, and form. Peace and happiness fails to prevail in the impermanence of all that is 'known' material world.

Some things we will only know in part, some things we will only understand in parts, some things we will only realise in parts. Some things we will never ever know or understand. Those things that we may never fully know or understand are best handed up to time and a higher order (call it what you may), towards which all our destiny converge in togetherness without questions, doubts, and differences. Watching the sunset, and the swans making their way home, there is serenity in the golden leaf that flew away herewith a prayer, a sincere wish, and an unconditional love. Time flies, suns rise and suns set. The soft pebbles on the shores touch our feet; the music of the night consoles without any instruments, the stars in the nightingale brings us a solace without words.

Life oh life! Let it be what it may be, let it be. Let it be, come what may. Face it, accept it, grit it, but grin and shrug it away. The spirit of life becomes an artist of infinite beauty, and a scientist of the soul. It begins to understand with compassion. It evolves and transforms. It awakens to the light of the Sun. It becomes energised. Like a river, the spirit of life capers to the sound of music. The spirit of life experiences life in the passage of time. Guided by the rain, the rustling trees, the masterful sun, the dissolving earth, and the teeming vast sky it takes a flight of delight to merge in the grand ocean of compassion, loosing its name, form, and intellectual ego.

Compassion is the essential nature of the soul. 'Maithuna' (coming together) is the merging marriage of twilight, the meeting together of the light of the soul and the light of the Cosmic Sun, at the dawn and the dusk.

The Sunrise and the Sunset are extra special moments of magnificent beauty unparalleled and perennial. The grand maestro manifests without words in profoundest silence.

We meet to share our experiences, in somewhat profound mystical sense. In time, we experience what we have shared in the briefest encounter. In time, we begin to see things as they are, rather than, as they should be.

Sorrow, grief, and loss come to us all. If we become divinely fully aware of this fact before adversities batter us, we are able to be alone in our own company without the necessity of 'all this, that and the other'.

Whatever act or deed, we may think, feel, and do; we eventually accredit or discredit none other than our own true soul divine. War is nothing more than a collation of fear from insecurity, anger, hatred, envy, betrayal, distrust, greed, lust, lure, desire, and political manipulation. Fear is the root cause of all diseases. Fear is the root cause of all unhappiness. Fear is the root of all evil.

Whatsoever we sow, thus we shall reap. In whatsoever we invest our time, our energy, our thoughts, our efforts, our whole that we shall eventually reap. All said and done, what really matters in all this, that and the other is what really sustains us when all else (this, that and the other) fails us. What really matters is whether you can be alone in your own company and be at peace with your spirit of life in the quiet moments.

When all else fails, when we are out on a limb, it is our duty, our human obligation to safeguard and nurture our spiritual integrity. All this, that, and the other does not truly matter. Life oh life! Let it be. Let it be what it may be. Face it, accept it, grit it, but grin and shrug it away. Life oh life! Let it be 'A flight of delight'.

Mr. Jyotikar Pattni and Mrs. Hasmita Jyotikar Pattni

November 2003

⚞ PREFACE ⚟

Salutations and reverence to eternity and eternal inspirations. I bow to the great almighty supreme God, who resides in your soul, in my soul, in the magnificent nature, and who manifests beyond the wholesome galaxies of the stars, the moon, the sun, the orbit, the planets, and the spiritual planes. Obeisance to every single individual spirit of life, and, every single scripture of divinity, that generates a word of wisdom. Time and eternity has afforded me this human life. I treasure it and cherish it as a precious gift, as if it were a blessing from eternal God.

Truth is a pathless eternity upon which God reposes. This truth manifests in our Soul – the very seat of God. The Soul is the purest nectar of compassion and beauty. The Soul is the crown of "all-pervading truth".

When words collect together to form lyrics, with utmost compassion, they begin to sound meaningful, profound, and energetic. The written word, albeit composed through a sacred process, is still a mere consolation of, compassion, expression, interpretation, translation, reconstruction and "that which is this", all incomplete in absolute sense. Life is never complete in absolute sense because there is an unexpected end to it too. Therefore, nothing in life is absolute, except the essence of life itself, which is soul divine bliss. Our life is a journey of the soul, in absolute sense (beyond the five multi-sensory realities) alias the sixth sense, which is the intuition and the insight. Self-discovery is an unfolding pilgrimage of light – A flight of delight.

Many persons claim to be holy and render words of wisdom to form their followers or to form followers of their organisation. Many teachers claim to possess the knowledge of life. Many preachers preach the doctrines and philosophies of religions. Modern religion is fragmented. There is huge scale segmentation, division, and segregation, of 'faith', because of 'reason' and 'cause', in the human mind. 'Faith' has become a convenience rather than a morale sacrifice to discover the soul, in an unfolding universe of uncertain time and uncertain environment.

The gap between the rich and the poor gets wider. The modern humankind is moving away from the 'roots' of 'altruism'. We are living in the world full of noise and haste. Many intellectuals have created powerful technologies, social infrastructures, economic warfare, political referendums, and institutional bureaucracies. This modern world of intellectual and ego power is full of heroism. Personality is never perfect. Personality is never absolute. However, few truly great saints, god incarnate savants, and sages have emerged in our centuries. These include Buddha, Krishna, Jesus, Mohammed, Confucius, Socrates, and others who have left significant wisdom. Their profound words of wisdom have been, reconstructed, and revived, perpetually with the elapsing time by profound discourses and sacred spiritual dialogues. These words of wisdom have been subsequently, reconstructed, compiled, and composed. Consequently, the original word has not remained a direct communication from the spoken word of the mouth to the listening word of the ears. Hence, we pledge our allegiance to faith with inferential reference and profound reliance on the written word of wisdom within an imperfect frame of circumstances.

On the one hand, we are struggling to survive reality and on the other hand, there is the innate quest for eternity. One is the survival of the fittest and the other is the free spirit of life that has justified its existence with true essential existence. Every single saint or sage or pious person striving to attain moksha (total spiritual liberation) repose on the pathless eternal truth that manifests in the soul. This eternal truth is the same for every single human person. The eternal truth manifests in profound silence of reverence in oneness with the soul. Great scientists and original thinkers like, Einstein, Darwin, Pluto, Archimedes, Marie Curie, Pythagoras, Trio, Isaac Newton, William James, Benjamin Whorf, Niels Bohr, Carl Jung, Krishnamurti, and others likewise have co-related the reality to the twofold aspects of truth. One is virtue of the fact and the other is substance of the existence. All great scientists of our centuries have considered the Vedas scientific in knowing and understanding (albeit not absolutely), the essence of existence. Fear creates a grey chaos between the divine eternal spirit of life and the ego. The 'ego' is constantly in conflict with the spirit of life and this conflict manifests in ailments, distress, and pain.

The goal of every life spirit is total spiritual liberation and total spiritual emancipation. Emancipation is to be free from the cages of the modern society, to be free from the fears of the reality, to be free from the religious doctrines (founded upon the sects, new theories, thesis, anti-thesis, synthesis, philosophies, and congressional debates). Emancipation means to be 'unconditionally' or 'absolutely' free, to be unconditionally and universally loving, to be enlightened, in, oneness of divinity with the soul, and the 'eternity' - to be 'unconditionally' free from 'falsehood'. This is self-realisation and it is more than just relatively, just perceptively, or just retrospectively happy. It is infinitely blissful and it is a harmony between life and soul.

I find that understanding ourselves is deeper than just knowing our personalities. When we understand each other in substance, in essence, we come to the same wavelengths and we communicate. Hence our existence becomes justified by our relationships being nurtured, by our essential substance being awakened, by our expression of the eyes, the spoken word, and the written word merging with the listening word in the compassionate human feeling.

Nurturing divinely, the human relationships, is beyond I.Q. In order to communicate with each other at the same level we require a oneness that we totally understand the virtue of the fact of life as well as the essence of the substance of the very existence. There is no complexity in 'what is' except in the ambitious urges and intellectual escapes that we conveniently undertake in order to reason and avoid our internal conflict.

Our basic problem is not 'the world around us', or 'the reality', that is the virtue of the fact. Our basic problem is within us, but we have to realise this profoundly not because the Vedas or some sacred anthology said so. The communication is a transformation process. Suffering in the process of transformation is inevitable. Even Buddha suffered. But when suffering is regarded in the light of discovering the naked truth, then this suffering brings eternal joy (delight), knowing that, our final beatitude reposes on truth, and that we are in harmony with our lives. Every new dawn brings us fresh opportunities, newer chances, and newer hopes. Take one day at a time. Slowly, steadfast, and consistently, persevere towards the twilight of the dusk, with beautiful orange sunset merging day to night.

Absolute truth does not manifest in, any temple, any church, or any mosque. It manifests in the shrine of our own spirit of life. It reposes in your soul, in my soul and in the soul of this magnificent nature. To communicate in 'word' of the feeling of this 'oneness' implies that we understand each other, we understand ourselves, we understand the eternal nature and we discover the word of 'oneness'. This kind of level of communication requires that we practice silence and quietness in harmony with great determination and zest. It is the discovering of oneself, of enquiring into the eternal truth. The divine power is an embodiment of 'energy' and 'eternal force' combined. This power is authentic power and it is a sacred gift to us by eternity.

I do not claim to be anything other than a mere universal spirit of life. Imperfect as I may be, I am trying to listen and learn the manifestations of your soul, of my soul, and of the soul of this magnificent nature. I am just an imperfect talent of life in an imperfect modern world. Reality is as imperfect as the experience it renders through living. Existence is essentially imperfect. However, it becomes substantially justifiable only when our perception transforms us into profound human fellows.

We never cease to learn. When we cease to learn, we cease to evolve and hence we cease to nurture the substance and the essence of the very existence.

Vedic wisdom is authentic elucidation of the spiritual nature of the soul and its journey in an absolute lifetime. The collective Vedic wisdom comprises *the Vedas and the Upanishads collectively known as sruttee (compilation of hymns, sacred lyrics, mantras, and doctrines of metaphysical, para psychological and philosophical union of the soul with the cosmic nature in time and space). Furthermore, the Ved-puranas (meaning historical inferences and sacred apocalypse) contain The Bhagawat Gita, Shrimad Bhagawatt puranam, the Guru Geeta, Siva puranas, the Ramayan, the Ved-shastras, the dhammmapada, and more. Ved-puranas are 'smritee' (historical anthologies).*

Vedic wisdom is some five thousand years ancient albeit it's exact origin is an approximation only. The Vedas are scientific, philosophical, and poetic.

When I began to write this book, I encountered severest adversities and many obstacles, all which were immeasurably beyond my control. The following activities brought solace to my wounded spirit: Creativity in fine arts, painting, playing music, dancing, cooking for others, reading anthologies, writing poetries, wandering with nature, being simply funny with children and old people, comforting grief, giving solace to lonely persons, sitting quietly in silence or mantra meditation, physical yoga on music, and, reciting the Vedas, Upanishads, and ancient scriptures. It is in these activities, that I feel closest to God and divine eternity. The Vedas inspire me substantially. My spirit dances to the rhythm of love with great profound inspiration and quintessence.

The human experience is a total creative experience in the talent of putting together in 'oneness', the thought, the feeling, the movement, the compassion, inertia of life, and the essence of the soul (extra ordinary insight). This experience albeit not absolute, is 'total harmony' bringing 'total happiness' in 'total freedom' of the mind, body, and the spirit of life. The journey of life is a pilgrimage of the soul through different, difficult, arduous, platforms of reality by virtue, yet interesting, awakening, magnificently blossoming and enriching discovery of the great richness embodied within the soul. It is an insight beyond the multifarious living. It is a sheer joy that transcends harmony upon realisation and brings us together to the very roots of our human existence. I welcome you compassionately and affectionately to share with me my "insight". May I hold your attention in 'togetherness' and wish you every happiness, harmony, joy, and love. May God grant you the serenity to accept the things you cannot change the courage to change the things you can and the 'great wisdom' to know the difference. Life oh life let it be flight of delight. Rejoice, dance, sing, rhyme, and play the music of love. Immerse yourself in the deep compassionate self-less, unconditional love. Love begets love. When your perception merges in oneness with my written words, glory will manifest in compassionate togetherness. Let us light the candle of delight in togetherness. Life oh life! Let it be a flight of delight!

1. INTRODUCTION 🐚

By the grace of God almighty supreme in whom we all take our final refuge. [1]

The final beatitude of life-breath (pranna) reposes on 'truth' (sattya). Soul is the seat of highest compassion, and, 'compassionate love' is the purest nectar of truth. Truth is infinite and infinite eternity is the sublime truth in the soul. In enlightenment only there is a delight of joy of infinite bliss. [2]

Beauty is pure glamour and charisma. Beauty is magnificent and eternally blissful. Beauty is artistically intricate and scientifically perfect. Beauty is the truth and the reality of life. Beauty is 'Mother Nature'. Beauty is simple and compassionate. Beauty is in the Sunrise and in the sunset. Beauty is in the glittering night-sky and in the vast ocean. Beauty is in music and in the finesse of arts. Beauty is in natural talent and in the soul. Beauty is in the eyes and in the word of expression. Beauty is in the form and in the formless silence. Beauty is in the truth and in the delight. Beauty is in the exquisite rivers. Beauty is in symphony. Beauty is in the rapture of the shores. Beauty is in the pathless pastures. Beauty is in the roar of the sea. Beauty is in the light of the lesson and in the delight of emancipation. This is all you need to conquer in absolute oneness of profound silence, profound wisdom, and profound living. I invoke thine divine light to bring you delightful beauty in all that you see and feel. Life oh life! Let me leave behind a trail of beauty, serenity, joy, hope, and light to all the rivers.

---

[1] He who knows not the eternal syllable of the Vedas, the highest point of wisdom upon which the Gods repose, what business has he with the Vedas? Only its knowers sit here in peace and concord with the magnificent glory of God. Know the magnificent nature, the all-pervading 'vishwaswaroop' cosmic form of God almighty. RigVeda 1, 164.

[2] The Upanishads are the sublime most constituent of the Rig Vedas. 'Delight' is the manifestation of divine love, 'Consciousness is the manifestation of the soul force and 'Existence' is the manifestation of the being. In delight, Brahman is reality. In love, Brahman is divinity. In consciousness Brahman is contemplation of the spiritual, vision alias the third eye. In 'super consciousness', Brahman is purest nectar of the vessel of 'Soma'. [Page 75 of The three branches of India's life tree by Sri Chinmoy/ Aum publication]

There are five aspects to every life spirit namely, our body, our mind, our dwelling, our work, and our nature. We want a healthy body in a healthy mind in a healthy lifestyle in a healthy environment in a healthy nature. Health is wealth, and good health is the core prelude to spiritual living. When the mind and the body are both healthy, then and only then is the spirit healthy, in an environment that is pure. To accomplish total freedom in our life, we need energy and strength. The 'life-breath' ('pranna) is a vital force of energy, and the breath we take in is crucial to survival. Total emancipation invokes the flame of delight - the fiery spirit of life, with greatest vigour and enthusiasm, to attain the inner power of the soul, and to attain the inner spiritual strength, to conquer the super-consciousness. [3,4]

When the spirit of life is in direct congruence with the magnificent nature, it becomes sublimely subtle and quiet. It begins to listen to its 'insight'. It begins to learn in quintessence. It begins to evolve in karmic progressions of the human life. It embraces 'delight' in compassion. [5] Oh child of nature, remember now, remember always, the sacredness of rivers, mountains, rustling trees, freshness of green pastures. Oh child of nature, remember now, remember always the beauty of the dawn and the dusk.

---

[3] Per Sri Chinmoy, the five distinct sheaths of relativity are: The gross physical; The vital force alias breath; The mental conscious; The Super Conscious vision; and; The eternal bliss or the pure. Three planes of matter are the gross physical, the body, and the subtle INSIGHT - causal. The vital force breath of life, the mental conscious and the super conscious governs the body. 'Pranna', is the vital force of energy emanating from food, atmosphere, and yoga (total way of godhead in purest form of living, existing, and, opening to the nature).

[4] Yajurveda 19.9: The self-discovering process must be ignited with the mightiest of all vigour. Aum, Tejo asi tejo moayi dehi, aum viryam asi viryam moayi dehi, aum balam asi balam moayi dehi, aum Ojo asi ojo moayi dehi, aum Manyur asi manyur moayi dehi, aum sahao asi saho moayi dehi. In profound Vedic wisdom, we invoke all the 64,000 energies of the nature and all the 72,000 vital life breaths to give us vigour, vitality, endurance, patience, fortitude, purity, good clean food (sattvic annam), good clean cotton cloths, good clean mind, good clean environment, good clean vibrations ascending and descending the seven chakras of the body.

[5] The great American philosopher Thoreau acclaimed Vedas to be scientifically soul searching. The firm belief of Sir William James is absolute truth in Isaac Newton as much as the Vedas for they both talk about the same things in almost different languages. Both are profoundly inspiring and illuminating.

When the silence of the profound prayer of the soul, the profound mantra (incantation/ sound), the profound twilight of sunrises and sunsets, the profound orb, the profound earthly atmosphere, and the profound para-existing eternity, altogether, merge in oneness, a fusion of delight emerges. It is in that oneness; we conquer the light of God and embrace it.[6]

'Truth' is a light of delight that manifests in a prism of enlightenment, comprising total self-dedication - sacrifice of life, grace, harmony, and divinity of the oneness of the soul and cosmic nature, fathomless faith and spiritual insight. Truth is compassion of the soul, and compassionate beauty is the truth. Nature is magnificent because god almighty supreme made rivers flow. Nature is but God's magnificent form in fire (the sun), Water (oceans), ether (the atmosphere), earth (the universe), Air (Galaxy), and Wind (Rain & storms). These constituents are infinitely meticulous and intricate. The Earth with its quality of smell, Water with its quality of taste, Wind with its quality of touch, Fire with its quality of glow, and Air (the galaxy) with its quality of sound. All these elements along with the element intellect make finite perception possible. Oceans, mountains, rivers, lakes, trees, forests, flowers, grass, deserts, valleys, singing birds, clouds, the galaxy, the universe, the life breath, the spiritual planes and beyond the wholesome sky, stretches the magnificent nature of God almighty supreme. In this supremacy that is beyond the finite perception manifests the infinite spirit of life. The cosmic nature is but God's beauty. It speaks for itself. This is the absolute truth. This is all you need know. This is all we need perceive in profound silence. [78]

---

[6] RigVeda1, 164: What thing I am I do not know; I wander secluded, burdened by my mind. When the first born word of truth has come to me, I receive a share in that self-same word.

[7] Per Ken-Upanishad, it is above the known nature and beyond the unknown fathomless skies and galaxy. It is infinitely sublime and it is an intuitive perception. It is the Universal God. When the poet unites sublimely and quietly with his poetry on God in oneness, he becomes infinitely awakened. He becomes the enlightened soul. Philosophy and poetry merge in oneness to express the insight and the super-conscious feelings of the seer (the personified spirit of life). Upanishads and the essence of pranna (breath of life) are inseparable. Therefore, a human kind is life energy spirit.

[8] Within infinite mysticism manifests the eternal truth of light. The beam of truth is eminent at the dawn and the dusk when all the rivers meet in silent prayer mode of the entire cosmos.

The prime focus and objective of composing my innate expression on the soul and its journey is to provide enlightenment, solace, and authentic compassion, affectionately, for the evolving spirit (the force between an identity and soul). It comprises rich contemporary poetry and experiential philosophies of human life. Life oh life let it be. Let it be a sacred experience of profoundness, and, let it be a compassionate life of integrity.

Life oh life! Let it be 'a flight of delight', depicts the flight of the river (spirit of life) unfolding in sacred pilgrimage of the essential existence. It is the cry of a free winged bird 'the spirit of life' – 'Hamnssa' within us that caper to symphonies of nature. It is the journey of human life, from gross physical existence onwards on to the final beatitude of truth in humanity, karmic evolution, compassion, sacrifice, devotion, and sacred dialogue of prayers.

'A flight of delight' is a magnificent portrayal of human life processes. A view portrayed by the eastern eyes, a view expressed by the western mind and a vision felt by the loving compassionate spirit of life. I am whispering into your ears through my written lyrics, 'I am in love with life'.

Music is my life. Music and poetry are complementary to each other. I am nothing without them. Music, art, dancing and poetry are my emotional roots. Life without music and poetry is a bare life without love and compassion.

Every life's spirit is a precious gift of nature. There is a structured plan for every breath of life on this earth. It is a plan that no 'man power' can alter. Every life breath has a defined wholesome purpose to fulfil. You and I may not always fully understand the ways of this unfolding universe. Conflict is but an inevitable means of realising that experience can only speak in profound silence retrospectively, introspectively, and, perceptively. It is the true content of self-discovery. No matter how brief or how elaborate the substance is, the content is more important than its form. So, pledge allegiance to your spirit, stand up, and deliver your true spirit of nature. Only through spiritual experience can we understand and perceive the true divine beauty. We have to become it (subtle beauty) to know the divine truth of the Vedas (composition of word, mantra, lyrics, poem, philosophy, music, and dance).

To be able to recite spiritually and to be able to listen profoundly beyond the five senses, in quietness and in awareness, is the essence of profound wisdom of the soul. [9]

The eyes of the eagle capture farthest vision. The mind of the dolphin perceives deepest emotions and thoughts. The memory of the elephant never fails. The intellect of the human person can reason and cause objectively or subjectively. The courage of the lion is fearless. The speed of the cheetah is unparalleled. The serenity of the magnificent nature is beyond the wholesome material life. The spirit of life takes a flight of delight with all the foregoing qualities of life and eventually transforms or evolves into a free winged spirit of eternity 'Hamnssa'. A flight of delight is a sacred journey of the soul, a penultimate pilgrimage of the atmospheric orb, based on life experience. Sacrifice is inevitably and essentially a joy, rather than a burden of life experience itself. It is an absolute means of justifying our existence rather than an intellectual reason because there is delight in the light of truth. Vedic perspective implies serene insight and right evaluation of life, retrospectively in karma (act). Vedic experience entails total growth of mind body and soul. Vedic experience is scientifically proven, authentic, and valid form of remedial measure. 'Saram' in Sanskrit means insight. Insight never follows noises, chaos, doubts, clustered intelligence, conditioned ego, error and terror, tragedies and misfortunes. Saram (insight) follows in silence in secret communion between the third eye and the cosmic eternity. Saram enters the blissful state of the lingham purush (human kind) known as the throat chakra and illuminates the lingham i.e., the head of the human kind. The spirit of life cries: 'Life oh life! Let it be the light of the glittering night sky. Let it be a glory of the sacred fire of the sun at the dawn and the dusk.'

---

[9] The Godhead has built this universe in a complex metamorphosis of worlds, which we find both within us and outside us, subjectively cognised and objectively sensed. It is a rising tier of earth's and heavens; It is a stream of diverse waters; It is a light of seven rays; It is a hill of many plateau's; It is an ocean of seven seas; It is a universe of seven continents. It is absolutely and infinitely intricate nature; It is a profound learning process; It is mindfully super-conscious; It is passionately compassionate and it is magnificently beyond the material world stretching into the divine world – "AUM TAT SAT" (thou art the absolute truth) and "SAT CHIT ANAND" (pure existence, pure consciousness and pure bliss). RV 1

Per Vedas, truth manifests in the soul. 'Truth' is perceived, discovered, nurtured, and realised, by its seer, through profound experience. This experience is a delightful light of joy that is expressed with an extra ordinary talent of the spirit of life. This talent is the insight to all super conscious avenues of the cosmic aura, the celestial aura, and the earthly aura.

Insight manifests in the multitude of light. Insight opens the third eye and travels through the Crown of the head. Insight reveals the path to salvation. It brings cosmic visions. Insight removes the gravitational force of the earthly matter from the human kind and elevates the human kind to a higher platform. Insight brings compassion with an extra ordinary depth of wisdom and it makes one smile. Insight removes darkness and illuminates. Insight becomes music of the spirit of life and the poetic lyrics of the true seer. Insight becomes the beauty of the magnificent nature. Insight becomes the nectar of eternity 'soma' (the highest point in galaxy where the truth infinite reposes) and the ultimate sublime sweetness of eternity in the crown chakra. Insight becomes the musician, the grand maestro. Insight becomes the player that capers to the heroism within the seer's heart. Insight makes the heavens smile. Insight is simply beyond words. Insight is the sky of the cosmic light and delight of the oceans. Insight is the rhythm of the valleys and the dance of the rivers. Insight is Shiva (God).

Light is the beginning of Godhead and light is the all-pervading truth. Delight is the life of God, manifesting with a smile of the universal oneness. Light is the all-pervading energy of God and delightful is God's energy. God is super conscious magnificent glory of blissfulness, consciousness, and altruism. Such is the daring fiery of the Agnee the sacred fire of the energy of God. Agnee first becomes insight and finally becomes the hue of the sun.

The foremost praises in Vedas go to 'Agnee', the infinite fire of the Sun, in delight. The light of the soul awakens, illuminates, and enlightens with 'Agnee' in delight. The Vedas never cease to glow in mantras (sacred incantations). 'Agnee' is the divine fire, the priestly minister of the sacrifice, the offerer of oblation, and the supreme giver of treasure and the everlasting infinite delight of light.

May the infinite light of the Sun 'never failing'; protect us from dull darkness and drudged ignorance. May the face of the truth in the orange hue Sun illuminate us. May the eyes of the truth grace 'insight' in our vision. May the heart of the truth embrace us in togetherness of soul compassion. May the formless infinite truth take the most beautiful form in the magnificent glory of the dawn and the dusk.

Vedas are composite sruttee (aggregate collection of sacred texts and verses). Sruttee is like a true mother, unconditional, universal, and impartial. Vedas provide the roots to scientific living. Vedas mean "knowledge of the truth". Vedas are the universally compassionate wisdom of God & Soul. Vedas do not conform to any specific group of persons, or institutional religions, or cults for that matter. They conform to the rudiments of essential divine life. Vedas teach us universally, consistently, practically, scientifically, and spiritually the true and rational substance of spiritual awakening. There are four main parts to Vedic wisdom namely RIG-VEDA, SAAMA VEDA, YAJUR VEDA, AND ATHARVA VEDA. The fifth one, which is UPA-VEDA, was added later to the 'srutis' (collection of Vedic verses and texts).

They were revealed by the Rishis (sages who wrote Sanskrit) to the four devas (the deity forces of life) namely Agnee (Rig-Veda), Aditya (Yajur-Veda), Vayu (Saam-Veda) and Angiras (Atharva-Veda). This is the constitution of Vedas. I would equate Vedas and Upanishads to 'Cow's milk' and Geeta to the cream from this milk. One has to fully appreciate and understand the Vedas before one can enjoy the Vedic rituals, customs, festivals, celebrations, and various sacred ceremonies.

Vedas give me solace. Vedas give me inspiration. Vedas support my spiritual life. Vedic incantations and sacred Vedic invocations are buoyed towards the Divine one (Brahman) and its divine nature (including sun, rain, sea, wind, fire, dawn, dusk, earth, and sky).

The Vedas bring together the twenty-four 'tattvas' (cosmic principles of existence), the human act, the entire cosmic existence, the infinite light of the Sun, and the formless vac 'Soma' (the nectar of truth) in an almost theatrical philanthropy.

The brief constituents of Vedas are mentioned below:

The Rig-Veda

The Rig-Veda is the heart of the entire Vedas with about 10,552 verses of hymns. Substantial wisdom is contained about spiritual peace, prosperity, and spiritual emancipation to a better world (a more uplifted life). Rig-Veda comprises four sub-sections namely the Samhitas, the Brahmanas, the Aranyakas, and the Upanishads. The Bhagawatt Gita is extended from the Aranyakas and the Upanishads. Rig-Vedas focuses on hymns and musical connotation of the hymns.

The Saama-Veda

Saama-Veda comprises mainly liturgical selections from the rig-Veda arranged for melodious chanting of shlokas and hymns. There are about 2,000 verses in all. Saam-Vedas focuses on sacred songs and poetic compilation of songs of praises in the highest Sanskrit rhythm. Vedas are also known as 'shlokas'/ (rhythmic hymns).

The Yajur-Veda

Yajur-Veda is also similar to Saama-Veda but focuses more on the condensed intonation of Vedic mantra chanting. The Yajur-Veda is divided into Shukla (white) and Krishna (purple black). Yajur-Vedas focus on 'mantras' (sacred words), 'yantras' (sacred symbols), 'yagna's' (sacred fire), and 'sankalpa' (sacrificial formulae).

The Atharwa-Vedas

The Atharwa Vedas comprises nearly 6,000 verses of prayers, ritual charms, and rites and are unique in their formulation. Atharva-Vedas focuses on practical arts and sciences, spiritual healing, and Ayurvedic healing. Scientific formulae, astrological science, and medical astrology come from Atharwa-Vedas. We shall concentrate on healing attributes of all forms of Vedas with emphasis on Vedic mantras and yantras.

The fifth section namely The Upa-Vedas, conveniently rather than originally, outlines the extended aspects of the atharwa-Vedas. There are four sub sections to their composition, namely:

Ayur-vedas

The analogy of Ayurveda is natural life and herbal medicine. It is the science of all naturopathy medicines, preventative and curative remedies, anatomy, physiology, hygiene, and metaphysical & physical surgery.

Dhanur-vedas

Aspects of archery and charioteering

Ghnadharva-Veda

Aspects of performing arts, dances, fine arts, and music

Shthapthya-Veda

Relates to metaphysics. Applied maths and applied physics. These include the visual arts, astrological sciences, scientific discoveries, engineering, architecture, sculpture, painting, modelling, and aircraft.

The Vedangas and Upavedas are collection of sacred texts and verses that augment and apply the Vedas as a comprehensive system of sacred living. For example, the Jyotisha Vedangas elucidates the Vedic astrological science and Kalpa Vedangas defines the rituals and rites in the public, private, domestic, and religious duties of a person.

Four other Vedangas are, expressly dedicated to the purity of mantra recitation through knowledge of phonetics, grammar, poetry, and the compilation of Sanskrit words as a complete literature.

According to the Veda's, the purpose of life is to accomplish spiritual emancipation (in Sanskrit know as 'muktee' or 'moksha'). The essence of Vedic wisdom manifests in compassion and the evolution of the soul in 'karma'.

Vedic wisdom does not preach nor does it convert anyone. It respects and gives utmost self-respect to every single lifestyle. It does not condemn. It reveres every single anthology as a divine seer's expression of the one infinite truth from different platforms. In every beautiful truth there will always remain a tint of imperfection, an oversight, or an error. In all imperfections, oversight, and errors, there will always manifest a tint of truth.

According to Vedas, all profound anthologies are a reflection of profound insight. It does not bring fear in reprimanding sin as such, rather it creates a fathomless hope of removing the darkness, the 'dull-ness', the ignorance, and the grey fog with the glory of Agnee in the Sun. It brings emancipation of the spirit. It looks at life and soul and it correlates life to space, ether, matter, air, water, and fire. Veda's are scientific. The birthright of the Vedas is the 'Himalayas', on the boarders of northern Indian, Nepal, and Tibet. It is an unparalleled wisdom of sages and seers of the Himalayas, in their way of lives. The compilations of Vedas were elucidated in Sanskrit over a period of three thousand years, based on profound insight, also referred to as 'divya-drashtee' in Sanskrit.

'Sannatana' (the eternal or the universal) Dharma (religion) comprises oldest and greatest of all traditions and cultures. 'Sannatana' Dharma is the manifestation of multifarious disciplines of universal truth. It is the union of God and the Individual human Soul. The core wisdom of which elucidate Composite Yoga's (Hatha- physical, Gyann- wisdom, Karma- righteous action, Bhakttee- devotion, and Nirvana- ultimate emancipation), Ayurveda (the medical science), Jyotisha (Vedic astrology), Samakhya (living samskarik alias social life), Vedanta, and Tantra-Yantra (worshipping rites and rituals). 'Sannatana Dharma' (universal Vedic religion) was founded by Rishis (sages & saints) in the Himalayan Mountains, in India. It is based on Vedic philosophy and Vedic mantras. It depicts universal consciousness and cosmic creation. 'Sannatana Dharma' supports and embraces all major religions of the world. Historically speaking the most ancient form of worldly wisdom has manifested in Sanskrit and Latin.

Vedas enlighten us about the evolution of the soul and its spiritual journey from before birth to death and beyond death. According to the Vedas, no one could possibly fully understand human life in absolute terms. However, it is imperative that we as humankind (manushyaavtar) understand that life is absolute and the infinite is unknown in as much as our five multi-sensory human functions are concerned. [10]

---

[10] Vedic mantras have cosmic energy, magnetic energy, electric energy, and spiritual energy.

The Vedas are endless wisdom founded by saints and sages and seers. The Vedas descended on to this earth as a vision of the seers. They are as ancient as ten thousand years, albeit their discovery is some five thousand years ago. It is the language of the revelation of the soul.

The belief of the believer belongs to the phenomenon itself just as the 'word' belongs to the seer of the sacred truth. The beauty of Vedas manifests in the art of the 'word', albeit impossible to capture the exact experience. It is an innate expression of the soul in the most intricate and perfect composition of mantras. The 'word', which comes out of the navel, is like the word that is meant most sincerely, in the most creative sense of the talent, for the most intricate aspect of the phenomenon. It is almost like the scale of a musical note ('sa-re-ga-ma-pa-da-ni), a profound word encompassing the life breath of the soul - 'pranna' and the divine truth of the mantras.

The dhammmapada (Buddhist wisdom) elucidates on the self-realisation principles and practice methodologically, consistently, and profoundly. It focuses on the spirit, compassionately. Therefore, the focus must be on the spirit and moulding the spirit entails self-realisation. Per the Ved-shastras (the anthological truth), the spirit must be awakened.

The light of awakening is awareness, a pure quintessence. Awareness travels in experience from base level to super-conscious level. It begins to ascend upwards from the gross physical level of gross basic lethal survival. The life breath (pranna) moves progressively on to the physical level of basic living. The vital life spirit moves onwards upwards onto the metaphysical level of the mental. The spirit of life then moves onto the intellectual and onwards to the consciousness. The spiritual light moves onwards upwards onto the unconditional super-consciousness and finally into the blissful vacuum of truth infinite. Aum Tat Sat (soul delight) illuminates the crown and merges the soul and God in oneness. The human personality has moulded in karmic evolutions of progressive human existence.

According to Vedic wisdom, spiritual emancipation ought to be a sheer bliss. In Sanskrit, it is "Sat chit ananda" (truthfulness- consciousness/ substance – blissfulness/eternal happiness).

Therefore, every ritual (act of spiritual practice 'sadhana') has to rhyme profoundly with absolute life. "Delight" is in the divine manifestation of the vast sky of cosmic light and the vast ocean of compassion. Delight is in the twilight of the dawn and the dusk on earth. Delight is the truth of the unparalleled beauty of the light of Sun. Delight is God and delight is the compassionate soul. Delight is the light of God and delight is the light of the soul merging in a fusion of universal togetherness.

The spirit of life soars with fiery passion. It capers like a wild 'master-less' river. It wanders like the powerful eagle and transforms into the free winged bird of life 'Hamnssa', past the shining fragments of physical and mental planes, fulfilling its desires and acquiring physical and emotional power of the flight of life. Its vision ascends beyond the wholesome beatitude into the divine supremacy of pure existence. Like the sunset and the sunrise, it moulds in its essential substance, with profound experience, in the passage of time.

I am a spirit of life that capers to nature. I love to be alone in quietness and I love to listen to the extra ordinary fathomless silence. There is no more fear in alone-ness. There is only divine bliss and it feels good. Alone-ness is not loneliness. In alone-ness we awaken our spirit of life and break free from the habitual material life. In alone-ness we learn to listen profoundly. When you silently immerse in quietness (subtle peace) with great intensity in my written words, it is then that you have actually listened to me.

What manifests in my heart, manifests in your heart too. It is the all- pervading force of life – 'spirit'. Focus your energy on the charioteer of your soul in profound silence. What we sacrifice really is our ignorance and dark ego. God's energy in return illuminates us with profound wisdom through insight in profound silence. The 'extra ordinary silence that cannot be adequately described in written words, but that which captures the delightful infinity beyond the infinite skies and the infinite oceans of eternity. The profound silence is pureness. It is divine because the insight, which brings the delightful joy of true light, is fulfilling. In profound silence, no earthly intruders prevail. It is an ancient peace of the simple primordial human existence. The quintessence of togetherness of the earth, the celestial, and the atmosphere is a light of delight of the twilight of the dawn and the dusk.

Our life is a gift from "Mother Nature Supreme". All that we materially accumulate to fulfil our desires and emotional power is 'matter' that belongs to ego comprising the mind or the intellect, desires and emotional power. Ego perishes with matter leaving only the subtle substance called the spirit. According to the Vedas, if we do sacrifice anything in our life, it is our 'ego', that which was never ours in the first place.

You and I are different rivers of energy flowing ultimately into the same ocean of eternity. Our life is elapsing with the unfolding universe, as it should. When we stop reacting to the chain of actions, we begin to evolve spiritually, and we begin our karmic journey, the journey of our life.

What is sought of the human spirit is a sacred sacrifice of the earthly flame of 'known impermanence' to the eternal flame of 'unknown' truth, that which manifests in the seat of our soul. Such a wholesome sacrifice requires unconditional compassion.

Invoking the flame of fathomless faith, in the Vedas, is a ritual of bringing together the earth, the atmospheric orb, the celestial planes, and the eternity in profound silence, compassionate prayers, hymns, mantras, poetry and music. When we discover ourselves, we perceive the manifestation of the lotus flower on which the nectar of truth beatitudes as God – Hari Aum Tat Sat. Truth is God and God is truth. This is the prelude of the Vedas. A mantra is a chant of sacred words put together collectively for the sacred weaving of the soul in oneness with God. It is almost a perfect musical knot of the sound, of which 'Aum' is the very first sound of nature.

Aum echoes and hums, in conch shells, in the valleys, in the rivers, in the ocean, in the forests, in the womb, in altars, in the nights, and in the atmosphere with the force of the divine wind – 'Vayu'. 'Hari' is the personified form of God that encapsulates the entire nature and the galaxy. It is the 'vishwaswaroop' (cosmic form). Aum is the cosmic connotation of God as a word, sound, and an echo in the atmospheric orbit with the force of wind. 'Tat' is the infinite eternity that has neither beginning nor an end and that which is majestic. 'Sat' means 'real truth' that is infinitely true beyond a measure of doubt or reason. 'Aum Tat sat' is that pathless eternity.

God may be personified into form and sacred word, whether it is 'Ishwar', 'Allah', 'Mungu', 'Maa', 'Ram', 'Buddha', 'Jesus', or 'Moses'. Theses are exemplified sacred most words that vibrate the personified God that is the beauty of truth. A mantra jaap (repetition in quietness) of 108,000 beads of any sacred name with an 'Aum' or a 'Ya' or a 'La' or 'Amen' as a prefix, has been proven to result into demagnetisation of karmic fields. The experience transforms a mentally conscious thought into a delight of 'insight'. It is said in Quran that by merely praising the lord with his ninety-nine sacred names, three times daily, one accomplishes light, provided the invocation is undertaken with pure profound insight and profound silence.

The praying ceremonies before the sunrise, before the peak sun and before the sunset are auspiciously sacred times. In Vedas, praying is a delight of union of the Cosmic light and the Soul in the twilight of the dawn and the dusk. Vedic praying comprises rituals and rites, full of colourful magnificence and sheer joy of togetherness between the soul infinite and the beautiful nature.

Vedas are the earliest gospel we have of man's immortality and these ancient stanzas conceal the primitive discipline of its inspired discoverers. Shrimad Bhagawat Gita is the mother of all Vedic scriptures, in which is illustrated the entire life process of Lord Vishnu alias the God Supreme and his Leela (the magnificent nature). According to Seers, saints, and savants of centuries, Vedas purport the profound wisdom of God in the most experiential sense of the existence. Such profound wisdom only manifests in the true aspirant's inspirational insight. This kind of insight is not a mentally intellectual wave, but a transcendental light of delight that is unparalleled and the best. Sanskrit has been referred to as the language of inspiration. Whilst I revere every single divine scripture, it is in the Geeta that I rest the spirit of my soul.

The essence of human life is to justify the existence itself by our collective human deeds (Karmas). It is not in our limited domain to perceive in full the metamorphosis of the unknown that manifests beyond the 'word', by mere intelligence. The nectar of altruism is beyond the five multi-sensory functions. We can reach it with our profound insight. The truth is in our soul divine and soul is the very seat of God. To discover this truth is a lifetime experience not an academic task.

Hence, the learning process of discovering the ultimate infinite truth in the passage of time is the ultimate pilgrimage of the soul. It is a process of learning. It is a process of learning about the ways of the nature and of the soul. Learning about the essential nature of the human soul by learning and understanding the essential cosmological eternal nature is Vedic wisdom.

The spirit of life said:

"Let me be! Let me be! Life oh life let it be what it may be. Let me be, let me caper, let me sing, let me play the music of my spirit. I am who I am. I am a mere talent of life that is imperfect as may seem but I am the spirit of life whose passion knows not the flames of desires but the beauty manifested in the oneness of eternity and earth. All that is between the other world and this world is love and compassion. All compassionate love is a warm glow of God. Life oh life! Let me rise in love and compassion."

"Let me conquer the almighty magnificent beauty of god that manifests in nature. Let me know the reality in its fullest and let me understand it compassionately. Let me know this earth in its most beautiful form. Life oh life! Let Beauty manifest in the vision my eyes, in my heart, in my perception, in my thoughts and in my insight. Let my eyes be the glow of a true seer. Let beauty become my inspiration. Let beauty be the reason for my life. Let beauty fill my senses with the magnificent Mother Nature divine."

"Let beauty be the 'sacred word' I speak. Let beauty be my poetry. Let beauty be the lyrics of my philosophy. Let beauty be the expression of the spirit of my life. Let beauty be profound and eternal. Let beauty become the beautiful spirit of life - the seer's spirit. Life oh life! Let me merge in delight with this fathomless beauty of the soul. Life oh life let it be a flight of delight. Let it be a journey of self-discovery pilgrimage of the soul. Let it be. Let it be a profound human experience of the profound wisdom of the soul in the most profound vision."

'Everyday' personality surviving the struggles of everyday life reveres the survival as a 'profound human duty' ordained towards the gross physical, physical, and mental planes of existence.

The duty of human being as a fiery mass is ordained towards the Agnee (fire) burning on this earth, the Agnee (fire) burning in our Stomach, the Agnee (fire) burning in our intellect), the Agnee (fire) burning in our five senses, the Agnee (fire) burning in our mind, and the Agnee (fire) burning in our consciousness. Sacrificing the fire of earth in 'sacredness' of devotion, prayer dialogue, and profound silence, for the delight of the light of fire in the Sun is but our human purpose. The life of a sacred seer dwells in sheer delight.

The personality is like an eagle; capable of seeing the farthest beyond the wholesome skies, yet it is engrossed in chewing its prey. Our spirit of life is embodied with that 'profound insight' to see the infinite truth beyond the boundaries of all manifestations.

Let us learn the eternal truth of life, in profoundness. Soul is a meta-physical manifestation beyond the metamorphosis of the matter and mind.

The personality (alias the lingham purush in Vedas) rotates and revolves, around its spirit, the substance, in moulds of experiences. This moulding process is a collective, aggregate, absolute life process, which does not just imply one lifetime experience but a continuation from and into another lifetime experience. This is the centrifugal force of fate and destiny and this is what I am referring to as 'Karma'.

A compassionate poet reaches far beyond the infinity with words collated together to form lyrics of rhythm and poetry of compassion. The intricate expression is an artistic expression through the caper of the heart. A Vedic poet recites, sings, and inspiringly invokes the light of truth with delightful aspiration, profound inspirational wisdom, and meticulous cosmic science. Each self-discovery is a boon from the vessel of God (Soma). The nectar of delight manifests in purest activity (sattvic karma), in purest self-sacrifice of profound sacred invocations to the light of Agnee (sacred fire). Mantra's (profound sacred sounds of sacred words) enlighten profound sacred silent communication between the third eye (the cosmic eye) which we refer to as profound insight and the crown chakra – 'eternity' (a point one millimetre above the pituitary glands).

A Vedic seer rejoices in delight! Life oh life! Let it be a flight of delight.

For a profound Vedic seer, the world at large and the vision of insight transpire in quintessence. To know this world and the other world in words (spoken, written or sound) is knowledge. However to understand in profound words (mantras), the surviving reality of this world and the eternal existence of the other worlds, is spiritual Vedic wisdom.

The karmic chain of action and reaction is a perpetual vicious cycle of life as long as that cycle is not demagnetised by our absolute insight. Journey of life is the sacred most absolute pilgrimage of the soul comprising demagnetisation of our karmic chain of many lives collated together in many 'Karmas' and many 'existences'. The present lifetime is a rare opportunity. When you and I, we begin to understand instead of knowing the 'root problem', deeply with our insight, we have begun to realise the 'root' of all human 'sorrows'.

Philosophy and poetry are inseparable. Philosophy defines the scientific parables of existence, whilst poetry expresses the artistic beauty of the sacred word in meaning, profound sound, and energy of the seer. [11],[12],[13]

It is but human to err. If humankind did not err, then the world catastrophes would not bring about the conflict and the chaos both in the world that we live in and within our mentally conscious mind. Our existence has become a mere survival of our ego based on disasters and tragic surprises. Our modern world is full of chaos and deep conflict.

---

[11] Sri Chinmoy says at the Bryn Mawr College, Pennsylvania: 'LIFE IS AN IDEA, LIFE IS AN IDEAL, LIFE HAS A SOUL, LIFE HAS A GOAL.'

[12] RigVeda explains Karma as a link between the roots and the main bark of a tree. It is like; the bark of the tree rests on the roots of the tree. Similarly, our Karma is the centrifugal force of the existence upon which activity manifests. We can influence Gods, nature, weather, harvests, peoples, nations, relationships, our own very careers, our friends and our adversaries, through the conscious, sub-conscious and unconscious intent of our act and its rites.

[13] May he delight in these sacred words of the Vedas that are manifestations of the soul divine. [Rv1]. I magnify God, the divine fire, the priest, minister of sacrifice, the offerer of oblation, supreme giver of treasure [rv1]. Aum we meditate upon the glorious splendour of the vivifier divine, may thou that is thee truth illumine our minds and may that is truth bring total spiritual liberation in us. [rv111,62,10]

Conflict exists between the "thought" and the "insight". The world we live in is governed by, the institutional, social, economic and political power of the 'i', 'me', 'my', 'mine', and, 'mind'. It is all 'thought'. The essential issue is that of chaos, mass division, disorder, and conflict prevailing in the world. This is a karmic result of many thousands of years of karmic evolution and involution. Once we remove the chaos, the mass division, the disorder, the conflict, the antagonism, the institutional emblem from our minds and fill it with deeper sense of understanding, we will automatically become quieter and calmer and we will automatically generate a different kind of warmth. We will give compassion and love in harmony.

Profound understanding with profound Vedic wisdom in profound silence transforms our karmic life progressively from the base gross physical into the subtle finest purity of pure truth. This progressive process of moving from the gross physical level to the finest subtle purity is a karmic evolution in seven phases. When the karmic evolution has manifested beyond the wholesome experiences of the conscious and the super conscious, the spirit of life is inspired into the eternity with divine bliss. The light of the Sun merges in oneness with the light of the soul in a fusion of delight! Eternity has transpired in soul, in sheer blissful delight. Aum is the sound and the light of the eternal sky that echoes and illuminates undyingly in benign silence on the ancient Himalayan mountain slopes. Under the great sky of the Himalayas, many seers are everlastingly present. They are enlightened souls that have conquered the beautiful divine truth. Nectar reposes there.

The enlightened spirit of life 'Hamnssa' takes a flight of delight. Life oh life! Let it be what it may be, let it be. Let it be, come what may. Face it, accept it, grit it, but grin and shrug it away. Life oh life! Let it be a triumph of truthfulness over falsehood. Let it be a triumph of light of delight over the dreary dull mundane darkness. Let it be a triumph of life over death. Let it be a triumph of death. Life oh life! Let it be triumph of joy. Life oh life! Let it be a journey of self-discovery in the bare essential existence. Let it be triumph of the spirit of life over the dreary mundane ego. Life oh life! Let it be a flight of delight.

2. LIFE OH LIFE! LET IT BE

Life oh life! Let it be. You only quit when you stop breathing completely, when your heart beat stops completely, and, when the spirit within you can no longer confirm to a physical state. Worse does not last forever. Let life be what it may be, let it be, come what may. Face it, accept it, grit it, but grin and shrug it away. Let it be, come what may. Let it be a flight of delight.

In this poem, I am roaring with deep passionate emotional outburst to elucidate my inner most thoughts on 'Life' - Journey of the soul, in the passage of time. What is life? In the flash of moment, life is an experience in time. The lyrics are coherently and specifically relevant to a battered person. We cannot continue to conquer our personal dreams and ambitions blindly without recognising the bareness of an empty stage of the numbed human earth filled with 'hopeless-ness' and 'helpless-ness'. We tremble at the thought of death. Come oh child of human let it be. Tragedies, epiphanies, and upheavals come uninvited. The spirit of life rises above all the sufferings and transient moments of human life to become a passionate talent of grand universal compassion.

Life oh life! Let me sing my song, let me dance, let me play the music of my life, let me write the lyrics of my poetry for now let me whisper silently my 'un-pitied' words. Let me smile with a tear of joy, as I share my vision with you. I am just a sentimental talent that cannot sigh in sympathetic sorrow but I embrace you affectionately in compassion and love. I whisper silently. Time flies fast; I hear a distinct drum beat from the celestial. Behold my precious prayer of solace. Oh traveller of life, in love and compassion hear the distinct sound of music. Let each moment become a footstep onwards towards the beautiful most magnificent void. The nightingale is mysteriously beautiful. Oh spirit of life, seek the truth, and experience the truth, for the dusk of the teeming world brings hope everlasting. Oh spirit of life, breath the freshness of the dawn thou art the dust, thou art the spirit of life, thou art the soft pebble, thou art the river, thou art the beautiful spirit of life. Oh child of nature, become a beautiful one, see 'beauty', feel 'beauty', and experience beauty, share beauty. Life oh life! Let it be a beautiful moment.

I cannot begin to sing the song of praise and write philosophies that are literally out of touch from the wretched reality of this earth. In order to express my compassionate wisdom, it is necessary for me to create an outburst of emotional sensation so that I can beg for your attention in understanding the essence of life. I cannot save a house that is burning in blazing flames alone nor can I force you to see my point of view, despondently. I am a mere talent whose words strive to dance, rhyme, and sing the music of the spirit of life. I am just a voyager in the journey of life, the passage of the soul.[14]

Life is a problem in as much as death is a great mystery! No human person has conquered death! Life oh life! Let it be what it may be, come what may! In the fiery passion of existence, the spirit of life soars in an outburst to create a manifestation of the hidden 'insight' trapped by the lures and desires. It is a cry of an aspiring person whose vision is split between the dark grey 'ego' in all the impermanence of this earthly survival on the one side and the delight of the insight on the other side. That is the 'paramatman', (eternal god 'infinite supreme') in the eternal vast sky, which is the same 'atman' (internal compassionate spirit of life -the soul) whose beauty manifests on one thousand one hundred and eight petals of divine lotus.[15]

---

[14] Imagine there is no heaven or hell. All that is visible by the naked eyes is the magnificent nature and empty space. All that matters is the magnificent glory and the beauty of Mother Nature supreme 'maa' whose imperishable first word is born of truth and whose truth manifests in the Veda. For she is the mother of Vedas and the hub of immortality. May she come to us in happiness and in sacrifice. May AUM protect us as GAYATRI the goddess of all pervading nature. May harmony ease the entreaty that is a union between the soul and the ETERNITY. [rv/tb/11]

[15] Almost like a child craving for the mothers' love, the flame of inquest, the urge to enquire and the innate outburst to reach the unknown breaks the hardened, stoned and even uncompromising ego. In the very outburst there is a deep praise to the flame of divinity that is the mother of all illumination: 'Oh invincible one, thou art visible in the flame, in the agnee (holy fire) here on earth. Oh divine mother, thou art never formless for even in your subtle most state Aum manifests in the sound, light, energy, ether, air, fire, water, earth, consciousness, and intellect. Oh divine mother 'prakrutti- MAA', may you bless the human mortals with thine boon to accept life as it is and to eliminate all the fears. Oh divine mother may you grant us victory over falsehood. Oh 'maa' may you bless us to become divine.'

⟪ LIFE OH LIFE! LET IT BE ⟫

Life oh life! Let it be what it may be, let it be. Let it be, come what may. Face it, accept it, grit it, but grin and shrug it away. It is "Today" that you have to live to your best and breathe your life to the fullest. "Tomorrow" is yet to be born afresh, anew. For 'today', let your heart sing a song of praise. Let your mind play the music comprising the most enchanting knots. Let your spirit caper to the heroism within you. Let your heart beat rhyme to the rhythm of love and let compassion fill it. Life oh life! Let it be what it may be, let it be. Let it be, come what may. Face it, accept it, grit it, but grin and shrug it away. Life oh life! Let it be.

Life oh life! Let it be what it may be, let it be. Let your past rest in memories, let your memories be a treasure of life well lived without regrets. Let your mistakes be human and let your humanity remain imperfect. Let it be a life well lived in love and let your love remain infinite. Fill your remorseful and battered heart with infinite love and let this love heal every wound in your heart. Life oh life! Let it be what it may be, let it be. Let it be, come what may. Face it, accept it, grit it, but grin and shrug it away. Life! Let it be what it may be. Let it be.

Life oh life! Let it be what it may be, let it be. Let it be, come what may. Face it, accept it, grit it, but grin and shrug it away. Life! Let it be what it may be. Let it be. Let your spirit rise above the wretched of this earth and let it touch the positive aspect streak of the eternal bliss. Let your soul become serene and let your serenity encapsulate spiritual strength. Let this strength be immortal to nurture your wholesome self amidst the noise and haste and waste. Let your life be a reflection of time, imperfect, as it may seem, it is still the manifestation of the very perfection. A phenomenon, we perceive to be God. Let it be what it may be, let it be. Let it be, come what may. Face it, accept it, grit it, but grin and shrug it away. Life! Let it be what it may be. Let it be.

Life oh life! Let my soul be athirst for God. Let me be a spirit of life. Life oh life! Let it be. Let it be, come what may. Suffering is transient. Let it be.

Life oh life! Let it be what it may be, let it be. Let it be, come what may. Face it, accept it, grit it, but grin and shrug it away. Life! Let it be what it may be. Let it be. Let your mind assure you that it is by giving gratitude and appreciation to the very gift of God that you become a hero of your own very existence. Let victory and not defeat be yours, through fearlessness, compassion, love, humility, patience, charity, sacrifice, penance, worship, and servitude. Let it be, what may. Stand up and deliver your very best of what is left of your breathing life. Die if you must, but die with integrity. Let your spirit free from the wretched of this earth. Let it be what it may be, let it be. Let it be, come what may. Face it, accept it, grit it, but grin and shrug it away. Life oh this life! Let it be what it may be. Let it be.

Life oh life! Let it be what it may be, let it be. Let it be, come what may. Face it, accept it, grit it, but grin and shrug it away. Life! Let it be what it may be. Let it be. Let your pains & sorrows rest at the feet of almighty God, whatever you perceive it to be. Let it be any sacred name, call it 'Maa', 'Allah', 'Rama', 'Mungu', 'Mosses', 'Buddha', 'Jesus', or 'Dyou'. Let it be what it may be. Let it be. Let it be the fathomless formless atmospheric orb of nature, let it be the divine ocean, let it be the eternal sky, but let it manifest in your soul. Laugh aloud, enjoy this present moment, and make this present moment a moment of joy. Let your worries diminish and disappear with the blowing wind and let your remorse & anxiety become obsolete. Let your pride be ashamed behind your dark ego. Let your intelligence stop reasoning the 'ifs' and 'buts'. Let your mind stop running after its five servants – 'what', 'where', 'which', 'why', 'when'. Let your mind be lit with fathomless faith. Let your life learn how to nurture and mould this faith. Let your brevity and courage, hold you, right and might. Let your might and brawn's transform the hopelessness in your heart into wonderful feelings of joy and let this joyful moment become the only moment worthwhile its living.

Life oh life! Let your entire trauma disperse. Let your negative anxiety burn away and become ashes on this earth. Let positive magnetic fields surround you wherever you go.

Oh this life! Let it be what it may be, keep smiling and let your troubles wither away with it. Let it be what it may be. Let it be, come what may. Face it, accept it, grit it, but grin and shrug it away. Let it be.

Life oh life! Let it be what it may be, let it be. Let it be, come what may. Face it, accept it, grit it, but grin and shrug it away. Let your dreams be there for life without dreams is like a bird without wings. Let your dreams refract the most beautiful vision of God and let this vision become the manifestation of your nature. Imperfect as you may seem to feel in your heart, you are still the very part of the perfection of God's creation. The magnificent nature is beautiful. All the beauty including the beauty of the moon & the stars, the trees & the flowers, the rivers and the oceans, the mountains and the valleys, the singing birds and the animals, the perennial grass, and, the rustling trees are in you. You have every right to be here on this earth, to laugh at the simple funny things, and to do the simple funny things in the simple stupid ways. Imperfect as you may feel, strive to cling to the perfection of God's nature and let it be a funny life. Let it be what it may be, let it be. Let it be, come what may. Face it, accept it, grit it, but grin and shrug it away. Laugh and let it be. May you become eternally beautiful.

Life oh life! Let it be what it may be, let it be. Let it be, come what may. Face it, accept it, grit it, but grin and shrug it away. Let it be, come what may. Let it be. Strive to cherish your wholesome self. Let the love of your mother give you comfort, solace, and security. Let your loneliness rest in the laps of your spiritual mother and let your heart find peace in your mother's eternal unconditional love. Let your wish be a cry of an innocent child, and let your cry reach God with the everlasting echoes of your mother's unconditional love. Let your wholesome self, free from the wretched of this earth and let this freedom be an emancipation of God. Let it be what it may be, let it be. Let your eyes express a sigh of contentment, let your thirst be quenched and let your spiritual mother take care of you. Let your spiritual nature guide you towards enlightenment. Let your spiritual enlightenment do good to the less fortunate, powerless, helpless, hopeless, and the innocent. Let your good deeds become your only life deeds. Let your life be a worthwhile, interesting, and a meaningful experience. Let your life be yours and only yours. Let it be what it may be, let it be. Let it be, come what may. Face it, accept it, grit it, but grin and shrug it away. Let it be, come what may. Let it be. Let it be what it may be.

Life oh life! Let it be what it may be, let it be. Let it be, come what may. Face it, accept it, grit it, but grin and shrug it away. Let it be, come what may. Let it be.

Life oh life! Let bygones be bygones, and let your disturbed mind rest in peace with a sincere prayer, a handsome gratitude, and a salutation to your father. Let your father know that you are proud of his distinction and let this sense of pride put a shine in your eyes. Let your wholesome self reflect prestige and distinguished calibre of integrity. Let your personal deliverance be honourable and eloquent. Let your brothers and sisters embrace you with dignity and pride and let there be no pity for life is an un-pitied struggle in its own right. Let it be known that you are a special person with special gifts and special talents. Let your spirit guard you and let your spirit heal you. Let your spirit bring strength and courage to you and to others less fortunate than yourself. Life oh life! Let there be peace, harmony, and happiness for now you deserve it. Life oh life! Let it be.

Oh this life! Let it be what it may be, keep smiling and let your troubles wither away with it. Let it be what it may be. Let it be, come what may. Face it, accept it, grit it, but grin and shrug it away. Let it be.

Life oh life! Let it be what it may be, let it be. Let it be, come what may. Face it, accept it, grit it, but grin and shrug it away. Let it be, come what may. Let it be. Oh let it be! Let your heart sing, dance, and play the music of the spirit of your life. Let your spirit be a star of integrity. Let your sense of humour bring lot of laughter's in the simple most beautiful and wonderful ways. Let your mind rest in the shadows of your peaceful dreams; let your life be full of joys. Just for once, let your life be a song, a dance, a rhythm of music, a composition of poetic lyrics. Let it be. Let your personality become a talent of compassion and let your talent of compassion conquer great love. Let it be, oh this life, but do not let your mind be disillusioned by the glamour, glitter, and passion of this universe. Life oh life! Let it be.

Life oh life! Be gentle with yourself and love your spirit of life. Dance if you must dance, sing if you must sing, laugh if you must laugh, cry if you must cry, play if you must play, but do not stop loving even for one moment. Life oh life! Let it be what it may be, let it be. Let it be, come what may. Face it, accept it, grit it, but grin and shrug it away. Let it be, come what may. Let it be. Oh let it be! Let your heart sing, dance, and play the music of the spirit of your life.

Life oh life! Let it be what it may be, let it be. Let it be, come what may. Face it, accept it, grit it, but grin and shrug it away. Let it be, come what may. Let it be. Oh let it be! Let your heart sing, dance, and play the music of the spirit of your life. Let the cosmic energy of the divine Sun ignite the flame of illumination and profound wisdom in your heart. Let the beautiful reflection of the glamorous Moon become the light of most beautiful vision in your eyes. Let the cosmic energy of infinite creation, infinite preservation of order, and infinite transformation of karmic evolution awaken the infinite spirit of life in your finite body. Let the life perish with the unfolding universe as it should, and let this earthly life elapse with the passing of time. Let it be life oh life.

Life oh life! Let your spirit capture the creative talent of integrity and let your spirit become a unique talent of integrity in the oneness of cosmic marriage. Let there be an echo of ecstatic joy all over the magnificent nature and let there be love in every single artery and vein in your body. Let there be compassion and warm affection in every single 'word' that you speak, hear, write, see, touch, feel, and sing. Let your spoken word be a charisma of creative talent, hope of harmony, and transforming energy to evolve every entity that connects with you. Let there be peace within you. Let peace spread everywhere you go and let there be peace all around you. Life oh life let it be what it may be, let it be. Let it be, come what may. Face it, accept it, grit it, but grin and shrug it away.

Life oh life! Let it be what it may be, let it be. Let it be, come what may. Face it, accept it, grit it, but grin and shrug it away. Let it be, come what may. Let it be. Life oh life let it be a flight of delight. Let it be a glimpse of the orb. Let it be a sacred peep into the highest truth. Let it be a human experience of 'twilight', of the sunrise and of the sunset. Let it be a dialogue of sacred prayers between the 'form' and the 'formless'. Let it be a congruence of fusion between the fire of sacrifice from earth and the flame of delight from the orb of the Sun. Let it be a united explosion of the 'form', the 'formless', and the 'intermediate' spheres in the night sky and let there be a meeting of million delights in one wholesome fusion of delight. Oh this life let it be a flight of delight.

Life oh life! Let it be what it may be, let it be. Let it be, come what may. Face it, accept it, grit it, but grin and shrug it away. Let it be, come what may. Let it be. Life oh life let it be a flight of delight.

Vedic philosophy on living the human life on earth:

We are born from the seed of germination to complete our specific karmic journey in accordance with our specific karmic map designated to us from primordial celestial. We possess a destiny that impels us profoundly in thoughts, actions, and spoken or written words. When we speak or act without being ashamed of ourselves, holding fast to this rule, to be faithful and true to our higher divine entity, our spirit of life, we evolve progressively, we become 'Hamnssa-Hanss' (swan-like). Each footstep we take is guided by our karma to journey across from the willing known abode to the unwilling unknown abode whose mysticism fervently expresses itself in all beauty.

We meet many varied persons in our life, from diverse walks of life, for some ('this' and 'that)' known or the 'other' unknown reasons. Most of the times, we assume and presume our circumstances, situations, thoughts, and feelings. We act, react, and get reaction of our actions in one form or another. At times, when sad events happen (whatever they may be), we may feel disheartened, disillusioned, astonished, or even amazed. We may not understand why they happen to us because we do not know. To be divinely happy is our human birthright. To sacrifice 'all' that we have to achieve spiritual peace and eternal happiness is our obligation. To realise this truth is soul searching. This happiness, bliss, tranquillity, depends on nothing and has no beginning or an end. It does not matter what we have done so far and what we have not done yet. All we need have to do is to surrender unconditionally, absolutely without a doubt to our true Self – our divine self (atman). This is the ultimate reality, not this, not that. The Self (atman) cannot abandon US, even if the mind rejects it, and the ego betrays it because eventually the individual self (atman) only merges with the grandeur cosmic soul infinite (param-atman) in delight (param-anandam).

One way to surrender to our true divine spirit is to just believe these words or similar words from any of the saints, sages, mystics, and psychics, whose ever-present grace is apparent.

The mind and the ego can somehow choose not to believe in this non-dual truth. Then, the mind can go to the source of the thoughts of the questions it raises.

- ❑ To whom is this perceived unhappiness?

- ❑ Who needs to be happy?

- ❑ Who are you the "I", the "ME"?

- ❑ Investigate this in fullest.

- ❑ This is 'atmana- vichara sauchatti' (self-inquiring investigation).

Duality gives birth to the 'I' and 'non-I' concept. The seer and the seen, the seeker and the sought, the lover and the loved, the good and evil, and this endless cycle perpetuates, as long as the illusion of duality persists as a conflict. Dualism of chaos can prevail between the mind and the spirit, between the ego and the spirit, between the mind and the body. Beyond the level of supreme soul, all animate and inanimate entities are dual.

The "me" concept generates numerous misidentifications, the primary being the idea that 'I am the body or mind' and is the worst of all. In fact, any identification with anything leads to a trap, which creates duality and interrupts the flow of immortality.

There is no escape from the dualistic world and misidentifications so long as the believer thinks he is someone else than who he really is or rather as long as one thinks he is a separate individual. Individuality is an illusion. Egoistic thoughts perish in due course of time and we feel changes! In actual fact, nothing really changes. All that changes is our perception of the mortal transient world of human existence.

All identifications with the unreal (emotions, body, mind, intellect, and finally the concepts of good and evil) eventually cease with death. When we remove the dualistic thoughts of 'this' and 'that', we learn to discard the "Me" or the "I" concept. When that is discarded the "other" concept will also be automatically discarded in time.

It is a matter of time only. The personality, the name, the identity, the falsity of ownership does eventually disappear with time. To realise this truth is the beginning of another journey – spiritual journey.

In a state without form and quality, a transcendental state of just pure awakening, the ego, and the personality associates with the spirit of life and dissolves completely.

In a state of non-duality, there is no seeker apart from the sought, no seen apart from the seer. This is the eternal "here" and "now", without the mundane past and the uncertain future. There is no other time. This is the state of fullness, oneness of the universal being, the state, which is beyond all identities but is the identity of all beings 'the infinite cosmic spirit' (param-atman). This is the state which is so near and but seems so far.

Just as we are sure that we are awake now, we should be humanly aware that we are neither the body nor the mind and thinking is not our real true divine nature. When we open and awaken by life's many betrayals, instead of shrivelling in fear, we become divinely happy realising the non-dual truth of the matter of life, without hiding it or even fixing it in many canny intelligent solutions.

To disappoint someone for the sake of being honest and true to one's true divine self, bearing all the accusations of betrayals and spite is upholding ones true integrity. Being faithful to one's own self (atman), being trustworthy to one's own true self (atman) makes one beautiful like the swan (Hamnssa). This is the god divine (Hamnssa so'hum) the soul divine (atma) not this not that. Alas in aloneness only the all-transcendental light of God illuminates us towards our true-life purpose, our real life goal! From light we came, towards light we merge. The soul is not born nor does it die. The terrestrial, the spiritual, and the celestial are the three worlds of existence co-related to the super-consciousness, sub-consciousness, and consciousness states of light.

May the merit of the divine light of illumination of the 'Sun-God' ('indra') bring happiness to all beings because the nature of this light is the very nature of all things and all beings. This is perception, this is conception, and this is inception of happiness. Not this, that, and the other.

'Devebhyah kam aavrrniita mrrtyumm a prajaayai kam amrrtamm naavrniita.'

For the sake of the Divine Great Spirit, 'Hamnssa' chooses to die. For the sake of the humankind 'Hamnssa' chooses to sacrifice itself like burning coal, never to die in spirit.

Once we have divine view, divine insight, although the delusory perceptions of 'samnsara' (mundane life) may arise in our mind, a somewhat beautiful 'hamnssa' (swan-like) will fill the empty space of being simply there for the teeming vast sky. When a rainbow appears in front of it, it is not particularly flattered, and when the clouds appear, it is not particularly disappointed either. There is a deep sense of contentment in this 'hamnssa' – the human swan. It chuckles from the inside in melodies constantly being amused in simplicity. This hamnssa is a state of being – 'Shivohum' (the Shiva that is the transcendental eternal 'param-atman' verily is the atman).

The spirit of life says:

"Life oh life! Let it be what it may be! Let me dance with wildness and let me feel ecstasy to the tips of my fingers and toes! Life oh life! Let me be who I am without cautioning me to be careful, to be realistic, or to remember the limitations of being out on a limb. I have borne the accusation of betrayal, I have been let down, I have been hurt enough, but what gives me ecstatic joy is that I have not betrayed the integrity of my own soul. Trusting in my own spirit of life, I can see beauty from within, even when the sun is not shinning every day. In all this, that and the other, I can source my life from God's presence, whatever you perceive it to be. Life oh life! Let it be what it may be, for I can live with my failures, stand still on the edge of a lake, and shout to the positive aspect of the full moon. Yes! I am crazy in love with this life!"

"When all else fails, I want to be alone, in my own company in my own home because I truly enjoy my own company in the quiet empty moments of a home that never betrays me! Life oh life! Let it be what it may be, for now let me be. Life oh life! Let it be a flight of delight. Oh Sun God, awaken me, illuminate me and take away the darkness of my ignorance. Oh divine Mother Savittree, the dynamic energy of the effulgent Sun grant me thine divine boon of illumination. Oh divine mother Samndhya (the consort of dawn and dusk), grant me thine divine compassion to understand this 'samnsahrir-maya' (illusionary known reality of all that is impermanence and mortal) and there from lead the spirit of my life onwards to immortality, whereat the delight of the light of sun forever illuminates."

The spirit of life Hamnssa says: 'Life oh life! Let me know thine essential existence in profound experiences.'

To know the existence in full is the light of the truth. To understand the existence in fullest is the delight of the truth! The human being is essentially a divine being with the essence of soul. Beyond the five elements (namely earth, water, fire, air and ether), the senses, the mind, the intellect, and the ego, there is a harmony-stillness-balance ('satt-chitd-ananda') that is unperturbed by 'all this, that and the other' noise, haste and waste.

According to Isa Upanishads we need to deliberately divide our attention at all times so that a portion of attention or time is devoted to the self, into self-discovery. This entails self-observation, self-awareness, watchfulness, mindfulness, and essential spiritualism based on nature's ways and essential experience of nature's healing energies. The Vedas say that the spirit of life (jivatman) is superior to the ego (ahamkar).

Pleasure and pain ('kaamah cha pidhah'), sorrows and happiness ('dukhah cha sukhah'), losses and gains ('bhrassah cha labhah'), ups and downs ('pragattih cha viklavah'), success and failures ('vijayah cha parajayah'), fortune and misfortune ('bhagah cha vyasanah') - These are transient experiences of the mortal finite world of existence ('Mrityoorlokka'), embodied within the ego or illusion ('aham eti maya') and the mind or memories of experiences ('manas eti anubhava'). Whatsoever is born out of karma must dissolve in karma. Matter ever changing; never remains the same with the elapsing time. This is the common sense of the Vedic life science that is based on normal logic, good practical sense, and truth by experience.

The purpose of every life spirit is to realise the elemental substances of the nature, the qualities of the nature, the qualities of time, and the 'satt-karma' righteous act or deed. To help another is a virtue, to hurt another knowingly or unknowingly is ignorance, and ignorance is stubborn-ness. Stubborn-ness is a sin. To refuse to learn the karmic lessons of life is a sin. The aim of every life spirit (jiva) is to liberate from fear and anxiety of sin.

'Sin' in the Vedas does not have literal implication. Sin or 'asatt-karma' implies a friction or a negative karma that gives rise to dosha-fault or vitiation in lifestyle, life, environment, and the world at large.

The Vedas speak of transformation from the gross state to the subtlest state. When a human being in his or her self-realisation experience reaches the final beatitude, the spirit of life, causes dissolution to gross states, like all the habitual attachments ('kaal-samnsahr'), false desires ('moha-praarthitah'), illusion (maya), ego (ahamkaar), and the falsehood ('asattmya'). From the dissolution of the mortal state of form ('saar-guna') which is like a mirage (maya) onwards to the immortal state of formlessness (nir-guna), the transformation takes place in divine self-realisation. The sublime state is a divine spiritual state, blissful, unperturbed by all this, that and the other ('satt-chidd-anandaaum').

'Yato vacho nivartante aprapya manasa saha anandam brahmano vidvan na bibheti kutas – chaneti' ('Taittiriya Upanishad B-Valli 2-9')

"Who so ever discovers and realises the bliss of eternal supreme infinite cosmic soul that which is verily the soul, becomes infinitely happy together with the mind and is anxiety free."

'Purusha-Param'atman-Parameishwaar' (cosmic spirit of god) and Prakrutti-Jagad'Amba-Parameishwaaree' (existence) are ever present together in each individual spirit of life. All 'gunas' (subtle qualities) are born out of karma (act, or thought, or deed). Prakrutti therefore is the causatal in the experience of 'kaal' - time. 'Purusha' is the cause which when associated with the prakrutti is born out of primordial karma to experience transient of human life in joys and sorrows. The spirit of life is the witness to karma and the life's encounters. When the super intelligence or the higher mind or the higher order (param-manas) is clouded by the ego and the lower intelligence (sense related), insight closed. The divine perception extends beyond the manifest into the un-manifest to realise the threefold nature of the existence and to realise the ineffable nature of the soul is the very essence of existential life. The existence verily is the divine nature. To realise the existence is satt-chidd ananda (truthfulness-righteousness-blissfulness).

3. ESSENCE OF EXISTENCE

Aum echoes, dances, rhymes, moves, creates, rotates, revolves, perpetuates, and causes eternal energy of SUBTLE creation to transcend out of pure sublime existence to the gross earthly planes of life ('pranna').

Vedic theory of existence:

'Samnkhya' means sublime wholesome metaphorical perception of cosmic creation that manifests beyond the finite into the infinite. 'Samnkhya' denotes logic of thought in a philosophy that is rationale and divinely inspirational. It is an innate wisdom or 'param-atman-jnanna' (divine cosmic wisdom) based on the 'atman-divya-drashtee' (pure intuition or insight). Manifestation of 'pranna' (life breath) can only be perceived through insight. No thesis or anti-thesis of creation can endeavour to elucidate in absoluteness the manifestation of transformation from 'Nirr-guna' - 'formless' to the Sarr-guna - 'form', un-manifest to manifest. Scientific postulates of Quasars and Cosmologist Herman Boehm, have established that light manifested from the subtle cosmic light that is beyond the atmospheric orbit of the universal earth, and the wholesome atmospheric orbit of the galaxy. This subtle cosmic light mystical as it may seem is a pure existential eternal celestial light of omnipotent God.

'One universal soul permeating all things, which in substance resembles sublime infinite molecule of infinite light' - Pythagorean hypothesis of light and energy.

Absoluteness is an infinite state of existence wherein there is vacuum and total formlessness ('shunya'). From 'shunya' (vacuum), emanated 'bindu-param-anu' (dot-para-atom) and from 'bindu-param-anu' (dot-para-atom), the anu finally emerged as a result of the law of karma (causation). Meta-physics, physics, cosmic science, and cosmic mathematics elucidate cosmic karma in experiential time (kaal), causing pure essential existence to manifest from cosmic formlessness to semi-formlessness (astral) to form (earthly orb).

'Vayu' (air/wind) is the Vata (pure ether and pure air) life force of cosmic pranna (life breath) that emanated from pure Akash (ether/space).

There is no life without 'Vayu' (air) and the orbit of existence will cease in the infinite 'Akash' (ether/space orb/ sky). Similarly, metaphorically, the human life breath is 'pranna' and without 'pranna' the spirit of life ceases to manifest in the 'bhautic' - matter state.

'Kundalini' is primordial energy of 'pranna' and cannot be appropriately elucidated in words. Vibration of the primordial energy causes transmigration of pure existence.

Pure awareness is static pure existence of sublime divine light that only observes, knows, sees, or watches. This pure awareness is the param-atman (cosmic soul) that which is verily the atman (individual soul divine).

When pure static power the seer is ignited with the inertia of dynamic energy the seen, current is formed. Similarly, when pure existential awareness mode initiates a circumference with primordial energy, the dance of cosmic creation happens mysteriously and mystically.

'Aum' is the first word in light, sound, energy, symbol, and maha-mantra of the Vedic Gods. From this extra-ordinary fusion, mahatt-tattva (pure intelligence) manifests.

The mahatt-tattva has a higher form 'the unmanifest', which is 'param-atman' or the astral body of the cosmic soul, and a lower form the 'sub-manifest' - 'consciousness or pure intelligence'.

From further exuberant contemplation of the vibrations, 'aham-tattva' (ego) transpires. The higher form of aham (ego) is the spiritual sense of self-identity (a true sense of identity) and the lower form of aham is the ego-sense of identity (egocentric) self-importance.

When 'Aham-tattva' and 'mahatt-tatva' united, the 'triguna' three qualities of nature became imminent - Sattva-rajjas-tammas (pure conscious intellect, motion, and inertia).

No single Guna (cosmic quality) can act on its own without the primordial energy – 'Kundalini'. 'Gunas' (humours) intercepted with cosmic energy, mahaad-tattva, and aham-tattva gives rise to 'mannas' (eleven gods and cognitive mind). The eleven gods in the human macro-cosmic entity that act with 'kaal' (time) in the 'param-mannas' (cosmic mind) are Dik, Vatar, Arka, Prachetas, Ashwini, Vanhi, Indra, Upendra, Mitra, Prajapatti, Chandra, and Manassa-vasus.

'Mannas' has two forms. The higher form, which is discriminative subjective form, a relative form and the lower form is functional, operational, cognitive form.

From the interception of the 'Tri-Gunas' (three subtle qualities of nature), 'Aham' and 'mannas', energy created the five composite elements of matter – 'pancha mahabhuttas'.

The great pancha-mahabhutas (the great five elements) of matter are ether, air, fire, water, and earth.

From these five elements, the cosmic intellect together with the cosmic ego began the wheel of karma to generate 'pranna', life breath nucleus.

From the interaction of life breathing force – 'pranna', the 'mannas' (cosmic mind), the 'pancha-mahabhutas' (five elements of matter), the tri-guna (three qualities of cosmos), aham-tattva (cosmic ego), 'mahatt-tattva' (sublime cosmic intelligence) and the 'prakruttee-shaktee', 'budhee' (cognition) manifested. Indriyas (cognitive sense organs) are karmen indriyas and janen indriyas. Karmen indriyas are the motor organs of senses namely hands, legs, anal, genitals, and vocal chords. The janen indriyas are proper senses organs namely the nose, the tongue, the eyes, the ears, and the skin.

The five senses that emanate from the interaction of the indriyas with pancha-mahabhutas are: sound, touch, sight, taste, and smell. The five functions that emanate from the karma kriya (inter-action) or dynamism of kinetic kundalini energy are tanmantras: speech, grasp, motion, procreation, and excretion. Karma transforms the un-manifest cosmic humours (param-gunas) into the manifest extended physical humours (param-doshas):

When the first two elements of the pancha mahabhutas namely 'Akash' (space) and 'Vayu' (air) combine it yields Vata (air). When the 'Tejas' (fire) and the 'Apah' (water) combine, it yields pita (liquid fire). When 'prithvee' (earth) and the fourth element of pancha mahabhutas 'apah' (water) combine, it yields kapha (earthly liquid mass).

These three doshas gravitate and gauge. Matter rotates, revolves, and perpetuates in causative cycles of karma. The 'sharir' (body) is in perpetual flux or dynamic equilibrium or changing mode. Every mode alters the state of pancha-mahabhutas (five elements) and consequently yields a manifestation of doshas (state of elemental creation), the 'koshas' (cells) and 'dhatus' (tissues), and the 'malas' (excretion).

The food we eat also comprises pancha-mahabhutas (elements). Food has a taste (rasa), 'guna' (virtue/humour/quality), 'virya' (potency/fresh), and 'vipaka' (after digestion smell). The digestion process is initiated by the agnis (various digestive acids and alkaline) and enzymes. The food either becomes a contribution 'kosha' (cell) or 'dhatu' (tissue and cells), as a vata, pita or kapha effect or otherwise it becomes Mala (waste excretion).

Ayur-veda (science of life) correlates the rog (disease) and the metaphysical state of human body. When a human being realises that beyond the sharir – (body/ matter), 'ahamkar' (ego), and 'mann/budhee' (mind/intelligence), there is a cosmic consciousness or metaphysically phenomenal intelligence, illumination of inner wisdom or insight or 'divya drashtee' happens in progressive stages from the gross to the subtle. Inner wisdom comes through subjective filtration of 'aham-tattva' (ego) and 'mahatt-tattva' (intelligence) through 'mannas' (mind) and 'sharir' (body). Consciousness or intelligent force manifests in all things, shapes, and all forms in one way or another including herbs, plants, and environment.

Albert Einstein was staggeringly amazed at the Vedic philosophies of creation and commented that it is far more important to have wholesome imagination than merely knowledge. The Vedas are scientifically wholesome. Vedic Wisdom encompasses knowledge, imagination, and intuitive vision.

Pythagorean said: 'In the universe, nothing really dies, it simply transforms itself.' According the 'Samnkhya-Yoga', there are three main sources of inner wisdom namely the perception, interception, and revelation.

In my imagination, from deep constant insight comes inspiration. From inspiration comes perception. From perception comes experiential interception. From experiential spiritual interception comes divine expression. From divine expression comes revelation.

Abstracts are metaphorical representations of what manifests beyond the surface of naked vision. Inner vision is abstruse to the external materialistic mind. The greatest scientists and philosophers of our times have used their inner most imagination to reach or arrive at a true postulate upon which a verification program of testing transpires.

Scriptures or srutees are a guide based upon inferential profoundness to intuition or insight or third eye vision. They are the means to understand and comprehend beyond the cognitive mind. Only in sublime, subtle experience can we become aware of the sublime and subtlest existence. Therefore, reasoning existence, imagining logically, and making rationale interpretation of our inner wisdom is centrifugal to pure divine experience of existential human life.

Various many scholars and philosophers have made a critical review of the 'Samnkhya philosophy of creation'.

It is not so important to debate upon the mechanism of primary imagination of the ancient 'Samnkhya', as it is important to enhance it further into our pure creative imagination of the wholesome creation process of the karmic cycles. The individual microcosmic personality is identical to that of the collective macrocosmic universal existence. Inherent in every human being are, the three gunas and the three doshas in percentages of manifestations.

Therefore, whilst the theory of creation is not perfect absolute personification of the true representation of the essential existence in reality, it may give us light into understanding that the nature is embodied with the three gunas.

The three gunas of sattva-rajjas-tammas exist in every atom, nucleus, molecule, electron, and micron. Beyond the gunas is the omnipotent vacuum – 'shunya' (eternal celestial). Vedantic creation is based on the omnipotent divine God 'Brahman-atman' (the eternal supreme).

Pure sublime existence is God 'Ishwaar' (Nirguna-formless), whose mantra representation is 'Hari Aum Tat Sat – Sat Chit anandam – Aum Tat Sat Swaha'. This is the invocation mantra of cosmic creation. The celestial is eternal bliss. Bliss is a perfect state of existence – 'sattva'. When pure existence merges with 'Aum-Maa-Uma-Aum-Mau-Aum' or shaktee (that which is construed as kundalini or primordial energy), a fusion of 'mahajyoti' – delight the meeting of two lights transpires into Tejas (energy).

Brahma is the omnipotent creator, Vishnu is the dynamic force of sustaining, and Shiva is the dissolution, destruction, and liberator of decaying matter. Brahma is pure sattva pure existential pure awareness. Vishnu is the pure rajjas pure preserver pure dynamism and Shiva is the pure tammas pure potentially static, dark potential kinetic force, pure destroyer, and dissolver of atoms, molecules, nucleus, and electrons with the vibrating primordial energy. Sage Kapil's ancient Samnkhya philosophy became the premise upon which Vedic life science was developed. Vedantic theory of creation begins with the omnipotent God. From Brahma emanates the great Maya (illusion).

From chaos and motion of the energy of Maya with the help of Gayatree - triguna adi-shaktee (the mother of creation saraswatti, laxshmi, and kali) came about Brahma-Vishnu-Shiva. From the Brahma-Vishnu-Shiva were created the cosmic Purusha – the seer and the cosmic prakritti – the seen. The seer is 'Shiva-atman-Acharya' the cosmic guru, and the seen is 'shaktee' the cosmic kundalini energy. From the fusion of the seer and the seen in a camouflage of 'kriya's' and 'karma' (motions and actions), mahatattwa (intelligence) was born.

From the interception of the maya-purush-prakritti-mahatattwa, omnipotent god gave birth to 'Shuksh-mata' (the subtle power of cosmic density) as the nucleus of karmic action. The prakritti comprises three gunas created by Maya (cosmic goddess of illusion) - Sattvic, rajjasic, and tamasic.

Followed by further kriya (chaotic motion), Aham-tattva was created as cause of delusion in 'mahat-tattva' (cosmic mind). Followed by further kriya, the 'pancha mahabhutas', the 'tri-guna swaroop' (three forms of gunas), 'mannas', 'devas' (deities)[16], 'indriyani's' (karmen and janen), gross 'tanmantras' and subtle 'tanmantras' were created. From further kriya, 'Lingha-sharir' (cosmic orbit) was created. From the 'lingha-sharir', 'Bramanda' (enormous gigantic egg) was created. All the gods entered the egg to become 'Vairaja purusha' (enthroned life soul – spirit of life). 'Hari/Brahman-atman' thus became 'Narayana'. From the navel of 'Narayana' was created the lotus of Brahma.

From the interception of three forces and three energies, the 'lokas' (spheres of existences), nine planets, constellations, stars, cosmic galaxy and 'rashis' (cosmic geography).[17]

Vedas repose on 'Gayatree Mantra'. Aum is the infinite omnipotent symbol of the first sound, light, symbol, energy, and matter. Aum is that infinite eternal bliss 'formlessness' (Nirguna-atman) from which the infinite came (jiva) and from the infinite came the form (swaroop). When this infinite is taken away from that infinite what remains is formless infinite. 'Gunas' were inherently transcended from the conscious level to the gross physical level in their existential state.

Therefore, beyond the conscious level of existence, manifestation cannot justifiably be shown in black and white except in divine perception with divine insight. 'Kaal' (eternal time) conforms to the principles of gunas (cosmic qualities of humour).[18]

---

[16] Vedic deities, devas, cosmic forces are some believe 84,000,0000 in total. 33,000,0000 devas on the ether orb preserve the galaxy. There are 64,000,000 cosmic energies 'kundalini'.

[17] The first seven great sages of the cosmos are believed to be Marichi, Angiras, Atri, Pulastya, Pulaha, Kratu and Vashishtta. The four mannas children are believed to be Sanak, Sanandan, Sannatana, and Sanatkumar.

[18] The Vatta or the Vayau times are 3-5 a.m. and 3-5 p.m.
The Vatta/Kapha times are 5-7 a.m. and 5-7 p.m.
The Kapha times are 7-9 a.m. and 7-9 p.m.
The Kapha/Pitta times are 9-11 a.m. and 9-11 p.m.
The Pitta times are 11 a.m. - 3 p.m. and 11p.m. – 3 a.m.

From pure Akash (space), emanates Vayu (air) that which spreads life or life breathe. Vayu in human being relates to the nerve force, nerve motor, inertia, and reflexes. Its inertia regulates Pita (fire and water) and Kapha (earth and water). Vayu regulates the circulatory system, the digestive system, the endocrine system, the reproductive system, the nervous system, the respiratory system, and the mental systems. Vayu is the 'pranna', life force of human existence. [19]

When power is ignited with the inertia of energy, current is formed. Similarly, when pure existential awareness mode initiates a circumference with primordial energy, the dance of cosmic creation happens mysteriously and mystically. Pure awareness is sat-chitt-ananda (a perfect state of happiness and bliss), in which sheer observation in silent quintessence reveals the wholesome pure nectar of divine immortal light (Amrutt-jyoti) of omnipotent God ('Hari'). Light never failing always illuminates in the typological heaven – celestial. Amrutt (immortal nectar) is similar to pure awareness. Being aware of the immortal soul of infinite existence, in purest sublime most existence, the human being (manushya) rises above the mundane gross physical level of survival mode and transforms itself into an existential spiritual being.

Cosmic consciousness or metaphysically phenomenal intelligence illumines a seeker with inner wisdom or insight or divya drashtee.

Life oh life! Let it be what it may be. Let it be, come what may. Face it, accept it, grit it but grin, and shrug it away. Let be a flight of delight. Delight happens in progressive stages from the gross to the subtle.

---

[19] According to the Swami Sada Shiva Tirtha, people may fall under seven different physiological physical constitutional humours. They are:

VAYAU (VATTA) – governed predominantly by air element

VAYAU-PITTA – Two doshic (AIR PLUS (FIRE + WATER))

PITTA   - (FIRE + WATER)

KAPHA – (EARTH AND WATER)

KAPHA-VAYAU – Two doshic (Air plus (EARTH + WATER))

KAPHA-PITTA – Two doshic (Water plus (EARTH + WATER)

VATTA-PITTA-KAPHA (TRI-DOSHIC) EQUAL AMOUNTS OF EACH DOSHA.

Firstly, the divine seeker or spirit of life becomes 'Arta' (depressed mode). Ayush seems full of Dukha (sorrows). He faces life and finds hard to accept the gross materialism. He has realised that life is full of sorrows. Having experienced mundane life, struggles, and sorrows, adversities and losses, he transforms into 'Jinasu' (enquirer and researcher). He transforms in karma and dissolves his karmic wheel by gritting his ego. 'Jinasu' wants to know innately, divinely, wholesome. 'Jinasu' then becomes 'Arthar'thi' (seeker of true spiritual wealth). In yagnas (self-sacrifices), he conquers. He experiences 'divya adhya-atma jyoti' (soul enlightenment). In time, he becomes Atman-Jnani (wise man).

No one can almost perfectly 'absolutely' elucidate the creation save for its perception in profound imagination. To the agnostic, the intuition cannot manifest beyond the mundane levels of survival, cognitive and animal instincts. Ayush (life) is causatal, sacrificial, purposeful spiritual life whose ultimate aim is moksha-muktee (freeing from the vicious cycles of sorrows). Dukhah (sorrow) arises when our mannas (pure mind) drift away in the illusion of Maya. 'Rog' or disease is 'piddha' (physical suffering). [20]

To diffuse the rog or disease, the Vedic Rishi or sage looked at the janma lagnesha (Vedic jyotisha birth chart). Based on this, determined the karmic pictorial view of the overall punarvasu-karma (previous karma that has resulted into the specific anxiety, loss, destruction, adversity, disease, sufferings, etc). The most important aspect of Vedic life science is the detoxification. Detoxification is not merely purification of the body, but also of the mind, the conscious, the spiritual composition, the emotional, and the psychological. Detoxification is the purification of the 'Pranna' (life breath) that becomes the digestive, the circulatory, the respiratory, prana (air).

---

[20] The mayic parts (the illusionary parts) are manifest 'draste' and unmanifest 'adraste'. These are 'naama' (name), 'swaroopa' (form), 'mannas' (mind), 'aham' (ego), 'satta' (existence), 'chitt' (consciousness), and 'atman-brahman-param-Brahma-anandam' (blissfulness). Existence, consciousness, and soul never perish with the manifest matter. These three elements of existence perpetuate in karma until eventually the karma cycle become no more. When Shiva the 'Mrutyunjayayah' (liberator of life from the bondage of mortal sufferings, karma, and maya) grants ultimate 'moksha' liberation from mundane earthly life, the 'jivan-atman' (individual soul goes into the seven spheres of immortality depending upon the karma.

Once the Pranna (life breath) is purified/ cleansed, the 'Vayu' (air) is balanced. Then the Agnee (the fire) begins to settle and synchronise. Then the Apah (water) begins to normalise. Then the bhumi (earth) begins to normalise in dhatus (tissues), malas (waste) and slowly the body resumes its peak functional performance.

The root of an illness or sorrow or pain or anxiety or worry or misfortune therefore is a karmic manifestation. To dissolve the adverse karmic habituation or lifestyle or (adverse thought and outlook) achit, punarvasu karma (previous life karma), rtu-sharir rog (invasive bacteria, fungi and poison), or 'Vyadhi' (illness) is the aim of Vedic life science. Our own ignorance of not understanding the conceptual framework of existential 'atman param atman' (divine being) brings us misery and rog (disease). Most karmic activities of greed, lust, desires, anger, lust, self-importance, emanate from ignorance and stubbornness. Like Aparadha (wrongful act), asatya (black lie), Aparinam (non-compliance with nature's rhythm), are some examples of adverse karmic actions. Being ignorant can be overcome by awakening insight and spiritual awareness in subtle spiritual experiences. Ignorance is overcome by collective divinity (adhyaatmaic brahma-gjnana anubhavatih), which extends to more than one life.

Individual human has a vikrutti-doshabhediya (current cyclical constitution of cosmic nature) in an inherent rashi prakrutti-doshabhedya (inborn elemental physical constitution). The later is considered karmic dosha-bhedya or a result of previous life karma.

The interaction of tridoshas -Vata-Pita-Kapha (the energising forces of nature) and the tri-gunas – Sattva-Rajjas-Tammas, produce cycles of kriya-karma (life process) namely speech, grasp, motion, procreation, and excretion, under varying vikrutti-yogs (life conditions). Human being is a cosmic entity (prakrutti) in relation to 'kaal'/ time the yogis (life conditions), vikrutti (the current climatic conditions), and punarvasu karma (previous karma). [21]

---

[21] To become the seer, yogi – Param-Hamnssa Shiva, the Vedas say that true seeker takes the path of the light, in the realm of the fire of the inner soul to become delight – param hamnssa.

The karmic element is a manifestation of the spiritual consciousness and the Sages are of the view that when the consciousness is in harmony, the mind and the body is in axiomatic harmony of dosha-bhediya (humours). Ayush (life), Ayush-karma (life process), and yogs (living states) are the three subjects of the objective Vedic rog-moksha (emancipation from disease).

When a 'jivan-atman' (the astral seed of karma, known as the spirit of life, that which in Vedic wisdom is also known as 'Hamnssa'), came into this world, 'Hamnssa' came naked with his or her hands empty. Life did not mean anything then to 'Hamnssa', as it was in a cosmic dream world.

Eternal supreme divine Mother Nature 'Maa' afforded everything to the 'jivan-atman' alias 'Hamnssa', with her three cosmic energies of creation, preservation, and evolution (retribution/dissolution/destruction).

Eternal supreme Mother Nature 'Maa' (divine cosmic eternity) gave 'Vital life breath' to the gross physical body, thereby connecting the 'jiva', as a person to this earth, its matter, and its intellect alias the mind. 'Jiva' became a spirit of life with a 'personality' and 'family', hence a 'person'. The body and the mind formed attachments or bondage with the illusions or the physical material world and disillusions or the social structures of the family. The ego (self-pride) then gave identity to 'Hamnssa' as a five sensory intellectual being – 'personality'.

The body is the 'kshetra' (field) of the astral seed of karma that is just a matter made up of fire, water, air, earth, ether, and wind. The mind is a collection of thoughts and perceptions of the intellect operating with the nervous system.

'Maa' gave the mind, the intellect, the consciousness, the will, and the vision. 'Maa' gave the heart, strength, courage, energy of seven spheres in kundalini (vital life breath), the nervous system, the stomach, the lungs, and the seventy two thousand nerves. 'Maa' gave felicity, welfare, fortune, luck, glamour, roof, clothing, food, and love. In time, the spirit of life, 'Hamnssa', is entangled and wrapped up with 'mine', 'my', 'me', 'I', and 'you'. 'Hamnssa', is engrossed in the falsehood of power struggles, and begins to feel too attached to everything that is 'not permanent'.

'Hamnssa' as a 'personality' begins to feel insecurity of loosing anything that is material in life and in this insecurity creates 'personal control' over everything and everybody. 'Hamnssa' as a person spreads fear, by, imposing on others, out of pity, sympathy, and sorrow. Hamnssa as a person thrives on chaos, crises, noises, haste, and waste. When 'Hamnssa' dies, he or she as an astral seed of karma cannot take with him or her anything or anybody. 'Hamnssa' as a 'jiva' will leave this universe empty handed too. 'Hamnssa' sighs in compassion and opens its insight to welcome the wisdom of God. God as a compassionate loving guru of the soul says to Hamnssa, 'My dear precious child, so, what are you claiming possessively as "mine"?' 'All that is on this earth is impermanent, dancing in the shadows of your mind as your very own illusion. What do you really control when you cannot have control over death?' 'Hamnssa' cries 'Life oh life, let it be!'

'God' eloquently speaks to 'Hamnssa' in soft quietness, through his insight:

"Your life is a journey of the soul in collective deeds (Karmas). Karma is the centrifugal force of life. You are the spirit of life that is surrounded by all that is not truly yours. Therefore as a spirit of life, one has to rise above all that is 'impermanence', and do the very best possible with keen aspiration to accomplish total spiritual liberation. It is but your human duty to discover your spiritual nature, your essential nature, and your compassionate nature."

"If someone has hurt you, then you must try to understand the essence of that hurt, instead of reacting back. Lest you forget, you must try to dissolve your hurting wound with profound compassion, profound wisdom of the soul, and profound simplicity. 'Pity' and 'sympathy' are mere reflection of fear, anger, and guilt. Compassion with 'integrity' wins."

"Enrich your human life with profound wisdom, love, and compassion for righteousness (dharma), courage in fearlessness (balla), serenity (sushiltah), fortitude, and self-same sacrifice (yagjna) of the mantra prayers and rites."

"Go placidly amidst all the chaos, noise, haste, and waste, and strive to evolve. Try to remain focused in meditation."

"I am the charioteer of your soul. Realise me with 'fathomless faith'. Eternity shall descent into the seat of your soul. Look towards the Sun with keen aspiration, to become a true 'karma yogi' (a Vedic soldier who is spiritually entwined with God). Become a scientist, become an artisan and become an obligatory patriot that has brawn, brevity, briskness, benignity, beauty, bliss, and benevolence."

"You are a spirit of life, who must realise the infinite truth of life. Truth is light and light is the delight. Beseech that infinite truth, to accomplish the journey of your life, with profound determination and unwavering mind. Learn profoundly to detach from the materially glittering embryo of this earth selflessly, learn to live your life without regrets, pity, sympathy, and remorse. Accept full responsibility for every single part of your life, retrospectively. Do not conclude and end in knowing others, this life, and yourself in knowledge. Understand the depth of every manifestation in profound silence. Surrender not! Follow valiantly the purest light, without doubts and veil of disillusions, for I am the charioteer of your soul."

When one unites in oneness, with the charioteer of the spirit of one's life, one shall accomplish total spiritual liberation. Our selfless devotion to humanity, righteousness, and religion alone will account for our Karmas. So with patience, let us learn to listen clearly and precisely and follow our spiritual intuition in profoundness.

Our mind and our ego capers to all the senses, in pity, lure, desires, and lust. Therefore do no let the attachments of this material world blind our super conscious insight from the infinite truth of existence.

The essence of existence is to justify our life process and to give our life spirit total spiritual liberation. This is the essential truth. It is our essential nature – compassion.

Let us take reflection of our 'life ship' now when you and I are as 'captain' of the 'life ship'. We are in the midst of severe adversities or severe livelihood, in the midst of noise, haste, and waste. We have become too involved with all that is 'heroism'.

To evolve in karmic life is to take a retrospective reflection of our life process. It is now that our 'ship' needs to change its course for the next future minute in the eternity of time. The next minute is another moment of our 'life ship'. Change is the way of this life.

Nothing remains forever. So, let us not grieve for what is not. Let us strive to be the survival of the fittest, no matter what, but let us embrace with warm compassionate affection the profoundness of the magnificent beautiful nature and the soul.

Let us learn to feel strategically powerful from within, with profound wisdom. Let us stand up and deliver our best, humanly in profound compassion. Let us justify our existence with authentic power – the power of our soul. Let us protect the righteousness, the pure, the helpless, the hopeless, and the ignorant. Let us realise that by shouting, screaming and getting angry we bring anguish to others and in return, we become anguished ourselves. We achieve only a chain of actions and reactions. It will not solve our problems. Let us have a positive attitude and be a patriot of truth. Let our life be an example to illuminate others. Let us give hope with our victory to religion (dharma) and let religion (dharma) bring joy and happiness to the distressed world at large. Let us give compassion selflessly to the less fortunate ones. Let us dissolve our enemies namely 'desire', 'greed', 'anger', 'lust', 'ego', 'social metamorphosis', and 'falsehood'.

No one is perfect. Life is imperfect. Transcendental truth does not repose in inactivity. Activity means life and activity is the means to discover the infinite truth that is hidden by the finite matter and the intellectual mind. What a humankind sacrifices is ego that is not permanently immortal. Our duty alone will grant us 'moksha' (total spiritual emancipation). Let us perform our duty with indifference in attitude towards this unfolding universe that is withering with the time.

All anthologies, somehow confirm that in the beginning there was nothing, in the end there is nothing. Perceptively, life must be a process of existence rather than mere survival, which of course is the reality that is imminent of the modern world. We live our daily lives relatively as a routine or as a task (things have to be done) without addressing the process of our lifestyle! Total transformation entails that we awaken the Arjun the true soldier of 'material warfare' 'life' in us and dissolve the enemies of Arjun (the spirit of life). These enemies are none other than the constituents that surround our own soul, namely, ego, desire, anger, lust, greed, social power, and falsehood (the 'mine' and the 'you are to be blamed or he is to be blamed or she is to be blamed' factor). Our lifestyle is a relative reflection of our 'Karmas'.

Karma is what we eat, what we think, what we say, what we see, what we hear, what we do, what we feel, what we make, what we create, and what we refract and reflect upon our own spirit. Our Karmas somehow retrospectively make our life a learning process and a journey in which we constantly evolve and change. When we mould and evolve, as individual spirit of life, we awaken to the spiritual light. When we change retrospectively, we change the course of direction of our lives and we follow the sixth sense. The spiritual awareness is the intuition to live divinely. It is then; we merge with the light of the Sun spiritually. We learn to listen to the divine bliss manifested in the seventh sense (the ultimate goal of every human life).

Therefore, the central theme of our entire life process is to discover soul. Soul is the very seat of God. When Atma (soul) and param-atma (God Supreme) unite in oneness, one transcends into pilgrimage of total liberation or total freedom termed 'moksha'. When an Arjun (the spirit of life) becomes profoundly wise, practices altruism, and lives a profound life, he becomes free from the bondage of sorrows.

Life and death do not argue with us! They just happen without argument. Birth is as pre-determined as death is albeit we claim to know one and not the other. Death finally comes without debates, arguments, discussions, or reason. It does not perform many religious conferences and dialogues. It just comes and stares at us unexpectedly, uninvited and unduly. It brings an end to renew a new beginning. No intellectual can argue about this truth.

'Hamnssa' (the spirit of life), is further obsessed, worried and distressed about something that is not real. 'Hamnssa' is feeling lonely, afraid, and anxious about 'death' despite the inherent wisdom of the soul given by the charioteer of his soul 'Krishna'.

When reason and cause come in conflict with the intellectual mind and ego, 'Hamnssa' feels helpless and hopeless in the suffering of grief. Hamnssa then seeks the 'param tatva guru' trinity 'Shiva' (the sole transcendental cosmic guru residing in the soul).

'Shiva' speaks with profound insight to the seeker of truth:

"What must live must suffer in sorrow. It is an inevitable law that no intellectual can possibly alter. Gita, Bible, Quran, or any other sacred anthology whilst being profound words of wisdom repose and merge in the oneness of eternity that does not have any paths nor does it have any language. This eternity is the soul. The soul therefore is the very seat of God."

"Evolving in karmic nature is surviving gracefully by transforming from the everyday noise and haste and justifying gracefully your existence by discovering this substance of life, the very essence of existence in profound silence."

"There is great harmony and immense joy in silence. Silence is blissful."

"Life is a wonderful experience filled with beautiful capering nature, enchanting music, compassionate love, infinite harmony, and simplicity. This type of experience does not require an intellectual I.Q. It requires an essential insight. In the highest and the purest form of activity manifests the eternal truth, which is divine blissful super-consciousness."

"Conquer it, fight like a soldier of 'altruism', and go progressively ahead in the karmic evolution. Only the brave and the courageous find their way to the end. This human life is full of differentiation. Therefore, be indifferent to all that is 'impermanent'. Then only shall you conquer your soul, the very essence of existence, and your essential nature."

Shiva elucidates a virtuous seeker's pilgrimage in brief:

"A person of virtue seeks truth with aspiration, inspiration, and inner strength."

"A person of action seeks enjoyment and power with intellect, thought, and, courage. A person of total inactivity enjoys nothing and remains in darkness, ignorance, and decaying death. He is stale and deluded. A virtuous person becomes 'Artan' (depressed, emotionally hurt, and afflicted knowing the naked truth of life). He seeks total sacred transformation and dreams of possessing bed of roses. 'Sorrow' is his painful possession and he suffers in silence. 'Artan' realises that there is neither beginning nor an end to life. Life is full of sufferings. We perish with our own pain albeit we came into this earth causing pain to our mother."

"'Artan' transforms and evolves into becoming a 'Jinasu' (true seeker and a genuine enquirer). He seeks knowledge and then profound wisdom of the soul. He begins to understand. 'Jinasu' then becomes an 'Artharthi' (the seeker of true wealth —Amrutt — nectar of truth that is contained in the vessel of 'soma'). He ceases to have sorrows of pity and has compassion. 'Jinasu' wants freedom, total freedom, and he sacrifices everything for freedom. 'Jinasu' becomes a 'Jnani' (profoundly wise) and he begins to identify with the oneness of the magnificent nature. The 'Jnani' takes a flight of delight into the eternal vastness of the clear blue skies and becomes a free winged spirit of life, the bird 'Hamnssa'. A virtuous person is born with the fiery sight of the eagle and transforms gracefully into the free winged spirit of life, the bird 'Hamnssa'. Rise O dear spirit of life; precious humble spirit of life. Know that in your humility, servitude, 'selflessness' and true sacrifice, my grace manifests the most."

Thus said 'Shiva' (the 'param tatva'/ cosmic guru of the soul) to 'Hamnssa'- the spirit of life. 'Shiva' finally concluded:

"My dear precious Hamnssa, in your aloneness, when the magnificent light of your sacrifice in mantra, prayers, devotion, hymns, music, and invocations, rites and rituals to Agnee enchant me in pureness, I dance in happiness. With my cosmic dance 'natraj' shimmers the entire cosmos and I fill your soul with eternal compassion and eternal light. Fathomless silence follows the murmuring Aum, where in glory is. Be happy and live your life in delight. Life oh life! Let it be a flight of delight. Oh Spirit of life, become free."

Essential nature of the human is spiritual according to the Vedas:

Freedom is stopping to argue, shout, scream, and becoming aggressively attached to the 'mine' and 'I'. Freedom is essentially becoming fearless. Fearlessness is a very difficult stage to accomplish because absolute fearlessness implies that death becomes weaker than life itself. The Vedic wisdom of life perches on fear. The root cause and reason of fear need to be conquered in full. Unless one becomes fearless, one cannot embrace death. The gist of Geeta and the very gist of the Vedas for that matter manifest in the conflict between the ego ('aham') and the spirit ('atman').

The ego manifests in the grand memory of the mind, cognitive intellect, and the body. Whereas the spirit is the soul divine connected with the higher intellect and the super intellect, that which is insight or the intuitive intelligence of god.

The ego is associated with the dreary mundane life, whereas the spiritual soul is associated with the sublime existence (eternal search in experiential journey of more than one lifetime).

'Ego' ('aham') versus the 'Self' ('atman'):

"The pursuit of truth and beauty is a sphere of activity in which we are permitted to remain children all of our lives." --Albert Einstein

"Fear makes us mortal" -- Pythagoras

Many mythological presumptions of the unknown celestial world project arguments in the minds of atheists, agnostics, scientists, and the intellectuals. Ego (that which in the Vedas is also referred to as 'aham'), is the core and centrifugal personification of "gross attachments". 'Gross attachments' imply that we conform to a body, a thing, a person, a system, an environment, an embodiment, a desire, a lust, a thought, an act, a defence, a feeling, a judgement, a visible vision, all this and more. 'Ego' in simple and basic conceptualisation is the "I" or the "me". Ego is the feeling of the personality that bears a name, prestige, status, pride, glamour, and pleasure, sensuality all this and more.

Spiritually certain sense of selfless existence is evident. If for example Mother Nature is, the grand mother that nourishes its new-born creation then the mother feeding the baby nourishes it similarly from the bosom milk. This selfless aspect is what I consider to be ego-less. Ego grows in everything but the self-less aspects of life that does not become oriented towards the benefit of the 'me', 'mine' or 'I'.

There is no absolute ego-less state in as much as there is no absolute ego state. Each personal identity is partly dark and partly light. The degree of the light and the dark in each personality vary with the karmic tendencies. Therefore, whilst ego is not born, the personality bears with it certain karmic tendencies, that which in Vedic terms is inherited over from the previous life time or previous set of family.

Karmic tendencies are visible in the behaviour of children in their early years when certain attributing act or speech is not a result of the child's immediate environment of present life family influences or parental attendance. There are certain behaviour that are tendencies of the child's own projections from the previous life experiences.

Traits in personality, albeit being exclusive result of genetic hypothesis, can be varying with specific qualitative inferential behaviours that cannot be accounted under child psychology to be related to its present life experience. Such variances in accounting for certain profoundly unique trait can be regarded in Vedic terms as 'carried over' from previous life experience, 'brought forward' to present life experience trait in the life principal form. The life principal or the breath of life is a subtle life energy that bears with it certain karmic tendencies. Like for example, the last breath of life principal at death allegedly contained cumulative effects of the actions and reactions (karma) of the individual life principal. These alleged tendencies are inborn in the present life principal. There are many mythological assumptions about the life principal theory and none of the metaphor has been seemingly proven right or wrong. The purpose is not to prove the rebirth thesis, the god thesis, or the life after death thesis. All 'this, that and the other' is a matter of arguments, debates, antithesis, and subjective to each individual life principal.

Finding a compatible fit between the earth (that which is the human body) and the atmospheric society (that which is the mind) in Vedic psychology is a process of evolution. The evolution takes place in experience. In experience, the life principal grows out of restrictions, constrictions, and restraints of the social demands, to gradually seek conscience.

According to Vedas, the human nature is an essential divine being capable of evolving in karma, by diffusion, dissolution, and rebirth. Essentially, the true self is the benevolent conscience truth of existence. When the life principal becomes entangles in the desires and profusion of the mind, the karmic life becomes perpetual in pain and pleasure.

Finding our true self-hood is the life purpose of every life principal and the Vedas regard the individual life principal to be a cosmological being.

The Vedas consider a strong well-balanced conscience to be an essential element of expression in the social context. A balanced conscience is also supportive of the well functioning ego structure. Under a well functioning ego structure, the lives principal relates and inter-acts with compassion, tolerance, and great self-respect without loosing self-esteem. According to Vedas, the ability to realise ones failings and short comings is a pre-requisite to the long-term strength of the true self. Failure is not regarded as an end, rather a mere turning point to another cycle.

According to Vedas, the individual personal failure is a weakness in one's own self. It is a karmic eruption. Eventually, the failure or adversity brings the responsibility of the failure to the weakness of one's own self. Under the self-discovery, blame does not shift elsewhere other than with the self and within the self as a weakness. The spirit to transform from weakness into strength progressively nurtures this weakness. Self-discovery comprises grand life lessons about the falsehood of the material world and the impermanence of the human world. Conflict is the nature of material life of collective human. Conflict can produce fragmentation between in the internalised conscience and the 'astral-ego' (the connecting link or interface to the social needs and social demands).

According to Vedas, ego ('aham') follows illusion or falsehood ('maya'). For ego to manifest in a body ('kaya') of matter ('bhumi') under the influence of mind ('budhi'), the social affiliation ('samsahr'), in condition and circumstances need to be presiding in events ('karma-chitra'). The scenario of life is a battlefield wherein all the physical senses ('indriyas') and ego ('aham') are like the plaintiffs suing for greed, lust, anger, rage, desires, wants, and power. The Self is like the defendants trying to survive, evolve, and defend the existence of the spirit in hard struggles. The process of present life struggles according to the Vedas is the dissolution of the previous karma and karmic evolution. The authentic self-confidence thus emanates from 'atmanabhayam' (fearless-ness based on virtue). The egoistic self-confidence emanates from autocratic power, political manipulations, and intellectualism.

The cycles of the evolutions are dependent on the astral karma, that which prevails at the time of the birth in constellations, permutations, and combinations of planetary positions in each circumference of life structures or aspects.

Therefore according to the Vedas, for example, one life cycle was left over before the complete dissolution of the spirit in spiritual karma, in lifetime, and then the cycle would continue in another lifetime. Such karmic progressions can be eminent from the Vedic birth charts.

Awareness implies realising the spirit. Awareness takes stages from the more darkness towards more lightness. The more dark aspects of life dwell with the 'aham' (ego) in greed, lust, anger, desires, attachments, wants, wishes, illusion of all impermanence, procrastination, and proclamations. The more light aspects, 'illumination of life' manifests in the spiritual growth in self-discovery experience. Sufferings bring sublimate quintessence that leads onwards towards the true light of life to realise the truth by understanding in experience rather than learned knowledge. Self-discovery process of understanding in profoundness the essence of the spirit is spiritual observation. Prolonged spiritual observation in profound experience of rites, rituals, ceremonial oblations, sacrificial oblations, mantra-manjaree, meditation, inspiration, poetry, music, fine arts, and finesse of the super mind, delivers a personality from the gross darkness to the divine lightness.

Perception is imperfect owing to inherent limitations of knowledge and experience. Perception always gives distorted picture of the categories of the subject, time, and cosmic space. Perception verily is based on the phenomenal world, phenomenal thought, and phenomenal idea.

The purpose of life is to experience it divinely and to enjoy it. One cannot enjoy the human life (manushyaayush) without human health (swastha). Albeit mortal life is full of 'piddhah' (suffering), 'vyaaddhi' (disease) and 'dukhah' (sorrows), it is the aim of all the Vedic wisdom and Ayurveda, to lessen sufferings by improving the quality of life to moderate the effect of adversities. To become healthy (swasthayam) and happy (sukhyam), the human entity (manushyaavtar) must shift from the 'want' mode to the 'need' mode. What do we need to survive and to evolve? At a sublime level, it implies realising the known gunas in progressive cycles of experience ('abhyaass-vissaardaam') 'life-action or reaction - duty- sacrificial deed – spiritual liberation' ('ayush – karma - dharma - tyaag - moksha') and time or kaal.

All the Vedas emanate and branch from the 'srimad-bhagawad-geeta' – lord's divine compendium. The Vedas are known as 'Ved-saamm'hhita' which literally means 'all-together' or collective or sum collective wisdom of the human entity and the cosmic entity. Beyond the existence, beyond the karmic orb, all things merge in delight. [22]

Here on human earth, all things dissolve in death. Sorrow, disease, pain, obstacles, loss, grief, rejection, resentment, torment, adversities, and mental anguish all appear in a human life as experience and a reaction of wrong doing - 'karma-vikarma' either due to previous life time (purva-vikarma) or present life time (apurva-vikarma).

The question then arises what is 'wrong doing' – 'karma-vikarma'?

'Selflessness' 'idda'nnan'mamma' implies that we do not own anything that we accumulate for ourselves. Servitude and satt-karma (right action) is based on merit, aptitude, ability, integrity, intent, effort, skills, honesty, sincerity, and attitude. 'Varna' (divine profession) generates these sublime gunas (qualities). Avarna (non-divine profession) generate tamasic gunas of lust, greed, hate, anger, avarice, jealousy, envy, falseness, theft, prostitution, and perversion. The Vedic godhead is based on togetherness ('samam') – togetherness of the three worlds namely the celestial (ethereal eternity), the spiritual (unknown-unseen), and the gross material earth (known – seen).

Balance ('sthirtha'), healthy collective function ('sarwa-swastha'), of the gross known physical earth 'drsstta-dravya-sharir' renders good health 'purnam-swastha' to the mind and the emotions (being associated with the spiritual world) and the spirit (being associated with the celestial world). Imbalance on the known material earth physically seen by the eyes 'drss'tte-dravya-sharir' imply imbalance in the unseen-unknown-spiritual world – 'adrss'tte-daiva-sattya-loka'.

---

[22] Human life is an Imperfection born imperfect and that, which also dies imperfect. The human world is an illusion/ 'maya' because it is impermanent, imperfect, incomplete, and more importantly because it is unhappy, mortal, and diseased. Desire causes attachment to all the known materialism and causes lust, greed, anger, aggression, control-ship, ego-power, possessiveness, mind-power, gross intellectualism, and warfare. To realise the unknown soul 'atman' and to be free from the bondage of sorrow, disease, and desires, therefore, we have to first conquer the known life in experiences of karma (human act).

The higher consciousness is divinity (that which is spiritual integrity). "Integrity" – self respect for the spirit of life and for the spirit of existence is the basis of divinity. When integrity is absent, all else is corrupt. Under corruption, exploitation, manipulation, and chaos prevail without pity. Imbalance in health prevails.

The divine nature 'prakritti' is our 'maa' supreme mother that must be hurting severely to have to make fiery outbursts in earthquakes, draught, tragic epiphanies, and destruction on earth. Destruction on the human earth ('manushya-lokka') transpires when divinity – 'param-sattya' is distorted by 'avarnas' (non-righteous activities like warfare, egocentric economics, selfishness, greed, anger, hatred, jealousy, envy, avarice, selfish desires, fragmented commercialism, and social corruption).

When universal humanity - dharma/ right conduct is globally violated by the 'collective ego', we witness chaos, and conflict. Conflict results into saturation in economics, dissolving economies (like the stock market crashes); after which physical dissolution in war manifests. Loss of Integrity implies dissolution, window dressing of crimes, pollution in thoughts, all these and much more.

Disease manifests because of corruption, pollution, politics, and ego power. 'Vedic sam'skruttee' is the 'wisdom of cosmic divinity' – 'daiva-divya-jjnana' narrated by the cosmic deities – 'devas', for life – 'ayush' on the 'paapi-manushya-loka' – imperfect human earth for attaining liberation – moksha from mortal sorrow.

The elements of falsehood that the collective ego has dwelled in for the last 3000 years are now saturated with the greatest shame in the fake spiritualism, aggressive commercialisation, propagandas, and political bigotry. Wealth obtained without virtue renders chaos, conflict, and eventually upheaval. The desire to live therefore entails the desire to live a righteous life to be able to enjoy the righteous ways of life by maintaining good health and simplicity.

Selflessness – 'niswarth nishkam karma', good conduct 'dharma' (righteousness and virtue), cosmic laws of happiness, peace, optimum health, real wealth, and longevity ('ishwaryeh-kriya-karma-Rr'tas'), are qualities (gunas) of higher order conducive to divinity - spiritualism – 'adhyaatmaic jivan' on earth.

Selfless action – nishkam karma means 'idda-nnam-mmama' - enlightened liberalism – 'moksha-karta' dedication and devotion to the well being of the society 'samnsahr' in a non-biased, non-discriminative, and non-prejudiced manner. This is the basis for divinity and universal existence. Vedas refer to religion as an eternal universal religion - known as 'Sannatana dharma' - Good for the entire existence altogether.

Knowing science does not necessarily make one a profound scientist. A scientist dwells beyond the surface levels of the gross survival and the gross form into the modes of true experiences. Therefore, only in experience one realises truth. When anyone claims to have realised the non-dual truth otherwise, it is a false claim. Plato agreed with the Vedic science governing the journey of the soul after death, albeit he arrived at his conclusions with his own independent investigations, observations, and experience.

Eternally, 'Kaal' (time) is 'nir-guna' (formless) at a 'Somam' point - highest ethereal point also known as 'bindu-marga'. Time becomes 'Sarr-guna' (qualitative & quantitative) with the 'maha-maya' – 'prakrutti' firstly at a spiritual level, secondly at an atmospheric level, thirdly at the environmental level, fourthly at the mental level and fifthly at the physical level.

The unknown metaphysical world comprises seven spheres (lokas) of divine existence known as 'daivyah-dhammah'. The first sphere is known as the eternity or the 'parammdhamma'. This is the zero point – 'shunya-nir-guna' for which the Vedas refer to as 'para-gate-bindu-margha' (beyond the atomic). Just below the 'parammdhamma' is the cosmos - 'Rr'tta'. This is also the immortal existence of cosmic deities. They are the divine gods comprising immortal cosmic deities like 'agnee', 'indra', 'varuna', 'vayau', 'rudra', 'nirritti', 'mitra', 'vassus', 'maruttas', 'yamma', 'soma', 'issanaay', and 'kaal-saarpa'. Adjoining the cosmos is the heavens 'swaargha'dhamma'. Following the 'swaargha'dhamma' is the sphere of the deities – 'devadhamma'. The abode of demi-gods is adjacently after the deities – 'divya-rishi-dhamma' (great spirits and great seers). Final and seventh abode following the abode of deities and demi-gods is the spiritual world the abode of ancestors 'pitt'ari'dhamma'. The Vedas refer to the seven holy spheres and below these are seven 'narrakka-lokkas' hell spheres that are mortal. 'Prithvee' earth is a 'paapi-lokkam'/'dhamam' (sinful place).

When we understand the language of the pure existence, we perceive its real beauty and nourish its real divine truth infinitely, without doubts. When we realise that we are children experiencing the existential life, and struggling to survive the gross mundane materialism with the impermanence of perishing body and ego, we become aware. This awareness in Vedas is referred to as inspirational insight.

Pure awareness is simple existential awareness which is also referred to as 'Sat-chitt-anandam' ('truthful'-'fearlessness'-'blissful') is the balanced perfect state of nature. Everyone is striving towards this goal. In this divine state, there is no malice, no jealousy, no avarice, no lust, no greed, no egocentricity, no desires, no anger, no aggression, no fear, no suppression, no oppression, no 'me'-'mine'-'I'-'my'. All falseness disperses gradually and the darkness of ignorance gradually disappears in divine profound experiences of spiritual awakening. Spiritual awareness eventually liberates us. What one cannot feel with the mind but because of which the mind perceives and experiences happiness that alone is the 'sat-chit-anandam parambrahma'.

The rotation and revolution of cosmic operation 'rr'tta-karma' is ever non-stop in time 'kaal'. Rr'tta-karma perpetuates in cycles of creation, dissolution, and recreation.

As the water ('jaal'/'appaa') cleanses the impurities of the earth ('pritheveee'); as the wind ('vayau') alters energy and force in eight different directions; as the fire ('agnee') gives the warmth of creation in the womb and dissolves the mortal matter in ashes; as the ether transcends the ten vital life breaths (dasha'prannah) from the gross manifest (sarguna) to the most subtle unmanifest (nirguna). The 'Rr'tta-karma' thus perpetuates.

Truth exalts the mind (budhhee) in divine/ Vedic experiential knowledge. Truth evolves in constant and consistent divine experiences, by practice of yoga 'communion' in devotion-'bhaktee yoga' and living in accordance with the laws of cosmic godhead –'rr'tta-karma yoga'. In the illumination process, the human spirit comes to realise that its individual spirit of existence is not different to the grand cosmological spirit of existence. When the two lights (cosmic light and the spiritual light) merge in the fusion of one grand illumination, there is nirvana (the state of total bliss). When love is revealed, beyond all this, that and the other, the spirit of life takes a flight of delight. Light of delight is the truth which manifests in the cosmic gods like Indra, Agnee, Surya, Vayau, Varuna, etc.

The essence of existence is elucidated profoundly in the Gita. Philosophy is perception of conceptual framework – 'Darshanas'.[23]

The true self is scientifically the cosmic self in the astral spirit and each true self is almost like the constellation of star in a specific mode and location. Each star in the galaxy has unique characteristic and nature definitively comprising an astral spirit or 'jiva-atman' of the main spirit. The main spirit is the soul. Soul can not be destroyed. The soul is the God and God is in the soul. The existence is in the God and God is in all existence. 'Param-atman' (eternal spirit/ soul) and the 'jiva-atman' (individual spirit of life) merge in one grand 'divya-atman' (enlightened soul) in experience.

---

[23] 'Purana-darshanas'/ancient primordial Vedic seers' perception of the conceptual philosophy of the science of life and essential existential nature are:

a. 'Upanishads'– Wisdom of the eternal Brahman and eternal celestial God. There are 108 in total. Eleven mains are Isa, Kena, Katha, Prasna, Mundaka, Mandukya, Aitiriya, Taitiriya, Shwetashwatar, Chhaandaogya, and Brihadaaranyaka.

b. Vedas are anthologies of the primordial 'Bharat' time (land of shaktee goddess Uma the consortium of Shiva-whose physical abode is the Himalayas).

c. Puranas deal with creation, conception, and details of 'kaal-yugs' (eternal time). There are 18 'puranas', they are: Brahma, Padma, Brahmanda, Agnee, Vishnu, Garuda, Brahmavaivarta, Shiva, Lingham, Naarad, Skanda, Markandeya, Bhavishyat, Matsaya, Varaah, Kurma, Vamana, and Bahagavatt.

d. 'Dharma Shastras' are compendium cosmic order and karma. The significant ones are: Manu, Vishnu, Yaajnavalkya, Angiras, Apastambhas, Kaatyaayana, Parashara, Sanmkhya, Dakshya, Satapatha, Atri, Harita, Usanas, Yamas, Samavarta, Brihaspattih, Vyasa, Likhita, Gautama, Vashishtta.

e. There are six main 'darshanas', they are: 'Yoga' by Sage Patanjali for the development of the mind and body; 'Nyaya' by Sage Gautama dealing with cosmic logic and cosmic rationale; 'Samnkhya' by Sage Kapila dealing with the existential nature and the divine human entity in relation to the cosmic existence; 'Vaishashikka' by Sage Kanada dealing with the atomic theory and nuclear metaphysics; 'Purbva-mimmimssha' by Sage Jaimini dealing with the rituals and rites; and; 'Uttarr-mimmaanshaa' or 'Vedanttaas' or 'Brahman Sutra' by Sage Baadraayanna dealing with the Upanishads.

f. Shrimad Bhagavad Geeta is the holy anthology of the ancient Bharata ('land of Arjuna') narrated by the incarnate Lord Krishna to Arjun the warrior. It is an anthology of soul.

'Divya-atman' (enlightened soul) is the ultimate point upon which the truth manifests. At this point, it is almost like the point of no come back or no turning back. The karmic evolution is no more and the soul had united with the eternal grand spirit of existence in 'absolute' illumination. Such a perfect bliss generates light as if there is no day and night anymore. The illumination of light never failing forever is enlightened. The 'divya-atman' (enlightened soul) does not transcend back to the 'manushya-lokh' (the earthly pastures), to evolve or involve in karmic cycles. The karmic cycles and evolution has ended. There is no more karma left in a 'divya-atman' (enlightened soul).

It brings our understanding of the fact that there is neither beginning nor an end to divine light. Divine light in the eternity ('ishwar-lokh') is never failing, forever illuminating. Therefore, the Vedic outlook to the life process is in the scientific evolution, scientific cosmic coherence, scientific mathematics of constellations, scientific parables of metaphysics, and scientific perfection of the existence. The unknown mysticism can not verily appropriately be known in black and white syllables of logic, rationale, and reason. Only with profoundest insight, the light of true mysticism manifests in the real imagination of the lateral intuitive thought. Life is, but a dream, a memory experienced in the passage of time, life is a river bound by karmic fate and an undeniable destiny.

Perhaps Hamnssa (the swan) has the grace and quintessence to give a lofty 'flight of delight'. So divinely loved in the sky, 'Hamnssa' returned on earth, for the love of humankind to chance a spiritual journey in time. Vaguely, a vivid imagination, almost like a dream, a longing out of the way places, distilled through the elixir of maya (illusion).

Perhaps that insubstantial gallant is a daring chance of the soul infinite to leap into the unknown mystical celestial.

Perhaps 'Hamnssa' longs to belong to its true home leaving behind the heavy earthen clay that is found in hard worked mundane role in memories. Perhaps, by beauty, the swanlike spirit of life (Hamnssa) renders to all, a glimpse of heaven. Yet, a poet's friend to Hamnssa does sometimes remain unseen, almost like divine vision. More like a soul uneasy in this earthly clay, trying to free itself from the earthen attachments, desires, lures, passionate lusts, all the competitive aggressions, greed, and wretched bigotry.

The spirit of life constantly wants to be elevated from the earthen clay of gross materialism because the happiness found thereat is impermanent.

Then happy hamnssa is at last in the face of the glorious sunbeam, divinely in love with life itself. When all the torments of the earthen clay have gone and been left behind, hamnssa (the spirit of life) laughs in happy play with the rainbow and greets the hue of the sun.

So takes hamnssa a flight of delight saying: "Life oh life! Let it be a flight of delight" with all grace and peace everlasting!

Atman - Hamnssa so hum. That spirit soul divine is our real true nature. It has never been born. It has no beginning, nor an end. I am that beautiful winged spirit of life!

No words can describe it. No example can point to it. No reason can explain it. No cause can take it or give it except the destiny in the grandeur soul of the teeming vast sky itself. The sky has never ceased. It has no limits at all. It is limitless. To understand this truth and to comprehend the eternity the human being becomes a state of existential being 'Hamnssa'.

"Aum Hamnssa Hamnssa So Hum" ('I am a divine spirit of life swan-like I am).

Great Spirit renders us a sacred opportunity in time to know 'prakruttee' (nature) in divine experiences of bare existence (rivers, forests, Greenland, mountains, highlands, trashing sea, great nightingale, the dolphins, and the swans). This is the beauty, know it in time, experience it in time, realise it in time, become it in time.

Invoking the inner intuition entails integrity. To become that which is the quintessence of nature requires talent of integrity. The sprit of life first becomes an artisan, then a talent of integrity, and then a scientist (who observes). When the spirit of life reaches a decisive point, it dwells in poetry, philosophy, music, sound, dance, nature, to connect with all beauty.

Integrity is the soul discrimination to filtrate the complex web of human intellect woven in karmic threads of the mind and the ego in all this, that and the other.

Water washes off the impurities of the earthly body, wind blows away the impurities of the bad atmosphere, ether transforms the grand sky constantly, fire maintains the balance between the three worlds, illuminates, and nurtures the spirit of earthly existence. Knowledge of the nature and the natures cosmic Godhead brings us awareness. Devotion and sacred rites of sacrificial fire, prayers, oblation, self-lessness, elevate our lower intelligence to the higher intelligence. Possession of refined good intentions and good ideas purify our higher minds. Integrity is being pious, truthful, unprejudiced, honest, and learned.

Life oh life! Let me be! Let me be a divine spirit of life. Let me contemplate my pilgrimage to reach the highest thought, to accomplish the profoundest intention, to keep a close watch over the nature, and to transform into a free winged bird 'Hamnssa' (divine spirit of life).

The Vedic rites, rituals, ceremonies, oblations, sacrificial fires, and pujas (sacred recital of mantras, shlokas, verses, etc.) are towards to collective spirit of integrity, virtue, and good health of human existence. The good health is not just the physical health but the spiritual health through integrity. The Vedas speak of purification of the environment with integrity.

4. INTEGRITY 🐦

Integrity with compassion conquers without pity and sympathy.

The spirit of life says: "Life oh life! Let me endure in the world of my own for I was born to love and not to argue, shout, scream, repress, suppress, justify, reject, object, inject, 'all this, that and the other'."

Integrity yearns for togetherness with a comforting prayer:

'May we together in communion provide for our common enjoyment. May we together contribute towards building the strength and energy of each other. Life oh life! Let the lessons we learn glorify each other without malice. Life oh life! Let us learn and share without envy. May our minds flow with pure intentions in one mingled current of good thoughts and may we each look after one another as genuine human kind. May there be self-lessness in the intention to preserve the integrity of righteousness to fulfil and to encourage another true seeker.'

Integrity belongs to the life's eternal spirit. It is righteousness, virtue, honesty, upright, valorous, victorious, fairness, humane, and humbleness.

No one being can take that away from another human being and mould it into its own shape. Subtler forces of the soul divine manifest in the consciousness, higher intelligence, spiritual will, righteous feeling, and perception.

Life oh life! Let no man touch your spirit. Guard it, nurture it, love it, and hold it closely to your awareness until it is fully divine. Hamnssa oh Hamnssa! Let no one dictate to your spirit and crush its beautiful white wings.

Ignorance is the knowledge of the physical mind. Wisdom is the experiential knowledge of the insight attained when the physical mind surrenders to the spiritual integrity of the soul divine.

Life oh life! Let no earthly pain grind your integrity with all this, that and the other into worthless ashes of power, pride, and ego. Life oh life! Let your integrity bring you divine strength to withstand and forebear bigotry, falsity, and betrayals. Life oh life!

Life oh life! Let no one speak against the integrity of your soul divine. All l else is lost, if your integrity is lost. Life's spirit is your divine abode, safeguard it with integrity. Life oh life! Nurture your divine spirit with sacred prayer of peace to pull you through all the strife. Life oh life, when all else fails us, the light of the soul divine never failing shows us the way to go. Life oh life! Let your integrity bring strength, love, light, and hope to your spirit.

The strength of being alive and aware amidst all life's betrayals, adversities, sorrows, pain, rejections, and hurt comes from integrity.

Integrity belongs to the divine soul. It is a sublime quality of the spirit of the seer. Profound integrity grants us the inner serenity during grief.

You cannot become the centre stage of this world and not notice the bareness of an empty stage of your own soul. Your stage is veiled by a world full of poverty, ignorance, and diseases. It is your stage that you have created for others to see you not for your own self to see your own reflection. No matter how powerful you are, no matter how intelligent you are, no matter how rich you are; you are equal to nothing if you do not have the talent to make yourself and others truthful, divine, and happy with integrity.

Do not seek pity and sympathy, and, do not give pity and sympathy to integrity of life. However, give great compassionate sentimental love, selflessly and it shall come back to you in great extra ordinary strength. Giving selflessly your compassion and love is the essence of human sacrifice that is obligatory. Therefore, grant your compassion not your pity; grant your solace not your sympathy to others less fortunate than yourself. For example, an innocent child, a wounded soldier, a widow, a frazzling old person, a dumb person, a deaf person, a blind person, a paralysed person, a sick person, a helpless person, and a hopeless person. If only we could rise above the trappings of the material rat race and realise that love can heal the most severe wounds of grief, there can be hope for grief to diminish. Love contemplates with the God given gift of compassion.

Love is an everlasting talent of the spirit of life. The glow of the sacred fire is aspiration. The mellow serenity of the waters is consciousness. The green pasture is hope. The tree is the courage. The coal is the warmth. All things connect somehow in a profound sense and no thing can make a human immortal in spirit except the sovereignty of its spirit of life in integrity!

Therefore, give compassion and humanity to all in particular to the persons suffering the pain of loneliness and fear. Every one of us suffers. There is no exception to this rule. Make no mistake about it.

Conquer the roots of your fear. Learn to understand it with love and compassion. Pledge allegiance to your spirit and take one step at a time, but stand up and deliver compassion to the less fortunate persons who are afraid and lonely out there in the real world.

When you discriminate and deprive 'integrity' in a life's talent (spirit of self-respect in a person), you have attempted to make a person helpless, hopeless, poor, and battered. A sick person does not demand your sympathy. A sick person seeks your compassion and love. A dying person does not want your pity. A dying person expects your "integrity" to touch the spirit of his/her life with dignity, courage, strength, and serenity.

When money is lost something is lost. When shelter, livelihood, and possessions are lost much more is lost. When integrity is lost everything is lost because character and integrity is the spirit of life. Adversities mould us so that we may nurture our spirit of life, as Buddha did.

Death awaits every human life. Death is the human destiny that no one can alter. Its consequences are mystically unknown as much as the spirit of life is unknown, unmanifest, and untimely. To reach the unknown mysticism of the soul, the divine most truth, one must understand, one must comprehend, and one must conquer the known existential nature (prakrutti). The self-discovering experience (abhyaas) of the wholesome nature (prakrutti) under life karmic conditions of time (kaal) is in its form, its contents, its behaviour, its conditions, its movements, its contentions, its intentions, and its modernisation.

'Dharma' is righteousness, 'adharma' is wrongfulness.

'Dharmasyahi raksatih raksatah evam satyam, satyam kevalam vijayitih'

One, who nurtures righteousness, is righteous. Truth always triumphs.

Talent of integrity therefore opens us to insight.

Where there is no integrity, there is no intuition nor is there any insight.

'Aapuuryamaanam accala-pratishttham samuddramm aapah pravissanti yadvat tadvat kaamaa yam pravissanti sarve sa ssaantim aapnoti na kaama-maami'

'One who is not disturbed by the incessant flow of the lust and desires, like the ocean which remains unperturbed despite all the rivers rushing and flowing into it in perpetual karmic forces, that person alone can achieve the divine peace and not the person who strives to satisfy the lust and desires of all this, that and the other.'

God preserves Integrity for its beloved devotee without the shadow of a doubt. A precious spirit of life devoted to godhead is like a nature's child born to be free, living in freedom from fear, and dying with integrity to be liberated from all, this, that and the other. Integrity invokes insight to make others happy and an insight to bring harmony and peace in our co-relationship with others. Many a times, it is necessary to let the cocoon of an un-blossomed spirit struggle so that its integrity remains unperturbed.

Insight is a divine light to learn, and to listen, and to discover without false pride. Insight enables us to acknowledge the eternity. Insight enables us to see infinite beyond the finite! How can we objectively distinguish between the partial impermanent material nature and the para-psychological and the metaphysical metamorphosis of the super consciousness without being that little bit creative about how we look at life in a broader sense of the phenomenon?

To be creative with integrity implies that we become artists of feeling with compassion and harmony this magnificent eternal nature whilst inquiring and learning from the experience as true scientists of the nature.

A suffering life talent does not want your sympathy or pity. A crying soul needs loving compassion. This nature is a soul too and it is crying for true compassion from you and me. All anthologies somehow somewhere in somewhat profound sense of the perception, primordially regard human existence as sacrifice. Buddha, Jesus, Prophet Mohammed, all symbolise sacrifice. Sacrifice of what? Sacrifice of us for others. How many of us give without an expectation of reward or return. 'Compassion' and 'love' are not something we give in order to receive back ego praise or a monetary reward.

Buddha, Jesus, Mohammed or any anthologist did not expect praise or monetary reward or ego praise, albeit their spoken words have been translated, interpreted, and reconstructed, to imply varying views. All these great saints, savants, and seers of our centuries talked about conquering the soul, the essence, and the substance in profound silence of oneness with Nature and God. The light of the soul is discovered in total self-less sacrifice. This human life on earth is a temporary, transient dwelling.

To explore and to experience eternal joy and eternal happiness, there must be a union of soul and 'Agnee' (the flame of god). This sacrifice is sacrifice of our passionate feelings and our subjectivity for objective compassion and objective humanity. How can we embark on the final beatitude of life experience without realising the form of reality that surrounds us? Therefore, the world at large is a reflection of our own human life spirit. It is what we truly are – transient human fellows.

According to Bible, grief has no boundaries and is inexplicable just as death is. However, we require to be serene within ourselves and to begin to look within our own soul with fathomless faith and undoubted determination to conquer the love of God. We cannot fully comprehend Gods ways or Gods plan and we cannot certainly change what has already happened. What Jesus does emphasise upon is the present day and the present bread that we eat. There is profound wisdom in this. It is logic and rationale.

Ram, Krishna, Jesus, Mohammed, Buddha, were true artists of humanity and true compassionate creative talents of nature. They all demonstrated by being incarnated wholesome of human kind that without being a creative artist about the intricate nature of the soul, one cannot possibly realise the soul.

To discover compassionately the oneness of the magnificent nature and the soul, we need integrity to sacrifice our intellectually power driven ego towards realising the artistic beauty of the divine truth (altruism of soul).

Vedic concept of integrity:

'Sattyam evam ekam brahmanah ishwaarya nirgunah, etatdevah bahutah jagadah' – One ineffable God and multifarious subtle cosmic deities (33); Indra, Agnee, Vayau, etc are such deities of the celestial.

When the terrestrial world becomes isolated from the spiritual and the celestial worlds of existence, the world at large becomes darkened by ninety-nine impurities.

Agnosticism, atheism, and corruption of politics, religion and social welfare give rise to 'Agham' (evil), 'Atidaaruna' (dreadful), and 'Ati-dukha-samvegah' (extreme pangs of pain).

Absence of integrity result into 'paapam' (sin), assatyam (falsehood), 'bhaya' (fear), 'vikarma' (negative karma), 'adharma' (chaotic irreligiousness like paganism, cultism, corruption, hypocrisy, individual profiteering, egotism, and political camouflage), and 'durahatman' (evil nature).

To be honest and true to ones 'atman' (soul) is integrity. When Integrity is lost, all is lost. The gist of Vedic Integrity is contained in the following hymn:

'Let the spirit of life not grow old, let the spirit of life remain a child-like entity of god, let the spirit of life nurture you through all the adversities, let no one touch its integrity'.

'Aartha' (material wealth) comes from 'param-artha' (cosmic metaphysical wealth of gods). When wealth is distorted with 99 impurities and 99 blind eyes (stubborn egos), the global 'maya' (phantasmagoria) becomes gross. The agham (impurity) pollutes the beautiful existence with the 'mahimoha' (false attachments), 'mahaad' (desires), 'irrshca' (envy), 'pratibhaskaam' (excessive lust), 'mithyajnana' (false knowledge), and 'krodha' (anger, hatred and 'asatmayam-durahatman' (opposite of integrity).

When seers and rishis experienced life, they voiced their profound wisdom to the human ears, to the listener, to the seeker as a life-long wisdom to attain happiness, health, wealth, and honesty.

Integrity is the most significant aspect of the spirit of life ('jivan-atman'). All this, that and the other are life attachments, etc and are only for this lifetime. The Vedic spiritual science is not spiritualism; it is based on the cosmic science of existence, and the natures laws 'Rrta'.

We are all the children of the same God. We are all creators of the same divinity. We all breathe similarly, speak, eat, and sleep similarly. We are altogether one soil, one soul.

Our father is one (that which is the param-atman ishwaar) and our mother is one (that which is the prakrutti-shaktee-param'eishwaryee mata). We are disintegrated only in physical, mental, and emotional nature. Our spiritual nature is one. Our essential existential nature is one. That is the Vedic divine truth. The quest for spiritual knowledge and spiritual foundation is 'bhava' or intention.

A person of integrity has the right intention, the right attitude, and the right outlook. When the spirit of life crosses the 'pancha-koshas' (five sheaths of food, life, mind, conscience, and super-conscience) in gross, subtle and causal states, it experiences 'daivyatman' divinity in 'kaal' (time) and eventually reaches the Brahman state. When it reaches the Brahman state it begins to feel 'yo ha masi aham masi aham Brahman aham ASI meva' (oh life, I am the god, I am the soul, I am the spirit of life).

'Shtulla sharira' (physical body is where there are the three humours of vatta, pitta and kapha, the five elements of ether, air, fire, water and earth, the 16 attributes, 5 sense organs, 5 organs of actions, 5 elements of mind. 'Shukshma-sharrir' (astral body), comprises the emotional. It comprises the senses of knowledge, cognitive sensors, elemental mind, emotions, life breath, intellect, ego, and the mind. 'Karrana-sharrir' (causal or essential body) comprises integrity the divine spirit of life, satt-karma (right moral), and divya (light). The human sacrifice is not a burden but a sheer joy of delight in experiencing like a scientist the true moulding human experience progressively in karmic evolution. It is hard to say whereat the karmic journey begins, but a dream manifests.

A person of integrity goes beyond the wholesome existence, beyond the psychological parameters, beyond the emotional parameters, into the divine nothingness with patience.

A seer's heart is compassionately artistic and poetic whilst his mind and consciousness is philosophical and scientific in that he is indifferent to impermanence. The spirit of life takes a flight of life and finds joy in nature - 'Let me caper, let me observe, let me experience, let me know, let me realise the atman.'

When Hamnssa is freed from the boundaries of agham (impurities), it takes a flight of delight across the blue skies in happiness.

'Let me sing, Let me dance, let me play the music of my life. I am who I am. I am a star on the empty stage of clear blue skies and clear blue oceans. I am a simple laughter. I am a joy. I am a dreamer. I am a lone rider. I am a bird. I am who I am. I am just a talent of life, imperfect, as I may seem. Let me sing, Let me dance; let me play the music of my life. I am a wounded bird that cannot fly anymore, but I am still a star on the empty stage, I am a Bird of the spirit of life – Hamnssa or short form 'Hanss'. I am the musical note, and I am a word that is compassionate and loving. Let me sing, Let me dance; let me play the music of my life. Let me caper to the melody of the night spirit, the moonlight, and glitter of the twinkling stars. Let me be the poet of all magnificent beauty. Let me gaze at the sunrise and the sunset. Let me feel the wind that blows with fresh breezes. Let me touch the ripples of the gleaming waters that reflect the mirage of the magnificent sky. Let me hear the mountains and the valleys that echo the sound of AUM, and infinitely more. Let me be a voice of compassion. Let me be a dreamer. Let me be a reflection of love. Let me be forever the quantum in the skies, and a distant star of destiny. Let me sing, Let me dance; let me play the music of my life. I am in love with life; I am in love with nature. For now, let me caper.'

A Vedic human being is a 'hamnssa' (free winged spirit of life born to be freed from the impermanence).

Our spirit is like a beautiful winged bird that flies across the blue skies and blue oceans and seven different earths and running rivers to capture the glamour and lore of the magnificent nature.

We are metaphorically like this free winged bird that experience's life from one point of vision to another point of vision. It is almost like taking different photographs from different points, under different time conditions.

To realise the true potential of our spirit, we need integrity not academic qualifications. We are afraid of 'alone-ness', thinking that it is loneliness (fearful boredom). We need to empty all our fears and inhibitions.

To understand and to appreciate the conceptual framework of 'fear', we must embark on a different platform. Fear takes away the inner child in each one of us.

Fear makes us mortals. Fear limits us to following falseness and becoming blind to the ethical conduct of the higher order.

When the inner child is abandoned, the body responds to stress. The result is ill health, distress, and catastrophe. When we look at any conflict, may it be a war, or a misunderstanding, or a hurt, or dismal propaganda, we may see a tint of fear underneath the sheath of physical brevity. Fear is fear whether it is hatred towards another out of insecurity, anger, frustration, or even trauma. Fear ('bhay') in Vedas block spiritual enhancement. Fearlessness ('abhay') means being aware of the obstructions and adversities but struggling onwards towards 'moksha' (spiritual liberation) with 'dharma' righteousness and right conduct and without expectations of the outcome.

When pollution becomes predominant in air, water, and earth, the Vedic 'artha' wealth becomes 'anartha' (materialism based on selfishness, egocentricity, and political power). Such 'anartha' renders sufferings firstly to the world at large in many tragedies, upheavals, epiphanies, trauma, distress, diseases, catastrophes, and uncertainties.

Fearlessness emanates from 'arthah' (balanced appropriation of wealth). When vocation is pursued for creating prosperity of the entire society based on righteousness, integrity and in accordance with the laws of nature, such vocation is considered to be 'nishkam-niswartha karma' (self-lessness). Wealth of the celestial 'param-artha' is provided for the enjoyment in moderation and appropriation economic wealth 'artha' in equal parts to the plant, animal, and humankind.

However, when misappropriation and fraudulent politics devolve, the economic infrastructure (socio-economic and political economy) becomes distorted. Distortion in the gross state affects adversely the subtle state and eventually the life span, quality of life, and livelihood. Livelihood, based on fear is a livelihood filled with high pollution, high political bureaucracy, hypocrisy, corruption, wars, terrorism, vendetta, and disintegration. Material welfare based on 'anartha' can become dismal, confusing, chaotic, uncertain, unstable, and even traumatically distressful.

Mass poverty and mass ignorance are two major aspects of existence that are probably the darkest perplexities. 'Ignorance' is the longest night according to Vedas.

All impurities emanate from the ignorance of the true divine knowledge of the soul, the cosmic nature, and the religion of universal righteousness. Conflict renders a gap, differentiation, and lack of discerning filtration. False knowledge is disruptive and half knowledge is empirical. When integrity is lost, the social, economical, and political welfare of the individual, the family, the community, the society, the government, the nations, and the world, is disrupted, disturbed, and vitiated.

Under vitiation, corruption prevails. The human entity is not merely a person, a personality, or a name. The human entity is a whole image of the cosmic eternity comprising the personality and the soul divine or the spirit of life. Without the spirit of life, the personality is nothing but a representation of ego, all that is falsely illusive. When the personality and the spirit of life combine in togetherness, there is soul divine compassion. The prevailing excessive materialism in the modern world is forcing all religions to jettison their metaphysical findings and ethical precepts as metaphorical.

A person of integrity is a wise person awakened through sufferings, grief, and the sentimental humanity. A person of integrity recognises the subtle elements of sound, touch, sight, taste, and smell in space, air, fire, water, and earth respectively. A person of integrity respects these five elements as resources of life, health, wealth, and happiness.

Suffering and pain, sorrow and grief, unhappiness and diseases, adversities and tragedies appear to awaken one's true divine self and to make one realise that the gross materialism, materialism, and egoistic intellectualism is mortal.

Life oh life! Let it be what it may be, let it be. Let it be, come what may. Face it, accept it, grit it, but grin and shrug it away. Let it be, come what may. Let it be.

'Hamnssa' grits at the realities of the modern world. There is fear and there is insecurity, making one realise that there is trauma, hurt, anguish, anxiety, sorrow, pain, suffering, and despair in all the surviving lifestyles. Oh the roaring streets, the busy streetlights, the rushing traffic, and the loud screams shall soon become quieter with the wonderful dusk. Nightfall brings one an opportunity to reflect upon the day's karma.

When 'Hamnssa' grits all the despair of the modern world, it (the spirit of life) weeps in tears of dismal compassion.

Life oh life! It is human to err. It is human to make mistakes. It is human to even wrong. However, it is also human to recognise the error, to realise the mistake, and to acknowledge the wrong. Life oh life! Life is full of sufferings and pain. Life oh life! Life is a sacred pilgrimage towards the soul divine. To suffer and to evolve in karma is but the grand opportunity rendered to one by the eternal time and eternal divinity. It is inevitable to become afraid, and to become dismal, for the human is born imperfect. Life oh life! Let the spirit of life awaken and understand with great compassion the despair surrounding the modern world. Life oh life! Let it be.

Satt-Karma (righteousness) associates a human being to its divine self, to its true self. Vi-karma or assatt-karma associates a human being to its ego state, the gross Personality State that thrives on excessive materialism. 'Hamnssa' sheds tears of hurt for its Integrity and speaks weeping to the gossamer of grand cosmic illusion (maya) and reality (sorrow):

"Life oh life! Let it be! Life oh life let me conquer fear before I can know myself. Fear oh fear. Let me know you. Fear oh fear. Let me even understand you. Life oh life! Let me righteously rise above the survival of all, this, that and the other dreary darkness. Life oh life! I am afraid of the dark. Let me see into the darkness of all my fears and let me find a light of hope in the tunnel of woven karmic webs."

5. DESPAIR IN THE MODERN WORLD ◈

The universal material body of the human being (manushya-sharir) is born of knowledge of material things and existence in combination. This is the knowledge of the self. Albeit the magnitude of the self-knowledge may vary in accordance to the karmic evolution, consciousness makes human beings both social animals and divine beings in a wholesome composition. This wholesome composition enables the 'personality' to awaken from the composite gross material level to the sublime metaphysical level. Here on karmic earth, all the 'known' materialism pulls the 'personality' (senses and the ego) to become grossly attached to it in desires, lures, greed, aggression, and temptations. There in the mystically unknown world, the unknown grand cosmic spirit of existence calls upon the human earth to realise the impermanence of the material mortal life.

Crying is an inborn inherent human nature. To cry and to express emotional sorrow is nature's way of associating with the falsehood of the mortal human life in attachments, illusions, desires, and ambitions. Fear is born in every human being as the opposite of blissfulness. Fear is a transient quality of the collective ego that builds the political economy of empires.

Social, economical, and political powers bring fear. The primary issue of the Vedic sociology ('samnsar-samaj'), economics ('artha'), and politics ('sabha') dwell in the root of all impurities ('aghamah'), deliberate offences ('aparaadhah'), and falsity ('asattmya').

The collective human entity has projected itself in personality, rather than an image of God or divinity. According to the Vedas, fear is the root cause of all negation, conflict, falsity, and despair. Fear is no longer pure fear in the context of the Vedic sociological perception. Under a fearful society, there is predominance of personality in the context of the mind, the intellect, the ego, and the emotions. The spirit or the divine soul is isolated, rejected, misjudged, and misappropriated in penances. Our Society seldom cherishes truth. During adversities and sorrows, one realises the ingenuity of relatives and friends!

The following features are predominant in a fearful society:

- Wrongfulness 'Adharma' which includes superstitions, cultism, unscientific outlook, blind faith, and hypocrisy.

- Falsity 'Asatmyah' which includes selfishness, greed, egocentric wars, hatred, jealousy, envy, bigotry, perversion, excessive materialism, propagandas, excessive ambitions, excessive desires, lust, prejudiced anger, discrimination, conflict, disagreements, obsession, insecurity, corruption, all these and more.

- Deliberate violence 'aparaadhah-hant' which includes international wars, terrorism, increased youth crimes, tribal wars, national wars, turbulence, upheaval, and serious critical disagreements.

- Commercialism without standards, ethics and morality.

- Uncertainty in workplaces, schools, and government.

The Vedic pillars of fearless state are selflessness 'nishkam niswarth karma', divinity and observance of cosmic laws of nature 'satt-rrttam karma', and trinity of value of the cosmic wealth 'param arthah' in 'dharma' (righteousness), 'artha' (distribution of earthly resources), and 'kaama' (desires of creation).

The Vedic philosophy of righteousness is not a mere theological anthology, rather morals of the individuals, society, ethics of the society, creation of universal wealth, health, and happiness.

The Vedas list six types living namely the divine living 'daivyayush', spiritual living 'adhya-aatmic', absolute pure living 'shunya-sattva', pure living 'sattva', directional living 'rajasic', and pleasurable living 'tamasic'.

Corruption, conflict (between the ego and the spirit), personal selfish greed, selfish ambitions, false attachments, egocentricity, and anger cause self-destruction of any society.

The aim of the Vedic counsel is to give a balance of all six states of living in proportion such that the universal existence remains in harmony.

However, the Vedas do place greater emphasis of dividing the time towards self-development, spiritual growth, and ultimately self-realisation. The purposes of one's lifetime periods can not therefore remain pleasurable forever. Hence, the issue is of caring for the welfare of others, the welfare of the universal society, for the good of all, and generating hope for tomorrow's children.

It is in corrupt society that savants like Jesus Christ suffered crucifix, many ideal social reformers like Mahatma Gandhi, Martin Luther King, and others suffered assassination. Are these individual acts not the same as terrorism, wars, and manipulative social, national and international imperialism?

When there is no harmony between the personality and the spirit, between the personality and the ego, and, between the ego and the spirit, a social influx of disparity prevails. Fear dominates the atmosphere, the environment, the society, the governments, the institutions, the welfare, the homes, the young, the older, and the weaker. Despair transpires in conflict in the personality. Conflict gives rise to chaos and eventually sorrow.

Personality in isolation without the soul divine

The personality is the centrifugal force of life. The personality is pulled towards the gross matter of the gross physical earth, by the 'ego' and the 'intellectual mind'. The personality being imperfect follows a set of systems, a set of patterns, and a set of bureaucracies that have conveniently transpired into the conscious mind by thought processes. Thought processes emanate from the historically established sociological, political, and economical systems. Thought transpires from frameworks of established personality rather the combination of the wholesome divine human entity comprising the mind, the ego, the higher mind, the spiritual intelligence, and the soul divine.

The personality is a 'collective mind' with 'collective intelligence', and 'collective action'. The personality is a life gene of 'collective human history'. This is the truth. The personality is illusively false because it is mortal.

The personality bears with it "history" that is not an eminence of 'total freedom' and 'total happiness'. The personality is embodied in the web of intellectual spectrum. Its survival is based on reason, cause, parameters, criteria, authority, academics, and, systems. Its survival is based on "what you see is what you get".

The personality functions through the status bound hierarchy of social, economical and political authority. The personality survives on, hierarchy of collective thought processes, conscious actions, deliberate reactions, and equations in 'action' versus 'reaction'.

The personality follows a chain of karmic thread, knowing the vicious chain but not necessarily understanding it with deep compassion. The personality always likes to create followers, to feel important and heroic, out of the authority, of being the 'technical knower' or a 'superior in charge'.

"Control" and "power" motivate politics, international political economy, and the gross collective ego. Control and power cannot manifest without greed, lust, desires, aggression (rage & anger), attachments, illusion, and falsity. All ego control and power generate falsity and heroism.

Personality on its own is the image of egoism. Personality without soul divine would project to be selfish. The intention, the motive, the aim, and the action purport personal heroism.

Despair has transpired in the modern world through the collective history of the collective human karma by the imposition of the personality in isolation. It is the little shadow which runs across the perennial grass and loses itself in the sunset. Personality is like the river (small, medium, large, tiny, wide, and long) that eventually looses its name, size, form and merges with the ocean to become one. 'All this, that and the other' dwell in the physical mind of the personality. The ego is the centrifugal identity of the personality. Social infrastructure is the mirage of this ego that dwells in materialism of all things. Motivated by desires and ambition, the personality is never satisfied.[24]

---

[24] The personality comprises the lower mind, the lower intellect, and the ego.

There is no perfect solution for the imperfect despair.[25]

The diminishing human value

Five thousand years ago, the world was a place of lesser diseases and lesser catastrophes than the world today. Five thousand years ago, the world was more peaceful and happier than the world today. Five thousand years ago, the world was less polluted and less chaotic than the world of humankind today. The beauty of human existence is shattered and the voice of beautiful human existence numbed by violence, fear, and tragedies.

So what are the powerful egos of the powerful nations proud of today? A world filled with miseries and diseases. A world filled with teenage crimes. A world filled with broken homes. A world filled with depression and pollution. A world filled with sex and violence. A world filled with jealousy, envy, and pride and political wars. A world filled with global poverty. A world filled with power conquests. A world filled with fear and propaganda.

No politician is free from the threat of loosing life at the hands of its enemy. A politician has greater enemy forces than any other entity. Politics and religion are the two most ridiculed aspects of our human life existence. Greed of power, the pleasure of controlling conquests and, the claim of 'something' has been the mode of historic global karma (action).

The collective human mind and the collective human ego are responsible for a collective human world filled with disasters. A world filled with wars, epiphanies, tragedies, recession, chaos, chemical pollution, ozone disturbance, water contamination, high disease rates, shorter life spans, life threatening diseases, camouflage, all these and much more.

---

[25] The Vedas advise that for a fearless state of mind, for fearlessness, all issues of the 'despair' or 'sorrow' or 'disease' or 'hurt' or 'trauma' or 'suffering' or 'grief', be perceived, understood, intercepted, and elucidated in completeness. Completeness entails combining the personality, the mind, the higher intellect, the soul, and the consciousness in addressing the issue of despair from an impartial, unbiased and objective perspective of the inward looking mind as well as the outward looking reality. In harmony and balance exists the value of the matter.

The modern human world dwells in brand names; new concepts, new frameworks, new umbrellas, new personalised names, and new forms of man made mirages. The core human values of health, fair proliferation, un-vitiated growth, happiness, and harmony have diminished but materialism has increased. Authority imposes with political power rather than divine truth.

The Vedic metaphysics is more for the welfare of all members of the society and made simple for those who are on the path of spiritual emancipation, divinity and godhead ('muktee-moksha jnanna marga').

Spiritualism has become the means of propaganda and commercialisation under different cocoons of politically powerful individuals each claiming to be right in their own territory.

Commerce and economy stand still saturated in nearly all western nations threatened by global diffusion of wealth, individualism, and personal political sovereignty being imposed upon us under different falseness. At whose expense are these 'so called political leaders' waging wars? At the expense of working class citizen known as 'the decent tax payer'. Money that is materially re-created money based on falsehood, hypocrisy, bigotry, political camouflage, and economic distortion, is fatal. It increases indebtedness, adulteration, and speculation. These are tamasic gunas (impure qualities) of the predominantly 'anartha-dhann' (false wealth). This kind of wealth is re-created by imposition, control, imperialism, warfare, chaos, camouflage, political corruption, and religious fanaticism. 'Daivya-Artha' (divine wealth) is like the air. We cannot see the air, but we inhale it nevertheless. Its pollution is felt immediately in diseases, tragic epiphanies, distress, and social chaos (increase in youth crimes).

Modern imperialism is 'fear' oriented on super exploitation of resources, welfare of people and bigotry (false propagandas). Peace is no more. We need to ask ourselves what has suddenly happened to divine mother earth in the last 5000 years. The world at large is filled with heroism of all this, that and the other. The modern money is generated with lesser honesty, lesser integrity, and lesser consciousness in most countries. Thus, the value of the money has diminished in technical terms.

When the outward looking mind ('etani/preyasman'), based on senses, the mind, the intellect, the ego, and the gross body thinks and works solutions based on mind conferences, intellectual referendums and political camouflage, there is synthesis of the thesis and the antithesis of all this, that and the other. However, this synthesis is temporary until another crises come along with another tragedy and another upheaval. Upheavals and tragedy happen because under the modern world problem solving takes place without inference to the cosmic laws or divinity or primordial Vedic wisdom of life or inward looking divine mind (divya manas/shreyasman).

Human is born in the image of God and it has the innate talent and capability to assimilate all the facts and information and then to comply and assist its higher mind or the super-conscious God. When decisions are based on incompleteness, inappropriateness, and inadequate assimilation, the consequences are dismal. A political human could achieve what the collective human could not achieve in 10,000 years if only it dwelt in the inner most insight and inner most intuition of divinity.

Vedic divinity always raises the questions: 'To whom is the benefit?' 'What is the intention', 'What is the motive', 'What is the remedy?'

Act, which protects the welfare of the society and the welfare of the children, is an honest act of good deeds, for example. Act which does not protect the welfare of the society and the welfare of the children is a wrongful act and the governments all over the world need charters for the protection of children's welfare, for the welfare of human integrity.

At the gross physical level, the world contains most dangerous toxins of the chemical warfare (nuclear weapons). At physical level, mass poverty, mass starvation, mass diseases, and political unrest, prevails, resulting into deprivation, suppression, and exploitation. At the physical level, the world is saturated. Saturation is dominating the world in all areas of trade and commerce and financial economy of currencies. At the mental level, the world is in great conflict between the declining interest rates and the high cost of inflationary living. At the emotional level, the world is faced with economic uncertainty because of which stress is adversely affecting lower income earners into various ailments and sudden tragic deaths.

At the meta-physical level, the world is generating greater mental illnesses and greater number of depressed persons. At the conscious level, the world is suffering falseness of artificial intelligence in many forms including computer frauds, illicit hankering, Internet violation, terrorism, perversion, and false political propaganda.

Everywhere, the world in crises and recession, is striving to implement reforms. There is no end to the number of reforms that have been pumped over the passage of five thousand years. Most of which have rendered either 'conflict' or 'confusion' in one form or another.

One political system imposes over another political system. One sociological system imposes over another sociological system. One economical system imposes over another economical system. The world at large is divided, disintegrated, fragmented, dissolved in its compassionate essence, and is full of 'uncertainty' or 'anxiety'. Eccentricity prevails everywhere causing havoc and chaos.

Political power is not authentic power

The first world war, the second world war, the Vietnam war, the triangular slave trade, the missionary compulsions, the division of the first world, the second world and the third world, are empirical projections of our collective human history. The collective human mind therefore cannot be different to an individual human mind, because the same warfare prevails in us all individually. As individuals, we are in constant 'conflict' between our 'true spirit of life' and our 'ego'. This conflict gives rise to hate, anger, frustration, anguish, stress, escapism, hurt, violence, rage, sex, alcohol, toxins, burglary, and more. We are either trying to defend a system or otherwise trying to follow the conflicting system of survival without actually trying to understand it.

Ego distorts the fundamental righteousness and the universal humanity with the individualism, excessive materialism, and imperialism. Growth in the political economy excludes divinity, spiritual growth, and harmony. We cease to bring about radical change within our individual perceptions. Our perceptions are filled with 'fear', or 'rebel', or 'rejection', or 'hurt', or 'doubt', or 'pride', or 'conveniences'! We survive and thrive on uncertainty and consider ourselves 'survivors of the fittest'! What are we surviving?

The modern man is engrossed in material power and creates a camouflage of social and economic rat race. We breathe and function through the superiority of "mind" presuming that, there is nothing beyond the mind, and the body, and the gigantic wholesome material world of wealth and power. The modern world is elapsing at a much faster pace than the world five thousand years ago.

The rapidity of the pace is attributable to the technological advancement, which the 'collective intellectual mind' has brought about. Growth in every sphere has organically saturated. Organic saturation has entailed the 'collective intelligence' to indulge in power warfare, stocks or currency exchanges, amalgamations, and nuclear wars to create 'inorganic survival'.

Inorganic survival has become the way of living in the modern world. The entire stock market and the entire global financial market is operating on the theme of 'share holder value', 'paper profits', 'accounting profits', 'tax avoidance', 'tax evasions', 'brands', 'mergers and acquisitions', 'inflationary trading', 'futile speculations', and 'massive re-structuring'. 'Micro-organic' growth has been recessed into deterioration, whilst inorganic growth has increased substantially. This is imminent from the 'east' and 'west' divisions.

Most of the enterprises that produce goods and services today, survive on "lowest cost" cheapest materials and lowest cost cheapest labour. Most successful enterprises thrive on the materials that come from the Far East, Asia, Africa, India, and any other third world economy referred to as 'East'. Necessities like rice, agricultural products, food, cotton, sisal, sugar, and leather come from the third world. In the passage of time, there must have been substantial production of essential materials, minerals and raw materials in the third world that have been exported to the saturated economies of the 'west'. This cycle of macroeconomic distribution of wealth is based on 'monetary power' of imperial exploitation.

The least powerful economies suffer the most. It is a fact, that, basic essentials like the rice, wheat and cotton still emanate from South America, Africa, Far East, China and India. These lands are most fertile and rich in production, yet they are the very economies that are suffering massive starvation, massive poverty, massive ignorance, massive warfare, and massive grief, massive camouflage, massive conflict, and massive chaos!

The world at large suffers from chaos and uncertainty from unexpected natural disasters, accidents, traumatic upheavals in climate, and many other natural forms of dissolution. The third world suffers greater loss of uncertainty from famine, wars, ignorance, and mass poverty.

One wonders why uncertainty prevails in the "known material world" in one form or another. What has brought our present world of existence in its present uncertain state? Perhaps this is what the Vedas are invoking one to examine with an impartial higher mind and consciousness.

If the intellectual mind is capable of producing such highly powerful technological advancements and such highly powerful institutional umbrellas, then why has the human mind failed to render a solution to end the despair 'human misery'? There is the conflict! Why has the collective human intelligence failed to render a simple solution to "sorrow"?

"Sorrow" is the same for the poor or the rich, for the east or the west, for the powerful or the weaker, for the small or the large, for the young or the old. Sorrow is universally the same sorrow, and to render a solution to end the universal human misery therefore there must be a transformation in totality not social and political reforms that please the closet of power driven authorities. Love is love. Love cannot be different in the east and the west. Love is compassion. Compassion is the same regardless of the caste, creed, culture, colour, race, society, or platforms.

Organically, the world dwells in a vicious cycle of absorption, manipulation, consumption, redemption, and exploitation. Inorganically the world dwells on the 'paper profit'. The creative intellectual and the recuperative material persons both survive on the vicious cycles of 'powers'. Organically, the gigantic industries, commerce and professional practice operate in vicious cycles of "institutional power'.

If one has established a social status, that is powerful enough to influence other powerful persons, in the commercial game, becoming part of the 'system' platform is imminently easy. There is manipulation of the original creative talent. There is absorption of the glittering talent (that which is not always real glamour). The organic process of competition, consumes, redeems, and exploits for "profit" or for personal benefit.

Power means everything. If one has power, name, social status, prestige, professional reputation, then one's personal character and personal reputation are overlooked.

Hierarchy of platforms and hierarchy of authority support the collective human intelligence in bringing about 'world economic crises'. The collective human history in its collective hierarchy of intellectual and egocentric powers has rendered rapid solutions and rapid conclusions. We have woven a karmic thread of action and reaction, in a chain of perpetual assertions. This is the naked fact! The super "para-person" inside our soul, whom I call God (shining in the armour of immortality and benign with one million petals of integrity) has been killed and murdered several times with 'institutional power'. No one will admit to be a fastidious person, to stand up and understand the shame of 'institutional power', but everyone, will claim to know 'everything' and to impose themselves onto others less powerful. Fear is breeding in mass ignorance, mass poverty, and mass confusion as a result of the power imposed by the collective human 'ego' with its collective human intelligence.

'Fear' reflects itself in many forms, including, pleasure, sorrow, thought, rage, aggression, regression, fuss, anger, rejection, rebel, discriminations, insecurity, lust, violence, indulgence, hate, anguish, irritation, loneliness, isolation, depression, all that and more. Either people are isolated or otherwise they form part of a group that thrives on propaganda, set of religious anthologies, and systems of hierarchy. Solitude is rarely respected. Solitude is rarely revered. Is this not too obvious then, that the world outside us is a mere reflection of what has happened to us 'within us', collectively? Only human has the soul as a divine spark to unravel the truth - God.

If you and I, we forget for a moment to look at the 'I' and 'you', and concentrate on 'our' human condition collectively. We will realise and understand with deep compassionate love that the human intelligence has manipulated, absorbed, consumed, copied, redeemed, and exploited true human talent of integrity with power. From childhood, one is taught to acquire brevity of mind and brevity of body to compete and to become better than others. This insecurity grows into an adult that becomes insecure and wants to protect and safeguard his or her power, position, prestige, house, car, and 'any' possession or obsession, with his or her acquired power, and authority!

When something goes wrong, the blame shifts downwards not upwards. The blame never becomes imminent in the higher power position. This kind of shift has become empirically evident in political warfare, violence, and discrimination.

Organically therefore, power emblem is everything in 'name', 'hierarchy', and 'social status'. Power breeds on power. Organic power operates on economic and political frameworks of complex intellectual formulae, 'repeating the system', and 'supporting the bureaucracy' out of fear, creating distinctions of human classes, 'personal charisma ', 'institutional knowledge, and 'authoritative position'. All that and more. There is no end to the cycle of structural survival.

Organic cycles dwell on 'monetary equations', with the power of wanting more and more. Organic cycles dwell on flesh and intelligence of 'greed' and 'lust'. Organic cycles operate on politics and economics of 'convenience' rather than 'deliverance' of truth. If one conveniently supports the bureaucracy and conveniently plays the game, then that person is a convenient leader or a convenient follower and the rest of the world is expected to either take it or leave it (bureaucracy). As long as one is under the umbrella of systematic bureaucracy and one abides to play the game of bureaucracy, one becomes an active player and a passive reciprocator. I use the term 'passive' because, in reality, the personality does not evolve in karmic life, and in reality the personality decays with the elapsing time.

Any power play does not remain a permanent feature of the person's lifetime. Organic power play cannot manifest to render peace and harmony albeit it deceives one with 'economic growth'.

The world of organic saturation and inorganic growth has rendered to us 'human crises', 'human misery', and 'human problems'. We survive in constant conflict. As a collective karmic seed of personality, we impose, rather than embrace the collective human existence.

The most powerful economies of this world attract the best intellectuals because the competitiveness in the circumstantial environment affords to maintain the high levels of recuperation.

Maximum power will be able to buy maximum talent. This is truly exemplified in the U.S.A, where, doctors, psychiatrists, medical professionals, lawyers, and MBA's earn three times more than the same professionals in the third world countries. Some of the world's best doctors and best professionally qualified persons have migrated to this political economy from India, Africa, Asia, Eastern Europe, and South America, because of the enticing recuperation in greater monetary pay.

What is the solution to resolve mass poverty and mass ignorance in Asia and Africa?

From the outer mind, and outer intellect, the solution would be to give monetary resources to the governments of those continents, to give aid grants and to set up schools, hospitals, etc. However, when the same issue is resolved under the Vedic ethos of value, the root of the issue is considered. The root question of the issue will dwell on what has made India and Africa poorer. What are the root causes of distorting Integrity?

Organically, the third world is indebted heavily in repaying their loans and aids given by the first world namely U.S.A, Canada, and Europe. The aid is a burden to the third world economy because; the cumulative interest aggregates to more than the amount of actual loan, over loan time scale. Inorganically, the world has become a desperate place with highest professional bureaucracy (medicine, law, finance, and others). The best intellectual minds and the best professionally talented persons are forced to ignore selfless servitude in their own third world countries. The power of money shifts specialist skills and talent from their needed territories into the powerfully covered veil of bureaucracy. The risk of sacrificing towards the mass poverty and mass ignorance is absconded for luxuries, comforts, and conveniences of life. In pleasure has manifested all the looms of personal desires. Fear emanates from the aggression to survive and compete.

There is fear emanating from those that lead in positions in the form of personal insecurity, personal shield, dualism, suppression, oppression, compulsive adherence, and threats. There is fear transcending unto the 'powerless', making them passive blind followers or abiding puppets.

The issue of fitting in the survival kit is not an issue of choice; it is rather an issue of cause and reason. Mundane Karma reasons to accumulate or struggles to survive.

Organic world of power play has brought about First World War, Second World War, and the many mini wars like the Vietnam, the east, and the west, mass poverty in Africa, India, Far East, South America, and Middle East and so on. Violence is the feature of collective organic power play. Violence manifests in many forms. Violence does not simply mean a gun and a knife. Violence means "stress", violence means "frustrations", violence means "personal hatred", violence means "personal pride", violence means "greed", violence means "lust", violence means "possession", violence means "obsession", and violence means "non-peace". If one is not at peace and if one does not have true spiritual harmony, then one must sincerely consider the collective organic power play with compassion to realise its true effects.

In collective understanding, one needs to discover and realise that fear is originating from collective human intelligence and collective human mind, in the collective historical period. Feeling insecure, making others feel timid, making someone feel less important, making one's personality feel superior to others, comparing each others power dressing, becoming miserly in spending to obsessively hoard more and more for more personal security and comfort; all that, and more.

The collective human intelligence and the collective human mind created the world we are in today. World filled with crises, and materially despondent environment. Speed has become our nature in everything. Speeding to win, speeding to drive, speeding to think in haste, and wasting resources. So can we actually deliver the truth in abstracts of 'half compiled thoughts'? Can we actually deliver the human solutions with our superior human intelligence and human mind power in haste? Can we put an end to the human misery in haste? Have we increased the human misery or decreased the human misery with our intellectual mind power? What are we so proud of in our accomplishments? The fact that we earn more money and the fact that we have greater status and greater prestige supposes that one is more powerful than another. It is all about material and intellectual prowess of being superior or better than others, is it not?

'Status' is the living yardstick of measuring a person! The karmic thread that the collective human intelligence has woven is merely a web of 'personal crises' and 'personal sorrow', for this karmic web of collective human intelligence has not brought 'total happiness', 'total freedom', 'total concord', or 'total peace'.

Inorganically, the world of power dwells in 'paper profits', 'paper passports', 'paper qualifications', 'paper recommendations', 'paper insurance's', 'paper licences', 'paper titles', 'paper growth' and 'paper transfers'; all that, and more. Inorganically, the entire global financial stock market is operating in a bombshell of uncertainty. Whilst there is no real term growth, companies show huge paper profits and as a result escalate their share prices in ecstasy of 'share holder value'. The price per share goes up whilst the salary per head gets cut off and the middle and lower management suffer the recession, inflation, and rising cost of living.

The top management continue to eat the cream whilst the labourers and the arduous working class continue to operate in almost robotic alliance of the bureaucracy in fear of mortgages, family commitments, status, reputation, and more. There is growing anxiety and 'weariness', in all that is 'known', socially, politically, and economically. Fear is fear, in any form shape or manner as long as it blocks or otherwise causes despair.

The modern world has reached saturation in every sphere of organic and inorganic growth in the political economy. Hence, the world dwells on artificial survival, created by the power of the intellectual mind and warfare.

Historically speaking, the mind (in conflict) has brought about many brutal camouflages. A few prominent examples are, the 'the Vietnam war', 'the triangular slave trade', 'the barter trade' (exchanging rich wealth in return for wants of life), 'the lowest cost competitiveness', 'the missionary campaigns', 'the colonialisations', 'the imperialisations', 'strategic wars', and others for the individual political quests. Sadly, we have inherited a collective infrastructure of political power that likes to project, impose, and control. When we loose control, we fear. We fear to loose anything we own. We are afraid to be hurt, to be humiliated, to be absconded and to be betrayed.

Despair in the political economy

The world at large is facing higher cost of living, higher inflation, higher property prices, and higher uncertainty of the saturated world financial stock market. The world financial stock market rotates and revolves around the inorganic growth of money.

Inorganic growth is growth created by diminishing real value of money, increased borrowing, and increased cost of living. Growth created by re-structuring the monetary investments from liquid form into tangible form. Lower cost of borrowing is a temporary temptation to invest in higher tangible costs, and higher cost of living. Living is ten times more expensive, more stylish, more power conscious and more uncertain than a millennium ago. If the stock market index keeps on rising, there should be 'real growth of the companies and economies' in 'real terms', resulting in real savings of the disposable incomes and real distribution of pure economic wealth. This is not true of the current world economic order.

In real terms, there is no real growth in an inorganic expansion, except in the shareholder value created by mergers and acquisitions, amalgamations and grand re-engineering. The survival is in sophisticated jargons of intelligent permutations and combinations of artificial money. The value of which is dualistic.

INSTITUTIONAL ECONOMICS AND FINANCE CAUSE ANXIETY!

Our world dwells in powerful institutions, powerful umbrellas of images, powerful economic game play, and powerful political game play. The millennium world has been a result of five thousand years of collective human history of institutional power play. Everything over the years has carried with it a symbol, a constitution, a reform, propaganda, a pattern, or a doctrine of ideological invasions. The institutional power play has manifested in global warfare, global imbalance in economic wealth, global discrimination, global divisions, global differentiation, global regression in capacity, global recession, global inflation, global crises, mass global impositions, and global nuclear threat! All these and more!

The institutional power play has resulted in the civilisation of, the money, the intellect, the ego, the super image, the thing, the value, and the brick walls. All that and more! Except the civilisation of the bare simple human existence! The human existence has been tormented with one disaster after another disaster. In the passage of time, the collective individual personality has created huge empires of personal prestige, personal fame, personal power, personal image, personal glitter, personal charisma, personal wealth, and personal name! All these and much more!

In as much as the world is institutional, the collective human personality is institutional too! The individual personality is no different to the entire world image! If the world image is that of power and exploitation, the collective human personality is no different to this. The despair in the political economy is an imbalanced state of the global wealth, giving rise to global sorrow, global diseases, global mortality, global insecurity, global fear, and global misery.

Knowing economics is an academic issue. Knowing economics is an intellectual task. Knowing economics and finance is a matter of the mind in the technological spectrum. Knowing economics is super intellectual matter. It is something that a super mathematician can extrapolate using complex equations and formulae. To know the microeconomics and macroeconomics is an institutional matter! Most institutes operate almost on the same principles of survival – "bureaucracy of economic and political power".

Strategy and business value operates on complex business and economic plans with most uncertain permutations and combinations, yet these business plans succeed to create value.

Is value a concept, a doctrine, a symbol, an ideological business profit for the individual personality or is value a 'core economic value' for the 'core standard of living'? Which value are we referring to? The real value of consuming a necessity of life or the value of an institutional individual compiling institutional financial extrapolations?

The financial directors, the economic investors, the strategic business consultants, and the tax consultants, justify their presence by maximum knowledge manipulation. Few examples include, tax avoidance strategies, international group structures to minimise taxation, manipulation of conceptual doctrines, shareholder value restructuring, book profit maximisation to increase the unit share price, and international exchanges. All these, and more. The value is the value of the paper money, which in reality does not have physical capacity to the 'mass collective' surviving resources or the distribution of real wealth. The end consumer is an average person, whose disposable income has remained more or less the same for five years yet the cost of surviving has multiplied tremendously.

Anxiety manifests everywhere in the spheres of collective average survival, for the fear of mortgage, loan, rent, petrol, lifestyle, and much more. A personality is constantly worried about rising costs and dwells in pressure, compression, stress, pity, and sympathy from the powerful authority.

Let us be seriously considerate about the sophisticated 'value chain analysis' and try to understand rather than to know the financial and economic magic of the monetary value of the buying power. It is simple that the one with the maximum power to buy will win the monopoly of financial and economic games, whilst the weaker person will just hurt more and more in dismay of imbalances of equations and deficits! This is evident of the world around us and the world within us! The world will follow an order of instructions as long as these instructions come from the top, the control tower, the institute, and the power terminal. "If you cannot win them, join them or else." Perhaps, as a collective human personality, we should design "value chain analysis models" and "strategic analysis" for natural disasters, like floods, drought, famine, hurricanes, tornadoes, storms, thunders, acute chills, earthquakes, wind gusts, tragic accidents, viruses, bacterial infections, diseases, and much more! Every intellectual knows of these epiphanies in concepts, terminologies, and words. However, fewer understand these epiphanies with deep soul compassion.

Institutional organisations of the developed world namely the North America, Canada, and Europe, have strategically moved their production bases and operations to third world countries. The 'cost of production' –'the cost of bricks and walls plus the cost of materials plus the cost of labour plus the cost of direct overheads', put together, in the territorial lands of, the Far east, South America, and Africa, tantamount to, a third of the 'cost of production', in the territorial lands of the powerful 'west'. By keeping the direct costs low in this manner, and enjoying the relishes of double taxation relief, the powerful institutions proclaim heroism in financial and economic strategies.

Two thousand years ago, the very same economies dwelled in triangular slave trade, missionary campaigns, and other barter trades to exploit and to harvest "economic profit" and "economic surplus" from the rich and fertile lands of Africa, China, India, and South America. Majority of the world's minerals came and still come from the fertile lands of Africa, South America, Far East, India, Middle East, and Australia.

Most of the world's basic agricultural products came and still come from the fertile lands of Africa, South America, Far East, India, and Middle East.

These fertile lands of rich minerals and rich agriculture are barren economies! Is this a coincidence or a consequence of collective human power play over some five thousand years? To know economics is easy. Every intellectual can know economics. Even a young school student can know economic formulae of micro and macro financial spectrums. Mathematical equations can put every financial implication in a formulae equation. That is not difficult at all! To know that the most powerful economies dominate the world economic order because of the fact that the financial power of buying and selling rests with their powerful unit of exchange, in the powerful frontier, within the powerful control towers of the stock exchanges.

The entire conglomerate of industries and commerce operate from the powerful territories of the 'west', albeit their basic commodity may be emanating and originating from the Far East, Africa, South America, and India. The control tower is also the exchange tower. The exchange of the unit currency, the unit 'values', the unit 'shares', and the unit 'price'.

Therefore, the institutional control tower of the value dominates the world! Where does anxiety come from? Does fear ('worries and disparities') come from the vast under-developed lands of the weaker economies or does fear (real anxieties) emanate from the global political, economic, and financial manipulation by the 'controlling frontiers'? Mathematically, it is not difficult to know that with the scarcity increases demand! Scarcity has been the 'anxiety' of the mind! In times when the availability of 'per square footage land' becomes scarce, know it that the cost of living and inflation are bound to be highest. Alternatively, where the economic power of the currency cannot dominate the buying power of the global currency, the cost of living is going to be high in relation to the local standard of living, not in relation to the saturated economies.

The burden of pain and torment will remain in the domain of the weaker, less powerful, and less capable rather than the more powerfully canny! Anxiety is another terminology for fear. In perceptual terms, anxiety, worry, disparity, submissiveness, passivity, all imply fear of survival!

Third world economies have never seized the opportunity to realise proliferation from the harvested fruits of their own lands. History has presented us a collective set of doctrines, ideologies, beliefs, propaganda, political reforms, paper regulations, paper realisations, progenies of perplex conquests and perplex political colonialisations.

The collective human history represents canny, greedy manipulation, and complex formulae of religious structures, religious fragmentation's, political conflicts, economic control, and financial domination. The most powerful intellectual economy controls the movement of the base goods and labour. The most powerful economy has always dominated and controlled the patterns of the global material trade, no matter what! However, hypothetically, if the very nature of the collective human ego did not project in conquests, colonialisations, imperialism, and missionary propaganda, the culture of mother Africa would not have been distorted and perhaps the African people would be worshipping the cosmic gods like the Rain god, the Sun God, and the Wind God.

Today, the third world countries have been left with the uncertainty of the sociological chaos. This sociological imbalance is not a result of the spiritual God, but the result of the collective human intelligence! The collective human personality is responsible for the crises and chaos! Let us understand the foregoing facts with compassion rather than cantankerous rebel, rejection, arguments, debates, and augmentative competitions in intellectual I.Q. The issue is of understanding why the collective human personality has over the collective history brought about the gap, between the rich and the poor, between the powerful and weak, between one nation and another, between one individual and another, between one frontier and another frontier.

The issue is that of despair. 'Despair' does not blame individuals, nor does it hold one particular entity responsible for the wrongfulness.

The Vedic wisdom calls for a global awakening to address the issue of global despair that has emanated from the global collective 'vikarma' or 'assatt-karma' or wrongfulness as a result of collective projections of the collective ego, collective lower intelligence, and personality in isolation.

The issue in the Vedas is not so much as who is responsible for what rather what is the remedial solution and what is the collective responsibility of the collective human entity as a combination of the personality, the soul compassion and the universal spirit of humanity.

The Vedas invoke one to investigate and examine corruption, disparity, dismal misappropriation of the resources, unfair trade, and the dualism of the ego and all this, that and the other (vendetta, hatred, anger, wars).

'Dualism' and 'double standards' can never render 'total peace' and 'total harmony'!

The real core problem of the human survival is "collective frontier" represented in ideological doctrines, patterns, super images, complex equations, inappropriate thought processes, imbalance vision, domination, manipulation, concepts, precepts, business strategies, financial value chains, price infrastructures, control, impositions, dispositions, suppressions, oppressions, depressions, afflictions, disparity, worry, anxiety, and much more. The political party is the foremost collective frontier, filled with dismal conflicts.

Every single survival of the personality is based on duality. Duality of mind, duality of thought, duality of living, duality of decision making, duality of the right and the wrong, duality of the power, duality of the control, duality of the bureaucracy, and much more.

How can one find a transformation and a New World economic order when one social institutional frontier barks at another, when one economic pattern cuts another economic pattern, when one political party dominates another political party? The core problem of duality cannot cease with reforms, referendums, academics, or conflicting mind! In real terms the gap between the rich and the poor gets wider and wider whilst, the political parties continue to bark at each other at the expense of the honest person's integrity. Real organic growth entails that the economy is healthier in as much as the environment is healthier and in as much as 'the facility' (like schools, hospitals, health care, etc) is healthier. When violence and crime rise rapidly, the press covers otherwise.

Uncertainty prevails in our daily life. It brings about 'anxiety' and 'distresses, and 'despair'. Uncertainty is the product of our own making if we acknowledge full responsibility of universal human intelligence and universal human mind.

Collectively therefore, the world dwells on hypocrisy of mind power. The power of any social, economic, and political institution manifests in 'pressure', 'compression', 'suppression', 'oppression', 'impression', and 'depression' of the person in one form or another. The collective human personality thrives on control, duality, power, domination, suppression, oppression, self-importance, self-pride, and acquisitions. The collective human personality dwells in 'dualism'; for example; dualism of, the 'east' and the 'west', the 'rich' and the 'poor', the 'intelligent' and the 'dumb', the 'powerful' and the 'weak', the 'assertive' and the 'passive', the 'dominant' and the 'submissive'. The personality functions with the frontiers of dualism.

The person with more money, monetary investment, more status, more position, more prestige, more institutional education, more academic politics, and more thrust wins in the modern world. Differentiation and discrimination prevails in the institutional power with highest forms of bureaucracies. The modern living has created greater uncertainty.

Uncertainties and conflicts bring about fear in one form or another; fear of loosing something or fear of survival or fear of dying. Despite the material world being fully known to the human intelligence and the human mind, there is still uncertainty about the very matter that brings about diseases, decay, decomposition, dismay, worry, anxiety, stress, pressure, all that and more despair. The human mind knows it all and yet it is somewhat dwelling in uncertainty. The human mind feels in fullest control of everything yet it becomes oppressed, compressed, and suppressed with worries, anxieties, stress, tension, and more. 'Institutional Power' does not remain permanent, if one perceives life to be a perpetual epiphany in absolute time. By far the greatest obstacle towards spiritual emancipation is fear.

Fear is physical and it has form that becomes eminent on our body and mind, as an ailment or aggression. Fear is environmental and it is subjected to the five multi-sensory human personalities. Fear is the root cause of all evil and all depression. Fear grows in dreary loneliness, rejection, and isolation. Fear comes in varying magnitudes. Fear puts a blockage in our minds. It diminishes our talent to nurture relationships. It makes us insecure in one form or another.

Anxiety utilises the greatest amount of nervous energy and creates diffusion of the body tissues, hence we see from a person who is excessively worried or distressed that this person wears off quicker. Fear has resulted from the darkness of avoiding the truth! Fear originates from social economic and political power – 'institutional power'. Reality brings competition and 'rat race' (the chase of surviving without a quest for retrospection). One lives relatively. One creates endless worries and endless mental anguish for one's self. One finds excuses and escapes and creates insecurity to those who depend on us emotionally. Fear spreads like a contagious life disease, under corruption, conflict, and uncertainty.

False dependency makes others follow authority blindly out of fear and makes authority operate in a manipulative manner out of fear of insecurity.

High technologies create power warfare all over the world, making our environment insecure, polluted, and risky. Computers are causing more havoc and more anxiety to the end users through rapid electronic hankering and viruses.

Most power driven high fliers reach their positions at the expense of others. This is not authentic power! It is not absolute. It shall wither away in due course of time. It shall become frail with the frazzled age! Institutional power divides people by race, culture, creed, caste, colour, thesis, anti-thesis, and frames. Institutional power is vicious cycle of rotations and it brings about fear or pressure in one form or another. Fear destroys the talent to be humanely funny and to be humanely caring. When you defy institutional power, the conclusion is either self destruction or destruction of your beloved. When you defy and rebel against institutional power, you hurt yourself and your beloved before hurting the institute. Defiance is always filled with rage, anger, and reaction. Institutional power brings warfare and chaos in our society. Anxiety controls most of us in some form or another as long as we are in enticed with the social power.

'What you pay is what you get' philosophy prevail in most of the institutions of the first world, a rather 'what you can control is what you should get' philosophy prevail in most of the institutions of the second world. The third world institutions thrive on 'what you can afford is what you can get' motto. Be stressed, remain stressed, and cause stress that is not essential. Power is manipulated for survival.

Blame is shifted to justify existence. To make a presence felt one imposes with aggression, assertion, verbal language power, and canny swiftness. Exploitation and corruption renders power that is a personal accumulation of breeding power - social power, economical power, and more political power. Until finally our body and matter perish with the elapsing time. Then on our 'death bed' we shall realise that it was all an absurdity! Then it is going to be too late to change and undo our life process and Karmas. Our life process matters today right here right now at this very moment whilst it is still alive and aware! We are constantly escaping and running a rat race without recognising the true values of life. As a collective human personality, we give value to everything except the essential spirit of life!

The modern society is constantly feeding on frozen fast food, 'ready' meals, and processed meat. It gives 'ready'/ frozen foods to children out of ill habit of rushing and running a marathon of rat race of institutional power in all this, that and the other. We refuse to sit quietly to listen purely.

"Stress" has become the living consciousness today and business stress generates all kinds of excuses to have alcohol, cigarettes, sex, fast food, red meat, and fast life. Toxins bring the immune system down. Toxins create excessive nervous energy. Toxins bring headaches. Toxins create degenerative ailments. Toxin pollutes. Stress is toxic related. From stress emanates anxiety and from anxiety emanates fear. Toxin is highest in red meat, alcohol, fast foods, and frozen foods and unprocessed foods. Toxins are high in caffeine, carbonated drinks, and un-boiled milk. This is now a proven medical fact known to most of us.

Most fast forward forthright young persons thrive on the exhilaration of competition. Life for the modern young person has become extremely hectic, stressful, competitive, and ruthless.

The spirit of life, (a deep compassion) has been squashed, by the personality (ego, mind, intellect, and sensuous body). One lives at the expense of integrity. One begins to find 'fault' and 'cause' in others. One begins to draw conclusion about an unaccomplished or distorted social person if he or she has fallen in the eyes of the society due to inadequacies, severe adversities, and incapacities.

One makes definitive assumptions about another's circumstances, and one thrives on talking about another's imperfections and about another's impetuous circumstantial conditions. One constantly passes judgement that is highly personal, subjective and strives to make the judgement look impartially professional by hiding under the veil of 'power' hypocrisy. One makes another helpless person more helpless by turning him or her away with our pity and sympathy. If one does not give pity or sympathy, one affords monetary tip (a little something) just to keep this person away. Admit it whole-heartedly that in reality a suffering person suffers pain only in isolation and aloneness. Rarely is there collective compassion without pity between relationships. If the compassion does arise in sorrow, it is also something that becomes a burden with time as the anxiety of one's own life over takes our priorities.

Perhaps the despair in the modern world needs a savant like Rama, Jesus, Buddha, or Krishna to be incarnated again.

We let things get beyond our control and then with our regret and remorse, we try to show our sympathy and pity. In essence we reflect the insecurity of the chaotic world.

One carries on being congress of the monumental churches, mosques, and temples proclaiming to be religious or otherwise agnostically super-power intellectuals (the arrogant and the stubborn). One constantly doubts others and in turn makes oneself canny. Speeches are made without having innate belief or trust in the spoken words.

We constantly compare ourselves with others and unknowingly feel superior or inferior. We draw up social yardstick of measurement based on the matter of clothing, housing, car, style, fashion, glamour, and status. We forget to 'just simply love'! We forget just to be simple. We forget just to be funny. We forget to laugh open-heartedly. We forget just to be human. We forget just to bring compassionate togetherness without any fear. We cannot simply be capable of being human. When we are healthy and fit and smart we presume that this state will never perish. We continue to give grief and aggression to others less powerful than us; thereby causing pain and misery to this other person without any justice whatsoever. We try to defend ourselves and we shield ourselves with our egos. This erupts in a grander war. Wars have not rendered solutions.

We are just running from one point of ego praise to another. The modern 'personality' thrives by creating followers and brings newer ideas with newer concepts to fascinate the 'stale' dark grey intellectual ego. When a personality feels the fear of loneliness, rejection, morale defeat, emotional breakdown, weakening economical conditions, the weaker personality becomes a follower of an 'umbrella'. If an umbrella renders temporary physical and mental comfort of convenience, the umbrella is conveniently suitable. Convenience and preference comes before relationship.

Our present day human relationships are built on physical, mental, and intellectual conveniences and preferences rather than the spiritual consciousness. We knowingly or unknowingly spread the contagious life disease – 'fear' - despair. Ego dwells in darkness, in vicious cycles of selfishness (vikarma), and personality greed ('moha' and 'mahaad'). Ego never identity emanates from excessive desires, gross attachments, and insecurity.

When sorrow comes to us, in our old frazzling body, we become angry, frustrated, and fearful. We run to material shelters of pleasures. We move to self-preferred umbrellas. We move from one medicine to another, aimlessly seeking for a remedy and cure. We find escape in short cuts like alcohol, cigarettes, drugs, or any other stimulants. Stimulation brings further anxiety and we thence suffer from insomnia or escapism. We grow out of our old partners and change them in the aspirations of being sensually different. We have made marriages and relationships like clothes. We change them when we grow out of them.

People are not clothes! Love is irreplaceable! Happiness cannot be for one moment and cease to be for another. It is either there or was never there. Love and compassion is not something we can barter for "if" & "but". Our preferences for people we love keep changing a million times! Our mind and our physical bodies begin to weaken with age. The physical pain is inevitable. Pain sits in every human body in some form or another, at some stage or another, without fail. The human body being born without infinite super powers cannot escape pain. If the problem is within us, the solution must also be within us, inwardly, in our consciousness, our own perception.

Pain is material; pain is part of the material nature. Pain is part of the human personality. Pain is the nature of the human mortality!

All physical comforts and luxuries of life end in more pain. We begin to tremble and seek comfort from doctors, astrologers, and professionals. We get frustrated within ourselves and spread anxiety to others close to us, when the doctor only touches the basic needs of the body and mind but does not cleanse the spiritual substance within us. We fail to acknowledge the truth! We fail to take full responsibility of our life actions. In this frustration, we drive others close to us into dismay of emotional distress. We spread our own physical pain to others close to us by constantly complaining, moaning, arguing, testifying, brooding, and crying. So what have we really achieved?

We have just become part of a contagious life disease. Our survival has become a one way traffic! It suits us fine! Does it suit the other person who is compassionately caring and affectionate? Anxiety and fear surrounds the helpless and the hopeless. Depression emanates fear.

The life objective of an anti-depressant should be to lessen the miseries of life and to lessen the physical pain. Modern anti-depressants create toxic harm in the long term that diminishes a person's mental aptitude to cope with daily life. A true anti-depressant should emanate from within our own very life support light "conscious", without which no one is alive. Awakening this life support entails spiritual awakening.

We fail to acknowledge that our past karmic life patterns were erratic. We ate without regard for purity of mind and body. We slept without any zest for the spiritual awakening. We drank alcohol and excreted wastefully. We, 'over indulge' in sex, smoking, and other forms of habits. We dwelled aimlessly, in power-struggle, dirty politics, and mental & physical manipulation of mind and intellect. We indulged in one form of pleasure or another. We enjoyed rich foods, wondering in aimless worries, arguing for importance, rebelling for anger, segregating, dividing, defying, acting and reacting with intellectual superiority, dancing in the shadows of the mind, antagonising and bringing anguish to ourselves and others! We gave fear and ourselves became afraid. When we are afraid, we are not fully aware.

The materially conscious arrogant personality survives with "ego" power. Ego must never ever be displeased; otherwise, hurt will spread like a disease.

Personality breeds on anxiety, thrives on anxiety, and spreads anxiety. If we let 'personality' adversely affect our 'spirit of life', then surely, 'personality' will perpetuate in pain and sorrow! If we let adversity and severe circumstances torment our spirit of life, than surely helplessness and hopelessness shall transpire! If we let our destiny be controlled by 'personality', than surely our spirit of life shall soon become insecure and finally 'trash-able thing'!

Fear is the biggest grey cloud between the Sun and the earthly human spirit of life!

The root cause of all evil and all miseries is fear. Fear brings helplessness and hopelessness. The power of the ego and the intellect is false and mortal. The true authentic power is the power of the soul divine that never fails us.

Fear generates anger, rage, envy, hatred, loneliness, grief, remorse, arrogance, self-pity, alienation, guilt, inferiority complex, and disparity. 'Fear' is the greatest enemy of humankind. When we become isolated and lonely, as opposed to sitting alone in quintessence and serenity, we generate 'fear'.

When we isolate a suffering personality, we bring fear to that person as well as ourselves.

The worse kind of fear emanates from psychological, emotional and physical insecurity. Uncertainties pervade everywhere. We are constantly tormented with anxiety, in fear and anguish. We are constantly worried and troubled. We are making our personalities become the centrifugal force of materially physical life without considering our responsibilities and obligations towards the spiritual evolution in ourselves and in our children.

We are constantly weary and conscious of ourselves in an inferior or superior manner. We are always comparing. Greed of power, the pleasure of controlling conquests and proclaiming has been the mode of historical global karma. The modern day money has devalued in its worthiness.

The human kind desires happiness and shuns sorrow. In sorrow, every single spirit of life is hurting.

War is just a physical manifestation of conflict, buried the fire of volcano that has erupted in lava of rage, fury, and destruction. Insolence and aggression do not imply brevity in as much as fortitude and compassion do not imply cowardice. Conflicts always render hurt, agony, pain, and eventually sorrow. It can be seen evidently that those parts of the global world that are hurting the most would strangely show most toxin, chaos, pollution, disease, catastrophes, disasters, poverty, tragedies, all these and much more. It can be evidently realised that the modern humankind has a shorter life span compared to its predecessors five thousand years ago. Life perishes most unexpectedly. When death stares at us uninvited, we feel insecure and afraid. We feel remorseful and regretful. The ego never ceases to argue, shout, scream, frown, defend, justify, make noises, waste precious time in meetings, and 'all, this, that and the other'. Death is a lonely visitor. It comes uninvited. Thousand sorrows seem so trivial compared to the grief of loosing a loved one.

The conflict that is within us is deeply rooted in our sub conscious mind. It is imminent in the trauma, tragedies, miseries, crises, upheavals, violence, crime, break-ups, and inflated value of the paper money, higher cost of living, and lower disposable income; all that, and more.

Most organisations that run on systematic administration, strategy, and board of powerful decision-makers operate on bureaucracy of one form or another. Organisations are surviving rather than existing. Organisations survive on collective bureaucracy, not in isolation. They thrive on power control and survive on its subservient servants and subordinate labour! Organisations bring a hierarchy of power and most organisations operate on the bureaucracy of power.

Intellectuals and business professors make it more than complex to justify existence of an 'everyday' humble person who is trying to cope with his anxiety to survive and to thrive on surviving in an ambitious web of becoming something; something that he or she is truly not in nature a reality! The minute we follow a set system of bureaucracy we cease to become creative artists. We become part of a web, the power web of intellectual spectrum that survives on intellectual reason and intellectually conscious mind.

We become monotonous robots surviving on patterns and structures of collective personality with collective ego. Can an intellectual system honestly control life and death? Does death bring with it an intellectual web of 'frameworks and structures' to argue and to reason with us? Can bureaucracy really listen or hear what it likes to hear? Systems duplicate, replicate, eventually recreate, and reproduce more complexities. This is the paradox of the intellectual power.

Anything we fear to loose, is a symbol of this power. For example, a job, a house, a car, an attractive looking body, a monetary status, academic prestige, economic prosperity and political structures. We derive a sense of comfort and security from all of these foregoing constituents accepting that they control our survival and living because we are either grossly attached to them or otherwise grossly dependent on them to give us comfort.

The dynamics of bureaucracies and powerful systems bring dependency of a kind that is somewhat difficult to challenge and impossible to defy. What we have created as human minds and as mental power is a social structure of thoughts, ideas, and emotions that depend on our daily life. Our daily life is shaped around material and physical constituents of needs and wants.

Deep within any 'personality' a person is the emotional consciousness of a prestige. A person is insecure, feeling lonely and is despondently dependent on others for physical, mental and sensuous comforts. When the expected comfort does not come, the personality person gets frustrated and dismayed in anger. It reflects and refracts 'fear' out of uncertainty and out of 'self-pity', 'dismay', 'sympathy', and 'doubts'. This important person, with important name and an important address is lonely, afraid, and anxious. From being nervous, and out of pride, this person is probably more anxious than you could possibly know. In some form or another, this person feels lonely and there is fear either because there is the insecurity of financial commitments or the insecurity of the marital relationship or the insecurity of the business venture or the insecurity of the family members or the insecurity of death. Nevertheless, there is some insecurity. This insecurity may drive this person to escape into alcohol, sex, institutional power warfare, grapevine of physical affections, or any other habitual pattern of mentally tiring the mind so that the mind can sleep conveniently.

Society is uncertain albeit it is 'the known'. There is more uncertainty prevailing in real terms all over the 'known' physical world than there is probably in the unknown metaphysical world of cosmic eternity. The entire game of speculation comprises doubts, dark grey illusions, self-inflicted conclusions, proclamations, assumptions, presumptions, hypothetical assimilation, thoughts, and 'conflicts'. The uncertainty in the unknown eternity is not from the virtue of the fact but from the inability to see it from a perspective that is not a mental thought process. The uncertainty prevailing the unknown eternity emanates from the absence of the insight or the deliberation of the mind. The uncertainty of the 'known' however is the result of the collective 'vikarma' (wrongfulness) that has given rise to fear.

Our mind therefore, is uncertain. Our mind therefore does not constantly remain the same because it is subject to moods and swings. Our mind therefore must be unreliable. Yet we keep on relying on it for producing all kinds of thoughts and all kinds of conscious contents that are convincing or that bear a reason or cause or feeling. We keep on running after its power. We live in that practical survival kit. We keep on changing our thoughts, as cloths and we keep on inventing new ideas and new technologies to keep abreast the new socio-economic and political environment. Our world is created and based on thoughts and we feel that only thoughts will try to find solution to all our problems and dilemmas. When we fail to find a solution to our problems through our minds, we turn to gurus, leaders, new leaders, new functions, new avenues, new environment, and new people. We try to find convenience of comfort to our thoughts and mental tortures.

Modern civilisation dwells on 'buzz', 'rush', 'wham', 'bang', 'waste' and 'taste'. Modern civilisation proclaims power that is not supported by life breath alias health. There are more stress-sufferers today then 2000 years ago. This is an undeniable fact. Money and worry walk side by side today for most highfliers. People have learnt intelligent ways to manipulate the simplest situation just to win over others and obtain that one extra point of ego praise. Modern civilisation is a civilisation of the "intellect", "sensuality", and "exotic taste" for desires of the tongue and the stomach. The intellectual and the physical gravity of all that is impermanent, rule the pleasure conscious society.

In 'dark self-importance' of the intellect filled with aggression, the mind wonders in endless thoughts of speculations, doubts, confusions, and conflicts.

When something has not worked out, it is the fault of another person or the fault of the company or the fault of the government, never the fault of the 'collective human intelligence'!

Power play manifests in the body exposure and power dressing. Power play is evident in substantial body language and psychological jargons. Power plays it all! If you have the good looks, powerful brains and highest paper knowledge, the world is in your pocket! Make no mistake about it.

This is the 'power conscious' modern civilisation. Brand names and designer labels play the market forces in contributing maximum profits with minimum input. The world of fashion is ruled by brand name, the world of technology is ruled by brand name, the world of business is ruled by brand name, the world of profit is ruled by brand name.

"Name", personalise anything and in due course of time, it will contain monetary value. Personalised car number plates for example, personalised telephone numbers, and personalised 'anything'. What has the modern civilisation rendered over the last two thousand years is a higher cost of living. Hence, our standards of living are ten times as much as they were two thousand years ago. Inflation may be minimal in books.

How then has the modern civilisation managed to evolve? Has not the modern civilisation of man made intellectual progression really diminished an affordable simple daily living into complex jargons of convenient inflation and rising costs of living?

The 'intellectual power' is not authentic power because it has brought more worries and more tension of cash flows and disposable cash income. The intellectual power warfare over the last 3000 years degraded human integrity in many dismal ways.

Political power must be superficial power then because it has not rendered any solace 'nor' has it rendered any universal peace nor has it afforded any genuine harmony. Uncertainty is the result of modern civilisation. The depth of uncertainty brings about fear of anxiety or fear of insecurity. Mass confusion and mass perplexities prevail everywhere. Albeit bewilderment is imminent, mind always wants to escape and provide comfort with diplomatic treaties and words that are not sacredly profound.

Political power that is based in isolation of the personality without the combination of the divine soul and the integrity create greater despair and greater fear.

There is no end to 'greyness' of fear brought about by modern civilisation. 'Grey' matter widens the gap between 'conflict' and 'insight'. 'Living and existing as human beings' is different to 'living and surviving the struggles of life'. Life is full of struggles. Yes. Life is a battle and life is difficult. However, living a fuller life entails that we conquer the falseness of the material civilisation.

When we realise that life is a grand university from which we learn progressively and evolve spiritually, our existence is justified. We are consciously results oriented ambitious minded individuals who like to be in control with our circumstances through our status and prestige. We survive our lives with intelligence and convince our conscious that 'this is so because of such and such, and it will be that because of such and such'. We constantly find consolations and temporarily feel good about them. We indulge in living and we enjoy life's pleasures and good things that come with our prestige, hard work, and mental power.

We find conclusions about problems and we consider them an end. We spend hours and hours of our mental energy into solving problems that are created by us in the first place. This web of humankind is not woven in isolation; it is a collective reflection of collective thoughts. You see insecurity prevails in everything that the mind sees from its thoughts because mind is seeking constant comfort in intellectual consciousness. Thought can never be permanent. Thought is under certain conditions of the life. Conditions of life always change. As long as the mind seeks comfort and as long as mind wants to secure comfort, this very 'mind' cannot conquer 'fear' in real terms can it?

If our mental consciousness is the centrifugal force of our living, we must turn to mental faculties to resolve the many problems of life. All the mental power holders should be able to resolve problems like grief, sorrow, sufferings, ailments, pain, loneliness, misery, tragedies, earthquakes, anxiety, stress, emotional sadness, hurt, anguish, frustration, anger, all that and more. The modern society intellectuals can do nothing for "sorrow"! The best one ever bothers to do is, give pity and sympathy in dismay! This is the real fact.

When we encounter a tragic death in the family, it brings with it an eternal echo of our impermanence! We grieve for our loss. We grieve for ourselves because we have lost all the given opportunities in a lifetime to undo a hurt or a slander or an aggression or a conflict. We become dismal because having everything (status, pride, prestige, name, power, wealth, things, houses, cars, positions, and money) we feel we have nothing. We feel empty! Death is a reminder that we are living on borrowed time and 'all, this, that and the other' does not really matter.

Becoming aware, we realise in profound silence that under the diseased roots, the tree collapses gradually because when the roots become diseased the bark and the branches show the symptoms and signs. The tree stops to yield fruits and the leaves dry out. The tree is diseased, wearing out, ageing, and even dying. Death is inevitable. Death is a constant reminder of our impermanence and mortality.

The chief cause of many ailments in the long term has been either, over eating or anorexia, or malnutrition. These conditions emanate originally from fear. The emotions arising out of rejections, dejection, guilt, false temptations out of insecurity, apprehensions, anxiety, ill actions, guilt, anger, grief, depression, suppression, loneliness, all that and more, generate impurity in blood. When there is impurity in blood, the entire nervous system (comprising seventy two thousand nerves and white blood cells and red blood cells), becomes despondently dependent on taste, sensuality, pleasure, stimulation and physical things.

People sometimes become obsessed, possessed and aggravated with tinniest little material thing and the smallest amount of money. The external power constantly innovated by the super powers and the super human intelligence must be deceitful because it renders involution rather than evolution of the society and the 'social person'. For example, a person thrives on chaos under extremely adverse economic tides without realising that the net disposable income has not really brought immense health and immense wealth despite all the mammoth drudgery.

We are too attached to things and we constantly want to possess more and more assets and niceties of life. Understanding this parable is much more significant than total detachment of things and material things. This is the gist of the many Vedic verses.

We need to be simpler and cleaner rather than smarter and expensive. Out of attachment, we are conforming to constancy of occupying our minds and we are always trying to be occupied consciously. We hold on to something or the other. Just because an intellectually conscious person feels in him or her, the social norm becomes that. It has become that!

Does the fear of feeling emptiness demand occupation and not self-discovery? Therefore, one must give importance to that idea, that social norm, that expectation of status conscious intellectuals. Is not self-discovery an occupation in its own rights then? What my spirit of life aspires with deepest inspiration is a forbearance of your aggressive attitude to profoundly unlock the source of 'emptiness'. One must sit quietly and enquire introspectively, retrospectively, and without all, this, that and the other. If an intellectually powerful and ambitious person feels that there is fear in emptiness, the institutional power expects others to adhere to this norm. However, whose norm is this? Who created this citizen's charter?

If one feels scared in being alone and being empty then there is definitely a profound spiritual stigma in the life of this person. As such this person needs to pinpoint exactly that specific element which brings, fear, or boredom, or 'lack of inspiration'. What is the true mirror reflection of this person's soul? Is this lonely person so ugly in spirit and so dull in compassion? Is this lonely person without true love and without talent of integrity? Perhaps fear emanates from all the insecurities and inhibitions.

Why is one so afraid to be alone?

If in discovering the fear one has to suffer the fear of 'profound silence' than one must suffer and discover the root cause of all fear. By merely pre-occupying oneself, the 'sorrow' will not disappear! Explore sorrow, discover its roots, and investigate it with, profound silence, profound insight, profound wisdom, and profound inspiration. Do it. Try it. A consolation of means is not an end to problems. When we become free from the vicious cycles of this mental thought processes, and when we discard the falsehood of the society for its falseness in totality, then and only then, we begin to channel our spiritual energies into discovering the answers intuitively with an insight.

Let us try to understand with deep compassion and with deep profoundness that fear is inevitably a condition of living as long as the mind is intellectually responsible for speculating, assuming, presuming, drawing, thinking, arguing, discussing, debating, making inferential references to knowledge, and more.

Let us try to understand the root cause of fear without any preconditioning of the mind and the referential knowledge. We know how to explain fear from knowledge and from institutional psychology. We do not want to know 'fear'. We already know it in all forms and shapes. What we truly want is to understand it with deep profound compassion and deep profound inspirational insight. Let us simply understand in simplicity that you and I may be different in our constitutional personalities, but our essential substance is the same – "compassion". Our souls understand the same "insight" – one that is true compassion. Our souls have the same deep compassionate love, albeit hidden, suppressed and crushed by the ego, the pride, the intellectual crown, and the social status. Renunciation of intellectual power for the compassionate understanding will deliver a profound wider view. Compassionate understanding will mould ones way of looking at this society, its economical and political metamorphosis. The mental faculty will extend to the inner faculty of the soul with profound wisdom and profound understanding. Revere life.

PSYCHOLOGY SHOULD INCORPORATE SPIRITUAL INSIGHT

How can intellectual mind understand with profound inspirational insight when the very person's ego contradicts in desires, each pulling in different directions in this very person's personal life? Psychology really entails an in-depth understanding and in-depth compassion of the consciousness that is supported by the human mind and the human intelligence. Psychology therefore has to be based on an innermost understanding of mind, not knowing the knowledge of how the mind works in a personality.

We all know that the mind works in crises and in conflict because if the mind worked otherwise in a personality, the world would not be place full of camouflage and wars. The world has become an uncertain place; therefore, the mind must be the source place of conflict. The root of fear therefore must be inset in the mind from childhood to adulthood.

The modern psychology places greater emphasis on how the five sensory personalities function. The core dynamics underlying the values and the 'conflicts' must manifest in the spirit of the person.

The spirit of life within a person is trapped inside the cage of self-conceived intellectual personality and dark 'ego'.

Every psychological evaluations and psychological remedies that work on the anti-depressant drugs to cure depression must therefore be hollow and ineffective. An anti-depressant drug will induce chemical activity within the physical brain to enable the distressed person combat restlessness. When the effect of the drug wears out, the person becomes even more withdrawn because now the person has to worry about acute headaches that arise in the area of pituitary glands. Depression as a phenomenon cannot emanate solely out of mental thoughts and physical lapses. Pain on its own is merely pain. This is the medical term for physical and mental pain.

However, when a person mentions sorrow it does not mean pain it means hurt. 'Hurt' is emotional and spiritual beyond the physical and mental sheaths. It is rooted in the spirit. Fear has generated from suppression, buried emotions, and apprehension in the sub-conscious mind.

Therefore, to understand hurt with compassion, removing the institutional umbrella of the intellectual mind power will enable psychology to realise with pure compassion that this 'hurt' may be a reason and a cause for karmic evolution. Evolution is a progressive step forward to abandon the past and a progressive question time to evaluate karma. The core issue that arises out of any hurtful suffering is the issue of compassion.

As long as there is no profound compassion within a person to understand, 'fear' in absolute terms, the person is not going to be able to realise the problem. The problem will just continue to become another problem and the cycle of pain will continue to reflect medical ailments that survive purely on taking pills & medications.

When pity, sympathy, or half-hearted compassionate love is afforded, because of either thoughtful act of compulsion or mind-full preoccupation of intellectual knowledge, the reciprocation of such help is contaminated.

It is better not to receive such help because after the help is given, the reciprocation creates greater conflict, greater distress, and greater insomnia. 'Pity' either in the self or to others is not pure love and it is not fearless love.

'Pity' implies that the person giving the pity is incapable of giving compassion and the person receiving the pity is helplessly incapable of knowing the difference between 'pity' and 'compassion'.

Psychology of human nature is elevated from the physical psychology of human mind. Psychology of human nature dwells into the person's inner most feelings. Based on the feelings of the spirit, it discovers the pattern of karmic involution or evolution of the spirit of that person. In bringing to the surface of the mind, the modern psychology can create a new birth to the 'hurting' person, such that, the attitude towards fear changes. New birth can only come about if the older ways of survival and the collective karma from past lives are dissolved. Dissolution to previous karma entails sacrifice. Death is that dissolution and dispersion of the older worn out matter of the body, mind, and the ego. Spirit of life dances freely from the worn-out shelter of the mind body and ego and becomes free of the fear of the pain of ageing. This is karmic evolution.

Most persons suffer pain endlessly because they are unaware of the spiritual strength or because they have not cultivated the spiritual essence. Cultivating the human compassion and the profoundness of the soul is 'awareness'. This awareness elevates us from the gross physical level of pain into the physical level of pain and then through graceful profound self-healing of the soul, we elevate our pain into the consciousness. When we transform our pain into suffering in the sacrifice of understanding the root causes and the root reasons of our karmic lives, we elevate ourselves into higher beings. When we understand compassionately with sombre solace and integrity that our lives have been a chain of actions and reactions, our known knowledge is superseded with our profound insight. The Vedic wisdom of togetherness talks about the looking from another perspective, from another platform, from another viewpoint, from another world, from another aspect, from another way. When we examine issues from the nature's way, we begin to listen in profound silence the essence of our own spirit, and there is the rise in the self in evolution of karmas. The divinity within us elevates to awaken us, to make us aware. The ancient Vedic seers said with dignity and integrity that we are born to give.

When we realise the essence of our own spirits, we are ready to give self-less, uncontaminated pure compassion to others. This pure uncontaminated compassion will not be pity or sympathy; it will be compassion and human warmth. Compassion will be a wholesome love, more affective and more therapeutic towards the wholesome individual, rather than the intellectual person, which thrives on affording short pity and brief sympathy with time constraints. Compassion is absolute. Compassion is unconditional. Compassion is totality. Compassion is infinitely profound no matter how small it may be. Pity and sympathy on the other hand rotate, revolve, and perpetuate in constant cycles of isolations, rejections, disintegration, divisions, loneliness, hate, rage, anxiety, anger, impositions, power, and fear.

The Vedic wisdom is life science and it was narrated to resolve and minimise the global despair in the modern world, to save the human beings from falling in the utter darkness as Isa Upanishads and the last chapter of the Yajur Veda caution us despondently.

The unity in diversity, the togetherness of the three worlds, the communion of the human race, the awakening of the dreary dull dark ignorance, and the illumination of the human entity is the purport of the Vedic wisdom. The soul divine compassion is necessary for creating a New World order.

Superfluous personality

Personality does not conquer without a reason or a cause. It has to depend on the mind and its lower intellectual power albeit speeding in all directions with different kinds of ideas and presumptions. The personality dances to the shadows of the grey thoughts in desires, personal greed, personal survival, personal pleasure, and personal importance. When someone pleases the personality in, monetary form, intellectual form, or physical form, the personality wants to form a relationship with this other person. It is all an equation. The mind knows only equations. The mind only sees equations. Personality breeds on fear in one form or another. Personality is entwined with the threads of survival in complex metamorphosis of reason and cause.

The personality only sees what the ego likes to see not what the spirit likes to perceive. The personality makes the conscious vision in thought, and forms the only kind of empirical concrete vision. The personality thrives on self-centred ego praises and status.

Can one separate 'fear' from 'vicious life' itself? Let us examine this closely with all our compassionate understanding. What do we understand from 'fear' and its sources? Does fear generate because the mind wants it? Does fear sit in the shadows of the 'dark grey brain' matter and cause all kinds of fuss without any due cause of concern? Does 'conflict' become benign with 'thought'? We want peace, do we not? Is peace the complete opposite of antithesis of war then?

Is it not a fact that we are continuously at war within ourselves and we are constantly in conflict in one form or another? If one believes in socialism and the other believes in capitalism, there is conflict. If one believes in Jesus and the other believes in Allah, there is conflict. If one believes in the knowledge of psychology and the other believes in the Vedas, there is conflict. Therefore, there you are. One cannot create peace as long as there is conflict. When you cannot create total peace of mind and total harmony of outlook, there will remain fear of insecurity in one form or another and there will remain doubt in form or another.

It is imperative therefore that, if we seek absolute peace, one must sacredly abolish the frontiers of the intellectual mind - Mind that is already preconditioned with ideas, habits, thoughts, memories, desires, contradictions, worries, anxieties, all that and more. Your mind and the mind of another person and the mind of another person are all thriving on different directions at different speeds with different attitudes and different knowledge. As long as there is aggressive non-stop intellectual mind filled with gigantic ideas and gigantic knowledge, the perpetual human solution to end human misery will only be temporarily synergies. The 'mind cycle' does not understand in deep compassion, it only knows and assumes with thoughts, ideas, and intellectual prowess of the academic and institutional knowledge. Despite the flaw in the bureaucratic decision making, the power of position always triumphs with politics. The truth of the matter is that we, you and I earnestly want to create a cease-fire of the perpetual 'mechanism' of vicious cycles of life and thus we want to step completely out of this 'wretched mechanism' of 'fear'.

Knowledge is good; knowledge is not bad as long as knowledge is scientifically utilised as a means of understanding something. Knowledge is a means of understanding not an end to knowing. Understanding 'fear' requires one to look at fear from an inspirational insight. The Vedas invoke us to understand despair, and to realise the limitations of it.

Let us profoundly sit quietly and discover in profound silence what it is that we are afraid of. Let us be profoundly serious rather than academically serious about the issue of 'fear'. Let us remove all the different umbrellas of thoughts, intellectual knowledge, anthological cultures, and anthological faiths. Let us begin to understand compassionately rather than inferring conclusions using our intellectual power and imposing our intellectual knowledge. Let us discover and understand what it is about life that brings about 'fear'. Let us be serious about discovering 'fear' rather than just knowing it with conclusions, judgements, referrals, and prescriptions. Let us understand life as it is unconditionally, without any inhibitions of the intellectual mind, and without any formulation of cultural barriers.

This nature is one. Therefore, 'fear' is fear albeit different conditions are attached to it. Fear is all that is "temporary".

'Thing' brings fear because we become insecure of loosing it. 'Mind' brings fear because in the shadows of it our thoughts dance in darkness. 'Life breath' brings fear because we do not know when it will stop.

'Job' brings fear because we are insecure about the bureaucracies and politics of the institutional powers.

'Money' brings fear because we are afraid of loosing it. 'House' brings fear because we have not filled with compassion and warm love but traumatised it with our worries and mortgages therefore it is not a home filled with our security but a house filled with insecurity.

'Thought' brings fear because we let a negative thought adversely affect us and in this adversity feel hurt, anguished, and lonely, therefore if we never hurt anyone in the first place; we would not generate this vicious cycle would we?

'Relationship' brings fear because we have not filled it with real compassion and real soul friendship but mere convenience of the body and the mind. Therefore, an intellectual relationship is not permanent. 'Man made 'Religion' brings fear because it threatens us with its man made thoughts of doctrines of sin and retribution. 'Superstition' brings fear because it is grey. 'Power' brings fear because we become helpless and hopeless at the magnitude of any power therefore we run and run and run and run aimlessly without any motivation, aspiration, or inspiration. 'Ego' brings fear because we are afraid of being humiliated and insulted, therefore, we safeguard our ego by reasons, causes, agreements, disagreements, consensus, etc. 'Insecurity' brings fear because when we are rejected, unloved, unwanted, we feel that we lack compassion and therefore we turn to a brutal substitution. 'Occultism' brings fear because the tantric powers of occultism are tantamount to magic, mental and physical fascination, which creates blind followers who are only seeking out a convenient security because inherently these followers have not discovered their own souls. 'Cults and personal religious leaders' bring fear because they divide and further create a havoc of truth with substantial manipulation, impress upon ignorant persons. 'Despair' brings fear because hopelessness is a condition that has transpired as a result of the consequential collective life karma in the collective karmic time. To understand the process of collective life requires a deep insight (astrological guidance), meditation, and spiritual awareness.

According to the Vedas, fear emanates from seven main aspects. Firstly, fear emanates from what we think, how we think, our "thought" ('achitta'). Secondly, fear emanates from what we eat, how we eat, when we eat, where we eat, which type of food we eat, our "food" ('annam'). Thirdly, fear emanates from what we do all day long, how we live, where we live, when we nurture our bodies, our "actions" ('dina-karma'). Fourthly, fear emanates from what we do, how we do it, what we follow and what we practice, our life "process" ('ayu-karma'). Fifthly, fear emanates from how we live our present day life, in a present situation, in a present attitude, in a present understanding of our "environment" (paristithi). Sixthly fear emanates from our wrong beliefs (ashraddha), seventhly fear emanates from our wrongful perceptions (assatyam). Fear makes us mortal beings. This is not our true divine nature. We are born to conquer fear in all experiences of life.

'Fear' therefore, must be related, directly and indirectly to 'Karma' (or our human life). Every single person innately seeks total freedom from the known gross physical, physical, mental and conscious levels of human life. We understand that this kind of freedom is not imminent in fear and we understand that total freedom of the soul cannot manifest in clinging to authority, intellectual power, leaders, and gurus.

The journey of discovering the self abandons the past and abandons the entire social power, authority, and leaders who create umbrellas of their own empires. Any kind of imposing authority comprising 'thoughts', 'intellectual frameworks', and 'physical fascination' is destructive and evil. Firstly, it brings about 'insecurity'. Secondly it creates 'division and segregation' amidst integrity. Thirdly, it operates on 'discrimination'. Fourthly, it survives on 'conditions of the mind and the body'. Fifthly, it yearns for 'self-praises of the ego'. Sixthly, there is always a 'conflict' in it. Seventhly, it brings 'fear' of uncertainty, threat of impermanence and aggression.

Any powerful person accepting self praises of hymns, songs and creates a whole set of holy anthology away and separate from the root of the main aspect of core sacred religion of the soul is a power conscious deceitful person trying to manipulate and trying to win the confidence of the mind through illusive thoughts and illusive practices.

'Sickness' brings fear because we loose our well being and we become total 'dark grey cloud' when we are ill. We fear the lack of confidence.

'Control' brings fear because we try to emphasise concern and care out of obsession, possession and deception of our own selfish motives rather that trying to compassionately understand what does a humble person (the subservient person in the eyes of the modern world) truly need.

'Emptiness' brings fear because in that state we are afraid of finding our real person.

'Fear' is a condition of the mind that is linked with the vicious cycles of the mind, thought, intellect, reason and cause. As long as there is that 'conflict' between the 'thought' and the 'insight' there is, fear. Fear must therefore be unreal in as much as the thought is unreliable and impermanent. This is my true diagnosis with compassionate understanding and deep profound insight.

Our material success should not stop us from becoming a better human fellow. If we do not understand and help each other then are we communicating socially? The material prosperity does not mean one should make reforms and renewals but not to renew as a spirit.

The physical power or the brevity of material beauty and form is not everlasting. It is unfolding. This is the kind of power that threatens, dominates, controls, manipulates, competes, compares, possesses, shouts, blames, fights, and it is the kind power that is constantly trapped in hypocrisy. Until we die, we thrive on, we struggle, we survive, we suffer, and we continuously change and evolve in our physical form. In the process of physical evolution, our spirit moulds.

Vedic analogy: Can you really read a Holy Quran, a Holy Geeta, or a Holy Bible to the Bull who cannot even stand still for more than five minutes? Stubborn, Proud, Selfish, Inconsiderate, Self-opinionated, Narrow minded, blinded by the colour red, Power conscious, and vengeful. The Bull hates the colour red! Similarly, an egocentric (power conscious) individual is destructive towards the uniformity of the colour red! (Which represents the same colour of blood in all living beings)?

Love is not equal to something else! Compassion is not equal to something else! It is simply love! It is simply compassion! The simplicity of truth is not in the matrix of complex statistical, economic, and financial equations. The simplicity of love does not, argue, or rebel, or hold endless debates about it. Truth is 'truth', in the simplest of all sense, and it does not need a language to understand it, only experience. To understand 'truth', what is begged of a personality is a total shut down of the faculty of the hollow mind.

What is beseeched of a personality is the self-less sacrifice in time, to discover in quintessence, the light of truth.

What is begged of the personality is to sit down to inquire in silence, in emptiness, unconditionally and with love as naïve as an infant child. What is begged of the personality is patience. What is begged of the personality is transformation. What is begged of the personality is humility!

Total absolute fearlessness can only exist in total absolute freedom of the total person in wholesome. This type of absolute fearlessness cannot prevail in the power of social, economic and political environment of the mind and intellect that remains in conflict and brings 'hopelessness' in others. Total absolute fearlessness is a sacred sensation that cannot be loosely associated with the rites and rituals of the institutional power of any kind. Total absolute fearlessness glows in the eyes of pure serenity and pure courage. Pure courage and pure serenity only manifests in pure absolute profound wisdom of the soul.

Pure truth or the naked truth is only one truth. That which is this eternal truth of the soul supreme divine. In the highest seat of the soul transpires this eternal naked truth. When this eternal truth pervades in the conscience, fear begins to diminish gradually and fear begins to turn into energy of pure compassion. Uncertainty begins to transform into certainty. Doubts begin to fizzle away as they do not matter anymore. To evolve spiritually is real power. This power is authentic power. To grow and to become powerful authentically entails that we address our Karma's (collective acts and deeds of many lives put together in the complex influx of human existence).

Authentic power of the soul enables us to co-relate our personality to our spirit. Authentic power of the soul enhances our vision with the unfolding world, progressively and retrospectively. Authentic power is focused on the absolute journey of the soul. When we conquer the light of the soul, we conquer darkness of fear. We conquer our cosmic body.

There is profound wisdom in all sacred anthologies and all sacred experiences without a single doubt. It is when we shut off the noise and conditions of the social, economic and political reasons, that we are able to see things from a fresh point of view.

Seeing this universal nature in its essential nature is holistic religion. Learning the altruism of the free nature is the Vedic science. Growing with the profound honey wisdom of the essential nature is Vedic wisdom. Moulding with the nature, evolving in core composition of gross physical, physical, mental, meta-physical, conscious, and super conscious levels of existence is true religion of human kind, is profound Vedic experience. This infinite truth is unparalleled.

The karmic thread of actions and reactions are entwined in anxiety. This web of 'collective life gene' is a result of many years of collective human ego and collective human intelligence dissolved to create, recreate, and procreate power. The karmic thread rotates, revolves, and perpetuates in aggression, regression, progression, abrasion, and resolutions. This collective karmic thread connects us all in somewhat profound sense.

In the passage of time, we all loose our name, form, and status bound ego, to merge in togetherness! What one truly aspires is total freedom from the known gross physical, known physical, known mental and known conscious life of this everyday "worries".

One has to discover and understand with deep compassion and profound silence that naked truth manifests in profound simplicity. The simplest and the purest, 'truth', is in the essential compassion of the soul. Experience it, feel it, touch it, sense it, see it, but perceive it in wholesome. Reality is lonely. In rejection, isolation, and loneliness, most persons become sad and emotionally depressed albeit wearing a brave facemask.

Most of us are too proud to cry for help and most of us do not even consider that we need help. It is imperative, that no one truly likes to ask for help. Therefore, if someone has turned on your doorstep for help, do not ever deny this person true compassion and love, no matter what; otherwise you could not possibly be human. We are born alone and we die alone. This is reality and this is the naked truth. No humankind power could possibly alter this truth. However, when we realise this truth, we begin to elevate and evolve in karma.

True light comes from the heart of the core philosophical wisdom that manifests on rites and rituals of poetry, music, and insight of the spirit of life. Aspiration and inspiration are the essence of the discovery of the delight of the soul. Knowing the truth and understanding the truth are two different aspects.

Understanding entails that one penetrates the 'emptiness' of the personality. Understanding entails a total transformation rather than millions of reforms in intellectual and mental faculties. Understanding entails that we seek the truth in the spirit not in the hollow mind filled with crises and problems. Understanding entails that we meditate in silence.

Understanding entails that we examine retrospectively, rather than in respect of. Understanding entails that we perceive with our profound insight of the soul. Understanding entails that we stretch our finite mechanisms of social animal traits. Understanding entails that we see beyond the reality. Understanding entails that we stop running, and rest at the tranquil shores at the dawn and at the dusk. Understanding entails that we cease to operate in a robotic manner. Understanding entails that we open to the grand maestro in our spirits in solitude. Understanding entails that we experience it rather than profess it by knowledge. Understanding entails that we evolve in Karmas. Realise that 'fear' is nothing more than the dancing shadows of the mind, jumping ego of the conscious, fluttering senses of the desires, passion of pleasures, and petty mindedness in "mine", "I", "my", and "me"! Understanding does not carry a shield with it; rather it cherishes simplicity, in the most compassionate manner, without any postulates, criteria, or social norm. Understanding does not restrict to a confined institute.

Understanding does not entangle; rather it undoes the karmic knot of karmic actions. Understanding entails that we diffuse the power conscious ego, and the proud mind with great compassion! Understanding entails that we become tranquil and serene not for the sake of it but for the great experience of it. If we cannot make anyone happy, at least let us not make someone more miserable! If we cannot create hope for anyone, at least let us not destroy the little hope there is in a personality.

Essential life process comprises good health (clean food, clean environment, clean cloths, and clean body, clean conscious), good holistic human Life filled with compassion, culture, humanity, truth, and 'good deeds'. We are nothing without the essence of our own spirit.

Our ego is false, our pride is false, our money is false, our pleasure is false, our life is false, until we have realised our real 'true self' – our spiritual self. Then and only then, we are the masters of our own life. Then and only then, will we be able to play the violin, and express ourselves in music, poetry, and the magnificent nature whose beauty manifests in the vision of our intuitive eyes and compassionate understanding.

Integrity and Self-respect is pre-requisite to any progressive step in life. A man's self-respect is all he has to help him in adversities. No honestly decent person likes to suffer.

Understanding entails honest person's integrity to grant self respect not abrasive accusations to another person who is bruised, broken and traumatised in anguish!

If one cannot respect "integrity", at least one must not attempt to destroy it by superior position, power, mentally deliberate decision, discrimination, and paranoiac insecurity. It is fine for a person of power to deprive another humble person of integrity, his or her justified right because the powerful person is protected by the shield of institutional power but a humble person of integrity is not. If one cannot respect integrity, one must not crush it and destroy it with authority and power! Integral fear is imminent in many terrorist activities and many anti-terrorist wars.

What is the root of terrorism? Is it not suppressed fear in anger? No fire fighting or warfare renders any solution when the warfare and fire fighting is geared at fulfilling a personality. No act of terrorism if manifested without first indicating its symptoms! The symptoms are global saturation, global confusion in stock markets, and global catastrophes in foreign exchange trade, hiked property value, and increased inflation. The main aim of terrorism is to defy authority and to terrify the mass. Any terrorism brings fear and uncertainty. Terrorism creates greatest fears in the modern world bringing global chaos, conflict, confusion, and disorder. Earth is wounded and hurt.

The Vedas invoke the Param-Brahma to bring to the world in dismal sorrow hope and remedial healing. This healing mantra is a mantra designated to invoke the energies of the celestial gods, the spiritual embodiments of the divinity and spiritual awareness within human entity:

'Aum khamma Brahma-atman Param-Atman Param-Eishwaar Jagada-Purusha Ayam Atman Brahma-atman Ekam Tat Sat Tat Tvam Asi Hari Aum Tat Sat.'

'Oh divine God, thy name is Brahma, Aum is your mantra. My soul is part of the divine cosmic God. The divine cosmic God and the individual soul are essentially one. God is therefore one. Thou are that one great supreme God Hari personified in many forms of divine manifestations.'

This prayer invokes the divinity within one to become divine, to become aware and to grit the fears and the despair of the modern world.

In Vedic philosophy, the terms 'moha' (all the gross attachments of the material world), and 'maya' (all the enticement of the personality) are related to 'samnsara' (the gross physical earthly society of norms and criteria). 'Moha' and 'maya' are two hands of this 'samnsara'. 'Kaama' (desires) and 'taamman' (lust) are the stomach and excretory organs of the 'samnsara' (the society). 'Irriccha' (wish of the mind and heart) is the bosom of the 'samnsara' (the society). 'Krodha' (anger) and 'lobbha' (greed) are the two legs of the samnsara (society). 'Maddha' (arrogant pride) is the ego of the 'samnsara' (society). 'Samnsara' is a dummy personality with all these and more material qualities. It operates on 'buddhee' (the mind) and 'vicchaar' (thoughts).

'Samnsara' or the society of humankind survives on the principle of 'duality'. Everything is, related, co-related, or inter-related to something else. There is a second to compare and compete. Fear prevails the minute there is duality. 'Ignorance' is the longest night of the 'samnsara'.

To understand 'Samnsara', rather than to know 'samnsara' is the first of the seven stages of the pilgrimage (or 'yatra') of karmic evolution. When the knower ('jinasu'), understands with deep compassion the many faces of 'samnsara', the knower turns and transforms into an 'Artharthi' (the reasoning pillar of the spirit of life). When the 'Artharthi' (the transforming platform) evolves in karma with profound wisdom, the 'Artharthi' becomes a 'Jnani' (a wise spirit of life). The personality shifts into the spirit of life mode and the spirit of life, 'Hamnssa', follows its intuition, its spiritual insight. The first three stages of evolution are associated with the body of the cosmic human in gross physical, physical and mental planes. The next stage, the fourth stage, is associated with the meta-physical (the perception and the transpiration), wherein the transformation transpires in totality. The fifth and the sixth stages of evolution are associated with the consciousness and super consciousness and the seventh stage in karmic evolution is associated with delight.

Everything animate or inanimate that is within the universe is controlled and owned by the supreme eternal divine God. One should not accept other things knowing well to whom they truly belong. Things cannot give immortality, true divine happiness, or even quench the thirst of the hungry spirit of life. All things are material appropriation of the gossamer wealth of the grand cosmic existence.

This is the essence of satt-karma (righteousness), satt-dharma (right conduct), and samma-pusthee-sukham (eternal divine contentment and happiness).

The Vedic godhead is built upon togetherness – 'vissvaa kutumbhkam'. The humankind has woven a web of intellectualism almost universally uniform. Our individual life is a 'micro-cosmic' representation of the universal 'macro-cosmic' reality. The conflict surmounting the grand universe is the same conflict within our families our immediate surroundings our communities our societies our nations, our world, and us at large.

"Do not believe in anything simply because you have heard it. Do not believe in anything simply because it is spoken and rumoured by many. Do not believe in anything simply because it is found written in your religious books. Do not believe in anything merely on the authority of your teachers and elders. Do not believe in traditions because they have been handed down for many generations. But after observation and analysis, when you find that anything agrees with reason and is conducive to the good and benefit of one and all, then accept it and live up to it."

~ Buddha

'Param Sukham' – Eternal happiness is beyond just 'sukham' happiness. It is a sublime state wherein 'sarwa-dukhah' - all the sorrows, 'sarwa-pidhatah' – all the diseases, and 'sarwa-vyaaddhi' – all the anxiety disperse. Eternal happiness is a beautiful state of happiness that eventually transpires for those who have, suffered long, cried, wept, and been hurt, searched long, tried, and experienced the wholesome truth. Let noble thoughts inspire us and nourish our spirit.

Yoga (communion of godhead and soul) or Atman-shanti (soul tranquillity) cannot take place in differentiation, fragmentation, and hurt of 'all this, that and the other'.

The giver of fear and the recipient of fear are both therefore wrongful. Integrity is non-negotiable. Integrity means observing the code of conduct conducive to the higher order. When we create our own code of conduct to suite our circumstances, then it becomes distortion, fragmentation, differentiation, individualisation, and commercialisation from the hypocritical personal intentions.

To state a good selfless intention and then to profit and to become richer at the expense of others means exploitation. It implies taking that which does not belong to us in the first place. Therefore, it is better to state the facts honestly and humbly without the fear of loosing the proliferation. Proliferation should become secondary not primary. Political propaganda will defend individualism in 'all this, that and the other' and verily there is chaos in one form or another. This chaos is imminent in the pollution, epiphanies, tragedies, sicknesses, stress, artificial lifestyles, unhappy homes, broken marriages, personal life crises, all these and much more based on comparison, aggression, competition, and justification of self-made personal sympathies.

We are not material entities undergoing a mystical experience; rather we are divine entities experiencing paradox of surviving the grand collective ego. The humankind is a divine entity that is journeying in the passage of time in karma to experience the collective hurt, sorrow, adversity, suffering, pain, and grief to associate itself back to its true essential spiritual existence. The spirit of life cries in dismal hurt, as it triumphs over great fears and embraces the collective 'despair':

'Life oh life! Let me face all my adversities as they are with great courage, profound spiritual strength, and greatest inner peace.'

'Life oh life! Let the storm manifest itself as a mere moment of existence, let me stand firm to this earthen clay with all my spiritual roots to experience karma. Life oh life! Let me evolve like the butterfly and let me break free from the cocoons of all this, that and the other. Let me evolve in karma.'

'Life oh life! Let me grow in spirit! Let me sacrifice all that is impermanence to the most beautiful most wonderful delight of the light of the spirit of my life in satt-karma (righteousness) and dharma (right conduct). Life oh life! Let it be an experience filled with adventures. Life oh life! Let it be moments filled with extra ordinary memories of divinity. Life oh life! Let it be a composition of lyrics filled with self-same words of sacrifice in karma. Life oh life! Let it be a song, let it be a poem, let it be a never ending music of the dance of karma.'

6. EVOLUTION OF KARMA

Time flies fast; the universe is unfolding as it should. Righteousness brings virtue, welfare, happiness, health, and global wealth. Whatsoever we do, we eventually credit or discredit our own soul divine.

The entire cosmos, from the very magnificent Sun to the very tiniest of the particle of nature in the smallest atom, molecule, and nucleus, is controlled profoundly with profound cosmic laws of the higher order. There is almost a perfect order. Like the sunrise and sunset, like the flow of rivers and the roar of oceans, like the rustle of the trees and the perennial grass, like the rotation and revolution, like the dawn and the dusk, like the stars and the planets, like the vastness of the eternity and celestial planes. Every single particle of nature, (whether the gross physical, physical, mental, conscious or the super conscious spiritual plane) is governed by scientific cosmic laws of karma.

This 'absoluteness' prevails within the context of karma in perpetual transient phases, cycles, involutions and evolutions. The law of 'health' in profound most sense prevails, as much in nature as in us. We are nothing without health. Good health is vital to human well being. Good health is absolute vital force of essential existence, the existence of good life breath.

'Sorrow' does not actually begin in the sense of first born word or first born creation in the first breath of life, and 'sorrow' does not actually end in the literal sense of the last word or diffusion of life breath. All creation is born from the pain and infusion of force and inertia and all creation perish in the pain of force and inertia of karma. Life in the literal sense is sorrow as long as life is force and inertia of action. Every single action comprises inertia. Inertia is the reason, inertia is the cause of movement and without inertia of Karma there would be no life process. To be in love with absolute life is to be in love with all that is magnificently beautiful and profoundly permanent like the galaxy, the stars, the dancing rivers, the roaring oceans, the rustling trees, the perennial grass, the sunrises and the sunsets, the glittering stars and the heavenly clouds. The entire cosmic entity infinitely goes beyond the blue skies in to the 'unknown' eternity.

Every single particle and every single entity of the cosmos operate on the inertia of vital life breath. The vital life breath brings energy, force and power in the air, and moves the rays of the sun into the orbits of ether and transforms the fire and the air into the currents of waters in the rivers and oceans that trash, touch, nourish and fertilize the bare earth. Every single activity is operating on the inertia of currents and the inertia of activity. This is the karmic cosmic life. Life means activity. Inactivity is stale. Activity involves and evolves in cycles like the low tides and the high tides of the ocean. Like the thunderstorms and the bright blue skies. Like the sunsets and the sunrises. Like the day and the night. Every life activity operates on 'rotation' and 'revolution'. Every Karmic activity is rotating and revolving in magnetic fields of vibrations.

The rotation and revolution of cosmic operation 'rr'tta-karma' is ever non stop in time 'kaal'. Rr'tta-karma perpetuates in cycles of creation, dissolution, and recreation. As the water ('jaal' or 'apah') cleanses the impurities of the earth ('prithevee'); as the wind (vayau alters energy and force in eight different directions); as the fire ('agnee') gives the warmth of creation in the womb and dissolves the mortal matter in ashes; as the ether transcends the ten vital life breaths (dasha'prannah) from the gross manifest (sarguna) to the most subtle unmanifest (nirguna). Truth exalts the mind (budhhee) in divine or Vedic experiential knowledge. Truth evolves in constant and consistent divine experiences, by practice of yoga 'communion' in devotion-'bhaktee yoga' and living in accordance with the laws of cosmic godhead –'rr'tta-karma yoga'. 'Satt-gjnannam' (true divine knowledge) together with 'satt-karma' (righteous act) renders 'satt-jivan' (righteous life), minimises the 'bhay' (fear) of 'rog' (disease) and brings 'sukham' (happiness) and 'Shantih' (peace).

"IshAvAsyam idam sarvam yat kincha jagatyAm jagat tena tyaktena bhunjIthA mA gRidhah kasya svid dhanam". (Sri Isha Upanishad)

Everything animate or inanimate that is within the universe is controlled and owned by the higher order call it God – eternal divine spirit (iswhaara-param-brahman-narayan-svarroppam-param-atma). One should therefore accept only those things necessary for oneself, which are set aside as his or her quota. One should not accept other things knowing well to whom they truly belong. When in a society, there is a misappropriation of divine wealth; there will be symptoms of fearfulness as a result of precarious parody of culture caused by corruption, wrongfulness, hypocrisy, double standards, and deceit.

When righteousness is metaphysically perturbed by wrongful possession, the laws of the divine nature are physically disturbed and hence the consequences are non-pious, non-truthful, prejudiced, dishonest, non-virtuous, and unwise.

Beyond the inferior cosmic nature comprising the eight material (five elements, mind, ego, and intellect) constituents, manifests the superior energy of the spirit of life. It is the superior cosmic nature where ego is no more. The reasoning of 'all this, that and the other' perish from the grossness to the sublime-ness. The existential nature belongs to God. The quest to conquer the infinite cosmic nature beyond the material plane for control and power only renders the collective egocentric human person more miserable. Control is never permanent! Power is never permanent; 'all this, that and the other' which becomes owned either in thought or action eventually becomes disowned, as death stares us all in the face of life. Just like the rivers merging into the ocean loosing their names, forms, shapes, and personal identity, becomes universally one grand ocean, our centrifugal forces 'jivan-atmanas' ultimately unite us in oneness of param-atman without a doubt. The mind and the ego eventually loose in their reign of control and ownership.

A fair quota of happiness is set aside for every existence, every household, and every karmic being. This is the quota of 'pushttee' (satisfaction and contentment). When we break the barriers of the necessities and dwell into the excess territories we are in possession and control of surplus wealth. Surplus wealth becomes hoarded wealth when it is not utilised for the good intent of humanity, servitude, growth, and expansion but for the self. The altruism of Vedas does not prohibit enjoyment. Enjoy a healthy life and proliferate. However, realise and become aware that a higher order does exist. The divine higher order does exist in right conduct, right endurance, right patience, right intent, right compassion, and right love. The question then arises 'What is right?' What is right is circumstantial! It is imperfect like the imperfect human world crying out in sorrows, pains, epiphanies, miseries, and depression.

'Selflessness' 'idda'nnan'mamma' implies that we do not own anything that we accumulate for ourselves. Servitude and satt-karma (right action) is based on merit, aptitude, ability, integrity, intent, effort, skills, honesty, sincerity, and attitude. 'Varna' (divine profession) generates these sublime gunas (qualities). Avarna (non-divine profession) generate tamasic gunas of lust, greed, hate, anger, avarice, jealousy, envy, falseness, theft, prostitution, and perversion.

The Vedic godhead is based on togetherness ('samam') – togetherness of the three worlds namely the celestial (ethereal eternity), the spiritual (unknown-unseen), and the gross material earth (known – seen).

Every Karmic activity generates a vibration of distinct oscillation of force and energy outwards into the cosmic eternity or a sublime inclination that continues to vibrate in the mind. Each karmic action continues to attract from the environmental surrounding and from the personality a magnetic conglomerate of field of energy and force. 'Like' attracts 'like', 'beauty' attracts 'beauty', acts of love attracts loving acts, malicious impurity attracts impurity, artistic talent attracts art, music attracts sounds, anxiety attracts fear, fear attracts power, power attracts power, and so on. It is almost a non-stop activity in a loop of like pattern of eight [8]. Every action is compounded by a reaction. Action continues to become reaction until demagnetised.

Satt-karma is demagnetisation by our own subtle sub-conscious re-experience, compassionate understanding, and resolution by change and transformation. This transformation is hereby referred to as a moulding process of progressive change. When we continue to demagnetise the karmic cycles, we elevate from the 'platform of life' spiritually and we begin to grow and mould into what I refer to as eternal truth or eternity at the outset of this book. This process of moulding and evolving is a positive, progressive inertia of karma crossing seven progressions from the base gross physical condition into the highest eternal super conscious truth, the seat of the soul.

Therefore, satt-karma is the centrifugal force of life activity and life activity only stops when life becomes immortal. Even in inactivity, there is activity as long as there is life breath.

Our progressive demagnetisation is known as evolution whereas our regressive continuous magnetisation is known as involution.

What is significant to our understanding is that whilst 'fate' and 'destiny' are inevitably dependent on each other, 'fate' is not permanent. Fate is changeable and alterable in as much as the demagnetisation process will continue to diffuse the magnetic fields of the 'fate' itself.

'Fate' is not a phenomenon of absoluteness, in that a river flowing with fiery currents can alter its direction if corrective measures and scientific electricity of positive energy, positive protons, and positive electrons diffuse the currents. Our human sacrifice renders such diffusion, literally.

In essence, the spirit of life journeys mortality on human earth. Every life in the passage of time is a karmic journey based on Aartha (desires, action, and wealth), kaama (ambition, causation, pleasure, passion, and rewards), dharma (righteousness, duty towards ourselves and to others), and moksha (spiritual salvation). The law of causatal life is creation, preservation, dissolution, retribution, transformation, and recreation in perpetual cycles.

'Adhyattmic-satt-karma' implies spiritual rites, rituals, ceremonies, culture, sacrifices, retribution, evolution, and realising the unknown mysticism of the Atma (soul). In the process of self-realisation, a spirit profoundly understands the impermanence of human life.

Human Personality wants to enjoy life. Everything in life becomes part of personality. Every human personality has a right to enjoy life. However, the soul must experience life in order to realise the impermanence of life itself. Sanchitta karma is the karmic manifestation of our previous life or past that has brought us to the present. Sanchitta karma is a metaphorical bank of karma. Either the metaphorical karmic bank can be overdrawn (collective negative karma) or it can be in credit (collective positive karma). When we experience despair, anguish, and adversity, we are presented with an opportunity to evolve. Every life spirit must move from the darkness to lightness, from the falsehood to truth, from the impermanence to the spiritual permanence, from the dullness to awareness, from the ignorance to wisdom, from the ego to the self.

To divinely give is a sacred human sacrifice that is but our human obligation and our human duty! To feed a poor hungry child in the Gatos of the muddy villages of India and Africa is not a great charity! It is our collective human duty ordained by the higher order in karma! How can one not see this? As long as the germ of differentiation and fragmentation is there, Bharati - Mother India or Mama Africa will not be freed from the deep painful diseases of the 'falseness' and vikarma (wrongfulness).

We must take and accept only what we can give back on to others. If we take something that does not belong to us because we have either not earned it or because we have no inheritable right over it then it must be dispensed off, written off, or passed on to others who are lesser fortunate, otherwise we become diseased, burdened, and eventually our life karma gives us pain. Love begets love. Compassion begets compassion. Silence begets peace. Beauty begets beauty.

The world is unfolding as it should and we are withering with its time and space. A spirit of life takes birth in 'hope' (aspiration) and exists in the essence of 'fathomless faith' (inspiration). Our life moulds in karmic cycles and our karmic entity merges in oneness with the eternal entity in divine bliss when we come to the end of our journey.

Life is a perpetual triumph over death. Every spirit is transient in physical nature and personality. Everything withers away with the elapsing time and the unfolding matter (earth), as it should. Life is a `never ending' process of 'change'. Life comprises cycles. Cycles of life and death, Cycles of good and bad, cycles of pain and pleasure, Cycles of happiness and sorrows, Cycle of success and failures, Cycles of Rich and Poor, Cycles of seasons and tides, etc. Life is a vicious cycle as long as life is body and matter. Inadvertently, we conform to this vicious cycle without realising that our life is a gift to us from God. We must therefore at least owe this much to the almighty spirit within us. At least listen to the call of your own soul; a silent cry from deep within you, a cry to set it free, a cry to lift it, a cry to emancipate totally. Wake up o dear friend and awaken yourself. Do not become an obsolete particle of the withering unfolding material world. The world is unfolding, as it should.

Everywhere there is a rise in mass poverty, ignorance, diseases, war, and pollution. The earth is perishing with time. Our material kingdom is a temporary house of comforts. Journey of life perpetuates beyond birth and death. It encompasses cycles of lives attributable to the eternal soul. A spirit lives beyond this mass & matter.

Karma extends beyond one lifetime experience. It perpetuates with the spirit alias-astral body of the soul until total spiritual liberation is accomplished. Karma (reflective actions and deeds) is the composition of many configurations put together. It is the reflection of our absolute life (different lives put together).

By our Karma, we shape our personalities and give physical conformity to our spirits. Karma is the reason for life. Karma is definite and perspective in relation to life in that it is limited to life itself and is a reflection of time and space.

Every single one of us is constantly evolving within our personalities during our lifetime. Karma is the intent or deed conducted with or without the knowledge of its consequences. Intent or a deed could bring benefit or loss in this life or the life after life.

Spiritual life of a human jive (astral body of the spirit) according to the Vedas is 120 years (provided the human life is totally free from toxic, stress, evil, fear, and pain). According to Vedangas jyotisha (Vedic science of astrology), human life span experiences karmic cycles based on the planetary configurations of the astrological birth chart ruling at the time of birth. The time a spirit enters this world from the mother's womb, the day, and the year are significant and profound in establishing the karmic journey of the spirit. In Kalyug, the age of falsehood, whilst it is not possible to have a long life a pro-rata proportion of the life is taken in relation to the standard Vedic human life. The standard Vedic life span comprises phases of cycles. A planet rules each karmic phase. Each planet determines the characteristics of the karmic life. It is explicit however in the Vedas that the birth chart does not provide an end conclusion and it must therefore be taken only as a guide. Almost like the personality profile.

In proportion to 120 spiritual years, therefore, each planet has a cycle starting in chronological sequence with, the Sun, Moon, Mars, Rahu, Jupiter, Saturn, Mercury, Ketu, and Venus. The cycles representative of phase for each planet in number of years, in respective chronological sequence comprise:

6(SUN)+10(MOON)+7(MARS)+18(RAHU)+16(JUPITER)+19(SATURN)+17 (MERCURY)+7(KETU)+20(VENUS)=120 SPIRITUAL YEARS. One can be born under any of the above cyclical phase and the life will continue thenceforth.

Life is a reflection of total experience for the soul unconditionally and conditionally under its karmic circumstances (pleasure and pain, happiness and sorrow, success and failure, gain and loss, rich and poor, life and death).

Listening silently can enable us to understand Karma. From our deeper and compassionate understanding of Karma, we come to terms with suffering and sorrow. We gradually become indifferent and immune to suffering. We feel freedom and relief from the burdens of fear, anxiety, social power, prestige, status, social configurations of greed, envy, lust, anger, and competition. Karma has an evolving nature. The passage of time encompasses multitude of five sensory experiences that are finite and measurable. However, the personality or the person withers in body with time and the nature of this limitation is unfolding with time. The body and the mind form personality and personality is limited to the perception of the five senses and matter. Karma evolves with the elapsing personality. It evolves in absolute terms with the absolute life in the absolute journey of life, perpetually. We can be definitive about our choices. We have the ability and the human gift to distinguish between the right and the wrong. We have the innate divine blissful consciousness to be Divine.

What seemed impossible yesterday appears possible today and what seems great illusion today may turn out to be great reality tomorrow. The physical evolution is occurring more rapidly then ever before. Our personalities and identities evolve physically and mentally whilst our spiritual soul perpetually evolves in a momentum of Karmas (reflective actions and intentions of the personalities and identities).

Spirit continues its journey beyond this physical metamorphosis of body, matter, and mind (personality). It evolves in absolute terms of life in a perpetual cycle of absolute change. The spirit evolves in the journey of absolute life. It perches on life experiences only to manifest its Karmas in the personified constituent of body and matter. Reality is survival and reality is a virtue of life.

Karmic activity involves three spheres of human life, namely, the family, the life of the 'life spirit', and the extent of the life breath. The third is the significant sphere because it is the most uncertain sphere of every human kind. Life breath will stop inadvertently and death is almost uncertain. Therefore, the nervous system contains magnetic fields of Karmas that have been released from the past.

Based on magnetic fields, our impulses draw us or withdraw us from situations or circumstances in the present.

To demagnetise this cycle, we need to evolve compassionately and profoundly until we are elevated from the 'platform of vicious life cycle'.

To justify our existence is to free from the virtue of life, in a process of spiritual evolution, based on profound wisdom of the soul.[26]

In Vedas, Yamma (the lord of death) describes how a Brahma purush manushya (incarnate individual human spirit) becomes immortal. He becomes immortal by becoming enlightened with the delight of light, in a fusion of togetherness with the twilight of dawn and dusk in, prayers, devotion, and profound mantra-meditation, and profound silence, recitals of musical Vedas, rites and rituals of 'agnee' (sun).

His enlightenment came from karmic evolution (evolution in activities).

Progressively, he was antecedently an 'Artan' (despondently depressed and afflicted). He realised that life is a bed of thorns and that it is a vicious cycle. From then on he became a 'jinasu' (the seeker, the enquirer) based on the profound wisdom of the soul. Then he progressed onto Artharthi (the seeker of truth) whereby he abandoned all the material illusions and strived to reach the super-consciousness. He then progressed into becoming a 'Jnani' (the wisely awakened). All progressive evolution of the soul is regarded as transcendental. An involution is regarded as darkness of ignorance, attachment to pleasures, desires, lust, anger, and ego.

'Jnani' is intimately engrossed with almighty supreme god in poetries, philosophy, meditation, mantra jaap, hymns, songs of praise, profound silence of compassionate embrace, and joys of enlightened delights. 'He is the Karma Yogi (evolved soul), the param (profound) bhakta (devotee), and a humble person.

---

[26] Per Vedic wisdom, food, and thought are vital forces of the life breath. By ignorance, the life spirit crosses the journey of life. By profound wisdom, the life spirit enters the boundless immortality of pure eternity. In the finite known mortal material world, there is no permanent happiness. Only in the infinite immortal spiritual world, there is bliss, happiness, and peace. To honor and to respect means to think of the land and the water and the air and the sky and all life of existence as having equal rights as us. We are imperfect humans performing our given task. Everything is a circle and we are each responsible for our own actions in a circle.

The soul transcends from one form into another form of personality or identity, replenishing its karmic cycle of evolution. In its transcendental transition, the mind memory is wiped away, as there is some time gap between death and birth. A mother's womb is a place where the spirit (astral body of the soul) sleeps the longest, peacefully and freely without its five sensory functions interacting directly with the environment. When a baby is born, it feels almost like waking up from a deep anaesthetic sleep. It finds itself in new habitual home (body) in a new environment. All it recognises is its mother's bosom and the rhythm of her heartbeat. Hence a spirit transmigrates and habituates into a renewed cycle of Karma's into another lifetime experience. We have the innate ability to make the choices of destroying our innate enemies comprising the negative Karma's (life actions and deeds).

Karma is one's own life reflection and Karma defines one's life purpose. Karma is primordial as much as antecedent to this life.

Negative karma emanates from greed (over indulgence, power hungry, over-materialistic, meanness and miserliness), anger (mental rashness and emotional selfishness), lust (multifarious desires and immorality), and desires or material attachments (the possessive self). When desires remain unfulfilled, one becomes frustrated and gloomy.

Our negative karmas (inconsiderate actions) reflect upon us either in this life or next (if you consider spiritual journey after death to be a fact) and make no mistake about that! No one escapes this law of action and reaction, no one.

'What goes around comes around'. It all goes around in circles.

Per Vedas, Karma can be of four kinds. The first one is the past karma (karma of our previous life). The second one is the present Karma (the karma of our life that we breath). The third one is the intended Karma (Karma which we intend to do in the future based on the stored up past). The fourth one is the future Karma (karma which we actually do in the future life, including next reincarnation).

Karma manifests in three states, namely the dynamic, the static, and the transcendental future (alias the spiritually perpetual form).

Karmas are guided by 'Gunas' (quality). They are namely, the 'Tammas', the 'Rajas', and the 'Sattva'. The Tammas is that which creates and recreates form and matter, body, and ego. 'Tammas'/ grounded senses manifest in the gross matter, physical body, and the physical mind. The 'Rajas' is that which manifests in the content of rich foods and activity of the mind and sensory system. The 'Sattva' is that which manifests in pure consciousness of the crown of the mind. The three qualities rule different energy points alias chakras (spiritual points) of our body.

Seven chakras: The first chakra is at the base of the spine-coccyx. The second chakra is in the spleen and the sex organs. The third chakra is in the solar plexus. The fourth chakra is in the lungs and heart. The fifth chakra is in the throat and thyroid). The sixth chakra is in the mind, intelligence, and super intuition. The seventh chakra is in the sublime consciousness or pure bliss of the crown of the head just above the pituitary gland. 'Sattva' being the purest quality, rules the sixth and the seventh chakra. 'Sattva' is associated with consciousness and super consciousness. 'Rajas' being the sensory survival rule the fifth, the fourth, and the third energy points. 'Rajas' is associated with the mind and the emotions. 'Tammas' being the matter rule the second and the first energy points. 'Tammas' is associated with the gross physical and physical matter.

See annex two for illustration.

Karma manifests in twofold aspects. One is the duty and the other is THE SACRIFICE. The duty is towards our stomach, the senses, and the excellent performance of the multi-sensory human being. The sacrifice is towards the spirit of life.

Sacrifice is not a burden. Sacrifice is a joy that transcends from the delight of discovering the light of truth.

According to the karmic philosophy, Jesus, Mohammed, Buddha, and others sacrificed the ego and the mind to super-consciousness.

We acknowledge the mind, the ego, and the body as a survival kit. However, the super-consciousness is beyond the survival struggles. It is a quest into the existence of the very substance. Sacrifice is the experiential self-discovery pilgrimage of the soul.

Karma is manifested in five different stages (or yugs not yoga) or circumstances. The first one is the Bala Yug (childlike, childhood, playground, and playing music, dancing, singing, etc.). The second one is the Brahmcharya Yug (the moulding into the world of reality with knowledge (or Veena Gjnan). The third one is the Kshatriya grahasta yug (the duty bound obligations of the enjoyment and reaping the fruits of the Brahmcharya yug). The third one is the Jnanna yug (wisdom by experience and self-discovery into Middle age). The fourth one is the Bhaktee yug (refrain from the world of matter through worship). The fifth one is the Vairagya yug (the renunciation of all maya-illusions and samnsara-social attachments).

After 'Karma' has progressed through the five stages, 'Karma' transcends in the purest and highest beatitude of truth infinite in sublime most fusion of delight. It merges the light of the soul and the light of the sun in twilight of delight. It brings together God and Soul, in profound prayer dialogue, rites, and rituals of Agnee, profound mantra-manjaree, profound meditation, profound silence of enlightenment, profound compassion, and profound peace. It becomes the link between this world and the other world. It leads us onto the moksha yug (liberation).

A Karma-Yogi (an altruist) is governed by Yoga. Yoga is union of two lights. In yoga, transpires silence in the final beatitude, (observance of silence with mantra-manjaree). A Karma-Yogi performs his duty in twofold respects (to sustain survival and to evolve in the existence). He dedicates himself selflessly to Humanity and Godhead.

A Karma-Yogi loves compassionately, unconditionally and universally. A Karma-Yogi understands and listens in profoundness.

A Karma-Yogi becomes an artiste of music, rites, rituals, hymns, poetry, philosophy, lyrics, mantras, and writing. A Karma-Yogi becomes a 'Jnani' (wise soul) by learning the profound ways of God, the spirit, and the universal soul. A Karma-Yogi keeps his body in shape by physical yoga and physical exercises.

The performance of Karma in every single situation requires five qualities in a person. The first quality is the quality of a Brahman (the seer). The second quality is the quality of a Kshatriya (the warrior or the Arjun with spiritual, mental and physical energy).

The third quality is the quality of a Vaishya (the creative performer and the prolific person with positive attitude. The fourth quality is the quality of a Shuddra (the labourer or the task person). The fifth quality is the quality of the quality of Ardhanarishvara (the oneness of unity and cosmic marriage of the Shiva and Shaktee or the he and she or the union of divinity or the eternal harmony). A harmony of momentum is essential for optimum transmigration of the human spirit.

The metaphysics of creation and the law of Karma and Gunas (qualities) state that excess of any constituent, in Gunas (qualities) and Karma's (action), will result in an imbalance either in 'Karma' or in 'Life'. Hence, we suffer pain emanating from, Sickness, Accidents, Death (loss of beloved), Job loss, Loss of money, Ill-habits (like alcohol drinking, illicit sex, etc.), changing physical conditions, Insomnia, Fear, Loneliness, Old age and many other adversities of life. Doubt begins to shadow our mental state and we begin to doubt most things in life, making us susceptible to most situations. Mental anguish begins to eat us. Our sensitivity becomes negative and our physical body begins to show signs of anxiety and worries.

According to Vedas, there can never be absolute inactivity nor can there be absolute activity. Therefore, the laws of Karma suggest that we remain indifferent in activity and find purest activity in the most inactivity. We are each entities of the sacred hoop of karma just as the trees and the stars and the plants and the animals and the sea and the rivers and the soft pebbles are.

When we become subjective and biased about our conditions, we accelerate inertia of mind and body in stress and anxiety. When the wear and tear of the mind becomes directly proportional to the wear and tear of the physical tissues, our immune systems begins to weaken, resulting into many ailments and diseases. When we reach our weakest points in life, we turn to medical help, then we turn to psychological help, then we finally turn to spiritual help, as a last resort. Some of us turn to astrologers and psychic healers for help. Depending on the magnitude of misfortune, we seek for the compensatory healing in some form or another and are willing to pay the asking price in desperation. We presume that it is a process in itself and we take life at its face value and change it without attempting to mould it. Such a change is short-lived and temporary.

Creation is beyond human conception. There is an inter-link of infinite eternity to the infinite of the mind and the finite of the mind and matter. This link is personified in the sound "AUM" and we awaken our chakras alias our spiritual energies thus by this one word that is the sound of infinite creation in the infinity of the infinite magnificent nature. The spectrum of collective creation is a giant web of karma.

By Karma then there is inter-link at every level in time and space. No one lives or can possibly live in total isolation. Every single being is somehow connected in somewhat profound sense. The past of a being is linked to the present, the present is linked to the future, and the future is linked into the next world and so on. Every single human being is linked with another human being and their actions and reactions are linked in somewhat profound sense. Living spirit of life is inter-linked with the departed spirit in the other spiritual planes. An individual reaps or replenishes making persons connected with him in a collective group or family or community or race or nation, part of this proliferation or dissolution or dispersion.

The food that we consume is extremely significant. The manner in which we consume food is profoundly significant to our mental consciousness.

Health is therefore the result of what we think and how we think. Our thoughts form preliminary karmic cycle of our karmic activity. Every single thought and every single food particle that we consume, digest, and excrete therefore affects our health. Being healthy is a necessity.

Our body is like a temple to our soul and our mind is like the doors of this temple. What enters through the doors (alias the mind) enters the temple eventually and finally affects the whole being (alias the spiritual being). What we feed our body brings a corresponding level of karmic activity in the mind and the gross physical senses. Like for example, eating red meat produces sensuous desires and aggression. Like for example eating pure sattvic foods comprising fresh vegetables, fresh fruits, freshly cooked hot food, freshly prepared meals, fibre, salads, freshly cooked rice, fresh yoghurt, fresh milk, pure non carbonated water, and lots of fresh air and sunshine bring fresh thoughts and clean outlook. Cleanliness is vital and cleanliness speaks for the clean person that there is a clean conscience inside the clean body.

Ancient science of yoga suggests we become that what we eat and that what we think. Karma Yoga is a composite term implying wholesome life activities which includes, the gross physical (the food, the environment, the body, the cloths, the things), physical (the body as a sacred temple), the mind (as the vision or the gates of the physical temple – body), the conscious (our feelings, emotions, and thoughts that flow to and from the nervous system), the super conscious (our deeper spiritual insight).

Our human character is built on the karmic activity of food, thought, and total human evolution. Character is the bark of our life tree comprising the conscious, the mind, the body, and the gross physical environment whilst nature is the root of our life tree comprising consciousness and super consciousness.

Character is integrity. Character is the aspiration and the determination of the spiritual will to become illumined. What we think, thus we become, when we believe it.

What we eat, thus we feel. What we do, thus we reciprocate. Character is what makes us from our food, thought and activity whilst human nature is what we are in essence. One is dynamic whilst the other is static. Our human nature is a gift of compassion.

Compassion is as flawless as the magnificent Mother Nature itself is. It is the gaze of our illumined eyes. It is the treasure of love. It is wealth, health, and happiness in bliss.

In 'all this, that and the other', all said and done, when we loose our integrity we have truly lost everything. In defending dharma (right conduct) with sat-karma (in righteousness), therefore, a true Yogi (beloved devotee of Lord Krishnan) holds fast to the purest integrity of his spirit.[27]

---

[27] Atma (soul) verily is Shiva and Atma-lingham (phallus of earthen creation) is verily the Shiva-lingham (phallus of the cosmos). Praise and highest praise to the supreme atman-lingham, to the Shiva-lingham, to the param-yogi (grandeur). The supreme teacher is the atman that is the guru (param-guru). The supreme teacher verily is the 'param-purushat-ataman-jivan-atman' (the one who sits in the soul). Atma is seat of 'tathagatih' (enlightenment). Integrity is divine. Integrity is like character. When that is taken away from us all is taken away. 'Vikarma' (false deed) renders dishonesty, disintegration, destruction, conflict, and chaos to all. Shiva is the lord of 'fearlessness'. As water runs fresh and free from the woodlands, so does new life and meaning come from Shiva.

Absolute life encompasses wealth, happiness, prosperity, and all that is materially and externally powerful. However, Absolute life requires us to be committed to absoluteness and infinitely sublime nature - The nature of the soul – 'atma jagrutti' (spiritual awareness). [28],[29]

SURVIVING VERSES EXISTING

Our journey of life comprises five progressive stages. They are the childhood, the adolescence, the adulthood, the middle age, and the old age. Childhood lasts to the age of twelve - twelve years cycle. Adolescence runs from the thirteen year to the twentieth year - seven and a half years cycle. Adulthood runs from the twenty first year to the fiftieth year - thirty years cycle. Middle age runs from the fiftieth year to the sixty-fifth years - fifteen years cycle. Finally, the old age runs from sixty-fifth years to death - usually third of total life. The apportionment in years may vary from one person to another person. However, the cycles are five evolutionary cycles and each cycle represents predominance of a particular karmic purpose.

---

[28] Karma: Action and reaction are equal and opposites. What we pull and what we push in life are mere forces of our mentally conscious mind together with the body (alias the bhumi – earth). Karma is perpetual, as long as action and reaction do not cease. In the Vedic experience by professor Pannikar, he says in part four A under S.U.VI.2040: Only when men shall roll up space as if it were a simple skin, only then will there be an end of sorrow without acknowledging God.

[29] Krishna – Arjun updesh (dialogue): Arjun is in the kshetra (stage of life) after seven births and seven cycles of evolution. The evolution, which has brought him to manushyalokh (humankind universe) or life as a purush (humankind) is progressive mould. This is not a mere coincidence nor is it in the control of Arjun's mind. Therefore, Arjun was confused and frustrated only because he was mentally reasoning and consciously trying to find a rational explanation of avoiding destruction. But without the destruction of the EGO and its enemies (greed, self indulging pleasure, desires, lust, anger, ignorance, attachment with the illusions of life's many excitements and exhilaration, and causing to conveniently comfort the mind), it is not possible to diffuse Karma. Karma is life and life is Karma. Pranna or the life breathe means ACTIVITY. In activity only there is joy of self-realisation. Performing our duty is activity. Our earth is more valuable than our money. It will last forever. It will not perish by the flames of man made fires, as long as the divine ocean and the rivers forever flow in circles. Thought comes before speech. The Vedic wisdom constantly refrains from talking senselessly and wasting energy. It encourages on silence.

IMPORTANT PHASES IN OUR LIVES ACCORDING TO THE VEDAS

The childhood, the adolescent, the adulthood, and the old age are four different karmic stages in every life. These four stages are represented by four ways of life respectively, namely, the scholar life, the householder or the working life, the post working life or the renunciation, and the total spiritual liberation life alias 'moksha'. According to the Vedas, the scholar life can stretch up to the age of thirty, depending on the magnitude of profound wisdom one accumulates. The householder or the working life lasts up to the age of sixty, presuming the maximum life span in Kalyug (the present time). The third stage lasts unto the age of seventy, and the final stage is beatitude onto total renunciation of the worldly or material illusions (maya) and its social metamorphosis (samnsara). These stages entail progressive development and moulding growth or development of the spirit within us. If we react and crash with crises, we become part of the decaying process of matter. Strong spiritual foundation implies easy and comfortable old age. Weak spiritual foundation implies difficult and painful old age. It is better to suffer materially than spiritually and emotionally. Albeit total salvation cannot always be accomplished in the modern age, the ultimate purpose of life is to elevate from the cycles of life and death. The ultimate goal of the spirit is to emancipate totally. The ultimate destination of the spirit is the spiritual world, whether you like it or not. This is a journey - journey of life. Life oh life! Let it be what it may be, let it be. Let it be, come what may. Face it, accept it, grit it, but grin and shrug it away.

THE FOUR PURPOSES OF LIFE ACCORDING TO VEDAS

Nature does not condemn us to enjoy life. We must enjoy life in the every sense of its valued constituents. Reality is the very virtue of the same magnificent eternity as is the sublime essence of the eternity in its substance. The entire human life span according to Vedas is divided into four karmic themes namely, *'Kaama'* (desire, passion, sexual, drive, religiously righteous actions), *'Artha'* (work, career, money, reaping the sensuous pleasures & material fruits), *'Dharma'* (righteous wisdom/knowledge), and *'Moksha'* (Spiritual emancipation). *'Moksha'* comprises *'Tyaag'* (self-sacrifice), *'Bhaktee rass'* (loving God unconditionally), *'Atma Nirwaan Dhyaan'* (total spiritual awakening) and *'Vairagya'* (renunciation).

Each of the foregoing karmic aspect manifests in every human life in a greater or lesser magnitude. Every single conceptual theme is inter-linked to one another. Education and knowledge with wisdom leads to undertaking righteous actions, which in turn lead to a healthy enjoyment. Realising the catastrophes of the material life, one must focus finally on 'Atma Nirwaan Dhyaan' (alias liberating the soul), which in Sanskrit is also known as 'Atma jagrutti' (soul awakening). The free spirit of life, without a single doubt, finally aims towards 'Moksha' (meaning total spiritual emancipation), with wisdom.

The Vedic wisdom places emphasis on cleansing of Karma's (life deeds and actions), and replenishing sorrows and miseries of life and death. It puts one into spiritual perspective even before one is born. It considers Hinduism and Buddhism to be complementary religions as both consider the total way of life. [30]

If you want power of knowledge, status and prestige, it is precisely what you will get, provided you sow the seed of ambition with wholesome sacrifice and wholesome dedication towards the prestige.

If you want mental and physical brevity, you will get it. This is the inevitable process of evolution. Status will be earned and status will be achieved and with it fame, prestige and material power; all that and probably much more. Status and prestige bring consolation in a transient circumstantial life mode; that which seems rather conveniently suitable and conveniently comfortable to the mind as long as the mind is occupied and buzzing with the fastidious lifestyle. It all depends on what you consider to be of value.

---

[30] According to the Vedas, the final beatitude of the pilgrimage of the human soul is towards its total emancipation from the material proliferation (maya) and karmic proliferation (samnsara or repeated births). The fundamental aspects of the pilgrimage which I am talking about are dividing into four stages or five stages namely: KNOWLEDGE, ACTION, WISDOM, DEVOUTION AND MOKSHA (TOTAL LIBERATION). Karma evolves thus over five stages in life. Worship is final beatitude that transforms the inner spirit of life into total spiritual freedom. Being humans, we have a sacred responsibility to take care of all existential life. To be human is a sacred trust. The human being is divinely capable of realising that this earth is sacred. Humankind (manushyaavtar) is born in the image of God, and as such, is capable of realising the sacred most divinity with great inspiration, great aspiration and great integrity to realise the truth. It is the Brahman itself because it is the micro version the gigantic macro cosmic Brahman. God is in us.

We slip from one form of pleasure into another like clothes. We grow out of old social habits and create new social habits. We grow out of our social preferences and we keep on pursuing new and different things out of boredom and disparity.

We keep on pursuing change as a technological rotation and revolution in keeping the pace with the latest modern world of survival. We accumulate experience and keep on accumulating experiences but thrive on to survive by getting forward in our career and enjoying our ambitious ride. We keep on expanding in knowledge and experience. Our bank accounts keep on growing bigger and bigger whilst our life keeps getting shorter and shorter. We want more and more power once we get power. There is no end to it. It becomes a habitual mental process of survival and it becomes a rotation of days and nights in mere pre-occupation of the mind. The 'mind', that becomes important, significantly powerful, and prestigious. We feel good. We feel good with our successes and we want to indulge in pleasures of life like sex and good food and good wine. Of course, who would not like to! We take things for granted. We find comfort in becoming despondently dependent on people and we assume and presume our relationships in an almost selfish manner of fulfilling our own desires and means. We feel burdened with stress by making quality time for our loved ones because there are other burdens wearing us out subconsciously in worries. We keep on moving from situation into another situation, being that extravagant, and we thrive on to survive as 'successful intellectuals'.

We begin to feel somewhat empty when suddenly our life cannot justify all the grief and sorrow it brings with it in its elapsing unfolding nature. One tragedy hits us after another. This kind of adversity comes into everyone's life at some point. Some experience it earlier, others experience it later, but it does manifest at one point or another. We come face to face with SORROW. We get hurt or we get disparity. We get ailment or we get tragedy. Nevertheless, we get sorrow. Then one fine morning, we wake up and realise that our life is monogamy of habits, routines, excuses, reasons, causes, pleasures, escapes, and a burden on our own spirit of existence. We realise that our money and our prestige can no longer buy us peace, harmony and happiness, and, we feel empty because we do not feel happily fulfilled. This is virtue of the fact without denial. This moment of looking back into the past retrospectively is looking at our karmic life and trying to address it with a revolution of outlook and attitude.

Until we have revolved in our absolute life experience, we have not moulded in karmic life. Our moulding retrospectively, in regard to the learning of the past, in respect to our present condition (at the point of realising), for the perspective karmic life is a revolution of one cycle completed with time and the astral body alias the spirit of life.

Realising our karmic life is justifying our human existence and stopping the rotation of 'survival life kit'. When the buzzing noises and haste stop rotating our mind and when the ecstasy of mental power ceases to render joy from many pleasurable indulgences, it is then we begin to evolve into our karmic cycles of life. We begin to look introspectively from within the reflection of our own life in a broader sense of its values and rites. Life has a purpose – 'salvation'. Life is an idea - 'dream from another dream'. Life is a sacred journey – 'sacrifice'. Life is a grand learning experience – 'profound wisdom'. Life is a flight of delight – 'enlightenment. Life has a reason in as much as life has a cause to be alive – 'Karma'. 'Reason' and 'cause' are not mere products of matter and mind. Life is beyond survival. Life is a journey of existence. Life is a journey of karmic evolutions and involutions. Life is perpetuity over death – 'profound silence'.

Once we have elevated ourselves from the 'platform of vicious life cycles', we have broken the perpetual curves of the digit eight (8) into the next digit, nine (9). In this mode, our life becomes a process of learning and growing with the experience. Truth is a struggle but the delight it brings with it is a sheer light of joy in the deeper sense.

Vedas talk of the law of, causation, compensation, retribution, and reincarnation of karmic life. Karma is the centrifugal force of life. Karma brings life. Karma brings cause and effect. A seed sown in the ground is the cause for the tree. A tree is the effect of this cause and a tree produces fruits that become the compensation of its existence. The fruits are either bad or good depending on the tree, the ground, and its roots. Every thought, desire, action, imagination, feeling, has a deep-rooted cause, effect, and reaction either mentally or physically. The chain is a cycle of perpetuity. Vedas give a profound example of a warrior carrying a bag of arrows on his back, arching a bow and arrow with his hands. Substantial thought process and mental conflicts finally end in one concentration of release of an arrow. The release of an arrow is equivalent of releasing karmic action from built up energy and power accumulated in thought, feelings, and emotions.

Hence, the arrow that is released becomes the 'most significant' release of present or current energy. 'Now', is what matters. Today is what matters. The arrows that have not been released yet are the stored up potential future Karmas. The archer can alter the effect of these unreleased arrows but the archer cannot alter an arrow that has been released out of anger, dispassion, rage, vengeance, hatred, greed, lust, or desire. The archer has to face the consequences. If however the arrows were released one by one to target the seven great enemies of life, namely, anger, greed, lust, desire, ignorance, discrimination, and egocentricity, then, the energies of the atmosphere would dissolve all the pollution. The environment would then become universally a grand school. There would be retribution and there would be demagnetisation or diffusion. Once life becomes a learning experience and once the archer that is the 'modern man' becomes aware of the karmic laws of causation, compensation, and retribution, life evolves.

The evolution of karma progressively elevates the spirit of life onto the higher planes and finally into the liberation of pure 'sat chit ananda' (eternal truthfulness-blissfulness-consciousness). What has happened in the past has already happened. We cannot change it. Like the arrow wrongfully released out of the archer's hands. What we can however change and alter is the future by transforming our attitudes, and way of life.

Vedas are scientifically profound in my opinion because, it is true that unless we regard life a sacred journey of sacrifices, we cannot change the future causation and dispensation of the perpetual karmic cycles. Destiny and fate are drawn from our previous actions and our previous causation and effect. We cannot alter destiny of death and destiny of 'what is born must die'. What we can however change is our future fate. The present lifetime therefore is a rare opportunity to evolve.

What the Vedas emphasise is that we begin the transformation now, here, when it all matters. At least there will be hope for the future and probably a better life after life. Sacrifice implies that we learn this profound wisdom of the soul, in profound silence. Vedas are composite wisdom of the soul. An individual personality is never isolated in reality. The individual personality is a karmic seed of collective human existence and as such, carries with it constitutive relationship, inter- relationship and co-relationship with other fellow human, the celestial world and the eternal world of God. This connecting thread is woven in energy, force, and compassionate kingship.

Vedas regard this as a complement, supplement, and an exemplification of fervour, consecration and delightful. In the heart of understanding this karmic thread, a seer is made aware of compassion, by profound experience. Only experience conquers a 'true expression', and only experience creates a delight of compassion in almost passionate penances of austerity. Karmic evolution is this profound experience.

'Abhaya' (total fearlessness), is the only way to eradicate all the pains and transform them into suffering for such austere penances. To give up that which does not belong to us in the first place is our obligation, our duty.

'Mokshah-mukteeh' (freedom), 'Satt-Atman-Sauchatti' (self-same enquiry in righteous thoughts), and 'param-premmam' (eternal love), are super-consciousness, consciousness, and sub-consciousness attributes of the cosmic human being.

The sun brings nourishment of heat and warmth to the earthly clay and universe leaving the perennial pastures to rest to the divine song of the compassionate sea, the music of the rain fall and the hymns of the birds and rustling trees standing bare with the wind. A super-conscious intelligence almost keeps the mother earth beautiful, extra ordinarily blossoming, happy, in flowers, and green pastures. The rivers continue onwards to the sea despite the stumbling blockages of rocks, wheel of the mill, and dark bark.

The three worlds namely the celestial, the terrestrial, and the spiritual world are directly correlated to 'freedom', 'thought' and 'love' respectively. The terrestrial world inter connects with the other two mystical worlds of existence (namely the celestial and the spiritual) unknown as they may be, in profoundest thoughts, existence, and love enduringly.

A blissful state of trance is a harmony of the three worlds, namely the celestial, the terrestrial, and the spiritual worlds. Such beautiful harmony in togetherness is an occurrence of chance. As the river continues it's onwards journey into the grand ocean despite being broken by logs and mills, so does a spirit of life eventually dissolve, 'all this, that and the other', in due course of time.

Hear me oh precious child of nature, hear me for I am a relative. No more, no less.

The spirit of life weeps in silence watching the grand nightingale of beautiful stars. It makes a wish upon a star. There is the melody of nightingale - the music of the night, the lyrics of the song of the spirit of life, and the beauty of the dancing river on the one side of the dreams.

There is the chaos of the noise, haste and waste of 'all this, that and the other' family upheavals distracting on the other side of the mind in recurring nightmares.

Karma bound to our family and attachments, we constantly strive to become detached from all this, that and the other.

The irony of death and dissolution is that, 'Death' is a lonely visitor. It comes uninvited. It visits every life breath. Thousand sorrows of hurt seem trivial compared to the grief of death because life is blown away and time no more is alive in consciousness (in thought) in sub-consciousness (in love). Karma no longer is alive. Life and death meet in congruence of destiny.

Every life is a drowning child of destiny as much as every death is a divine manifestation of the grand profound love of the grand profound unseen tranquil world of spirits.

When we encounter a tragic death in the family, it brings with it an eternal echo of longing to belong to the compassionate world of eternity without a doubt. It brings the 'mystical' compassion together in congress with the kicking chaos of the survival. It renders an immigration from the platform of 'all this, that and the other' to the New World of spiritual evolution. It brings to us an eternal insight. We find insight in aloneness. Aloneness is different to loneliness. Let us understand the significance of sitting quietly alone in profoundness to listen to spiritual insight, to learn the truth of mortal human life.

The spirit of life having travelled thousands of rough roads finally arrives at the plateau of soft pebbles on the beautiful lining of the shores.

Absolute beautiful freedom is only a typological theatrical moment of time at the dawn and the dusk. It is almost like a trance of pure bliss.

Such bliss is like the eternal celestial state. It is like a blink of the eyes. When the eyes blink, at the clasp of the eyelashes, there is the dream vision on the one side, which is a beautiful eternal heaven. When the eyes open, there is the chaos dancing wildly in reality of 'all this that and the other'. This is the dance of 'karma' when it is alive and bliss when it is in the sleeping mode.

Becoming aware implies that we leave behind 'all this, that and the other and transport our inner spirit of life intrinsically 'onwards' towards our true-life purpose. It does not really matter, all said and done, now the time is past and gone forever.

Profoundest awareness leads us gently, kindly, and compassionately towards a platform of reverence to our true self. Our awareness opens our insight to the truth that leaves behind 'all this, that and the other'. Profound awareness makes us see things differently, somehow and brings to us an opportunity to awaken with the experience it renders. Becoming aware, we congress in 'togetherness' at the dawn and the dusk to bring together the three worlds (namely the celestial, the terrestrial, and the spiritual (ether)), in prayer invocations, in sacrificial light (candles), mantra-manjaree (invocations of peace mantra), sacred hymns and eternal peace oblation.

Between the human world and the spiritual world, a constant unseen communication creates an innate yearning to love profoundly as if the earth and the spirit of life were one. This constant unseen communication is the measure of our consciousness. Becoming aware we realise that under the diseased roots the tree collapses gradually without anyone realising it because of the blinded ego being the bark and the arrogance of the mind being the branch of the tree. When a tree collapses the bark and the branch, show the condition and the symptom. However, under the dark soil rots the diseased roots of the tree. In Vedic Wisdom, unless we treat the spirit of life in satt-karma (righteous acts) and dharma (righteous conduct) the roots of our life will continue to rot.

Compassion is not manufactured in the mind. Compassion simply occurs and it emanates from events. Growing and learning in time, we experience life. Evolving and moulding the spirit of life, we learn significant lessons about ourselves and about others and sooner we realise that another person, whom we may call a visitor only, brings us the opportunity to become compassionate. Learning is becoming aware.

Awareness implies that the negative karma (that which is the resulting action of the collective grand ego) is dissolved in deep profound compassion towards the self with profound respect for the self. Becoming aware and alive means that despite 'all this, that and the other', the true-life purpose of the spirit of life transpires in self-discovery process of living life. Life is a never-ending process of learning.

Transmigration of life takes place in ones mind. Every moment is a new moment. Every moment is a learning experience in karma (act), chitt (thought), 'pramana-prayoga' (observation), 'gjana' (wisdom), and 'pragatti' (evolution).

Old moment dies, new moment is born. This is the wheel of 'samnsara' (the illusion of human life in 'maya' (attachments) and 'moha' (desires). 'Chit tam eva hi samsaram-mayam' (the thought is itself the illusion). Every moment, our life is a new life and an old death. We die in a past that is gone. We come into the world from a past journey in time, into the present journey in time. Our present life here on this earth is a perpetual karmic transmigration into the future time. The karma dissolves in eight-fold process of learning. From the gross metamorphosis of the melodious earth to the infinite 'shunya', light travels to become twilight and eventually pure 'delight' whereat the sun never sets. When life fades away, the Great Spirit shall carry onwards to the unknown mystical world of spirits to accomplish its journey. It may come back to the earthen clay without shame if it is so ordained by karma.

Pain without austere penance is pure gross physical and mental pain. Such a pain is congenial disease and there is no end to it. However, when pain is no longer a torture but an obligatory suffering for demagnetising negative Karmas, we evolve in light towards twilight of de-light. Life is a process of learning of the soul infinite supreme. Happiness transpires in quintessence.

The spirit of life longs to belong to divinity. In divine experiences, it longs to become an immortal light. It longs for 'maitri' (togetherness or friendship), 'karuna' (compassion for helpless), 'mudita' (joy of wishing good to all), and 'upeksha' (forgiveness of overlooking the faults of others). Vision is all we need to learn. This vision is the spiritual vision. It is the right view towards the 'samnsara' (wheel of life).

In the introduction, it is mentioned that Saram (insight) never follows noise. Saram (insight) only travels in profound silence of profound solitude. To understand 'sorrow' as a collective phenomenon, and to realise the infinite truth of the soul, the personality must begin to learn in silence. The personality must become a creative artist and a technical scientist. The Vedic seer listens, watches, senses, perceives, attends, observes, searches, enquires, understands, and meditates in profound silence.

From the Vedas, there is a beautiful most enchanting analogy:

Do not look back. Do not try to bring back the lost time. Look 'now' as the only moment available to change the future. Here is the right moment to learn everything. Learn all you can from the mistakes of the past. It is only human to err. Accept the shortfalls. When we look back to dwell in the past, we loose all our hard efforts. It is in the 'now' that life breathes and loves.

What we think that we become. What we speak that we are obliged to do. Only in right words which are good and beautiful and true, there is light of truth. Therefore, our speech is very important. Once we have spoken our words, we become slaves of our spoken words. We have to realise and learn through experience of human life, that 'satt-kriya' (right deeds), 'satt-karma' (righteousness), 'satt-dharma' (right conduct), and 'satt-jivan' (right life support- livelihood) helps us not to hurt others. Sorrows emanate from the buried hurt. The Vedas say that we have to learn the paradox of letting go of the dreary mundane life of all, this, that and the other and move onwards towards the freedom of the spirit of life in watchfulness, awareness.

All said and done, don't look back. Be gentle with yourself. Go placidly and be alone if necessary. Make peace with yourself and bring sunshine into the lives of others less fortunate than yourself. This is the greatest sat-karma. When you are afraid no longer in the empty moments of aloneness, you have found your way home into the beautiful world of stars and magnificent galaxies spinning around in the nightingale with its glitter. Follow your dreams, your own dreams. Follow your path, your own path. Let no one touch the integrity of your spirit. Nurture your spirit for it belongs to you. Close your eyes and open your spiritual vision and you will never cease to be happy in all that is beautiful.

Life oh life! Let it be a flight of delight. Let it be a process of awakening the spiritual consciousness that is the pathless beauty of the delight of many lights. Oh this life, let me be still and ready for I want to make things right, to listen to the intricate sounds of this earth and to mend the sacred hoop of all nations. There is nothing to gain by being afraid in a world of chaos, conflicts, and dismal hurt. We must believe that things can mend, things can become better, and hope can be given to the future generation children. We must learn that love for possessions is unreal love and a grand weakness of human life. The ancient Vedic seers used to believe that no matter how much possessions and how much wealth one has, eventually one dies empty handed and eventually we are led to witness that we are born to give. Our human life purpose is to learn, to love, and to give life hope. Life oh life! Let the ancient wisdom of the Vedas bring light to the indigenous spirit of humankind to mend and to heal many of life's puzzles and conflicts. Life oh life! Let it be a process of learning.

Dance if you must dance. Sing if you must sing. Cry if you must cry. Laugh if you must laugh. Play if you must play. Rhyme if you must rhyme. Just do not stop loving for even one moment in your life. Just do not stop the music of the spirit of your life. Just do not stop longing to belong to the eternal world of beautiful light, despite all said, and done in 'all this, that and the other'. A true Vedic seer learns in great patience and never ceases to learn. Be patient. Be calm. Be peaceful. Watch, observe, listen, learn, let go of the past, and live to learn and love endlessly.

Life oh life! Let the rivers run fresh and free from the blocked logs and trees, through the woodland spring, and bring a new meaning to the inner perception as I stand still and steady amidst all the noise, haste, and waste. Life oh life! Let it be a beautiful experience of freedom, joy, and happiness. Life oh life! Let it be a pilgrimage from the mundane earthly city to the distant mountains whereat no one dare disturbs and whereat there are no enclosures of all this, that and the other. Life ah life! Let it be breathe of freshness, let it be a quintessence of profound wisdom, let it be a light of delight. Let it be a flight of delight. Life oh life! Let it be a flight of delight. Let it be a process of learning.

7. LIFE IS A PROCESS OF LEARNING

I made a wish to the falling star that I may never cease to learn.

Oh divine mother of profound wisdom, I faint in disparity of the uncertainty prevailing around me. Shower your mercy on my arrogance and deliver me from my pride. Grant me hope, and kindly awaken me in silence. Grant me delight of learning the true existence of the spirit of my life and bring light to my heart. Oh divine Agnee, enlighten me with your profound effulgence, and bring me delight with your glamorous radiance. Grant me solace and grant me divine harmony so that I may be able to listen to your magnificent nature that capers to the rhythm of compassionate love, sounds of enchanting music, and poetry of altruism. Oh divine mother of profound wisdom; grant me patience, fortitude, and great strength so that I may never cease to learn.

Life is a process of learning. Each day is a new experience. Life is difficult and full of struggles. Only death brings cessation to toil, drudgery, and sufferings of the mind and matter - personality. Every problem presents us with an opportunity and a challenge to change and to evolve. Life is constantly evolving. If we do not perpetuate 'change', than we cease to evolve in matter (physical personality) and in substance (spiritually).

Until we die, we thrive on, we struggle, we survive, we suffer, and we continuously change and evolve in our physical form. In the process of physical evolution, our spirit moulds. When the spirit has moulded progressively and found absolute compassion in the personality, it begins to reflect authentic power. We, sow the seeds, bear the fruits, pledge in pleasure, reciprocate the consequences, and, we reflect and refract our life relatively, perceptively and retrospectively. Everything must change. Change is the nature of all things. Just as the rivers never move backwards, the humans are born to liberate and to be free onwards from the bounds of the earthly clay towards the ocean of liberty and infinity. Every step is a lesson. Every experience is a divine lesson of learning the karmic life in discovering and realising the self – that which verily is the atman – soul divine.

We cause and reason. We create and recreate. We act and react. We do and undo. We effect and affect. We sow and reap. We are linked at every level of our lives, in time, space, and perpetual cycles of change. For instance, in relative terms, 'yesterday' (past) is linked to 'today' (present), and 'today' (present) is linked to 'tomorrow' (future). Like, perceptively, this world is linked to the galaxy of planets, stars, protons, and electrons. Like, you and I are linked to one another and to other persons and other living entities. Retrospectively, we are somehow linked to the departed spirits (ancestors).

Collectively, therefore, our life is inter-linked with Karma (collective, continuous, perpetual act or action). Every single act (mental, physical or verbal) in our life is an act of Karma. Every action is a deed (meaning moral act). We are constantly evolving in the conscious-dream-sleep-awake cycle in perpetuity.

Our life is an aggregate reflection of our spirit, the journey of which is beyond the spectrum of time and space. We cannot even encapsulate in wholesome, the true magnitude of the eternal metamorphosis of the unknown extra ordinary manifestation of the soul. The human life process is a wholesome experience. The human experience is a learning curve stretched between life and death in perpetual cycles of change. Nothing remains forever, except the human experience as a memory or a lyric or a picture or a song or a dance or a retrospective reflection of the human spirit. We all become history as composite matter, but our substance 'the absolute life' goes on as the world unfolds itself with time. There is no end to perpetual human experience. The composite human experience purges in pleasures and reflects in sorrows. Is there an end to decomposition of matter? Is there an end to sorrow? As long as there is breath of life in 'life' there is suffering and pain, inevitably.

Life is but an aggregate experience brought to our conscious by time and karma (our actions and deeds or tasks alias what we do, what we say, what we think, how we do, how we say, how we think, etc.). Higher knowledge is a faculty of life experience comprising moments of divinity and profoundness. The human experience goes beyond the five sensory functions and beyond the composition of our brains and brawn. It encompasses infinite, absolute experience of absolute life itself – 'the human life processes'. Perhaps we need to extend our processes of learning to the whole of the natural existence.

Life is full of sufferings, adversities, turmoil and sorrows. Can we ever conquer "sorrow" in just one snap shot 'bang!'? Can we end our miseries and loneliness in just one big bang? Can we buy happiness with the power of matter? Can we possibly buy a selfless mother's unconditional love with money? Is decomposition an end or a means? Can we possibly presume the unknown and can we in our presumption assume how another fellow human person feels in his or her spirit? Can we fully understand and comprehend the one word "sorrow"?

Perhaps we need emotional I.Q. to end sorrow (material warfare!). Perhaps we need to configure the fuller aptitude of the word "sorrow". The human intelligence has not been able to create a cure to end 'sorrows'. Therefore, this one word "sorrow" must be beyond the human intelligence. It must be beyond the comprehension of the five sensory functions of the human matter. It must be beyond task. It must be beyond the physical brevity of mind and matter. It must be beyond the institutional powers. 'Sorrow' does not end, by intelligence, or by conclusions, or by presumptions, or by assumptions, or by speculations or by reactions, or by powerful researches!

Sorrow is grief. Sorrow is physical pain. Sorrow is anxiety. Sorrow is anguish. Sorrow is worry. Sorrow is apprehension. Sorrow is exhilaration of sensory functions. Sorrow is ageing. Sorrow is emotional hurt. Sorrow is guilt. Sorrow is desperate loneliness. Sorrow is fear. Sorrow is anger. Sorrow is self-pity. Sorrow is power warfare. Sorrow is exhilaration of the senses at the expense of others. Sorrow is all that and much more.

The ending of sorrow nay the dissolution of sorrow is indeed the result of collective compassion that only transpires through love. Love is the healing comfort to every emotional wound. Learning therefore commences with compassion and affectionate unconditional love. Learning the grand lessons of karma, one walks in beauty, across the great mysterious silence in peace. Such unparalleled compassion can only manifest when we surrender our ego and self-pride to the institutional intelligence alias the collective intelligence, in the profound hope of becoming sublimely quiet. We need to begin with the right attitude and the right perspective to listen to our inner most voice, retrospectively (addressing the entire aggregate life process). We need to learn about all things which support the sacred web of human life that which is the unparalleled beauty of the nature that divinely almost sacredly takes care of us.

To begin the process of learning, we must ignite the divine flame of self-awareness, with great love and compassion; to observe and to watch the extra ordinary manifestation of the soul, in quietness, and alone. Then, and only then we will begin to understand the soul – the very seat of God. We shape our destiny by our Karma (collective continuous act). To understand the progressive process of life, we must therefore surrender ourselves unconditionally to the author who is seated in our soul as the charioteer of our life. I call it the inner voice or the spirit of life. Life is thus a school of collective experience in the most absolute sense.

Humankind cannot weave the entire web of human life. We do not have the authentic power to create the web of life albeit we claim to do so. We are just various threads within the whole spectrum of human web. We reflect or refract our thoughts and actions on to others through this spectrum and thus connect to one another. Accordingly, whatever we do to the web, we ultimately do onto ourselves. All threads connect somehow, prospectively, respectively, retrospectively, infinitely, absolutely, and relatively. The spectrum of human configuration is complex and paradoxical. It is beyond the perception of five senses. No one could possibly become a true master of the human spectrum, no one. The web is imperfect as much as the thread itself. What is true however is the realisation of the imperfection of all that is transiently unfolding with time. Our intellect, our body and our mindfulness that has emanated from life experience, dwells in perpetual cycles. When we realise and mould, our mindfulness changes and the change is but a learning growth based on experience and self-discovery. This is Vedic learning - the learning of existence, in beautiful divine experiences. Therefore, collectively, our aggregate life experiences tantamount to a perpetual learning process of the soul that has no proven beginning or a proven end.

Absolute freedom really implies profound happiness and profound joy in the most profound sense of the absolute life. This is a blissful transcendental state. It is the spirit of absolute life. Let us nurture this truly divine bliss. Let us try our best in embracing the little child in us with love and compassion. Let us take one step at a time, one day at a time, but let us begin to learn to listen.

Talking and competing intellectually will not accomplish anything absolutely. We have carried on the vicious cycle of 'excuses' and 'reasons' to make us feel important.

We decompose the profound human relationships with ludicrous warfare of greed, selfishness, and aggression. You are trying to prove your point of view; some one else is trying to prove his or her point of view. I am trying to prove my point of view. Is this really learning?

Atheism, agnosticism, fanaticism, pragmatism, or any "ism" founded by the social criteria of man made progeny; to me is absurd and hypothetical. All foregoing categories, claim, suppose, assume, presume, hope, and believe in abstract of life rather than the absolute life process. Therefore, until the spirit has awakened absolutely and begun to listen quietly in profound silence, it has not conquered the soul – the real seat of God. Thesis or anti-thesis renders endless arguments, discussions, debates contradictions, and confusion. One cannot possibly count the exact number of stars in the night sky, can you?

Learning does not stop with knowledge. Knowledge acquired at school, institutions, and books is not absolute wisdom. It is an accumulation of technology, certified skill, and means, to execute a professional task in return for a reward or price. Knowledge is stored as memory and knowledge is applied several times in a similar manner with same standards and inferences to the past. This is institutional learning. The mind learns and accumulates in various ways to meet the challenges of life in practical and academic causes. Knowledge has been established with the passage of time by criteria and facts. It has been laid by the governing bodies and institutions as a projection of many skills put together in technical terms. It is a communication of words and figures conceptually and retrospectively to derive at a means of accomplishing the task at hand, whatever it may be.

Spiritual learning however, entails greater magnitude of learning than knowledge. It entails self-discovery of perception and the vision with which perception is further enhanced by learning about the collective life process. This kind of learning requires us to listen without buzzing ideas and noises of words. It requires absolute listening for the absolute truth with an absolute attitude.

This universe is not separate from us. We are connected to it somehow and our problems are connected too. Therefore, if one is in grieve trouble, so is the world projected by one's spirit. The world at large is a collective reflection of our own spirit.

The state of this universe must say something profound to us and we have to listen profoundly in order to learn about it. In order to perceive the life process of the soul, we must stop contradicting and antagonising conceptually. We must become intensely immersed in seeking out the spirit within us. We must unconditionally listen to the grand soul quietly. We must learn to recognise that every grain of sand is divinely sacred.

Learning entails love and compassion to understand humanely. This is true religion; the way we live with others; how we live our lives; the way in which we live our lives; the way in which we perceive others. Our attitude and outlook towards life form our perceptions. This is real learning. This is spiritual wisdom and this is the only religion that is truly religious for the soul. It is the learning of the spirit and its place in life.

The issue is not whether to believe or not to believe in Religion. The issue is not to become a hero or a follower of "ism" religion. The issue really is a total transformation of your sprit. Transformation is the beginning of learning the wisdom of the soul, understanding its place and ceasing to run a marathon of 'rat race' of pleasing the ego. Transformation is breaking free from the ill habits of the mind. This process is referred to as the process of self-development, which is profoundly beyond the euphoria of psychological, material, and physical developments. Transformation of your spirit can take place only when you have stopped conditioning your mind with buzzing noises and ideas emanating from the electricity of modern technology and power.

'Religious faith' therefore does not render solution or an end to the issue at large. It is merely a means for the 'true belief' to manifest in spiritual perception. True religion must merge us to our roots, not separate us from our roots. Like the rivers flowing in all directions, finally merge in oceans and lakes. Faith can bring hope and transformation in our lives only when we nurture the human relationships; like beginning with the immediate family and those who matter most. It requires work and effort but at least it is the real religion. When we fail towards our immediate families, we have to try again and again but to never give up the hope of compassionate togetherness. When the mind ceases to be manipulated by greed, envy, ambition, lust, anger, status, social powers, indulgence, pleasure, reason, illusion, ideas, contradictions and antagonism, the spirit finds silence, quietness, and alone-ness. It is in this quietness, that the personality begins to listen and learn in abundance. One will realise the same issue differently.

Have you ever tried just sitting quietly without any buzzing noises of words and thoughts, in front of a beautiful stream of river or seashore? It is a wonderful experience. The moving water has this energy in it that is serene and extra ordinary. When you get the feeling of great energy and goodness, anonymously serene, you begin to create a New World of "empty space". In this state, there is no more fear and anxiety. Most of my inspiration emanate from flowing rivers, dancing tides of the sea, beautiful mountains, night skies, rustling trees, singing birds, and the rhythmic sound of music. In the most adverse circumstances, one seeks solace from the compassion and love manifested by the magnificent nature. Nature has an extra ordinary beauty that is always connected to our spirit of life. Learn to listen to simple but most profound music. Learn to listen to our own nature, our own soul. Our earth is very much a grand womb of our own divine mother.

Life creates experiences through our personalities or identities. Whilst creating multitude of experiences, we evolve either externally by intellectual knowledge, status, position and material wealth or we evolve spiritually internally by authentic power comprising compassion, love, wisdom, and harmony. Life is a perpetual process of evolution. Nothing ever remains the same forever. Everything in life perishes with the withering unfolding universe as it should. Life unfolds with eternal time, diminishing in form. The intuitive talent entails one to change the manner in which one listens. For example, stopping to condition one's mind with million and one thoughts, ideas, and noises, and, starting to empty one's mind of all the worries and noises and ideas. Stopping all the wrong habits and starting to re-build and renew from scratch if one has to but to begin to learn intuitively. The sense of hearing is the last sense a dying man looses. It is the very first sense that begins to perform life's rhythm in a new-born baby. Stop, listen carefully, and find time for peaceful solitude. Look towards the sunrise and keep consistent early morning watch of the beautiful- wonderful-magnificent- awakening nature. Learn to listen to the music of the blossoming nature. Learn to listen to your soul. Nurture your spirit. Let no man touch its integrity. It belongs to you and only you have the right to its life. Everything withers away in due course of time. Nothing remains forever. Pleasure does not last forever. Money does not buy us happiness. Money does not buy a selfless unconditional mother's pure love. High society never stands by us in times of difficulties. No one aspect of our material life is a permanent feature.

Our biggest problem by far is that we presume permanence in the comfort of power, pleasure, sex, alcohol, food, things, and environment. We cling to our habits. The human life has always been insecure. We compete and compare without gravity of substance. If only we could stop living a life full of noise, haste, power warfare, material waste, decomposition, and stress. If only we could become profoundly and sublimely, quiet.

Universal love manifests in your heart. Conquer it, enrich it with compassion, and give it to others less fortunate than yourself, and it shall come back to you in great strength. Let us learn how to love compassionately and affectionately. Let us give substantial compassion not pity to others. A long-suffering soul has learnt compassion, an erratic pain only shouts and screams. The sound of music is almost inter-linked with the Spirit through what is considered the sixth sense or the intuition as one may refer. Spirit is almost like a pivot providing the momentum of energy and force in our life and body. We need to keep a balance on this pivot (the spirit) at all times and we need to be meticulously scrupulous about the sensitivity of the pivot (spirit).

When the rhythm in our lives is somehow lost, we loose our momentum and balance in life. It almost resembles a worn out violin, with its strings ready to break. We need to find time to be alone and to listen quietly to our spirit. We need to restore back that momentum with wisdom, love, compassion, and integrity. In the process of restoring back the momentum in our lives, we grow and mould into better individuals. We become aware of how others feel and how the surrounding environment feels. We come out of our habitual nutshell. We begin to understand and we learn substantially the sublime manifestations of the soul. We learn from the gross tamasic to sublime sattvic levels.

When there is no more spirit in the soul, the soul no longer sustains a physical form; hence, there is no sound at all. The multi-sensory functions cease. The soul however continues its journey into para-existing planes and whether one likes it to be re-incarnation or not, it perpetuates within the nucleus of time, space and eternity. It may be a myth that every star represents a dead spirit. It may be a myth to perceive heaven and hell based on Holy Scriptures. It may be idealistic to conclude that a soul is reborn. It may be too eastern to perceive re-incarnation. Whatever it may be, it is certain that the soul does not stop with the dead matter. The soul does not decompose with the dead body. It is not important nor is it relevant to our living spirit, the after life process.

What is important to our living spirit is the life process. So why can we not just be what we are and make what is possible of our lives today, now and at this moment. If we knew what is going to happen tomorrow then we would become deities and Demi-Gods. It is not possible for us to determine what will happen tomorrow exactly but it is possible for us to prepare ourselves for tomorrow. It is like sitting for an examination. We can only anticipate and we must anticipate to the best of our ability. We must be able to discover ourselves, to learn about ourselves and to learn about our human nature. We must be able to understand the 'collective human soul'. [31]

Therefore, the art of listening stretches beyond the capabilities of hearing. It requires us to become profoundly silent and quiet, to welcome and to follow the rhythm of the sounds that caper deep within our spiritual entity – the soul. Knowing and understanding compassionately are different. Knowing stops with the mental consciousness whereas understanding compassionately draws from within us an insight to super-consciousness.

We have a choice to make; either to get closer to the real spiritual substance within us or to hold on to the withering material earth. When we take the fullest responsibility of our own actions and our own lives, we cease to blame others for our shortcomings. We begin to seek the truth. We begin to evolve spiritually and we begin live a human life. The passage of spiritual awakening is the journey of the soul. This passage is a process of learning. Our life is a circle; our karmic intent is an energy thrown in to life circle.

I cannot sit here and pretend that I am not part of reality. No. 'Reality' is where we must begin if anything. The process of listening and speaking is one to one communications merging in congruence with the profoundness of the word. It renders guidance and it renders solace. When we begin to live for others, we have actually begun to live for the spirit of our life. We begin to learn to listen profoundly and we begin to learn the true nature of this universal life force. We begin to transform from being intellectual structures to humanly simple and compassionate spirit of life.

---

[31] Silence is the absolute poise or balance of body, mind, and spirit. The human person, who preserves his self-hood self-respect, is ever calm and unshaken by the storms of existence. Soul divine, who has learnt to listen in silence, finds silence mysteriously beautiful and wholesome. Silence unperturbed comprises quiet moments of stillness, in quintessence. R.v.

LEARNING AND REALISING THE HOLISTIC TRUTH

As we journey into the first ten years of the new era, saturation will prevail in world economies; world catastrophes and disasters would have increased rapidly. It brings to our minds one very significant message, which is a common echo of all crying spirits of life. "Our society is as uncertain as our environment". There is 'fear' in all of us. Our minds have turned into 'robot like logic centres' that function on 'thoughts' and 'memories'. We as human kind envisage 'tomorrow' based on our 'present' state of mind that is nothing more than a mere product of many chaotic years of human conflict put together in divisions, segregation and discrimination. If really the chaotic world today is the result of the 'human mind' of the collective 'yesterdays', then surely there is something wrong somewhere in the mind itself.

The mind as a powerful intellectual mind can no longer resolve the problems of the world in chaos. Nor can this intellectual mind resolve the problems of our inner conflict comprising, uncertainty, confusion, violence, rage, hatred, warfare, pain, sorrow, loneliness, anxiety, insecurity, phobia, aggression, ignorance, stubbornness, sensuality, sexuality, diet, fitness, daily habits, all that and more.

What is really amazing is the magnitude of proclamations by numerous doctrines about God and Religion based on subjective divisions of 'thoughts' on the one hand and the 'external power' that prevails in the bureaucracies of 'institutional minds' on the other hand. Most religious doctrines in the modern society are a propaganda that has been put together by the powerful human mind. The modern world is full of commercialism and heroism. What the collective mind sees from its complex metamorphosis of thoughts deem appropriate and adequate for the time being because it is the only manner in which it can form conclusions and assumptions and presumptions intellectually. If the modern developed world is not in peace and harmony then surely there is something the human mind has not accomplished collectively from the past karma – It is a gap between the ego and the spirit of life. I understand with deep profound insight that to look at the core issue, we need to become impartial, dispassionate, impersonal, indifferent, and unconditional in our mental aptitude. We need to realise the holistic truth in togetherness, in wholesome, with a sacred insight that is not conditional.

As long as we discuss and hold conversations with an intellectual I.Q. and try to reason and cause intellectually with the power of the mind, we are going to look in different directions. We never ever look at anything in simplicity for the naked fact of the naked matter itself, but we look at an issue with an already complex mind full of problems and conditions. If the mind is filled with problems and aggression, can we really meditate on systems and platforms and follow these pathways into discovering the holistic truth? However, if you and I, we hold our eyes together unconditionally in profound silence, without any inhibitions of anthological words or varying religious umbrellas, there is 'hope' that perhaps we will understand the holistic truth together as two spirits of life. Learning is experiencing profoundly with reverence to the soul. I was born to learn!

Otherwise, you will claim that you are right and the other person will claim that he or she is right and I will make a false claim based on my intellectual words. No, I do not want to claim anything please. There is no such thing as perfection in anything that is life. What seems relevant to my deep insight is not the journeys start and the journeys close, but the life process. Let us 'in togetherness' try to understand with profound insight, the millennium world. The world that has been long suffering, wars, disparity, mass poverty, mass ignorance, mass confusion, mass chaos, mass disasters, mass loneliness, mass uncertainty, mass complexities, fears, and threats! Let us understand compassionately, profoundly and silently.

The issue of the human earth is 'human misery'. The holistic truth is that all that has been created, recreated, revived, and restored by the human mind is an intellectual camouflage of reason based on thought and perplexities. We understand 'in togetherness' that 'human mind' has brought about 'fear' and out of 'fear' invented a word called 'evil'. Therefore, from the childhood, the mind is conditioned; to see things and believe things because certain things are wrong and certain things are right and rebelling is a sin. Hence, the society churns more and more violence, crimes, political revolutions, religious destruction, sects, cults, and schools of thoughts, all that and more. The core words like 'evil' and 'sin' and 'right' and 'wrong' are not uniformly same for every individual, because these conceptual words are created, recreated and revived by the human mind in spoken word or written word. Out of fear, we have created, recreated, re-constructed, re-invented, and revived religious sacredness with mindfulness of intellectual warfare!

To end human misery is to end sorrow and to end this wretched warfare of intellectual metamorphosis. Let us understand 'in togetherness' that total sacred transformation is essential and crucial to overcome this huge camouflage of human uncertainty. This transformation is not just a consensus addendum of making diplomatic treaties or signing peace treaties between nations and between persons. It is a transformation of "us" in total love and total compassion, with total devotion and total sacredness towards absolute wholesome existence of humanity.

Total sacred transformation entails that we (you and I and another one) in togetherness realise that unless we discover the naked truth by learning the life process in profound silence with profound insight, we will never understand the word "sorrow" in wholesome.

In the ancient times, when people used to worship the Sun, the Wind, the mountain gods, the Rivers, the fire, the sounds, the Oceans, they did not use the Bible or the Quran or the Geeta or the Gurus or the institutions! They simply invoked the fiery energies of the beautiful Mother Nature and loved the beautiful Mother Nature simply without any complexities or jargons. Then the world was more peaceful a place. Does this not prove that the intellectually oriented powerful human mind has not been successful in preserving the pure unconditional love! Today the word 'love' has been degraded by all sorts of physical and mental manipulations. Where is the selfless unconditional love that manifests in every one of us hidden today? Where is that consideration of pure loving sacrifice to bring solace and humanitarian compassion to others rather than for the self? 'Love' is loosely used in all sorts of circumstances. The modern intellectual powerful mind has configured love with thoughts; every single aspect of it. Grief has also become a psychological process of consciously following the psychiatrist (who is in conflict) and doctors (who are in conflict). Therefore, the result must be conflict, i.e., grief has not ended sacredly holistically, but become dark affluent memories. Knowledge and mental thought process has never been able to diffuse "sorrow", albeit doctors, astrologers, congressional leaders and gurus strive to mentally tame 'sorrow' by mental thought systems, patterns and structures. Thriving in 'conflict' is not an end but a means of surviving. Learning this essential truth is learning to love the entire wholesome existence, as beautiful, sublime and sacred. It is an indication of transmigration.

Each one of the mentally powerful persons on this earth is struggling alone to survive and fulfil his or her own personal success, career, achievement, desires, and creating havoc! Every single mentally powerful person operates almost in a 'closet' style life – 'You mind your own business; I mind my own business. Let us get on with life'.

Where and how is deep compassionate understanding of the core problem manifested in thought analysis and mental evaluation please?

We understand in togetherness, that our living, in which we claim to be survivors of the fittest, is a mess. The world is in a mess. The society is in a mess. Our minds are hiding under the façade of intellectual mind power.

The human mind is an essential tool to make definitive profound choice for the inner most cry of the spirit of life, not a mere neurological centre. We have created undue conflict between one God prevailing in one mind and another God prevailing in another mind. We must transform together otherwise there will never be hope for peace. Your mental consciousness is made up of set of ideas, beliefs, values, ethos, traditions, concepts, attitudes, memories, thoughts and more. Your thinking pattern conforms to a certain mode and the other persons thinking pattern conforms to yet another certain mode. As long as there is a pattern, there is bound to be division and conflict. As long as there is more than one proclaimed naked truth, there will never be universal peace on this earth. Academic religion and academic gospels of churches will never render the truth.

Truth can never be more than one. Truth is only one. It is a holistic truth. This truth discards every single mental faculty of the mind and reposes on profound insight. When the mind is discarded and overcome by profound insight and profound wisdom of the soul, we begin to transform our outlook to life such that we realise beauty in nature and we realise that truth is universally the same whether one is a Christian, or a Muslim, or a Hindu, or a Buddhist. This truth is holistic truth in the most sacred sense. This truth is not realised by following systems of meditations or systems of anthologies or systems of bureaucracies, but it is realised in profound silence of profound activity of the profound super-consciousness, a faculty of the spirit which listens to learn with profound insight.

Holistic truth does not depend on intellectual camouflage of the systems. Holistic truth is the sacred most truth that manifests in self-discovery process of profoundness. Wholesome transformation means total sacred transformation of the personality such that there will be no more mind and ego; such that there will be no more reason and cause; such that our understanding is unconditionally selfless towards one problem, one issue - 'sorrow'. When we divinely understand sorrow with integrity, we will realise that there is a destiny of time, which we cannot alter, but learn to move to it.

Learning and understanding in profound silence with profound wisdom of the soul requires total sacred transformation. One learns from letting go of the past, letting go of the mind, letting go of the ego, letting go of various man made religious doctrines, letting go of various intellectual camouflages.

The mind must want to think beauty because the inner cry of the spirit of life is truly in love with the magnificent nature, that magnificence which is unparalleled. Infinite beauty cannot be compared. This beauty is not temptation. This magnificent nature is illuminating with purest sensations of delight. When our conscious becomes one with the magnificent beauty of the divine Mother Nature with fathomless faith, we find eternal peace. We have touched the supreme naked truth. We learn about our own true divinity.

We understand in 'togetherness' that this life breath, which we claim to be ours as a permanent feature, has an uncertain end, over which we have no control. Therefore, what is of paramount profoundness is "control". We try to control situations, people, minds, thoughts, actions, and reactions, all that and more. We just simply enjoy controlling. When our own life breath is not in our control, we emphasise and exercise control over other person's lives because we simply find emotional comfort in the power it brings to our ego. Nurturing relationships holistically is not about controlling people's emotions or feelings. It is about setting people free so that they can express their utmost talent in the sacred most manner in the fearless world of love and compassion. The personality must let go of the egocentric control and understanding in profound silence. Then the personality will transform holistically in the most profound ways. Then there is karmic evolution. The spirit of life walks in beauty and to behold in his/her vision, the sacredness of the lofty sunsets, and the beautiful ocean, and the nightingale, to learn and to hearten universal love, universal compassion and universal religion of humanity.

CONSCIOUSNESS

Whether one is a Christian, whether one is a Muslim, whether one is a Hindu, or whether one is a Buddhist, the quest is the same in as much as the content of the quest itself. Spiritual liberation or moksha cannot be accomplished in one big flight. It is a pilgrimage of progressive evolution. Only very rare souls reach the infinite bliss divine without being re-born into the karmic cycles of life and death.

All things come to and end and all ending begin with a new beginning. This is the law of existence of eternal time. Let us become the master of our intellectual minds and not the subservient slaves of the conscious thought. This mental power has created all that is physically and materially the social, economic and political world. We feel that the framework to finding answers to all our problems and sorrows manifests in that mental power. We make our brain the central management of our life process and we consider that this is where the buck stops. In our minds, in our mental power centre, fog transpires. Through this power centre, we create attitudes, differences, east and west, habits, escapism, reason and cause. We survive on this mental power. We thrive on the academics and institutions. We repose mentally on all that is 'known' fact of survival.

Whether one is a Christian, a Hindu, or a Muslim, the consciousness of the mind is uniformly composed of set of conscious, sub-conscious and unconscious values of life. Although within the 'values', the traditions, culture, superstitions, ethos, family roots, cultural ties, religious perceptions, knowledge, and survival (comprising sex, food, excretion, sleep, and habits) are different from one person to the another person. Whether one is Eastern or Western, one still has consciousness comprising "Values"; otherwise, one is not humankind. Every consciousness therefore is operating on the same principle - Surviving the fear, anxiety, and sorrows of everyday life and indulging the physical existence with pleasure, greed, aggressiveness, and demanding socials.

The essence of consciousness comprises set of values and ethos. Your consciousness does not operate differently to mine albeit the ingredients of the values and the ethos may differ to bring varied intellectual perceptions, lifestyles, and outlook to life. Consciousness or divine eternal bliss is not different for the east and the west.

Eternal joy and eternal bliss divine consciousness and total spiritual liberation is the same universally. Being born as humans to this mother earth is a sacred trust in itself.

Essentially, Vedic lyrics regard sin and guilt in a rather peculiar awareness of learning the limitations of the finiteness of evil. Evil is not permanent. Evil is a condition, that redeems, resolves, and dissolves with truth. Truth triumphs in the end, no matter what. Truth is inevitable. Truth is the light of the sun. When the light of the sun manifests in the heart, the consciousness, and the mind, a transformation transpires imminently.

Between the darkness of earth and the divine light, a grey cloud of ignorance prevails. This grey cloud is chaos, crises, confusion, pollution, evil, trauma, ailment, blur, mist, toxic, all that and more. This grey cloud of mass ignorance and false pride moves and transpires with 'ritta' (mercy) and 'dharmman' (compassion). The universal truth of 'Agnee' is ever effulgent, ever eternal, ever radiant, everlasting and eternal. Its light never ceases. Dissolution of the darkness, destruction of the evil, eradication of the loud noises, burning of the waste (unwanted evil), redemption of the fastidiousness, and the transpiration of personality, are the progenies of axiomatic deliverance to mercy.

Through mercy of Rudra (dissolver, destroyer, and giver of death) arises compassionate transformation through Varuna (the cosmic compassion). This total sacred transformation is a profound purification and detoxification for the grand awakening to the sacred cosmos, whose sacredness is in the light of Agnee in the sun.

If the universal problem is 'sorrow' then the universal consciousness must also manifest in one eternal truth. That, which is the super consciousness and that is this truth itself, embodied in the oneness of a marriage between the soul and the eternity.

To know the essential creation in the green pastures and the grains of the germinating soil, to see the eternal heaven in the blossom of a beautiful rose, and to behold the joy of delight in your open palms, imply that your perception has transpired progressively onwards onto the magnificent truth.

The transformation of delight travels through seven progressive phases namely the gross physical, the physical, the mental, the emotional, the conscious, the super conscious, and the eternal vacuum of purest delight.

Uttishtthata jagrata prapaya varrann nibodhata ksurasya dhara nishita duratyaya durgama pathas-tat kavayo vadanti.   (Keno-Upanishad 1-13-14)

Arise, awake, having reached the divine perception, become aware or enlightened. For the path (journey of life in the passage of time) is surprisingly sharp and arduous to tread. Thus, say the ancient Vedic wise.

Self-observation leads to awakening. An awakened mind has pushed its thought deliberation and consciousness to the limits of potential possibilities. Human being and God are identical in essence but different in forms. Human being is the manifest, the God is the unmanifest as the personality, and the sprit of life is. Human being is to be fulfilled God is fulfilled. Our essential nature is born for the purpose of health, longevity, happiness, selfless obligation, and universal peace.

The Vedas are sound philosophical perception of our wholesome human entity and its relationship to the wholesome cosmic universe. According to Vedas, it is only through the human incarnation that moksha (liberation) may be accomplished. The Upanishads suggest that the self (jivan-atman), not the eternal god 'param-atman', is to be realised.

Various Vedic gods like sun, Indra, vayau, varuna, soma, etc., in divine forms ('saar-guna-divya swaroop') are demythologised symbols of perception just as a word is Aum for example. When a human being attains bliss ('siddhi') through constant spiritual practice ('sadhana') in dynamic reality, he or she becomes one with the supreme God infinite ('nirguna-swaroopam'). The celestial is ever illuminated; whereat the sun never sets or rises. It is here on the human earth, that we experience the 'jyoti-samndhya' twilight of the dusk and the dawn. 'Samndhya' is the consort of the Sun god that makes the dawn and the dusk possible. Mind/ (manas) has external mind (etani) and internal mind (manahi). Perception is imperfect owing to inherent limitations of knowledge and experience. Perception always gives distorted picture of the categories of the subject, time, and cosmic space. Perception verily is based on the phenomenal world, phenomenal thought, and phenomenal idea.

To give is a great joy. To give knowledge rightfully is divine bliss. To give divine wisdom to humble soul is the greatest sobriety to enrich our own soul.

Beyond the finite existence, beyond the motions of rotation, revolution, and perpetual cycles of time, beyond the grand galaxy, and beyond the atmospheric orb, the para-existential celestial ordinance ('jagad-purusha-param-atman-param-eshvaar') is forever illuminated. Thereat, the sun never sets and the grand cosmic motion comes to 'bindu-shunya' (stillness of absolute vacuum). This 'nirguna param-atman' (formless divine eternal infinite cosmic soul) is similar to the 'nirguna atman' (formless soul). Atman (soul) like the param-atman (eternal soul) is impartial to the cycles of karma and dissolution. Atman verily is the param-atman and when we recognise this truth, we have elevated ourselves to realise our own true self. The manifestation of the 'nirguna-atman' in swaroopam (form) is the 'prakruttee' (nature). 'Prakruttee' (nature) is causal in the soul state, astral is in the ego and mind state, and physical is in the body state of pancha-mahabhuttas (five elements). 'Prithhvee' (earth), 'Jaal' (water), 'agnee' (fire), 'vayau' (air), 'akash' (space), manas (mind), 'budhee' (intellect), and ahamkar (ego) are the eight constituent parts of the 'swaroop-prakruttee' (manifested nature).

These 'ashtha-tatva' (eight aspects of material entity) together with 'jivan-atman-pranna' (karmic spirit of life) form the 'navv-niddhee-navv-tattva' (nine part human life). The Human life spirit, causes 'karma' (movement/action/act), thus, through its five senses (sound, touch, sight, taste, and smell), sense organs (hands, legs, anus, genitals, voice box, nose, ears, skin, eyes, tongue, and nose), and the navv-tattva (nine elements). Human life is an Imperfection born imperfect and that, which also dies imperfect. The human world is an illusion or 'maya' because it is impermanent, imperfect, incomplete, and more importantly because it is unhappy, mortal, and diseased. Desire causes attachment to all the known materialism and causes lust, greed, anger, aggression, control-ship, ego-power, possessiveness, mind-power, gross intellectualism, and warfare. To realise the unknown soul 'atma' and to be free from the bondage of sorrow, disease, and desires, therefore, we have to first conquer the known life in experiences of karma (human act and righteous sacrificial deed). The process of evolution is the process of learning profoundly the lessons of life. The answers lie within us. Only we need look beyond 'all, this, that and the other', to realise that it is never too late to live our dreams, our life purpose, and our bare humane existence, for the beautiful adventure of being alive. Before we get a glimpse of the truth, we inevitably touch the chore trauma of hurt. It becomes necessary for us to learn to love ourselves.

Understanding hurt entails that we look deeper with greater reverence to our true self and with greater compassionate love for our true self and that of the true self of others. Understanding hurt implies that we discover our pain gradually from the gross physical sheath onwards towards the physical sheath and beyond 'all, this, that and the other' into the mental and psychological sheaths, and beyond into the spiritual insight. Hurt requires us to be faithful to our spirit of life and to nurture the metaphysical wounds.

Rejections and discouragement have worn out the spirit of life as it sighs to the chaos and reflects in hurt. The spirit of life cries in desperation for encouragement.

The most horrendous aspect of loosing control is to loose awareness! When awareness is lost, we separate ourselves from the universal world of existence. Finding insight in profound experience eventually entails dissolution of "ego". Insight can never be found upon thesis or antithesis of 'all this, that and the other'. Insight occurs when the intrinsic longing persistently never failing pursues faithfulness – faithfulness to true self – to the soul divine.

Insight is not manufactured in circumstances, events, or life experiences. Insight simply occurs when our profound outlook to life alters and realises wholesome. Every profound experience therefore renders us an opportunity to look beyond 'all this, that and the other' into the mystical yet beautiful world of metaphorical existence.

Finding insight in profound experience makes us realise things from a different perspective. Hurt invites us to question the self-same sorrow from within intrinsically, profoundly, and with the spirit of life. When all else fails, we resort to the spirit of life, to sustain us profoundly, with respect, with integrity, with dignity and without a single doubt. The Vedic wisdom elucidates our living life as a shadow (chaayya) which runs across the pastures of karma and diminishes with the sunset; mortal end of one cycle.

The spirit of life having travelled thousands of rough roads finally arrives at the plateau of soft pebbles on the beautiful lining of the shores. Life oh life! Let it be! Let it be what it may be. Let it be come what may, accept it, face it, grit it, but grin and shrug it away. Life oh life! Let it be a moment in time, a moment to learn, and a moment to live in profound experiences of the soul divine, a moment to sit quietly, and a moment to be.

We can only free ourselves from the burdens of all this, that and the other by harnessing our spirit of life, detaching it from the falsehood of the grand ego regime. Becoming aware, we realise 'all this, that and the other' from a different perspective – from the perspective of the spiritual world. Absolute freedom cannot be possible because of the perpetual cycle of darkness and lightness. Absolute beautiful freedom is only a typological theatrical moment of time in the dawn and the dusk. It is almost like a trance of pure bliss.

Sacrificial oblation of peace and harmony offered to the world of spirits at the dawn and the dusk in various prayers, hymns, and mantras brings us awareness of the world of existence. It may not be imminent in the short term but it brings about progressive awareness.

Profoundest awareness leads us gently, kindly, and compassionately towards a platform of reverence to our true self. Our awareness opens our insight to the truth that leaves behind 'all this, that and the other'. Profound awareness makes us see things differently, somehow and brings to us an opportunity to awaken with the experience it renders. Between the human world and the spiritual world, a constant unseen communication creates an innate yearning to love profoundly, to learn profoundly, to share profoundly. Every experience in our life is a grand lesson towards one and the only one truth – All said and done our life is dying with every tick of the clock.

Human beings living in the world of human existence need to break free from the narrower concepts of liberation, education, and growth. Perhaps what is needed in the modern existence is the liberation of all things support life breath like the ether, the air, the water, the fire, and the earthly clay. Perhaps what is needed in the modern existence is the education of the soul. Perhaps what is needed in the modern existence is the growth of the soul.

The spirit of life confronts thousand thorns and thousand sorrows before it reaches a plateau of soft pebbles. The spirit of life opens to the beautiful world of spirit eventually whereat the chaos is no more and whereat the chaos seems dreary, mundane and trivial. Growing out of hurt entails discovering the true spiritual self to profoundly love, to follow one's own dreams, and to adventure life. We are born with a sacred trust in our spirit.

Love is life and life is love. Life is to live and love and let live of others for their own sakes and for their own purpose. It is better to die in great profound love than to live without it. If beauty embraces the spirit of life in great profoundness, death matters not in so much as what really matters is the beautiful moment of love. All said and done, we reflect in hurt, and we evolve in hurt. We learn to become compassionate, we learn to love. Learning to love our soul and having respect for our soul is the greatest lesson. Every human being is a child-like spirit of life capable of divine experience. To experience true divinity and true divine beauty, one must become a 'hamnssa' (spirit of life that is a swan personality) – 'Aum satt-chidd-ananda-hamnssa so hum'. 'Hamnssa' - swan personality is as delicate as a new born baby, as soft as the petals of the lotus flower, as tender as the child's heart, as sharp as a serpent, and as calm as the ocean. Divinity mantra:

"Aum Jaya Satt-Chidd-Anandam Parahabrahma Aum Purush'ottama Param'atma Aum Shree Bhagavattee Sammetha Aum Shree Bhagavateh nanamah. Aum Tat Sat Swaha-Hari Aum Tat Sat swadha swaha. Aum Hamnssa Hamnssa So Hum. Aum so hum. Aum so hum."

This is the maha-mantra of the divinity in Vedas. It takes us beyond the form 'saarguna' into the zero-formlessness ('nirguna'shunya'), and beyond the zero-shunya into the eternal divine bliss 'parabrahman'parammatman' (eternal celestial). Individual cosmic soul is the microcosmic spirit of this grand macrocosmic spirit. 'Atman-parramattam-assi' (God). Cosmic energy capers to the rhythm of cosmic karma to descend from the sublime most state to the gross state in glorious divinity. Chanting the divine mantra of divinity, a devotee never ceases to enjoy life because it has the friendship of the higher order. Life is blessed with endless divine experiences. To realise this non-dual truth, one has to become as subtle and as divine as the new born baby that does not know the ego in 'all this, that and the other', but knows only the divine warmth of the selfless love emanating from the mothers' bosom. Merging in oneness with the supreme god like a new born baby in a 'child-like' divinity voids all the dualism of 'all this, that and the other'. The Vedas and the Vedic wisdom elucidate the cosmic arithmetic, cosmic algebra, cosmic geometric, cosmic trigonometric, cosmic physics, cosmic quantum science, and metaphysics of the cosmos. Vedic mathematics and the number science of quantum metaphysics is cosmic science.

The Vedic astrology, Vedic yantras (geometrical configurations of cosmic elements), Vedic mantras (scientific words of incantations, meditation, yoga & chants), Vedic tantras (scientific remedial rites and rituals), Vedic shlokas (invocations and praises), Vedic hymns (poems), Vedic puja (ceremonial ritual), Vedic agnee-homage (sacred fire of tribute), and Vedic prayer, all inter connect consistently, relevantly and significantly. When there is a collective urge to learn the sacred web of life, the animate and the inanimate will axiomatically liberate without all this, that and the other.

The Vedas make a constant and consistent reminder of universal prayer of peace invocation – sarwa kutumbhkam shanty prarthana trisamndhya. The child-like prayer to the celestial eternity known as God or higher order – 'prarthana eta-ishwaar'param'atma param'brahma jagadda'datta anadi-ananta purusha' (prayer to the one without the beginning or an end, supreme cosmic soul divine) is as follows. Prayer of the Spirit of Life – inner child to the eternal father 'Sun':

"Tvameva maata cha pitta tvameva, tvameva bandu cha sakkha tvameva, tvameva vidya dravinnam tvameva, tvemeva sarrvaam mamma deva devam."

"Aum sahanau vbhavattu sahanau'bhunaktu sahaveerym'karvavahye tejas'vinaa vadhi'tamastu maa vid vishaa vahaiye."

"Aum shanno deveer abhissth'taya aapo bhavantu peetaye shanyor abhi-sravantu nah."

"Aum shanti shanti shanti".

Thou art the divine mother and thou art the divine father, the giver. Thou art the charioteer of my soul and my sole guardian. Thou art the light of divine wisdom and the glory of truth. Thou art the whole cosmological existence put together oh divine one, bless our human world of existence with peace, blissfulness, harmony, compassion and love. Oh God, may we in togetherness provide, contribute, generate and share the universal spirit of good will, spiritual strength, and divine light of Vedic wisdom, in self-lessness, peace, and love. Oh divine mother and selfless father give us strength, give us all the necessary wisdom, skills and material things to accomplish this most difficult passage of material existence in time.

Aum, the Brahma, peace to the celestial, peace to the spiritual, peace to the terrestrial.

"Asato ma sada gamayah, tamaso ma jyotirr gamayah, mrityoor ma amruttam gamayah". Brihadaranyaka Upanishad – 1.3.28

"From collective falseness to divine truth, from darkness to light, from death to immortality".

Oh divine celestial Sun, obeisance to you. Oh divine Sun, let us be free from diseases born out of three humours.

Before the physical creation there was only the mystical Brahma-param-atman supreme divinity - that which we refer to as the celestial or the mystical unknown. "Aum" is the first self-same three lettered word of the first sound of this Brahma. It may be written as "uam" (first cry of the newborn baby), "maa", "mau", "mua", or "uma", all of which refer to the same sound of divine supreme God Brahma or the celestial unknown. This is the eternal universal truth, this is the most beautiful realisation, and this is the most enlightening wisdom that is beyond the finite manifestation of the gross physical, physical, metaphysical ego, and the mind.

'Yan manasa na manute yena hoor mano matamm tadeva sat-chit-anandam-Brahma tvam viddhi nedam yad idam upasate.'   Keno-Upanishad 1-5

Therefore, happiness is not a condition; it is not a known phenomenon of the manifest. Happiness is a state of being. It is a divine experience in the total sacred transformation from the gross to the sublime most state.

The spirit of life having experienced life in all its stages of karma comes to the sublime stage of spiritual awakening. The spirit of life says:

"Life oh life! Let Indra (the cosmic illuminator) light the candle of delight in my half sleep state."

"Life oh life! Indra oh Indra, kindly acknowledge my sacrificial fire here on the earth as the smoke and seven coloured fire arise from it."

"Light oh light! Sun oh sun, make me desire-less, wise, immortal like the radiant light of your rays. Rudra oh Rudra! Shiva oh Shiva! Dissolve me; bring death to my mundane earthly bonds and earthly memories. May I be removed from the impermanent falseness of all this, that and the other. Maa oh Maa! The all pervading cosmic divine mother please grant me compassion and transform me oh Varuna (cosmic deity of compassion). Life oh life! Let me be a free winged spirit of life! Let me journey and experience the most beautiful and the most wonderful aspect of my human life in a state of divine enchantment."

"Life oh life! Let me become a desire-less state of existential being. Let me be as wise as 'Brahman' (the cosmic Brahmin) and let me become immortal like the radiant 'agnee' (fire of the sun). Let me be self-existent like the star in the nightingale. Let me become full of bliss like the beautiful divine ocean. Let me become all that which is the total fearlessness. Life oh life! Light oh light! Let the spirit of my life forever transpire into delight of light through my self-same sacrifice.' Life oh life! Let me not fear all this, that and the other."

"Life oh life! Let the spirit of my life merge together with the sacred sacrificial fire in fullness, in total sacred transformation."

8. TOTAL SACRED TRANSFORMATION 🌀

Total sacred transformation is the essential foundation to spiritual awakening. Sacrifice is a human obligation offered to time, eternity, and soul, in prayers, mantras, chants, hymns, and houmam (sacred fire).

'As smoke and sparks arise from a lighted fire kindled with damp fuel, even so, Maitreyi (seer of Agnee), have been breathed forth from the eternal all knowledge and all wisdom...They are breath of the eternal.'

Upanishad - Brihadaranyaka

Agnee is the divine fire of god, of which the orange orbit is the supreme life breath beneath which is the glory of pure light and pure consciousness.[32]

Sacrifice is not a burden. Sacrifice is transformation from the unreal into the real, from the untruth to the truth, from darkness into the light. The magnificent eternal nature, is not tempting to the naked eyes, it is blissfully illuminating. The self-imposed ordain of discovering the eternity is not a burden but a sacrifice of the human experience. Only in experience can a human kind grow and mould into a higher form of super-consciousness to merge in oneness with the super-consciousness itself. Therefore, sacrifice is really a transcendental sacred journey of life because in sacrifice we mould. Sacrifice is a sacred precious opportunity to breakthrough from the karmic planes of human existence and mundane survival. Sacrifice is secular. It requires total collaboration, in a total perspective, experiential and transcendental performance of 'yagjna' (the collective fire of sacrifice).

---

[32] Per Isa Upanishad 15: THE FACE OF THE TRUTH IS HIDDEN BY THY GOLDEN ORBIT, O SUN THAT DO THOU REMOVE PLEASE, IN ORDER THAT I WHOSE LAW OF BEING IS TRUTH INFINITE MAY BEHOLD ITS INFINITE GLORY.

SACRIFICE – THE NAVEL OF TOTAL SACRED TRANSFORMATION

'Yo devo agnau yo'psu vissvamm bhuvanam aavivessa Ya osadhiisu up vanaspatisu tasmai devaaya he namoh namah.'

Oh divine Great Spirit who is the fire Sun, the water Ocean, and who is present in all existence alike. To this divine Great Spirit Agnee, we offer supreme salutations and supreme sacrifice.

The profoundness of the word 'YAJNA' in Vedas is tantamount to expressing compassionate quintessence of the sacred revelation of Agnee (divine fire). The underlying insight of the power of Agnee, the composite wholesome sruttee (profound sacred words of mantra) of every cosmic energy, force and inertia is unparalleled to none. The supremacy of the agnee and the smoke of sacrificial fire are 'absoluteness' of the cosmic power of the Sun.

Yagjna is the sacrificial fire of Agnee on the karmic plane of human existence, to the 'Agnee' in Sun.

'Yagjna' (sacrificial offering to Agnee) is the representative illumination offered to illuminate the human soul, in total collaboration. Firstly, Yagjna comprises 'Satt-Kriya' which means sacred rites & rituals in 'mantras' (sacred holy words), 'shlokas' (sacred praises), 'pathd' (verses of Vedas), and 'shanti houmam' (togetherness of peace offering to every cosmic plane). Secondly, 'Yagjna' represents the self-less sacrifice of compassion 'Satt-karma' (act of pure deed in pure compassion). Thirdly, Yagjna signifies 'Satt-Kartreye' (pure soul duty, ordained to merge in 'oneness' with God in destiny). Thirdly, 'Yagjna' profoundly offers in act, rite, and ritual, in Sanskrit it is 'Satt-Karya' (motion of merging the soul and the cosmic eternity in havan – sacred fire ceremony). Fourthly, 'Yagjna' commemorates 'Kranti' (patriotism of cherishing the truth of Veda in blissful freedom of total spiritualism).

"Yagjna" (Sacrifice) is the most reliable ferry for human fellow to reach the infinite purity of the Soul. 'Yagjna' is undertaken by the aspiring spirit of life for invoking the light of delight of the effulgent Sun to take away all the ignorance, dreary dullness, and sins.

Sacrifice is offered to the of power of Agnee in the Sun (the sacred fire), upheld in profound reverence to Soma (the vessel of nectar of truth) by Indra (the illuminator and the inspiration), Varuna (the compassionate preserver and the compassionate fair judge), Rudra (the transformer and the evaluator), Vayau (the wind of quintessence), Kuber (the ploriferator), Issanaya (the sacred facilitator), and the cosmic energy of shaktee (vital life force). What we eat and what we think, we become that. How we eat and how we live, thus we make our relationships and thus we nurture our relationships. Nurturing requires sacred sacrifice of the ego.

Total sacred transformation ('T.S.T') begins with total change of lifestyle. To change our ill habits into good habits, to tame, our mind, body, and ego. 'T.S.T' entails us to change our narrower visions into broader visions of absolute life. Total sacred transformation changes our aggressive attitude into graceful quieter spiritual aptitude. Sacred transformation changes profound personality into a compassionate spirit of life, which is revering, caring, sincere, and compassionate. Humanity becomes the essence of life. 'Selfishness' turns into 'selflessness'. 'Reason' turns into 'insight'. Transformation entails learning - learning to be compassionate. Total spiritual transformation evolves with sacrifice and redemption.

Sacrifice means living for one's real self and living for the benefit of others not for the adversity of others. We owe it to our essential nature. This is the Vedic selflessness.

'Soma-Amrutt' (the nectar of truth and the purest juice of Godhead), is considered, as being the equivalent of the nectar of milk contained in the mother's bosom. It is the purest form of nectar that brings immortality to mortal life. 'Soma' is the vehicle of immortality, and 'Soma' is upheld upright in the highest northern point in the cosmos. When 'Soma', is invoked through sacrifice, it releases a drop of purest form of nectar that is as powerful as making a blind man see and a cripple walk. Under 'Soma', manifests the five worlds and it is the ultimate reveller of truth infinite. 'Soma' is God's eternal nectar.

The highest act of God or eternity is 'Agnee' the sacrificial fire, the cosmic priest, whose powers bring constant renewal and transformation through Rudra (the transformer, the karmic master). According to Upanishads, 'Asvattha' tree is a unique tree that has its roots above the ground and the bark, branches and fibres below the ground.

This tree has two distinct branches. One main branch enters the meshes of dark soils and darkness (implying ignorance, dullness, tamasic, and inactive) and struggles through the rough earth, to come out into the sunlight. During its struggle to come out of the dark soils into the sunlight, it fights the odd obscuring difficult earth. The other type of main branch always remains upward towards the sunlight. It's movement is upwards and it's aspirations is upwards.

Here on the universal existence of earthly plane, the human fellow sees all the darkness and ignorance of the uncertain 'known' earth within and around. The 'Aswattha tree' is like a human personality.

The human fellow has the ability to sacrifice the lures of life, the greed of life, the aggression, power warfare, the sensuous or lustful attachments, the attachments to material things, and the possessiveness of owning everything and everybody, i.e., control. This in Vedas is aspiration to realise the truth. It is through 'selfless' sacrifice, the human fellow destroys all the impermanence and purifies its branches, bark, and roots, to welcome compassion; the delight of illuminating light from Agnee. Sacrifice progressively evolves 'delight' from the gross physical sheath, into the physical sheath, into the physical intellect, into the physical mind, into the mind proper, into the intuitive mind, into the 'over-mind', and finally into the super consciousness. Delight enters the super consciousness in five fold orbits of eternal bliss. Delight firstly becomes 'ananda' (happiness). Delight then becomes 'ananda-Atma' (the real happiness of the soul). Delight then becomes 'param-ananda' (eternal happiness). Delight then becomes 'ananda-Purusha' (infinite happiness). Delight finally becomes 'sat chit ananda' (the happiness of infinite supreme eternity – the nectar of immortality). When the spirit has moulded progressively and found absolute compassion in the personality, it begins to reflect authentic power.

The issue is not a choice between 'east' and 'west'. Nor is it a choice of white or black or brown. Nor is it a choice between ballroom and monastery. Nor is it a choice between church and mosque or temple. That is not the issue of the core objective. The real issue is the delight of the light of the soul and the light of the sun merging in a fusion of true compassion. The issue is to conquer sorrow. The issue is to realise the supreme infinite truth. The issue is to transform. The issue is to mould progressively in karmic cycles.

A remedy to cure anxiety and depression is complete only when we begin to correct our Karma's and spiritual being (karmic roots). It is like curing the roots of a diseased Bonsai tree instead of cutting the bad leaves and branches only. When we cure the roots (the karmic threads), the bark of karmic tree will begin to bring out stronger leaves and branches anew.

So, let us cure the roots first by our karmic demagnetisation, otherwise, our life support light and existence will continue to remain dark and dull, tormented in perpetual chain reaction of sorrows.

A pure devotee eats fresh, pure and soothing foods so that he feels pure and harmonious. The food we eat is extremely important. A sound mind in a sound body is the basis of transforming from the illuminated state to the enlightened state onwards to the delight state. Austerity means a dedicated pure mind, a dedicated body, pure, compassionate loving heart, and an awakened soul. An awakened soul is simple, humble, pure, child-like funny, and sincere. Creativity of talent entails in a precise sense, that we become scholars of the faculty of our souls.

As creative artistes, we become disciples of our souls. As scientists, we make our souls our profound Guru. We transform our perception such that we look at our soul as the lotus of God, we become compassionate and harmonious, we forget about 'what is not' and that we focus on 'what is' the sole truth of life searching experience. The ultimate question or the crucial issue is what does one want and what does the spirit of life need in deep compassion. Do we want to survive the struggles and sorrows and keep on surviving, to keep on struggling, and to keep on reasoning intellectually or do we want to conquer the core essence of the very existence? In trying to determine rationally, what we want, we really need to shift from the faculty of the mind to the faculty of the heart. We need to transform from the intellectual I.Q. to the creative talent of discovering just simply for the sacred experience itself and not for the reason or cause of the mind. Just for the sheer delight of the illuminating experience of insight. Profound wisdom (spiritual wisdom) is for Christian, Muslim, Hindu, Buddhist, Jew, Sikh, African, Agnostic, or any other human individual. Everyone is an equal creation albeit different characteristics and different physical properties. Just as the particles of a rose and the particles of a carnation are different in appearance, yet they are both beautiful flowers of the same garden.

True religion of the soul does not discriminate. It embraces science; it embraces all religions of the world. It embraces every lifestyle. It embraces every living soul. What we seek is within us, in our soul. It is there all the time. If we gave up the intellectual debates and sank in quintessence of serene tranquillity, it will make itself known to us in profound delight.

There is a childlike wonderful person hidden in us all. We need to bring this great human quality to the surface of reality and try to give forbearance, compassion; love and encouragement to the hopeless without prejudice whatsoever. The global leadership needs to remove that veil of discrimination and canny differentiation. It needs to give hope to others less fortunate.

Do not destroy hope in others. If you cannot do any good, at least do not make an already hopeless person more hopeless! Giving 'hope' is like giving supplementary oxygen to a breathless patient. The Great divine spirit made all alike. Hope is to give life and livelihood without discrimination, prejudice, personal manipulation and canny facets.

Every Holy Scripture, (be it a Bible, or a Quran, or a Geeta) manifests on common elements of truth based on reasonableness and fairness. Our purpose in life is not to challenge, defy, and manipulate the common religious hypothesis and anthologies. Whilst I revere every sacred anthology, it is in the Geeta, that I rest the spirit of my life. Geeta is my natural spiritual mother and Geeta is the mother of Vedas. The implication of Vedas is towards the total liberation of the spirit of life.

TRANSFORMATION OF ATTITUDE

The world catastrophes and social antagonism emanating from the anti-thesis (rebellious cults and sects) or agnosticism (total non-believers of God) can only bring more chaos and more misunderstanding. It is easier to be cantankerous and critical, than it is to be sincerely correct. This modern attitude of defying without a thorough or total or complete understanding of a particular subject or scripture or a way of life renders emotional problems and increases the gap between "substance" (altruism i.e. metaphysical) and "matter" (mind and physical). There is no end to defiance and antagonism. Stubbornness implies unwilling to see the better side of the true perception.

The entire galaxy put together and the entire space put together would not be sufficient to measure the extent of "greyness" (or non-gravitational protrusion) of the gap created by antagonism and agnosticism.

The catastrophic modern religion places emphasis on symbolic brick structures like the church, the mosque, and the temple. Historically speaking, men have created a complicated jargon out of the everyday meaning of the word 'religion'. Religion and culture have really lost their root values. Everyone wants to proclaim, claim, presume, and assume the best.

Every Holy Scripture is an anthology of its seers, and every anthology is addressing the human life process. Therefore, take refuge in your own spirit first, before embarking onto the various intellectual conferences of mindfulness. Empty all the pre-conditions, speculations, ideas, and buzzing noises, and try to contemplate in silence. In silent beatitude and in quietness one will embrace this magnificent most beautiful nature of God almighty supreme. The mindfulness with the ultimate mantra 'Aum' is a sacred transformation from the buzzing noise.

All living creatures are life forces of this one magnificent nature and every life force carries one colour of blood red. Is this not scientific enough then to prove that the original creator of every one of us is one God?

Dividing and segregating people and compartmentalising monumental religions do not render salvation or emancipation. Institutional religions and monumental religions are structures of intellectual jargons camouflaged by the congress of power conscious individuals.

Everyone is claiming one thing or another. So when do we find time to sit in quietness to learn and to discover the magnificent soul?

Understanding profoundly like a true scientist 'what is' the known and realising the limitations of the known enables us to be that 'which is' sublimely immersed with the unknown in deep compassionate human experience.

A total sacred transformation is merely a shift in attitude wholesome with a holistic heart and a sacred mindfulness. A shift in attitude is a far-reaching revolution that is going to imply discarding the façade of the socio-economic and political orbit of conflicting ideologies and 'man' power. When the collective human spirit looks at every particle of the earth as a sacred most powerful centre of energy, self-respect and dignity would be restored back.

Sectarianism and Cultism only annihilates culture, true religious wisdom and traditional family values. Firstly, cultism takes away the essence of culture and tradition embodied in a person's family roots. It fails to recognise and appreciate the ancestral wisdom in totality. Secondly, because it provides satisfaction and accomplishment to the ignorant, proud and self conceited individuals. Individuals with half knowledge who are incomplete fools for albeit they know 'no better, they proclaim to be righteous, proud and self-conceited (narrow minded and stubborn). Only when you make a comparative evaluation of the world's history and culture can you be in a true position to make a firm and conclusive claim. Thirdly, because Sectarianism and Cultism practice acts of rituals and rites that are fundamentally oriented towards 'Kaal' (or the spiritual ghost) the proprietor of 'Kalyug' (an epic in Sanskrit meaning 'the age of falsehood'). Fourthly, it diminishes the real family tree in essence by drifting away the future generation children from the main family body and causing the family tree to have lesser branches. Consequently, families are left with lesser branches and lesser leaves and lesser fruits.

If one is born into a Christian family, why should one change one's origin and become something else, something other than what one's family is? Is one ashamed of one's family ancestral tree, one's own karmic roots? By merely transforming oneself into a Buddhist or a Hindu or a Muslim one does not become better than others! Similarly, if one is born into a Hindu family or a Muslim family, why should one change and transform into Christianity or a Sectarian Cult? One is not even reasonable and fair to the family values, culture and traditions of the very roots of one's parents, so how is one going to be logically fair to the cult in the evolution of the spirit? Often Cults and Sects follow an unconventional and unfair mode of worship that propitiates the ghostly spirit of 'Kaal' (lord of Kalyug or falsehood) and fulfils the egocentric individual without due consideration for family values at large or conventional traditions and customs.

Cult and sect Ideology is as bad as monetary power. The more power one has the more access one has to the world of ideological religion. Political religion is based on institutional frameworks of ideological doctrines, patterns, and criteria.

A carnation cannot become a rose and vice versa, albeit they are both beautiful flowers of the same manifestation of nature. Every flower, every leaf, every branch, and every bark constitute beautiful personality of individual life tree.

Each individual tree is a manifestation of the same nature. Every tree is rooted to the same earthly bonds. If by converting oneself one accomplishes God, then the entire quest for soul-searching truth and the self-discovering process of spiritual awakening becomes despondently dependent on the impermanent feature of the mind! That is somehow not appealing to my common sense. However, what is an appealing common sense and rationally scientific logic is that transformation of attitude towards the whole living experience will bring wholesome holistic awakening that is not subject to a means of convenience.

Religion has to be based on logic, rationale, spiritually holy rituals, holy rites, holy customs, authentic culture (culture based on spiritual roots), integrity, and above all virtues worthy of cherishing beyond one life experience. Reasoning intellectually is to argue or to debate about religion which is based on "ism". Religion as a modern practice is highly subjective, complicated and too personalised. Every single doctrine is trying to preach something new and something that is not oriented towards total sacred transformation. Religion is a way of life. It is the composite holistic life of our spirit. Only Truth triumphs in the end, not falsehood, or bigotry.

Therefore, let us be objective and hold our hands together compassionately, with gentleness and begin to discover the simple but most beautiful essence of our common constituents. Let us begin to be genuinely caring towards each other in simple daily life. Let us first give hope to each other. Let us communicate with each other. Let us work together. Let us just be honest and truthful and let us pledge allegiance to the human spirit. One does not need languages or institutional religions or intellectual supremacy or material means or social metamorphoses to reach the soul divine bliss. One does not need the segregation and divisions surmounted by the structures of this society.

One does not require inauthentic sects and cults to awaken spiritually. One does not need to go to churches, mosques, and temples and hold endless propagandas, and endless conferences to make one important or to make one less afraid! One does not need to become a leader or a follower of an umbrella to merely adapt to a personal ego or a personal intellectual mind out of ignorance or uncertainty of the quest.

All one truly needs in order to reach the divine eternal bliss of God is to be divine from within. Divinity encompasses many faculties of humanity. For example, to be loving, to be simple, to be cheerful, to be kind, to be truthful, to be patient, to be wise, to be non-violent, to be generous without hesitation, to be helpful, to be a listener, to be a self-less leader, to be a profound son, to be a compassionate brother, to be a big hearted father, to be an unconditional lover, to be a free citizen, to be a servant of humanity.

Total sacred transformation is a progressive step ahead in the moulding karmic evolution. A total human experience discards all that is impertinently conditionally transient in its make up, all that has been formulated on fragmentations of the individual intellect. Transformation therefore, looks from within with profound wisdom and profound attitude, feels compassionately the sublime nature of the soul, and is that which the God enlightenment itself is.

All major religions of the world contain some form of truth in them and some form of good in them. Pluck out two good points from every religious anthology and sincerely abide by these plucked "goodies". For example, the centrifugal force of the Bible manifests clearly in the serenity of the mind and compassionate wisdom of the soul. For example per the Quran, Allah protects his sincere devotee and holds his hands at the time of death. One who is selfless is a true Muslim. For example per the Geeta, the soul transmigrates into different stages of transformation based on its karmic evolution. Furthermore, there is profound truth in the magnificent nature, in that manifests oneness of truth albeit sages call it by various names. For example, per Dhamapada, Buddha becomes nirvana based on oneness of truth by merging in oneness with the infinite beyond the skies and making his soul the very seat of God almighty supreme eternal. He thus ignited the sacred flame of self-realisation through a process of learning and discovering the soul. Buddha found joy and bliss in suffering hardships and adversities during his quest for truth. Just this much is enough for one's journey of life to be prolific, in emancipation.

Total sacred transformation is what we need, not anthological faiths. Anthological faith is a mere tool of reference. Anthological faith is not there for us to use it as an end. No. What we reflect in our life is our own spirit of life. All the activities, acts, physical endurance's, vital forces, mental faculty etc. are based on our deep rooted faith in ourselves. This faith enables us to create, control, conquer, and finally totally transform. It is the divine will that is the chariot of the soul. Therefore, we all have the innate ability to be divine to be sublime and to be totally transformed. Transformation requires us to remove the 'I' and 'you', the veil of 'ist' and 'ism', the 'ity' and 'am', the gravity of 'me', and 'my', the uncertainties and doubts. Hinduism, Buddhism, Christianity, Islam, Hebrew, Jainism, and other anthological faiths are merely philosophical doctrines of personal god, God perceived from different consciousnesses. Transformation is the attitude of looking at it from the intellectual and mental point of view, with a broader wholesome attitude to the soul; the universal soul (param-atman) as being one to the individual soul (atman).

'Heaven' is a subjective phenomenon, which is perceived differently, from major anthological religious faiths like Christianity, Islam, Hinduism, Judaism, Buddhism, and others. However, the heaven that the beautiful dawn and the beautiful dusk bring forth is unparalleled. This is the composite collaboration of the magnificent Sun. The spirit of life says to God:

"Ah God, give me the beautiful vision and the beautiful insight! This is enough for me to enjoy the heavenly sunrises and the sunsets, the heavenly pasture, the heavenly flowers, the heavenly mountains, the heavenly rivers, the heavenly ocean, the heavenly silence! Ah God if all that I see is your magnificent unparalleled beauty, then who shall deprive me of my heaven on earth! Ah God my fathomless faith knows no limits in your beauty."

FATHOMLESS FAITH NOT ANTHOLOGICAL FAITHS

Collectively if these 'consciousnesses' were merged, there would be only one eternal ocean wherein the truth manifests in pathless eternity and one eternal sky where truth echoes beyond the infinite blue skies, into the infinity of empty space, and beyond the infinity. The written words help us to know who the 'unknown' is, what the 'unknown' is in abstract terms.

However, when we understand profoundly with compassion, we begin to first face this world of impermanence and its reality, we face the truth of mortality and impermanence, we acknowledge and accept the matter, the gross physical earth, and the physical earth. Realising the reality of this matter and all that is impermanence, we grit the naked bitter truth of mortality and we begin to grow and mould into compassionate spirit of life with profound inspiration and profound wisdom of the soul.

We transform and we evolve in experience. We finally grin in delight and rejoice as transformed spirits of life. As transformed spirits of life, we shrug off the past, the earth, and the material impermanence of name, status, and form and, we begin to conquer sorrow in profound compassion and soul wisdom.

When we get this rebirth, in total sacredness, we have become the free winged, 'Hamnssa' the eternal spirit of life who is ready to take a flight of delight with eternity. This kind of transformation is like transforming from the fiery eagle into the compassionate seagull. A wholesome transformation in faith is essential rather than trying to make words our convenient perch or follow-up or trail finder or personal comfort.

Faith is threefold human faith emanating from within us as faith proper or faith of the spirit of life. Firstly there is the humane (humble) faith or the compassionate faith that can only be sattvic or pure when it becomes a centrifugal force of worshipping and invoking the divine eternal bliss – Sat- Chitt-Ananda. The humane faith reposes on Hari-Aum-Tat-Sat which means God is the charioteer of thine soul, Aum is the sound of invoking this eternity and truth is the beatitude upon which the infinite reposes. Hence, the infinite reposes in thine soul. The second type of faith is passionate faith through which the person invokes and worships various deities or semi-gods and Demi-gods to fulfil sensuous desires and greed, and to repent lust. The third type of faith is tenebrous faith through which the person invokes and worships the unsatisfied, dissatisfied, hungry, obscure, impure, earth-bound, spirits, ghosts, and many false occultists. Tantric practices and occultism operate side by side within the same 'tamasic' (pungently egocentric) yantras and obscurely damaging mantras. Therefore, those that follow tenebrous faith and those that create followers of it are both classified as 'occultists', 'cultists', or 'sectarians'. They drift from the root truth.

There is no such a thing like the eastern or the western culture when it comes to the conquest of the soul. There is only one eternity. There is only one truth albeit saints and seers call it by different names. It is the truth infinite. 'Absolute truth' is the same truth that exists in your soul, which exists in mine. Your faith and my faith are 'faith' comprising 'values of life', albeit 'values' itself are not the same.

Therefore, what is really needed to be sacredly transformed is our 'will' and 'faith'. When our mental blockage is removed by clearance of anthological faith, we are left with the purest form of faith. We have faith in the sunrise and sunset, because we have the innate faith that there is an extra ordinary super being para existing beyond the wholesome reality of this earth that we cannot see with our naked eyes. Call it the grand maestro, or the eternal higher order. There is only one kind of faith that a true seeker needs, i.e., 'fathomless faith'. Fathomless faith does not entangle the mind in the entrapment of life platforms. The kind of faith which I am referring to does not entertain debates and nor does it participate in debates. It is a 'fathomless faith' that is based on purity of thought, indifference to all that is 'not permanent', compassion, mercy, sacrifice, great patience, profound wisdom, and fortitude. Like an infant child when sucking milk from the mother's bosom does so instinctively based on the faith in the bond of love between the infant and the mother. The infant knows that the mother's bosom is selflessly unconditional to it. It is a faith beyond doubts.

Our soul quest needs an unconditionally binding faith in our universal Mother Nature and the profound word of wisdom that is the nectar of sound, music and eternity. Profound faith does not argue nor does it entertain an argument. Profound faith is based on profound wisdom and, it is not to encourage defiance, antagonism, conflict, or contradiction. It is to encourage spiritual growth, bring solace and comfort to grief & pain. Profound faith is transformed from the noise into profound inspiration of the profound silence and profound quietness. Profound faith is a healer. Profound faith listens. Profound faith guides and acts as a reference point in a sacred anthology. Hold on to any wise scripture as a ship would hold on to its anchor to harbour the shores.

One reads the Bible, the Quran, the Geeta, the Dhamapada, the Gurugrantha, and more not because one wants to preach or proclaim a personified faith based on religious ideologies but because one wants to enrich the consciousness.

A sacred anthology is a composite praise of the same eternity so why should one not enjoy reading the Bible or the Quran? Anthologies are not considered as an end to follow or to be followed on quotes. The spiritual quest did not suggest that one becomes that or this. The spiritual quest is this wholesome transformation based on creative talent of integrity and profoundness to discover one's true divine self.

There is only one faith of the spirit of life, the fathomless faith of the transformed (awakened) spirit of life, to take a leap into the magnificent 'unknown' knowing that it is within us, in our soul. This awakened spirit of life merges with the 'unknown' eternity almost like a naïve innocent infant sucking milk from the mother's bosom. It wants to naturally rather than it has to or it is compelled to or it is conveniently appropriate or it is based on reason and causation. The natural instinctive want is based on trust and faith rather than a mentally conscious desire of intellectual supremacy or ego power.

Your choice of spiritual liberation has to be profoundly impeccable to the integrity of your own spirit of life and every single act or ritual must liberate you as a spirit. It is easier to be critical than to be correct. We are not born to judge others. No particular formulae for one will be the same for another. Therefore, the subjectivity of various religious practices and institutional segregation do not bring remedial healing. There is substantial growth in cult practices today; the controllers of which attempt to divide and manipulate the many complexities of man made code of institutional religious conduct. Sects and cults have manipulated the ancient anthologies completely and reconstructed Holy Scriptures to give renewed meaning under renewed organisations, and under renewed umbrella. Is true anthology really subject to an organisation, a sect, a religious congress, a religious institute, or a fellowship or a cult or a reformed revolutionary church movement?

Really, anthology is divinely sacred and divinely soul searching. Really, my heart longs to love and to be loved as much as yours do. It is simple really, that I want to laugh as much as you do. I want to share your grief and pain because it is part of my life process too. It is an uncommon human life process. Yet, it is common compassion and love. A Child gives love not because it wants something in return but because it is innocent. The Vedas encourage us to become childlike and not childish. We have to survive but to evolve is our innate nature and to transform towards the universal understanding, is awakening.

We are different ships anchored at different harbours on different shores at different times. We merge in the ocean of eternity and are subjected to common conditions of life 'sorrow', no matter what. Our ships have to follow the local rules and regulations whilst it is anchored on the shores and whilst it is perched on the harbour. However, when our ships are in the deep oceans we have to follow our intuitive faculty of commanding and being the captain in the most profound sense. Hence an error of judgement may render the ship against the tides and may result in a fatal accident with nature. Such is the philosophical boundaries of the profound wisdom of the spirit, which implicitly encapsulates the collective human life process in karmas. We learn and we never cease to learn.

Every scripture is the root for its holistic word that becomes a sacred lyric in Sanskrit, Latin, Hebrew, Arabic, Chinese, Tibetan, or any other form. Whatever the scripture is, it is a composition of its seers in the most inspirational sense of the words and the scripture becomes an anthology by compilation of many profound words into lyrics. Some encapsulate the poetry of the magnificent nature others project the way of holistic life. Every single religious anthology contains good common wisdom.

Anthology is there as a guide for the common purpose. Not as an end. We must not utilise religious anthologies, as an end to self-realisation, rather, as a means to spiritual growth. Progress towards the ultimate goal of life (total emancipation) comes from "experience", which is a profound human experience. We must mould and we must evolve progressively even if it means one step at a time. What is significant is that we understand compassionately rather than know something because someone said so or some word said so. For example, Christianity places great comfort on sincere wholesome repentance, knowledge of the Bible, universal human love, charitable deeds, meditating on the rosary beads, and church services. Islam evolves on spiritual purification by undertaking serious fasting during the month of Ramadan. It dedicates to fixed charitable contributions to the poor. It is committed to praying five times between sunrise and sunset, including chanting salient mantras (incantations) of 'Allah' (supreme God), in the rosary of 99 beads five times a day. The Quran combines infinite knowledge about Allah (God) and actions to perceive Godhead. Islam encourages visiting Holy places for pilgrimages.

Any human occupation comprises some culture and some Holy Scripture with some good points. Therefore, do not discard any occupation or lifestyle. Respect every single occupation on this earth regardless of the sex, caste, creed, and colour of the skin, or status. Salvation is not in the knowing of it, but in the deep compassionate understanding of the two sides to human personality (the dualistic nature of personality), and evolving into a free winged bird of life spirit. Salvation is about becoming united with that which is the 'eternal truth' divine eternity in the most quintessence of the pilgrimage. Salvation is the sacred pilgrimage of discovering the truth, realising the truth, and rejoicing in delight for the truth. Hinduism & Buddhism is a way of life "total living".

Every action has a reaction. Our Karma's are a reflection of our own actions and our future life will be a reflection of our own present karma. According to Hinduism or Buddhism, Karma goes beyond birth and beyond the current or present life.

Ultimate journey of life is towards soul salvation. Until we have realised ourselves, we keep on evolving in the web of life and death. Therefore, instead of being critical and argumentative about whether or not one is superior to the other, learn to acknowledge and respect all forms of life on this earth without duly changing your own spirit of life. One does not know how many hair roots one exactly has on one's entire body and head, yet one is aware that one's body and head consists of hair; some more than others. Such is nature. No religion or sacred religious experience is ever worthless. Religion to be truly religion is an experiential process. Total sacred transformation entails that we stop comparing that which is not the truth. For example the truth is that every life is transiently perishable with the unfolding universe and death awaits no one. A naïve infant sucks the mother's bosom not because the infant is intellectually able to distinguish between one form of nectar and another, but because it has fathomless faith that the nectar is the mother's purest milk. The truth is that all rivers finally merge in the ocean of seas or lakes. For example, there is delight in discovering the light of truth in profound silence. None of the foregoing statements refer to anthological annotations from ideological religion, yet every one of the simple facts is a naked truth in its own right with integrity. Earth mother, Star mother, Divine mother, Great mother, you who are called by thousand name, may all humankind realise that we are all germination of your oneness. Life oh life! Let it be congregation of togetherness, to dance and to rejoice together.

Therefore, to accomplish spiritual emancipation, we need to transform from the 'word' knowledge into the 'experience' wisdom. This total sacred transformation will not become dependent on the written words of the anthology but it will repose in 'twine silence'. A transformed spirit of life will listen and learn in silence. A transformed spirit of life will not be afraid to be alone. A transformed spirit of life will not impose nor will circumstances and worldly conditions impose upon him or her.

By our very own super consciousness, we are able to perceive the divine bliss. We are able to become divine. We are able to disregard and eliminate substantial confusion and chaos created and brought about by the anti-thesis. All human beings have the compassionate nature to become divine. By being divine, we are able to digest only the best food for thought, stomach, and emotions. We are able to disregard the polluted, the manipulated, and the cantankerous matter, with compassion. We are gifted to focus on the core substance. The spiritually divine subtleties entail helping the world to save it from the cultural genocide, precariousness, and parody of altruism.

'Maa', (call it affection or compassion), binds us humanely, unconditionally. A mother's love for an infant is unconditional, self-less, and compassionate. Thence the infant feels secured, and thence the infant wants the milk from her bosom. Then the mother was all right but now that the infant is a big and proud, powerful, personality the mother is not all right. What is not all right really is the infant's attitude of not understanding that ageing is a decaying process, and life is full of 'known' perplexities. What we are doing in the process of sacred transformation is giving back to the Mother Nature eternal supreme what never belonged to us in the first place – 'the sacred life platform. By this sacred transformation, we give hope and mend the sacred hoops.

What is meant by the sacred life platform is not the eternal absolute life. What is really meant is the 'attitude' of possessing all that is not permanent. Like 'breath of life' itself is not permanent hence taking for granted the comfort in our breath at the expense of our life experience means we have been really dumbfound and ignorant of the naked truth. Every single life elapses with time. Time stays but life does not stay. Life goes with the unfolding body and mind. The mind weathers away and the body wears out. We do not realise this truth and hence we fetter!

Our own extra ordinary consciousness manifests in the universal love of sacredness based on simplicity, divinity, and blissfulness. To be able to be a poet of this magnificent nature, we have to transform our vision of it. We have to understand with a deeper insight and we have to begin to learn about unconditional life. We have to be a great talent of integrity, to be creative, to be original, to be compassionately unbiased, to be unconditionally objective and to be humanely loving towards others. Understanding with an unconditional attitude would imply that we are looking at life from a sacred point of view. A sacred life is a profound life. Profound in word, spoken, written, and read, profound in breath, profound in the five sensory activities of touch, taste, sight, hear, smell, profound in karma, profound in relationships, profound in perceptions, profound in our habits and lifestyles, profound in basic thoughts, profound in extra ordinary thinking, and profound in silence. Self-realisation experience is profound.

The basic foundation to all walks of life must be compassion without which no one could possibly be truly religious (virtuous living and profound existence). Compassion enables us to love, compassion enables us to become more forbearing, compassion enables us to take an unbiased view, and compassion enables us to help others. It is about being a positive contribution to the welfare of others not to live and enjoy at their expense. Compassion is about giving respect to life. Compassion is about earning respect not demanding respect or imposing respect. Compassion is granting simple smiles, simple laughter, simple fun, solace and warm affection to the innocent child, the orphan, the widow, the helpless, the hopeless, the ignorant, the dumb, the less fortunate, the crippled, the lonely, and the weak. We are all creators of the same love.

Our existence is justified, only when we are spiritually awakened in substance and in essence. It is essential universal human compassion that binds us like the gravitational force as benevolent human being in our inner most emotions. We must therefore never ever forget our origins and our roots. Our ancestry represents us in personality and our parents and our fore-parents are part of us. We are all branches of this emotional root. To honour and to respect our true divine spirit of life entails that we think of all – the land, the waters, the plants, the trees, the animals, the beautiful divine existence. May we find in the ancient Vedic wisdom, the spiritual courage and the spiritual light to bring hope to all the nations, to heal and to mend the sacred hoops of all wounds alike.

We cannot conquer the holistic avenues of life in dialogues and written words without duly revering our own roots. Our own roots, no matter what, have nurtured us when we were infants. Therefore, they are somewhat significantly special, no matter what. We owe some gratitude if not all to most wonderful persons whom we refer to as parents. Culture, family values, family traditions, and family customs form part of our duty (karma-yoga). It is a sacred ritual rather than a mere obligation. In loving and forbearing compassionately manifests the sheer joy of delight.

Total transformation begins at home. The total transformation process begins by addressing our daily timetable of schedules, habits, activities, and our entire survival kit. The total sacred transformation begins with simple matters like food, clothing, bathing, brushing, body cleanliness, environmental cleanliness, relaxing habits, mental attitudes, physical indulgences, sleeping habits, eating habits, all that and more.

In wholesome sacredness, it is a shift in habitual daily rituals. Regulating our eating habits, for example, is to nurture and nourish our body. Transformation is changing the type of food we eat, changing and transforming the way we feel, renewing our 'outlook', changing the way we think (mentally & consciously), the way we look at life, and the way we exert creatively. Transforming our attitudes involves changing the way we listen, the way we breath, the way we live, the way we work, the way we nurture relationships, the way we talk, the way we look at others, all that and more.

Everyone has every right to enjoy life, to be right to be here on this earth, to be successful and to be ambitious. Everyone has every right to be rich, to be big, and power. This is the very essence of physical and material world. Transform the complex attitude into wholesome simple quintessence of attitude. Sacrifice does not entail one to switch off from performing as a multi-sensory sensuous human being. Sacrifice does not mean that one ceases to act as a father, a son, a daughter, a mother, an employee, an employer, etc. It means that one takes time out for one's soul to understand it and to nurture it.

Sacrifice entails that we forego certain rudimental accessories of life like toxic, wasteful intake, wasteful exertions, and changing our daily habits. Habits build our personalities. We are trapped in a habitual process, of daily life, that is highly stressful, full of toxic and full of noises and haste.

Total sacred transformation can take place only when one as a wholesome person holistically transforms in your daily habits and attitudes with a binding faith and will. The process is a gradual progressive one step at a time, one day at a time. A sky scrapper was not built overnight. What is significant to the philosophy and numerical physics of the skyscraper is that tremendous energy went into the process of putting together the thought, effect and statistics into the foundation stage. 'Habitual' evolution is a detoxification process of transforming what we eat, how we eat and what we think and how we think. It is Yoga of the body and the mind. It is a transformation for the self, from the self, in the self and within the entire body. The body is the shrine for the soul, and the spirit of life is the governing self in the entire Godhead. Detoxification of the mind body and soul is the yoga of purification.

Yoga is a communion with God. In Yoga, the Yogeshwar Jiva (the personality) evolves in multifarious pure activities. It rests on four limbs. Like the four seasons (winter, spring, summer, autumn). Like the four samdhyas (sunrise, noon, sunset and midnight). Like the four quarters. Like the four pillars (north, west, east south). Like the four vows of righteousness (namely 'self-lessness', detachment, dedicated devotion, and renunciation).

The satt-karmic activities of purest type 'sattva' are of four folds. Firstly, the duty; Duty comprises the Karma-yoga of servitude towards humanity, the performance of one's daily duty in total detachment. Duty is also to the soul, in the recitals of the sacred verses at the sunrises and sunsets, the recitals of kirtan raas (musical hymns of God), and many other colourful rites and rituals. Secondly, the Bhaktee-yoga (pure devotion or compassionate divine love comprising sacred dialogue of prayers, selfless meditation and mantra-manjaree – chanting or repeating mantras); the communion, in Vedas, is referred to as maithuna or the meeting in togetherness of the soul and Agnee (sun). Thirdly, the jnanna-yoga (the profound wisdom of the soul like self-realisation); learning in experience. Fourthly, the Vedic rites; Rites comprise Raja-yoga, cumulative practice of physical asanas (postures). Rites include gandharvas (musical sounds), mudras (movements), mantra (sacred word), and prannayam-breathing exercises), profound silence of profound meditation on objects, on nature or on mantras, Bandhas (rites), sacred sacrificial fire called the havan, the agnee, and many other rituals.

DETOXIFICATION OF MIND AND BODY

Fasting in an anthological perspective is a religious sacrifice. A sacrifice to the higher phenomenon, that is responsible for creation, preservation and dissolution or evolution. Fasting may be perceived differently from different anthological faiths. Like for example, the Christianity fasting talks of Jesus giving up food, as a gesture of abandonment and forfeiture, of gross physical and physical earthly sins of the people of Jerusalem. For example, In Islam, fasting is a gesture of abstaining, the sensuous survival of the gross physical, physical, and mental levels of the material human life, for propitiating the almighty eternal supreme God 'Allah' in the seat of the soul.

For example, in Hinduism, the five different fasting sessions during the year relate to sacred self-sacrifice. Firstly, obeisance to the ancestry spirits (known as the 'shraad'). Secondly, to the celestial orbits (fasting on the cycles of the moon like 'ekadashi' and 'poonam'). Thirdly, to commemorate the cosmic divine energy 'shaktee' (like the nine days in April and nine days in October). Fourthly, to revere auspicious days, like the birthdates of cosmic deities, cosmic gods, and savants. Fifthly, to balance the ill effects of the mall-positioned planets in ones karmic birth chart. For example, in Buddhism, fasting is undertaken to build up the roots of the spiritual awareness so that the stamina comes from the awareness rather than the gross physical, the physical and the dancing shadows of the mind. Fasting, according to anthological faiths, is a purification rite.

Vedic fasting however places emphasis on detoxification of the mind, body, and the soul. It is a cleansing process of the blood, the digestive systems, the excretory systems, the reproductive systems, the endocrine systems, the nervous systems, the respiratory systems, the circulatory systems, and the mental systems. To accomplish greater heights and to accomplish greater insight, one must welcome and receive greater inspiration and greater purity. In purest form of activity manifests purest thought, purest vision, and quintessence of profoundness. Fasting is relevantly a sacred most activity of the body wherein the body begins to sustain on the moving energy of the spirit in canals, arteries, and veins. During a total detoxification program, a personality abstains from the gross qualities of the 'tamasic' (slumber) and 'rajjasic' (passionate) thoughts, food, and activities and undertakes to transform into the 'sattvic' thoughts, food, and activities.

The 'sacrificial nature' of the human personality is the nature of every life spirit to know this world as it is, to taste, to dwell in it, to suffer in pain and to elevate from pain. When a personality begins to elevate from 'pain', it transforms progressively from the 'pain' state into 'essential human sacrifice' state in the profound aspiration to realise the profound inspiration. This profound sacredness in Vedic fasting is termed as detoxification of the mind, body, and the soul. The ultimate aim of every Vedic fast is to become pure. Sattvic - pure Yogic person has developed a total way of sacred life over many years with strong solid foundation from the youth.

The energy of the sattvic person is operating on the insight of the third eye. Constancy, consistency, and compassion rule this person. The sattvic person becomes indifferent to everything that is matter and thrives to be happy with all that is simple, pure, and holistic. Every activity, every thought, and every ritual is performed with one intention only; to know the soul and to understand its life on earth. The Sattvic or the pure person never drinks unfiltered or un-boiled water. For example, the sattvic person always drinks boiled milk. He or she eats freshly cooked rice, potatoes, and green vegetables with freshly prepared chapattis (wheat bread). He or she eats plenty of fresh fruits and green salads. He or she drinks non-carbonated water and non-carbonated drinks. He or she observes holistic detoxification fasts of water and fruits only for one to three days, on a regular basis.

He or she calms himself or herself down with plenty of breathing exercises and the sattvic person meditates in quintessence. He or she feels that this human life is a divine gift from god and therefore the body is a sacred temple for the soul. If the bark of the tree has to grow higher and leap in the air to reach out to the eternal manifestations, then the roots have to go deeper and much firmer into the earth. Sattvic person builds stamina and energy from within, and regards food as pure energy for the pure spiritual growth. Earth is female earth, who is the daughter of cosmic divine mother eternal supreme. Sky is the male cosmic galaxy, the son of the gigantic infinite power of the divine eternal omnipotent God that manifests beyond the wholesome skies and beyond the infinite space. The human person is the seed of the earth and sky meeting together in activity hence; we are the seed of karma. In essence, our essential nature is karmic. The seed of Karma is the compassionate spirit of life.

Our soul is unconditional, compassionate, and humane. Whilst our karmic seed is the seed of germination of many lives put together in a collective human life. Our essential nature is pure static love; Infinite love, manifesting beyond the infinite skies, and beyond the infinite wholesome eternity in an almost holistic truth of divinity, order, and charisma. The eternal truth manifests within us, in the seat of our soul. Truth manifests in 'compassion'. To reach this truth, the 'life tree' needs to be purified in the bark (the body systems), in the branches (senses), and finally in the roots (perception and attitude).

Different faiths consider different fasting methods and different fasting styles. There is no such thing like this or that. Only what is practically feasible according to a particular body type.

Every human person in Ayurvedic wisdom comprises the five elements of the earth, water, air, fire, and ether. The entity may comprise these elements in varying magnitudes.

According to the Ayurvedic shastras (the science of human anatomy and human nature), every person falls under the following categories of constituent elementary composition of the 'pancha bhautic' matter:

1. VATA: Mainly air composition, in which, the person is highly active and rapid. A pure vata person cannot sustain a long-term concentration and a pure vata person is running, rushing, trying to think million things at a time. The pure vata person chews his food very rapidly and hence suffers indigestion and constipation. Furthermore, the pure vata person eats at irregular intervals and is not constant in following a rigid timetable. The ruling planet for such composition is Mercury, with Venus as a supplementary planet and Saturn as a complementary planet.

2. PITTA: Mainly fire composition, in which, the person is nicely built, loves action and can be fiery, passionate, highly-strung, and erratically impulsive. Because of hectic life, and high energies, the pitta person often feels that activity is important and essential part of living. To be actively in high-pressured job is satisfying. In the high-pressured gross involvement, the person might pay less attention to foodand may suffer from acidity. The ruling planet for such composition is Mars, with Jupiter as supplementary planet and Sun as complementary planet.

3. KAPHA: Mainly earth and water composition. This person is slow, has a laid back calm attitude to life. Kapha person does not get upset too easily. Kapha person enjoys his food and eats slowly. Such persons normally get plump or fat and find it a lethargic to exercise. The ruling planet for such composition is Moon, with Jupiter-Saturn conjunction as supplementary planets and Venus as complementary planet.

4. VATA-PITTA: Composition of, Air, and Fire elements. This person is talkative and very active. A vata-pitta person can evaluate situations from a detached point of view and is compassionately expressive. The ruling planets are Mercury and Mars, with Venus and Jupiter forming the combination of wisdom arch. Saturn and Sun clash and bring transformation in vata-pitta composition.

5. VATA-KAPHA: Composition of, Air, earth, and water elements, as a conjunction. The person of this composition is beautiful, artistic, compassionate, and acutely intelligent. The ruling planets are a combination of two conjunctions namely Moon-Mercury as primary conjunction with Jupiter-Saturn as secondary conjunction, and Venus-Saturn as complementary conjunction. Such persons suffer and mould in their suffering. They are never at peace with themselves because they feel the world around them is always moving in constant competitions. This is also a performer's combination.

6. PITTA-KAPHA: Combination of, fire, earth, and water. Such persons have well balanced energies of life and can become natural healers because they can generate natural energies from their constitution. The ruling planets are a combination of three conjunctions namely Mars-Moon as primary, Jupiter-Venus as secondary and Sun-Saturn as complementary. Albeit, very serious life, they are naturally funny and can entertain. This combination may be attributed to an entertainer, a doctor, a healer, a teacher, a dancer, and a musician.

7. PITTA-VATA-KAPHA: Combination of all five elements. The conjunctions of such personalities are not elucidated in depth except that there are three ruling planets and three secondary planets with clashing energies and clashing forces. Such persons are jack of all trades and master of one or two proficiencies. The earnings of such persons may be from more than one source. Such persons often suffer bouts of depression, because of the world miseries and global imbalances.

Vedas do not permeate punishing the body such that the mind does not remain under control. The Vedic fasting is geared towards building the harmony of momentum between the physical, emotional and spiritual energies. Therefore, for example, during fasting and detoxification, one looses his or her temper, the fasting is nullified, and the karmic effect is negated. The magnetic fields of karma continue to form more magnetic fields and hence more camouflage in and around the person. Furthermore, the karmic involution does not evolve into the total sacred transformation.

Total sacred transformation only becomes imminent when the detoxification has been undertaken with a keen will to understand profoundly the energy aspect of the fasting without flaring or fleeing into pleasures. The core principle of fasting in Vedas is one must strive to gradually build up the energy instead of abrupt and abrasive manner. One must therefore try to extend fasting, holding of breath and physical exercises to the maximum comfortable point. Beyond the 'maximum comfortable point' the body begins to produce acid. Detoxification in Vedic terms implies that a person gracefully transforms.

The progressive, evolution of attitude is a moulding process commencing from fiery 'eagle' constitution, moving upward, onward on to the compassionate 'dolphin' constitution, gradually becoming the happy 'elephant' constitution, fearless 'lion' constitution, and finally turning into a free winged bird of life whose spirit abounds only with the clear blue skies. Plenty of laughters with plenty of oxygen and plenty of water are recommended during detoxification program. Be funny, be simple, and be joyful.

In Vedic wisdom, one must leave one-seventh fraction of the hunger unsatisfied. The practical reason for this is that the stomach will be gently able to digest small quantity of food rather than large quantity of food. Detoxification includes numerous pure activities like fasting on water, basking in the sun, being sober and sublime, living in the open air, being near rivers and mountains, being with the nature and eating a very light simple diet.

Detoxification does not merely imply flat fasting. Detoxification is a total purification of the mind, body, and consciousness. In this process, we eliminate the past in totality, we cleanse the circulation of blood by drinking plenty of water, excreting the same via kidneys, we sacrifice our needs, and we learn to life like simple human fellows.

The secret of being healthy and happy at all times is truly never to over eat. The stomach is sacred place of divine energy fire and the stomach according to the Vedas is the centre of food. Food is 'Annam Brahma' (germination & nourishment of divine God). A pure pious celibate eats pure food in the presence of divine fire 'agnee' (which we call candle). Stopping intake of food whilst observing the profound silence of compassionate meditation and compassionate mantramanjaree - incantation of sacred word, is similar to doctors putting a patient on 'nil by mouth' before an operation and before an examination under unconditional state. Fasting is healthy as long as the body can sustain it without feeling punished. Fasting must be progressively built with constancy and with determination of will.

Many schools of thoughts have gone into the phenomenon of fasting. Many authors and many persons claim their system is better than others. My personal view is that you listen to your body. Do not punish your body. If you punish your body, and fast with rage, that fasting is not counted at all.

Fasting is a pure experience with pure awareness. Even if one eats fruits and salads and drinks water but sustains on very little food, that fasting is counted as long as the intake of water keeps the level of hydration normal. The minute the body begins to get dehydrated, fasting becomes negative and it produces hormones that counter react with the purification process.

Renunciation therefore implies that the body must automatically feel lighter once we gradually make it lighter. Obsession and obesity are as harmful as anaemia and anorexia. Such conditions are not healthy conditions of the body. Healthy body entails eating pure types of food like fruits, vegetables, freshly cooked wheat, freshly cooked rice, hot potatoes, salads, soups and plenty of water.

Unhealthy foods contaminate our blood circulation and therefore increase our desires, block our ability to communicate with the essence of our spirit, and increase our personal urges. Furthermore, all heavy foods increase our cholesterol and our pulse rates. All heavy foods furthermore give slower digestion and from the slower digestions, we become stressed. Avoid entering fasting programs that are dangerously inappropriate to your body. The Vedas tame us to listen to our body.

I have undertaken many types of fasting over the last twenty years and I personally do not recommend that one undertake complete fasting of not eating at all for more than one day maximum. The reason for this is that it is better to build up ones stamina gradually than to abruptly punish the body. I find fasting on alternate days is better sometimes when the body cannot sustain longer fasts. My personal preference is fasting on water only for twelve to twenty four hours. Drinking plenty of water and not eating detoxifies our immune system, makes us more agile, and brings more stamina. Furthermore, my particular 'prakrutti' is used to eating light meals.

My detoxification process involves plenty of breathing exercises with plenty of yogic exercises and plenty of water intakes and abstaining from food for one day to two days with non-stop mantra-manjaree (constant repetition of sacred mantra, silently). I extend the length of time gradually and gracefully. I find fasting for twenty-four hours more beneficial than fasting for three days maximum. Fasting must be a sheer joy and one must be able to enjoy the glory of feeling lighter and healthier. Vedic wisdom does not encourage vigorous fasting programs without due consideration for the immune system.

Vedic wisdom puts greater emphasis on transformation of habits and transformation of the manner in which we consume our food. Furthermore, constancy, consistency and relevancy is more important than erratic programs of fasting that cease after certain years.

Fasting is healthy as long as it is undertaken throughout the life existence. Fasting one to two days, a week on water is beneficial in strengthening our immune system.

Our body is like a gigantic globe, in which our stomach is the largest city with many gates. From our stomach emanates energy of food (Annam Brahma) into the various smaller cities. If we eat pure wholesome foods, the various smaller cities within our gigantic globe will absorb pure form of energy and purer blood. Blood is centrifugal force in our body and blood circulation determines nearly every single bodily activity. If therefore, we purify our blood and make our blood thin, healthy, and full of vital breath, minerals, vitamins, then our body as a gigantic globe of cities will function in harmony.

The prime objective of Vedic fasting is to create harmony in our blood circulation such that the level of toxic is kept to bare minimum. We unconsciously repeat the great Gayatree mantra twenty one thousand times in a day by 'Sa'-'ha' inhale and exhale cycles of breathing. This is the unconscious Gayatree shaktee in pranna or breath of vital life force. Green plants aid in tap (meditation) because firstly it produces oxygen, secondly it purifies the air, thirdly it detoxifies our environment, and fourthly it produces a calming 'chi' energy flow in the air. We take in pranna gasping the first life breath and take out shuddering in our last breathe of life as the vital force of life leaving the matter (bhumi) and intellectual mind (svahar).

According to Vedic astrology and Vedanta (the guidance), there are two ways one can cleanse the karmic toxic of adversity and ill fate - The external (obligatory offering of rites and rituals) and the internal (mantra-jaap or the incantations of mantra in profound silence). The external way comprises obligatory sacrifice. This entails detoxification and purification of the blood, cleansing of the air, cleansing of the mind, cleansing of the body, recitation and offering of mantra to Agnee sacred fire known as havan, humanitarian servitude, propitiating the planet by wearing of respective gemstone and charity. The Vedic karmic astrology is based on nine active planets, nine active houses, nine active effects, nine active causes, nine reasons, and nine resolutions.

The gemstones for respective planets are as follows:

Planet	Day	Gemstone	Short Vedic Mantra:
Sun	Sunday	Ruby or Garnet	Aum hreem hreem surayaye namah
Moon	Monday	Moonstone/ Pearl	Aum aim kleem Chandramaasaye namah
Mars	Tuesday	Coral	Aum hrim shreem mangalaye namah
Mercury	Wednesday	Emerald	Aum aim streem Buddhaye namah
Jupiter	Thursday	Yellow sapphire/Topaz	Aum hrim kleem hum brahaspattaye namah
Venus	Friday	Diamond	Aum hareem sreem Shukraye namah
Saturn	Saturday	Sapphire/ Tanzanite	Aum aim hrim shrim Saneshcharaye namah
Rahu	Sunday	Hessonite	Aum aim hrim Rahuvey namah
Ketu	Saturday	Cats Eye	Aum aim kleem Ketuvey namah

Many persons prefer fasting for purification of the body toxic. In the Vedic culture however, fasting can be induced to balance the energies of the adverse planetary effects and karmic effects on ones life. Fasting alone does not render greater total sacred transformation. Fasting together with pure holistic activities like listening to hymns, recitation of the holy words, silent repetitions of the mantra jaap (sacred profound devotional incantation) on rosary beads, profound silence and profound compassionate understanding of the nature, should all form part of the wholesome total sacred transformation.

Per Vedas, fasting for the days of the week to invoke energies of the respective deities, planets, cosmic forces is as follows:

SUNDAY – SUN – ENERGY OF THE AGNEE GAYATREE COSMIC CONSCIOUSNESS OF BRAHMA SUPREME PURE (PRAJAPATTI). The Sun represents the first born of the effulgence. It is the soul of "time" and "form". The Sun is the creator of all objects, ingredients, and deities. Sun is the also known as the cosmic father. Sunday is a day for peace offering to the togetherness of a union of the Sun and all the planets revolving around it.

MONDAY – MOON – ENERGY OF 'ARDHANAREESHWARA' (SHIVA-SHAKTEE ONENESS/ cosmic guru 'Rudra' merged with 'pranna'). Moon rules over the oceans, rivers, and rains. It brings compassion in the vast sky, and the vast atmospheric orb. It is compassion for the calming waters.

TUESDAY – MARS – ENERGY OF THE SHAKTEE IN PUREST SATTVIC FORM OF MAA DIVINE, TRINITY OF BRAHMA VISHNU AND MAHESH IN ONE DEITY CALLED GANESH (THE ELEPHANT HEAD). It is personified god of gallant wars. The war between the 'kaal' (dull, dark, grey, ignorant, pungent, dusty, and contaminated mass) and the 'Mangal' (the blissful).

WEDNESDAY – MERCURY – ENERGY OF THE BUDHA, VISHNU, AND ALL THE INCARNATIONS OF GOD INCLUDING JESUS, MOHAMMED, ETC. Mercury is the planet of 'budhee' (intellect and communication). Mercury is an unmarried young beautifully handsome prince. It is the son of the moon.

THURSDAY – JUPITER – KING OF ALL PLANETS 'BRAHASPATTY'. Jupiter is the planet of pure intellect, pure speech, pure mental powers and the greatest teacher of all planets. Jupiter controls and rules science.

FRIDAY – VENUS – ENERGY OF THE BEAUTY, WEALTH AND GLAMOUR LAXSHMEE/ THE CONSORT OF LORD VISHNU THE PRESERVER. Venus is pure cosmic glamour, and radiant sensuality. It is an embodiment of love and sex. From Venus comes all the passion of life.

SATURDAY – SATURN – ENERGY OF THE TASK MASTER AND PURE STAMINA OF HANUMAN (THE SON OF WIND) AND FIERY GODDESS KALI (THE FIRE OF DESTRUCTION OF ALL ILLUSIONS). Shanee is the son of Pluto and is the lord of Saturday. Shanee/ Saturn is the cosmic planet of solitary and solidarity and has emanated from the fusion of Sun and 'Chaayya' (the sixth wife of the sun – chaayya means dark shadow).

SUNDAY – RAHU (dragonhead) and KETU (dragon-tail). Both belong to the ambrosial mysticism of grand illusion. Rahu and Ketu are associated with retribution, redemption, resolution, and transformation through mysticism or secrecy.

Another way is the internal way comprising regulation of cosmic energy by profound meditation, profound mantra-manjaree jaap (repetition of sacred 'Aum' in silence), and profound compassionate transformation. The internal way is a life time process and it is an evolving process. It is as 'what you see is what you get'. Therefore, if we see the sky (the vast openness and the vast eternity that is beyond the finite visions) we get an aspiration to take a flight of delight. If we see the earth (the noisy finite), we get the struggles, the pleasures, the pain, and the sorrows, the urges and so on. The external way is as if you get what you pay for in terms of your sacrifice. Vedas recommend a combination of both.

In Vedic astrology, every rite, and every ritual of propitiating planets for removing our negative planetary influences, can irradiate our karmic past into a neutral state. Furthermore, it does not render total sacred transformation. It helps in the parable of the core principle of knowing our existence and understanding our existence with deep compassionate 'insight' the essential nature of human existence.

The essential nature of human existence is a sacred sacrifice in knowing the fire on earth and the progressively evolve in understanding the fire that ascends to the 'yellow hue liquid' of the Sun. Knowing the earth is realising its nature, 'life oh life let it be'. Understanding profoundly and learning profoundly is a total sacred transformation of the human survival into the essential human existence. A cry of the spirit of life to be free and to be elevated from the gross physical and the physical contamination - 'Life oh life let it be a flight of delight'. From delight we came, into delight we return. This earth is a vicious platform of perpetual cycles of life and death wherein only mortality in sorrow prevails.

Detoxification focuses on 'attitude'. The wholesome attitude to life, the wholesome attitude to food, the wholesome attitude to pleasure, the wholesome attitude to thinking, the wholesome attitude to surviving and the wholesome attitude to self-realisation. Detoxification cannot be appropriately complete without cleansing and purifying the entire microcosmic human spectrum of existence. Detoxification according to my experience has to be elevating from the past. It has to give rise to new fresher view, to evolve onwards, to respect and to honour the existence, to perform righteous karma.

Detoxifying in essence implies change that is a progressive change and that change is the inertia of progressive karmic evolution. We cannot merely fast without the transformation of the basic attitude to life.

Our fasting must purify our thoughts and our attitudes because it is through our mind that thoughts dance in the shadows of our consciousness. When we fast, what we are actually doing to our body and mind is gracefully building inner stamina and inner 'inertia' of positive health.

Doubt is evil; doubt is the shadow of fear. Darkness is the ignorance of not being able to discover the eternal truth of the para-existing eternity and regarding the entire cosmic eternity as an 'unknown' imagination when in fact is that cosmic eternity is within us. The 'known' is really all that is uncertain and all that is impermanence. The 'known' brings us doubts and from 'doubts' we become afraid. To have doubts is to become a sick person. When we have doubts we become mere coals that burn when it is hot and that remain untouched when it is cold because of its black soot. Alternatively we become misused.

To be free from the vicious cycles of Karma, we need god-will, soul-will, and fathomless faith. Detoxification therefore comprises essentially the removal of 'doubts', 'conflict', 'uncertainty', and 'darkness'. Total sacred transformation begins with dissolving the root cause of uncertainty 'fear' in its absoluteness.

Only when 'fear' and 'conflict' are dissolved and destroyed by the forces of 'Yamma' (the god of death) and Issanaya (the god of destruction), can the cosmic bliss transform the cosmic energy progressively upwards and elevate us from the gross physical entity of matter.[33]

According to Vedas, spirit can travel in two directions; the north – upwards or the South - downwards. The north is the light and the south is the darkness. Darkness is below the gross physical earthly soil. Darkness carries with it, slumber dualism. In the heart of Vedic philosophy, 'light' was discovered in the sacred 'agnee'. Agnee is fire of the soul, as agnee is the fire of the sun.

In the art of the nature, devotion, dedication, and purification invoked 'inspiration'. Varuna (the merciful), Indra (the illuminator), Vayau (the air), Kuber (the ploriferator), and Rudra (the transformer), Issanaya (the facilitator), Apah (the calming waters), Agnee (the divine fire), Yamma (the dissolver), Nirritti (the breaker), Vasus, Marutas, Pusanas (the cosmic inertia), thus became the pioneers, of upholding, "Soma", the vessel of nectar in the northern most hemisphere of the cosmos. Aum Tat Sat reposed and the light of agnee became an illumination of Gayatree mantra in seventy two thousand cosmic energies, sixty nine thousand divine forces, and eighty four million atoms of the hundred and eight thousand magnetic fields. 'Aum' thus became the supreme divine truth of the 'Omnipotent God infinite supreme eternal'.

During the detoxification process, we are shutting off the loom of desires and the loom of greed. We are transforming our inner cosmic energy. According to Upanishads, detoxification begins in the mind and ends in the 'insight'.

---

[33] Yajur Veda: May our human life be prolific through self-sacrifice. May our human life breathe, and thrive through sacrifice in progressive transformation of evolutions. The lyrics of the compassionate soul create hope. Every self-same word of sacrifice is to emancipate.

The spirit wants to transform from the unreal material world of matter and uncertainties, to the real world of 'eternal truth', in profound karmic experience of blissfulness. The spirit of life wants to transform from the darkness of ignorance that wonders in the looms of desires and dark grey shadows of impermanence, into enlightenment of delight of the light of agnee (in Sun). The spirit of life wants to transform from the perishable mortality into the infinite immortality. The spirit of life wants to transform into an enlightened soul with profound wisdom and infinite profound Brahman the imperishable omnipotent Guru, in profound silence. Detoxification cleanses the body.

Detoxification can be of five types. Firstly, detoxification program of fasting on water only. Secondly, detoxification program of fasting on fruits only. Thirdly, detoxification program of mantra manjaree without breaks for example repeating 108,000 jaap over a period of one week continuously with just simple light sleep and simple light food. Fourthly, detoxification program entails refraining from eating rich foods in order to bring our energy chakras into harmony and balance. Fifthly, detoxification program of graceful Hatha (physical) yoga on music with water, fruits, light meals and hot bath soaks.

Eating light helps to keep the body healthy. Keeping the body fit helps with asanas helps to build stamina. Keeping the body nourished helps. Keeping the body free from any toxic like chocolates, cigarettes, alcohol, and red meat; helps. Keeping the body re-hydrated helps to rejuvenate tired torn muscle tissues. Eating plenty of fruits helps.

Fasting sustains us from various tamasic foods (gross, impure, and pungent) and various rajjasic foods (sensuous). Fasting transforms our activities and thoughts. It transforms us into Sattvic (purest) persons. It makes us ready to invoke the profound god of compassion and love –'Varuna'. It makes us connect with the merciful compassion of 'Varuna'. We try to avoid repetitive cycles of sorrow in shame, ignorance, and darkness. We try to shun away the realm of our true essential nature. In vain, we touch the wretched of this known earth and in vain, we cry. We seek solace of loving compassion so that our tears find profound wisdom, but in vain, we receive pity, self-pity, and sympathy. Our integrity is constantly questioned and we feel afraid, lonely, bitter, battered, shattered and confused. Everything is in circular motion, and we are responsible for our own karma.

In conflict we aimlessly live projecting to be a super power prestigious person with powerful status, powerful name, powerful bank account, powerful house, powerful car, powerful 'anything'. We constantly try to compare ourselves to others and in vain, we become sad. We are struggling in every single spheres of our life with intellectual reason and cause. We want more and more things. We are never satisfied. All things to humankind, all power to humankind, all glittering material wealth to humankind; yet, the humankind remains somewhat engrossed in the darkness of sorrows and the darkness of ignorance projecting to know it all but feeling somewhat shattered. A spirit of life that cries out in deep compassionate love and deep compassionate outburst has realised the impermanence of this world and in deep compassionate profound silence seeks to shrug off step by step the 'perpetual sorrowful past', shrug away in demagnetisation, the vicious cycles of karmic magnetic fields.

Prophets and holy savants like Jesus, Mohammed, and Buddha all had very similar altruism to the elapsing world of intellectual humankind - "THE OUTLOOK TO LIFE, AND TOTAL SACRED TRANSFORMATION". We have what we seek within ourselves. We only need give our whole for it to unveil.

'Rudra' (the transformer), 'Indra' (the illuminator), 'Vayau' (the purifying vital life breath), 'Tyaag-Agnee' (the sacrificial force), 'Ushas' (total human welfare brought by the sacred sunrise), 'Ashvinis' (the twin delight of light), 'Kuberayae' (the ploriferator), and 'Issanaya' (the facilitator), carry the 'kumbha' of divine sacrifices onwards onto the compassion of Varuna and in deep compassion invokes the compassionate force of the cosmos Varuna.

In 'kirtan rass' (glorious songs of praise) and in 'gandharva leela' (musical manifestations), the cosmos awaken the god of compassion. During the manifestations, the sound explodes from the seven musical notes into seventy two thousand rhythms and the rainbow from the light of Agnee (in Sun) embraces every single rhythm of the sound of music. This fusion creates an explosion of sixty four thousand colours and the cosmos creates nightfall of countless glittering stars with the compassion of Varuna. Varuna transforms the fiery energies of the sacred sacrifices and dissolution into compassion.

COMPASSION OF PURE LOVE IS DIVINITY

Jesus did not leave behind any authentic written words, nor did Mohamed or Buddha in fact. Their messages were voices of the spoken word of gospel transmitted with profound inspiration and profound aspiration with a profound purpose of transforming the materialistic being into the cosmic being. The sacred spoken words have been interpreted, constructed, reconstructed, and annotated after almost thousand years hence. As such the 'sacred words' have not remained 'original spoken words of profound wisdom'. However, the divinity of the lyrics concerns, THE UNIVERSAL human fellow, THE UNIVERSAL love, THE UNIVERSAL compassion, THE UNIVERSAL truth in the NATURE, THE UNIVERSAL glory in the freedom of the soul, THE UNIVERSAL manifestation of the divine bliss, THE UNIVERSAL profound wisdom of the soul infinite being. The implication of Jesus being redeemed on the crucifix is substantially profound and substantially significant to the compassion of the modern world.

Perhaps, the personified lord's Holy Spirit is hurting more now than it did then. Perhaps, the prophets and the alien divine energies and forces may be hurting much more now than they were hurting ten thousand years ago. Is not such a hurt evident in the number of traumatic tragedies and traumatic accidents and traumatic endings?

Is not the present state of the world enough evidence to all those powerful intellectuals that death does not come invited and that there are certain aspects of human life that are not in the intellectual domain. Human mind power has not been able to control death and natural tragedies, nor has the bureaucratic powers of this modern world accomplished world peace. At least in the ancient times, the errors emanated from ignorance of not knowing the difference between the right and the wrong.

The modern world heroes cannot avoid the wounds of this unfolding world in ignorance though! Despite knowing it all, the modern mind chooses deliberately, to ignore the profoundness and the sacredness of the simple way of living the profound life. If one would study the Sermon on the Mount profoundly, with deep profound transformation of attitude, than, there may be some hope for a progressive karmic evolution. But mere study without transforming the inner self is half knowledge.

Total sacred transformation dwells in the profoundness of the spiritual will. To be creative, one has to have a will. To have a will is to love compassionately. Life is to live and love. Life becomes a journey of sacred experiences and life becomes a manifestation of eternal truth divine when you are wholesome in love with it. When one is in love with life, one smiles and understands genuinely that 'selflessness' is profound. In profoundness manifests, poetry, philosophy of sacred words, music, dancing, compassionate servitude to humanity, songs of nature, blissfulness, and true religion. Universal religion loves every single soul and every single manifestation of this nature as eternal divine bliss. Love is the supreme most religion and without love, there cannot be a ritualistic observance, or a holy bath, or a sacred pilgrimage. The experience which love generates is a sacred pilgrimage in its own rights. Pure love contains warm compassionate embrace, whereas pity contains cold attitude. Pure love does not shun people. Pure love embraces people and especially people who are torn apart and hurt. When one cannot embrace a torn apart and hurt individual with deep compassionate love, this cold selfish attitude is usually met with betrayal and bigotry. Shutting out people emotionally and deliberately only brings about shame in a relationship. In the long term, it becomes obvious that it is out of ignorance people are trapped in their own little disillusions and it is out of ignorance, people are behaving in a cold manner.

The three worlds namely the celestial, the terrestrial, and the spiritual world are directly correlated to 'freedom', 'thought' and 'love' respectively. The terrestrial world inter connects with the other two mystical worlds of existence namely the celestial and the spiritual unknown as they may be, in profoundest thoughts that inspire. To die amidst the struggle for 'freedom' and 'love' and 'self respect' is better than living in the dreary wretched submission as the weakest. It is human to make mistakes but not at the cost of loosing the integrity of our soul. All fears demean but all compassion wins. Whilst it is true that there are no absolute remedies for absolutely perfect health, it is still worth adventuring the lateral remedy of karmic diffusion in deeds, mantra, peace oblation and sacrificial light for spiritual awakening. What really matters in 'all this, that and the other' is that we take time to heal true spirit of life and we take enough time to appreciate the bare existence of life itself. Understanding and having courage to be spiritually stronger means we simply become part of a beautiful bare existence, in the most extraordinary ways.

Circumstances, conditions, and events may drive us shadily into narrow paths in obstacles, troubles, and restrictions. Troubles will never disperse. Filtering energies is like straining contamination and straining dirt. The strainer is the perception or the insight that sustains the true spirit. It is based on experience rather than knowledge of 'all this, that and the other'. Filtering implies seeking out the right guidance and seeking out the right counsel. Filtering energies help us to transform our inner spiritual vision. From our experience of encountering negative energies, we realise that the impact becomes negative and the consequences become hearkened. We discard and move the thorns of confusion, perplexities and infusion of 'all, this, that and the other' with karmic diffusion. Filtration of energies can be extremely vital particularly when the worn out energy within needs to be re-built. Insolence and aggression do not imply brevity, in as much tenderness and compassion does not imply cowardice. Chat does not necessarily imply profound wisdom, as silence does not imply ignorance. A discussion or conference does not necessarily always imply progress as aloneness does not necessarily mean incompetence or inadequate.

Sustaining psychological troubles and sustaining hurt is very difficult indeed; much more difficult than a physical injury because the earlier is not visible or comprehensible to the external world of human ego.

Strength of spirit shapes up our life purpose, and our long-term happiness. Strength of character can make our life become what our inner spirit of life aches for and what our inner spirit of life longs to do. Filtering energies enables us to see beyond the appearance of reality and beyond the superfluous face of the surviving world. Transmigrating, coming through emotional pain and growing with the self-discovery of hurt in profound experience of living the adventures of life is one way to release the trauma of hurt. Acknowledging fully the nature of the hurt, and discovering it progressively, one day at a time with profound love, compassion, and spiritual strength is one way of resolving hurt. It takes time and great patience. Hurt cannot heal absolutely, just as a broken glass cannot be put together to become unbroken. The vicious chain of hurt begins in fear and ends in a grand warfare or eruption. The result of fear is always dismal frustration of the dead time; time that becomes empty without any grand memory of beauty and instead time that fills with dismal frustrations of 'all this, that and the other'.

The spirit of life weeps in silence watching the grand nightingale of beautiful stars. Sighing with batter, it makes a wish upon a star.

There is the melody of music, the lyrics of the song, and the beauty of the dancing river on the one side of the dreams.

There is the chaos of the noise, haste and waste of 'all this, that and the other' family upheavals distracting on the other side of the mind in recurring nightmares.

It does frighten us in nightmares and illusions! Our internal peace is distorted and it is time for us to look back at 'all, this, that and the other' with eternal insight and sigh in profoundest compassion to 'all said and done'.

Rejections, disappointments, betrayals, lie, trauma, torment, hatred, hypocrisy, greed, lust, anger, aggression, noise, arguments, screaming tensions, stress, all these and more will shatter the true self. When all else fails, we resort to the spirit of life, to sustain us profoundly, with respect. Certain hurt can be deep rooted due to various trauma, discouragement, rejections, abuse, conflicting family ego, 'all this, that and the other', in various upheavals.

Karma in not knowable, rather it is understandable. Death puts us into this karmic quest, retrospectively.

The diseased collective karma requires diffusion in rite, rituals, ceremonial sacrifices, obituaries, oblations, prayers, mantra-manjaree (invocations to offer peace), and hymns in togetherness.

From various experiences of adversities, I have learnt a grand lesson from the eternal world. All said and done, sacrificial oblation of peace and harmony offered to the world of spirits at the dawn and the dusk in various prayer modes brings us awareness of the world of existence. It may not be imminent in the short term but it brings about progressive awareness.

Profoundest awareness leads us gently, kindly, and compassionately towards a platform of reverence to our true self.

Our awareness opens our insight to the truth that leaves behind 'all this, that and the other'.

Profound awareness makes us see things differently, somehow and brings to us an opportunity to awaken with the experience it renders.

Becoming aware, we congress in 'togetherness' at the dawn and the dusk to bring together the three worlds (namely the celestial, the terrestrial, and the spiritual (ether)), in prayer invocations, in sacrificial light (candles), mantra-manjaree (invocations of peace mantra), sacred hymns and eternal peace oblation.

Between the human world and the spiritual world, a constant unseen communication creates an innate yearning to love profoundly.

Becoming aware we realise that under the diseased roots the tree collapses gradually without anyone realising it because of blinded ego being the bark and the arrogance of the mind being the branch of the tree. When a tree collapses the bark and the branch, show the condition and the symptom. However, under the dark soil rots the diseased roots of the tree. This is the vicious regime of the egocentric 'me', 'I', and 'mine'. All said and done, we become aware of 'all this, that and the other'. In the strength of true light of awareness manifests the great strength of BEAUTY.

The soft pebbles have travelled in time to eliminate rough unpleasantness of life. All said and done compassion triumphs in the end no matter what. Love endures the spirit of life no matter what.

Spiritual awakening implies that the negative karma, that which is the resulting action of the collective grand ego, is dissolved in deep profound compassion towards the self with profound respect for the self. Becoming aware and alive means that despite 'all this, that and the other', the true-life purpose of the spirit of life transpires in self-discovery process of living life.

All said and done, one set of system will never agree with another set of system unless there is a mutually compatible interface. The interface is the link between one world and another world.

Perhaps an adapter that translates the frequency of one world to the frequency of another world is needed to make a father understand a son and vice versa.

This translation process involves foregoing the language of the mind and adopting the salient language of the spirit of life. The spiritual evolution leads us towards light and delivers us from the collective hurt in wonderful most magnificent experiences of truth. It simply opens the doors to discover with our own spiritual strength and inner wisdom. Happiness is the birth right of every spirit of life. Therefore, hurting spirit of life needs deep compassionate sustenance that touches it in profound love, profound sense, profound energy, profound fusion of light and profound friendship. Karma has brought us to where we are and karma will take us to our final destination. The spirit finds its course eventually like the river eventually meets the ocean. All said and done, if karma is fate than we can alter it with our spiritual will.

Therefore, one person may hurt another person and so on, but has this very same person not hurt himself or herself in a greater way by bringing a potentially dangerous destiny closer with time. Who is a looser? The originator of the disguised, fragmented, and masked manipulator of love or the person who reciprocates hypocrisy with utmost compassion and love yet preserves his own integrity? If circumstances and the social powers hurt us, should we therefore reciprocate this hurt with love and compassion or react with more hurt. Love begets love, and in the end, love wins, no matter what. Fear breeds fear, anxiety brings more anxiety, hatred breeds hatreds, spite breeds spite, anger attracts frustrations, conflict blocks the intellect, etc. In love and compassion, we shrug away our negative forces of life like rejection, dejection, dispassion, hypocrisy, falsehood, darkness, ignorance, and unjustifiable fears.

When a spirit of life is truly in love with divine life, it sings in ecstasy of freedom with the divine Mother Nature and love brings delight of endless joys in the simplest and the smallest ways. When one is truly in love with life, one does not bother about the matter and the mind. The mind is the most uncertain place and the thought is the unstable field of energy. Therefore, whatever the mind and the thought decide for you and me will not remain the same forever. The naked truth is that we are part of a serious decaying process. The sooner we realise this truth the better it is for our compassionate nature. Life without true compassionate love is a bare life without any laughters or joy.

Knowing the techniques and super techniques of yantra, tantra and yoga shaktee in depth as a science will only increase one's knowledge and hence grant one a superior power to know every aspect of the human life in material and spiritual sense.

However, if the life spirit has not evolved naturally with total sacred transformation of true compassion, the methods and techniques cannot necessarily grant salvation. True loving compassion automatically transforms a conscious spirit of life and true loving compassion is the essence of total sacred transformation. Therefore, without total sacred transformation there cannot be total salvation.

Total salvation is the goal of every life spirit. Total salvation cannot be accomplished in techniques and methods but in love, compassion, sacrifice, and benign self-discovery process filled with natural and most beautiful experiences of sacred living. If one were, sublimely quiet, in a sublime mind, in a sublime consciousness, in a sublime compassion, would not this person's super consciousness automatically become sublimely divine and blissful? One must automatically be in love with sacred life with a keen will and pure love. Love is all embodied life breath of every spirit. Love is passion and love is compassion of the spirit of life. Love is a sensational feeling and love is universal sublime most truth. Love is the cause of life and love is the reason for life. Love is the faith of heart and love is the nest of human hope. Love is the trust of solace and love is the comfort of grief.

Love is the reflection of human trust without any conditions and love is your true reflection. Love is the emotional and sentimental talent of life and love is the very essence of existing beyond the survival. Love is your life for you are a lovely flower in the garden of God in the infinite sense.

Yes, you are the very charismatic talent of life. Do not abuse and destroy this beautiful talent with your intellectual manipulations and egocentric desires. Make love your true reflection and make your smile a warm compassionate embrace of harmony and eternal peace. Yes love is the joy of life and love will bring true nectar of happiness. Love heals every wounds and love cares in the simplest most wonderful ways. Love nurtures and love understands. Love does not rebel, argue, and shout. Love is simply great and love is simply the supreme truth of life. Love is life and love is consolation. Love is solace and love is harmony.

When your life is in harmony, it sings, it dances, it forms lyrics of compassionate poetry, it looks at everything with a philosophical sacredness, and it simply becomes a sheer joy. Love is the almighty power of God that is unseen, yet deeply and profoundly manifested in the most natural way. Love is forever a musical scale of eternal joy.

There is no substitute for the word 'love' except a free loving spirit of life that flies across the vast blue skies and the vast blue oceans and sings the glory of the Mother Nature. This magnificent love is portrayed in 'Hamnssa' as beauty. Beauty is all that it becomes, and in delight it sings to the world:

Glory is yours! Glory is mine! Victory is yours! Victory is mine! Hail the magnificent rainbow that stands between my beautiful vision and the gigantic most beautiful Sun. Hail the raindrops that sing in my ears, the drizzling sounds of the tears of joy. All that is gone in aimless wonders and messy disasters is now behind me, for now I see only the bright orange hue of the Sun, for now I seek only the eternal truth, for now I am ready to take a flight of delight. Life oh life let it be a flight of delight, let it be.

Love brings tears of joy and love rejoices in altruism. Love makes us feel simply good in the simplest ways. Love opens our insight to the magnificent, most wonderful eternal nature of God. Love makes us like the free winged bird of life, the free spirit of life 'Hamnssa', locked up in its beautiful insight of beautiful charismatic Mother Nature.

You and I, we emanate as humankind from an embryo of our mother's womb. The energy and life that breathes in that embryo is beyond the perception of the human intelligence albeit many scanning technologies can visualise it. The entire cosmic germination is simply magnificent. Similarly, the wholesome existence manifests on the parable of the embryo principle. The orbit surrounds the Earth and we are all little lives within this huge spectrum of Mother Earth.

In love and compassion we rise. With love and compassion, we strive to become profoundly humane. In love and compassion, we sigh. Our essential human nature is 'loving compassion'. In love and compassion, we grow, in love and compassion we dwell in our existence and in loving compassion we sacrifice our essential time and energy.

'Aum' became a symbol from the extra ordinary fusion of sound and light of transformation, and Aum thus became a symbol of three letters in culmination of one symbolic fusion of ecstasy, inspiration, and delight. Adoration to 'Aum'; salutation to 'Aum'; prostration to 'Aum'; devotion to 'Aum'; sacrifice to 'Aum'; meditation to 'Aum'. Silence to 'Aum'; glory to 'Aum'; Victory to 'Aum'. Hail to 'Aum'. 'Aum' echoed all over the atmospheric orb, and Varuna with his compassion and love made the entire cosmos sing and dance on the great Gayatree mantra. The rivers of the terrestrial, the spiritual, and the celestial meet together.

'Aum Tat Sat' the trinity guru Tattva Shiva performed 'mudra-tandum' (dance of compassion) whilst the entire atmospheric orb of the cosmos transformed into 'sat-chitt-annand-parramannand' (blissful joy). Profound compassion and profound wisdom of the soul can enable us to transform our vision with spiritual awakening insight. That every living creature is a soul creation of God almighty (satt chitt ananda Brahma) and that God almighty resides in each one of the living creatures. Without this compassion, we cannot enhance into the spectrum of Godhead nor can we reach out to our inner spirit. Compassion in harmony is wholesome and eternal. A compassionate devotee of God cries out for a grateful heart, an artistic heart whose pulse beat rhymes the music of the sounds of Aum that echoes in the valleys and the mountains and the rivers and the oceans. La, the devotee is a meticulous scientist who patiently learns to listen in profound silence, the essence of his Guru that is God (Hari Aum Tat Sat) in his soul.

Invoking trinity guru Shiva in threesome cosmic powers (of creation, preservation and transformation) and threesome energies (of inspiration, courage and strength, and wholesome charisma), the transformed spirit of life takes a bow to the glorious most magnificent energy of the sunrise to welcome the awakening delight of Agnee the illuminating light of the Sun and opens the doors of its mind to let the 'insight' in. Total sacred transformation entails therefore that we look beyond the wholesome orbit of life into the eternity. Total sacred transformation entails total awakening with the magnificent nature, the world within us, the world outside us and the world in between. Total sacred transformation is a progressive karmic evolution in our absolute life. In Sanskrit 'divya-drashtee' means pure sacred vision. Sacred vision is pure beauty.

Pure beauty is sacredness of pure love that manifests only in quintessence - The kind of love that only begets endless love and endless compassion with fathomless faith and great aspiration. Love transforms us into our true nature. Love unites us with nature as rivers unite with the divine ocean.

Total sacred transformation is a sacred journey of profound sacrifice within us in silence of sacred love and profound reverence of profound wisdom of the soul.

In Vedas, the Fiery Agnee in the Sun, the calming Waters of the 'Apah' (seven oceans), the atmospheric Orb 'Tatva', the motion of the wind 'Vayau', the vast fathomless sky 'Attall-Pattal', the vacuum of pranna or life, and the earthly germination of fertility, is controlled and transformed by the cosmic guru Shiva (the evolutionary). The cosmic power of ultimate moksha (ultimate liberation), that in Vedas who is the 'param tatva guru' trinity 'Shiva' never ceases to dance with nature in 'oneness' of 'natraj' (a 72,000 fiery step dance-nrityam), Dhyaan (silence) and profound reverence of the nature in poetry, music, philosophy, hymns, and mantras. The cosmic eternity and the entire nature never ceases to perpetually, rotate, revolve and charm its magnificent beauty because Shiva (the cosmic power) never ceases to caper in oneness with nature. Shiva is the ultimate guru (paramtatva guru) and Shiva is the ultimate trinity of Moksha (spiritual liberation). It is 'Shiva' that grants final beatitude to Soul. Shiva is the master of Yoga and Shiva is the master of all dances. Shiva is the master of all warriors and Shiva is the master of all Earth (humankind) and its celestial or the spiritual life.

Through Shiva's third eye or the cosmic eye, we see the entire gigantic eternity of the wholesome cosmos of the universal eternity.

The vast sky, the planets, the cosmic deities, the cosmic forces, and the cosmic energies form part of this wholesome cosmos. The seven earths, the seven oceans, the seven orbs, the seven celestial spiritual planes, and the seven-auricle orbits form part of the wholesome cosmos. The universal rotations and revolutions, the universal momentum of active planets, and the night sky form part of the wholesome cosmos. The 108 trillion stars form part of the wholesome cosmos. The unseen stars of destinies form part of the cosmos. The other para-psychological and metaphysical manifestations of the cosmic soul, all form part of the wholesome cosmos.

'Rudra' is the cosmic transformer, the cosmic force of evolution, and the cosmic force of change (in creation, preservation, and transformation). Glory is to Rudra and praise is afforded to Rudra. Rudra is the transforming force of eternity within us in our third eye situated between the two eyebrows and above the nose in the middle of our forehead.

'That is the wholesome eternity; this is the wholesome infinite nature. From the fullness of the wholesome eternity, comes the entire wholesome existence. When the fullness of existence is taken away from the fullness of eternity, only fullness remains. This is the eternal omnipotent power of one without a second.'(Brahmajnana –V. -110)

Understanding with deep compassionate love, makes us divine because we come to realise 'what we were' in our karmic actions and when we mould, evolve and transform, we extinguish our flux (continuous succession of changes and evolution).

Our deeper compassionate understanding of our karmic life is a transformation process of purification and detoxification of our mind, body, and consciousness. Total sacred transformation prepares us for a gigantic awakening experience of wholesome, of enlightenment.

When we come to understand that attachment or grasping or being too habituated to particular things and particular forms binds us into this world of desires, pleasures, and power.

Understanding with deep compassionate love negates or neuters our karmic magnetic fields of actions, reactions, deeds, and retributions. It brings us to confront the one single truth of life that is death. Looking at our death and intermediate state, we recognise and understand compassionately the distinctions between virtue and vice, self-less unconditional love and conditional love, unconditional super-consciousness and conditional consciousness. Our lifetime experiences are transformed and evolved. Our absolute life (the life of our spirit) evolves into a sacred journey of its own right. The profound wisdom that we inherit from the supreme 'insight' as an inspirational energy of divine bliss makes us transformed into human delight. The light of wisdom makes us delightful human beings, compassionate human fellows. We are caring, kind, considerate, loving, warm, unconditional, and aware.

We are transformed from the power conscious eagle into compassionate bird of joy 'Hamnssa' who is the free spirit of life. Seven streams of spiritual wisdom join to congregate poetry, philosophy, metaphysics, sound, mantra, mudra-dance, and delight of twilights.

This brings us to the point of spiritual awakening. A beautiful divine state of enlightenment, wherein light of joy and delight of truth manifests in word, work, speech, activity and life breathe. Only devotion of pure love manifests in the heart, and our living becomes a sacred pilgrimage of the soul. Awakening to the essence of our soul in Vedas is known as 'Atman Jagruttee' (which means opening to the cosmos and uniting with the cosmic forces). This merging or the marriage of communion between the individual soul finite and the cosmic soul infinite is known as 'ARDHENAREESHWARA MAITHUNA' (merging of 'force' and 'energy' into the power of the sun that manifests as delight in the Soul).

In Vedas, the progressive process of transformation brings the spirit of life to a point where it wants to rather than it has to merge in sheer delight. Delight of the insight now focuses on the core cosmic guru called 'param tatva guru' the enlightening power of the third eye that is a centre point between two eyebrows and the forehead. It entails understanding this essential nature itself in deep compassionate love and illuminating light of the Sun in Gayatree (the illuminating force).

From the planes of gross physical existence wherein the personality is engrossed in looms of desires, the personality gradually transforms in karma. To understand evolution, the personality becomes a talented artiste of the grand maestro God infinite. In deep loving compassion, the personality moulds into a beautiful talent of life, compassionate loving soul 'Hamnssa'.

The personality evolves firstly in knowing and understanding the material life and its values. The personality begins to learn in silence, the profound meaning of life. The personality opens to the 'insight'. The personality looks at the karmic plane of life and death. The personality transforms into the spirit of life in progressive karma. The spirit of life has transformed in long processes of profound learning and inner growth. The spirit of life has evolved, and is now awakening to the cosmic spirit of eternity.

The new dawn brings with it illumination, enlightenment, glory, and victory. To embrace this illumination in deep compassion, the spirit of life pledges allegiance to its 'insight'. Take the fresh breath of the new dawn to embrace the delight of twilights.

In reverence to nature, 'Hamnssa' recites poetry to the divine awakening:

Life oh life! Let it be a beautiful joy of sacredness to enjoy the running streams of rivers and the dwellings of the spinning mills.

Life oh life! Let it be a wonderful experience of the fresh dew captured on the morning rosebuds young within the nest a hearth for sacred fire the holy flame of the sun.

Life oh life! Let me become the strikingly beautiful scene of the rainbow or the thundercloud above the mountain.

Life oh life! Let me become the waterfall in the heart of a green gorge, and a vast prairie tinged with the orange hue sunset.

Ah life! Let me pause a while to worship the instant of the beautiful dusk that waves goodnight to the tired, worn out, energies of all this, that and the other on the busy streets of modern cities.

Life oh life! Let the spirit of life meet the morning sun, the new sweet earth, and the magnificent silence in aloneness to discover and to unveil the beauty of soul divine. Life oh life! Let the energies of the kundalini become the flash of the firefly in the night. Let the breath of the spirit of life become the shadow which runs across the grass and looses itself in the sunset.

Life oh life! The land I stand on is my very own body! It is the same matter within me. Hear me oh four quarters of the earthen clay a relative I am of the universal brotherhood spirit of human kind. Oh mother earth, grant me strength to understand all the sorrows of the existence that I may be like you in compassion and in love. Oh mother earth, with your powers only I can face the force of the wild winds.

Life oh life! Let our bare feet touch the consciousness of the mother earth and feel the sympathetic compassion of our ancestors as we walk across the green pastures. Let me understand the pain of another. Let me share.

Life oh life! Let healthy feet hear the very heart beat of the sacred mother earth. We are all flowers in the garden of the Great Spirit. We share common roots to the divine mother earth.

Life oh life! The garden is a beautiful manifestation of divine god because it is one voice yet different colours, different traditions, different cultures, different shapes, different names, and different minds. Oh divine spirit let there be peace and harmony in all. Oh divine spirit of karmic transformation, let there be spiritual awakening!

Life oh life! Let it be a flight of divinity. Let it be a moment of delight.

'Aum ekam Brahma Sat-chitt-ananda. Aum tat-twam-asi. Hamnssa Aum soham. Aum Atman Param-atman ekam jyott.'

'Aum' is the universal truth of one universal Brahma (universal cosmic spirit – purusha), that is the absolute infinite truth prevailing in the absolute sattvic state of divine truth, divine light and divine blissfulness. Aum is that divine cosmic self. Aum is the universal sound, light, and energy of that divine transcendental universal cosmic spirit that which is the manifestation of atma (human soul) itself.

The atma and the cosmic soul (param-atman or Jagada-atma) are therefore the same divine light of truth. The spirit of life offers obeisance to seven oceans, seven main rivers, seven worlds, seven spheres, and seven spectrum of Agnee (the divine fire).

In the light of 'Agnee' the sacred earthly fire of sacrifice, the spirit of life welcomes the divine insight (divya-drashtee).

The light of Agnee is invoked, to awaken soul compassion in delight, and to create a fathomless flame of fathomless hope, fathomless faith, fathomless love, and fathomless delight.

The fiery spirit of the Sun is invoked, the vigour of the energy of the Sun is invoked, the valiant valour of the Sun is invoked, the fury of the fire of the sun is invoke, the conquering light of the Sun is invoked, to move onwards towards freedom, awakening, and unveiling the truth.

The rainbows beautiful arch, the waterfalls, the running rivers, the grand ocean, the vast prairie, and teeming sky tinge sacredly with the glory of the sunsets and the sunrises.

In delight the wise, 'Jnani' (knower of truth and preceptor of true wisdom); gallantly opens the gates of its third eye, namely the cosmic eye, to let it the profoundest 'delight' enter the pure consciousness. 'Jnani' says:

"Life oh life! Let it be a flight of awakening to the radiance of agnee (the sacred illumination of sun). Life oh life! Let it be time to commemorate almost in pulsation of the three states of being. Life oh life! Let it be moment of revelation of the divine truth. Life oh life! Let the dawn and the dusk be the moments of twilight of the divine vision and let me glimpse into the eternity whilst I am in the state of transcendental delight. Life oh life! Let the radiance, which has become the glorious awareness of the beauty of my soul be the light of my spiritual delight. Life oh life! Let me become the light of delight of the truth itself and let me triumph over all that is impermanence and false."

9. AWAKENING TO OUR SOUL DIVINE ⤻

Self-realisation is a beautiful experience of awakening to the divine cosmic nature of our infinite soul. The pilgrimage is unfolding in time.

"Sun-ward". Let the spirit of life sing the morning glory of the sunrise.

"Oh glorious sunrise, let the spirit of my life awaken to the magnificent unimposing orange hue light of your Agnee (fire in Sun). Sun oh Sun! Let your light enlighten my soul as it enlightens the entire sky in grand illumination. Sun oh Sun! Let your light be my first delight! Sun oh glorious Sun, your duty is extra ordinary and your duty is God ordained! Sun oh glorious sun let your illumination, a self-less expression of delight; bring transcendental serenity, hope, and fresh energy. Let the spirit of my life follow your glory and let its shadows fall behind. Let it reach out for the nectar of truth from the vessel of Soma (vessel of eternity). Oh Sun the universal provider of light and illuminator of all ignorance and darkness, enlighten the spirit of my life."

"That thou art, O almighty supreme God. That eternity is absolute truth infinite. That infinity is blissful. That bliss is sublimely true. That divinity is beyond the wholesome sky and beyond the infinity. That same truth is within me. That is the same joy, without which all this is not real. That is the wholesome harmony of my soul, that which is in the magnificent nature, and the eternity. That thou art, O almighty supreme God."

The entire galaxy, the wonderful sky full of glittering stars, the momentum of planetary motions, the intricate earth the wholesome nature moves in an almost 'non-stop' phenomenon. Our Earthly nature is in such magnified order, that beauty manifests even in the tiniest of the natures' substance. Such is the charisma of God (whatever you perceive it to be). Nature and spirit are identical in "form". This is the basis to spiritual awakening. What is in the nature is within our human body and vice versa.

Spiritual awakening implies culture and wisdom of the very human nature. Spiritual awakening entails cultivating the intricate and the most beautiful constituents of nature, compassion, nourishing the well being of our soul and humanity. This is 'altruism'. This is pure happiness. This is your human duty towards humanity and God (whatever you may perceive it to be). Like the duty of the galaxy is to preserve order and nature. Like the duty of water is to quench the thirst. Like the duty of the Sun is to provide light and chemical metamorphosis of existence. Like the duty of the parents is to nurture & nourish their infants and children. Like the duty of the children is to preserve their parents with utmost sincerity. Like the duty of the doctor is to save life and bring good health. Like the duty of the governor, administrator, and management is to serve, protect, guide, direct, and maintain the welfare of the people serving the common objective – "health, wealth, and happiness". Like, the duty of a Guru is to be selfless and impartial in giving wisdom; Like, the duty of a soul/ Jiva (astral soul 'Hamnssa') is to be worthy of the human existence and to be responsible in the satt-karma – righteousness, virtue, and spiritual awakening.[34]

---

[34] May the fire that is the sun illuminate us in our intellect. May the waters that gleam and germinate bless us with happiness and joy. May the wind that controls the entire spectrum of nature bring renewal and transformation. May the earth that is the embryo of fertilisation and Karma bring to us proliferation and sattvic food (pure food). May the wholesome galaxy of the magnificent nature, comprising Soma, Indra, Varuna, Vanaspattaye, Vishwadeva, Kuberaye, Issanaye, Rudra, Agneeye, Yamaye, Nirrittaye, Vayauvey, atal-patal, prithevee, ranta, rapa, roshadhye, Surya, Chandra, Mangla, Budha, Brahapattaye, Shukra, Shanni, Rahu, Ketu, Devo, Devi, all that and more, Vishwadeva. Mahakala rest in peace. [THE ELEMENTS OF NATURE PER VEDAS]. THE MAGNIFICENT NATURE is the representation of the sargoon swaroop of ETERNITY itself and this sargoon swaroop of eternity reposes on AUM. AUM is Brahma and Aum is the first born word. Aum is a sacred sound, a meaningful vibration of nature, a cry of the first born child, a hymn of God, a word of truth, a symbol of ETERNITY and a mantra that unites the individual soul with the magnificent eternity. The divine power who has bound this girdle around us, who tied us together and yoked us in one, the divine power under whose direction we progress, may this ultimate divine power that reposes with shaktee Gayatree lead us onto the other shore and free us from our bondage's and attachments and Karmas. Oh daughter of faith, born of fervour, Oh sister of all sages who moulds the world as an elapsing universe grant us GIRDLE powers of insight and wisdom, grant us ardour and vigour. [av.vi.133.1.460/awakening and coming of age]

A Vedic seer, with profound insight, affords the foremost praise to divine Mother Nature.

"O divine 'Mother Nature', you are always there for me, no matter what."

"May the wind blow swiftly, gently with freshness of the morning dew. May the sun, set and rise in utmost compelling benign serenity. May the clouds build a celestial of motion with the mountain peak. May the mountains and valleys echo sounds of eternity with the wind. May the rivers flow sweetness, may the herbs bring sweetness. May the oceans make the sounds of whales in their calm waters. May the harmony be for the altruism that manifests in the glory of my heart."

When the personality (alias the lingham purush) and the eternal energy alias (Shaktee in the form of Sri Gayatree) unite in oneness in utmost purest sensation, then there is the fusion of a true word in delight, the first born form of cosmic marriage. Then the truth emits light and delight emanates from the spoken word. The fire of the sun (as agnee) becomes the illuminator of the mind, the harmony of the waters (as apah) brings serenity and peace, the force of the wind (Vayu) brings transformation, the space and the galaxy (akash patal) brings about infinite wisdom and the earth (prithvee) opens its orbits to our insight so that we can with our third eye see that which is this truth divine bliss (Aum Tatvam Asi Swaha Aum Tat Sat Hari Aum Tat Sat swadha swaha). The awakening to nature takes the form of rising to the crown of the purest plane, the brahma-loka. Therefore, we arise from the human reality, the manushya-lokka into the divine eternity, sattvic lokka.

Divine marriage is cosmic union involving the entire universe to the entire outside world. It is a special oneness. Like the oneness of he and she. Like the oneness of a man and woman. Man is a personality uniquely embodied with constitutive relationship. The constitutive collaboration is firstly between the eternity and the soul, secondly between the spirit and the cosmos, thirdly between the Sun and the soul, fourthly between one soul and another soul, and fifthly between the ancestral and the living.

This relativity of connection in compassion exists between not only Man as a personality and God as an eternity, but also between mankind as person and his fellow men as other persons. [35]

According to the Vedas, we are a manifestation of the very nature prevailing around us. We are the human form that is the cosmic form. The metaphysical world is our soul. Therefore, the profound words in the Vedas are awakening the magnificent nature with their deep philosophical altruism, poetic rhythm, sound and musical rites and rituals.

Per Vedas, we as humankind ought to know the earth first; its reality and its ways i.e., the human works that sustain us. Labour is but a means of survival and to labour is to earn our daily bread that is pure (sattvic). Only when we have harvested the fruits of our humankind can we embark upon the pilgrimage of the soul. This is exemplified in the case of Buddha who was born a prince Sidhartta, got married and had a child called Rahul. He finally bid farewell at the age of 33, to the world of humankind and embarked onto the pilgrimage of his soul. It is imperative, that the shelter we sleep under is made of multifarious blessings of purity, joy and utmost compassion.

In Kalyug (age of falsehood), it is not practically feasible and possible to embark upon pilgrimages in forests blindly. Therefore, pilgrimage of the soul can take place whilst living in the very society and fulfilling everyday duty and Karmas but with an indifference of attitude to all that is not permanent. The discipline, which we need, is the same as Buddha. What is pertinently significant is that we grow, we mould, and we evolve gracefully but truthfully and faithfully in all earnest way. What is significant is that we change our habitual lifestyle and practice altruism almost like making a sacred word more profoundly sacred by practice. When our shelter that is our home is pure (sattvic), compassionate and full of devotional worship (Bhaktee) it brings peace and harmony to our circulating blood, our immediate environment and our immediate contacts.

---

[35] Thus, the seers of Vedas desiring with excellence and meditating with undivided devotion to the seven heavens embarked upon fervour and consecration. Thence was born energy, force, and kingship. Let the Gods bestow them upon this humankind. Togetherness is divine. The earth is the sacred grain and the sacred loaf that sustains us daily. The earth is divinely maternal. It never ceases to give. So, shall we be patient and learn from our struggles to honour this earth.

Therefore, our home is a place where our mind and body repose. It is a home of the sacred "us" (Brahma purush). This earth is our 'clothing home' and the other world is the eternity or the vastness of the spiritual home. This is natural truth, it is simple, it is magnificent, it is eternal truth, and it is the supreme truth. One needs to fully understand the only beautiful truth, with one's divine insight. Profound silence with profound insight opens the gates to the profound sacred truth. The eternal truth that manifests in one's soul is the same truth that manifests in the divine magnificent nature, in calm waters and still mountains. We have what we seek within our soul. To realise it we need to be calm and persevering. We need to open to natures galore.

Our dwelling (home) is the umbrella provided by God. Our work (purest forms of activities) is our vital force of circulation force for the blood. Our purest devotion and profound mantra-meditation render bliss from the cooling waters of the rivers and the oceans. Weather and conditions of our material life are identical. They are both unpredictable. We may claim, as much as we want to and we may possess and be obsessed, with all that is materially known yet impermanent. Eventually, the 'umbrella' is needed to shield us from adverse conditions of life just like the sharp heat of the sun and the throbbing tears of the rain. Our 'umbrella' is our body and our home in which we reside. Hence, our body and our home must both be equally pure and profound. Otherwise, we would not endure in adverse conditions of life. We purify our circulating blood with our mantra jaap and we purify our excretory system with our mantra jaap. Purification and detoxification to the human body is very crucial.

Our profound silence brings to us, the illuminating light force of the divine Brahma. Agnee (the sacred fire) of Sun unite us in oneness with the divine flame as eternity. This is simple and appealing co-relationship of our material nature to the cosmic nature. We are what our home is made up of and our home is what we think and speak. Our home is a sacred most place for it is a shelter for our body and mind and the astral body. Our attachment should not be on the bricks but in the love and compassion of the surrounding air and atmosphere.

Our attachment should be in the beauty of nature and the beauty of the soul. Vibrations are created by us as we speak. Therefore, be careful when speaking. Every written or spoken word carry with it energy and vibrations.

The eternal most wonderful spirit of life capers to the rhythm of compassion and love, and knows no maestro so grand to reach the infinite eternal truth, in the pathless infinity of the eternity except the soul divine. The soul is the very seat of the grand maestro and it is filled with delight.

'Delight' is the wholesome sacred effulgence of the light of Sun (Agnee) that manifests in composite sound of seven notes, composite vision of rainbow, and a composite syllable 'Aum'.

The divine flame of fire Agnee and its effulgent energy Gayatree:

"Aum eternity divine bliss, Aum eternity peaceful, make me sacred"

O divine light of eternity, lead me kindly, lead me gently, lead me in silence. O divine light, illuminate me wholesome, take me from the wonderland of this earth (Maya – unreal) in whose known reality manifests my sorrows, to the endless joy of the eternal world.

O divine light, enlighten me with the love of your divinity and the flame of your eternal truth, deliver me from my sinful body with your merciful affection and embrace my imperfections with your compassion.

O divine light let 'Aauummm' echo in the valleys, in the rivers, in the seas, in the mountains, in the air, in the forests, in the empty space, and deep within me.

O divine light I invoke thee with my sacred word come and enlighten me with your sacred light.

O divine light I invoke thee with my sacred word "Aum". Let there be peace all over the world, all over the galaxy, all over the celestial planes and deep within me.

O divine 'Aum', we meditate in silence, Aum we pray in silence, upon the glorious splendour of the vivified divine bliss. May thou that illuminates all, illuminate our mind, intellect, and the consciousness. O divine light, may you delight in the sacred word 'Aum', peace to thine glory.

The first mantra in Vedas invokes the Agnee or the sacred fire of the sun:

I magnify thee O God of the divine fire, the priest, minister of the sacred sacrifice, the offerer of oblation, supreme giver of treasure.

"Aum agneeyeem ile' puroheetam yajnasya devam rrttvijam hotaram ratnadhatamam Aum."

Translation: Sacredness is purity. Sacred fire is Agnee the divine light of delight. In sacredness of Agnee, repose all the energies and all the forces of the seven worlds. In the sacredness of fire that comes out as the very first fiery energy of God, we meditate in profoundness to the rest of the cosmic forces. Namely: Indra, Varuna, Visnuva, Yamma, Issanaya, Vasus, Rudra, Marutas, and Pusanas who reside within us in different spiritual chakras or spiritual planes. To invoke peace to the three worlds is a constancy of Vedas.

Gayatree is the mother of Vedic mantras and Gayatree is the illuminating energy of Agnee. Gayatree is a she in that there is threefold energies comprising, the spark, the flame, and the smoke that transcends in the universal cosmos. She is the 'savitur varenyam bhargo devasya dhimahi dhiyo yo naha-prachodayat'. She dwells in all spheres namely, Bhur (the earth), bhurvah (the worlds of various becoming between the earth and the eternity), svahr (the world of light of three heavens) and tat (the world of truth). Many tantric practices have taken the nectar of this core energy into the spiritual practices of the seven chakras and have done so either with have the usage of the sacred words or have the mantra itself.

It is a dismal decay of the energy of the word when word can no longer conform to its original connotation. Hence, recital of AUM with the intent of invoking our inner flame of profoundness and the outer world of existence with illumination is sufficient provided that aum becomes the spark, the flame and the smoke of sacredness from which emanates profound vibrations of the sacred sound of gods. When 'mind' and 'word' merge in the oneness of a sacred sound, not only is the word a sacred meaning of God but the power to transcend the mental plane. Music is the mother tongue of humanity and compassion blossoms in music. God is the supreme musician and God is the grandest maestro.

Agnee resides in the crown chakra implying purest state or the AUM. Aum is the ultimate Brahman and Aum is the ultimate truth that is the AGNEE in the crown chakra. To awaken this chakra, one has to become sattvic or pure in activity, and sattvic or pure in practice of religion and life. Invoking the sacred fire, we invoke our inner most flame of spiritual awakening. [36]

Every cosmic force is energy, divinely infinite, within the orbit of our own mind, body, astral bodies (the spirit), and the soul. It is scientifically what we consider the magnetic field surrounding the spiritual energy of every vital chakra within the human body. To awaken our chakras and to awaken our mind, body and soul to the nature entails that we put ourselves in the wholesome perspective of the earth as the physical plane of existence, the celestial as the seven divine spiritual spheres, and the spiritual plane.

The existence of Godhead manifests within us on seven principles, which are as follows: PURE EXISTENCE [SAT]; PURE CONSCIOUSNESS [CHIT]; PURE BLISS [ANANDA]; KNOWLEDGE AND WISDOM [JNAN]; MIND & INTELLECT [SVAHR]; LIFE & NERVES [PRANNA & BHUVAR]; MATTER [BHUR]

---

[36] Agnee is the only cosmic power that is sublimely pure in existence because it is expressed in seven energies namely 'kali' (or the divine force of the cosmic eternity without which the purity of the eternity could be polluted), 'karali' (the terrible), 'Manojava' (thought swift), 'Sulohita' (blood red), 'Sudhumravarna' (smoke hued), 'Sphulingini' (scattering sparks), 'Visvarucci' (the all beautiful). [Page 69 of Sri Chinmoy's book 'Three branches of India's life tree Vedas-Upanishads-Bhagavad Gita). According to the Vedas, Kali, which appears fiery, is a fire to destroy the evil and fight the warfare of the Kalyug. Kali in reality is golden beautiful as the colour of the sun itself. Kali fights against the hostile forces but she is the all-pervading compassion of nature whom many persons misunderstand in phenomenon. Her dynamic qualities are not aggressive; they are assuredly re-affirming the spirit of life. Kali loves perfection and Kali is a perfect beauty of the cosmic universe unparalleled. Kali is also our inner beauty, which elevates our soul into the higher consciousness – the super consciousness. Aum khama brahmah Aum yo ahamasi aham premmam aum satyam evam mama jyotihm aum shanti shanti shanty. In all thine existence, oh divine creator may thou bestow upon us love and compassion, integrity and honesty, and, light of the divine Sun God Suryah into the soul. May we rise above the dreary mundane earthly existence into divinity. The Vedic evolution does not happen in isolation or in solitude. The spiral karmic dance congregates all-together, all the cosmic deities, the earth, the planets, the stars, the sky, the cosmic soul, and the spiritual world to work onwards towards freedom beyond fears.

The vital force, known as 'ayasya angirasa' is the eternal force of the cosmic entity that essentially implies the limbs of the divine cosmos. The vital force made speech immortal. From speech, the agnee (sacred fire) became thus immortal. The vital force made breath eternal, air thus became immortal. Air thus blew beyond death. The vital force carried the eyes beyond death and made the Sun immortal light. The vital force carried the ears beyond mortality and made sound immortal, in currents of winds, storms, and energies of directions. The vital force then carried the mind beyond death and made the moon immortal. The vital force then created the life out of light. The vital force then created the points in the galaxy known as the EAST, WEST, NORTH, SOUTH, NORTH EAST, SOUTH EAST, SOUTH WEST, NORTH WEST. The vital force then created from the congruence of the Sun and the Moon, the galaxy comprising the SEVEN planets namely MARS, MERCURY, JUPITER, VENUS, SATURN, RAHU and KETU. The vital force then created the ministerial orbits comprising DEITI-Gods.

The chief deities are namely, SOMA (the vessel of nectar in the north), YAMMA (the god of death in the south), VARUNA (the god of prosperity and proliferation in the west), INDRA (the lord of trinity and Brahma infinite truth), VAYAU (the god of winds in the north west), RUDRA (God of devotion and liberation in the north east), NIRRITTI (God of destruction in the south west), leaving AGNEE (fire) in the south east. KUBERA (God of wealth) was created by the vital force as the left arm of the TRINITY GOD, whilst ISSANAYA (God of wisdom) was created as the right arm of the TRINITY GOD. The trinity god was thus created as BRAHMA, VISHNU, AND MAHESH. Brahma-Sat sitting in the crown, Brahma-purush sitting in the naval, Vishnu residing in the left limb, and Shiva residing on the right limb each with its power of pure bliss, wealth and wisdom respectively. Sheesh Naag (five faced cosmic cobra) was created to uphold PRITHEVEE-EARTH (as the daughter of the vital force and God eternity).

Life was thus breath unto the earth and cosmological forces danced in seventy two million rhythms to generate vital life (pranna) in three distinct spheres namely the EARTH comprising the BHUR, THE CELESTIAL comprising the BHURVAH SWAHR AND THE HEAVEN comprising AUM TAT SAT. *'Aum Tat Sat Swaha. Hari Aum Tat Sat Swaha'*. This is mantra of the cosmic system. It is the accord of highest cosmic point beyond which only Aum murmurs in silence and beyond which there is only emptiness.

Each plane is represented by chakras in our body. Each chakra is surrounded by an 'aura'. Each aura has an 'orb'. The seven chakras (spiritual points corresponding to the eternal universe) ruling in our body are as follows:

THE CROWN chakra, which represents the pure existence or the divine, bliss Brahman God 'AUM TAT SAT'. It is similar to the soma point of cosmos.

THE COSMIC EYE OR THE THIRD EYE chakra located above the eyes and in the centre of the forehead is the sixth chakra associated with pure consciousness. This is the insight point or the divine vision point.

THE THROAT chakra is the fifth chakra and it is associated with the pure bliss. This is the emotional region of poetry, wisdom, expression, and life.

THE HEART chakra is the fourth chakra and is associated with the wisdom and knowledge as combination of an artist and a scientist.

THE SOLAR PLEXUS chakra is the third chakra governs the stomach and intestine. The third chakra is associated with the mind and the intellect of the cosmos.

THE SACRAL chakra is the second chakra governing the spleen, the kidneys, and the sex organs. The second chakra is associated with the life and nerves of the cosmos.

THE MULADHARA –ROOT chakra is the first chakra at the base of the spine in coccyx. The first chakra is associated with the matter of the cosmos.

Per Vedas, there are seven earth's (seven major continents), seven great mountains, seven great rivers, seven great oceans, seven spiritual planes and seven material planes, seven great seers and sages, seven colours of the rainbow, seven chakras (spiritual energies) embodied in a humankind, seven planets apart from the moon and the sun, seven great planes, seven great valleys, seven great musical notes in one music scale, and seven atmospheric layers.

See annex one and two.

The entire cosmic nature is divided into groups of seven spiritual spheres and seven spiritual orbits. Each 'energy' contains seven auras, seven magnetic fields, seven atoms, seven protons, and seven electrons. Every karmic cycle therefore, has phases of seven unit of time. Per Vedas, the evolution of absolute human life, if transcendentally progressive, is seven times, seven karmic cycles, seven stages, and seven life times. A human life is considered sacred most life bearing seven sacred knots - GROSS PHYSICAL, PHYSICAL, EMOTIONAL, CONSCIOUSNESS, CAUSAL, SUBTLE, AND SUPER CONSCIOUSNESS. Our metamorphosis is almost exactly similar to the cosmic nature.

We move to and from the gross physical knot of pleasures, indulgences, sensuality, taste, escapism, etc. The gross physical knot keeps us attached and bonded with all that is materially glittering and this gross physical knot pulls the physical knot comprising our desires and ambitions into the illusions of the earth. The emotional knot is like a border and it is the ego. Most of the times, the ego tries to reason and the ego tries to find comfort in the mind and body. The consciousness is the mind that is attached to the ego. CAUSAL, SUBTLE and SUPER CONSCIOUSNESS are three divine knots of nature embodied in human kind and when the light of spiritual awakening delight enters the causal and passes into the subtle, one becomes blissfully happy – SAT CHIT ANAND. This happiness is not a conditional happiness. It is eternal happiness – PARAM ANAND. When the spirit has progressively evolved into the seventh knot, it realises the soul with eternal truth – AUM TAT SAT.

I consider that there are seven progressive stages to this purest form of bliss namely, PLAY & ENJOY, READ & EXPAND, GET TO KNOW LIFE, experience 'SORROW', UNDERSTAND 'SORROW', PROFOUND WISDOM, PROFOUND SILENCE and bliss. One cannot know life unless one has tasted and lived it. Therefore, life is imperfect in as much as the experience it renders. We only strive to accomplish that truth with our limitations and shortfalls. Hence, we can never be masters in absoluteness but mere seers. The sound of music echoes in different wavelengths but eventually the seven musical knots of the sound merge with in one sound – 'aum', 'am', or 'mm'.

The number seven represents the planet Jupiter (Jupiter is regarded as the Guruvey Brahaspattey). 'Jupiter' or Brahaspattey in Sanskrit is the lord of the nine planets[37]

Thursday is Guru Brahaspattey day and Thursday in Vedangas is auspicious for invoking the sacred energy of the Gayatree. Thursday is also the dawn for sacred sacrifice. Thursday is auspicious day for healing the energies of the cosmic forces within our human entity. Jupiter is associated with yellow gemstone, either the yellow sapphire, topaz, or amber. Through the cosmic powers of Jupiter, Lord Vishnu was incarnated, as a dwarf. Brahaspattey is regarded as a pure sattvic Brahman. He is identified with the lord of all deities, 'GANESH', in the form of wisdom and knowledge and with 'ANGIRAS', the priest of all deities and lords of sacrifice in the form of germination, light delight and science of manifestation. Brahaspatteyeh controls and governs all the nine planets including the Sun and Moon. Jupiter is known as the Guru of Galaxy, the matter, and the celestial planes. Brahaspattey is known by the cosmic intelligence as 'GURU BRAHASPATTEY'. He is priestly, co-operative, inspiring, and a self-less teacher, illuminating, radiant. His vehicle is AN ELEPHANT who is a symbol of profound wisdom, and large store of knowledge. In one hand, he holds a scroll of sacred knowledge. On the other hand, he holds the disc of Vishnu to cut through, the illusions of the world, the universe, and the celestial worlds. Through his conch mantra sounds vibrate the galaxy and through his serene reverence beatitude of blessings are showered unto beings, deities and gods of the galaxy. Guru Brahaspatteyeh maintains harmony and brings peace. Jupiter (Brahaspatteyeh), is the cosmic guru of Agnee (Sun). Through his guidance and inspiration, the entire cosmos became immortal and transcendentally infinite.

THE SUN is the abode of Brahma prajapattee (the omnipotent god of trinity and one absolute truth eternity).

---

[37] Source: Healing with the power of gemstones by Harish Johari; RigVed: Brahaspatteyeh (Jupiter) is born in the sky with seven faces and seven rays. No rites or ritual ceremony or mantra is complete without invoking Brahaspatteyeh. Brahaspattey per Upanishads is known as a guru because he is the intellect and speech of the Viraat Purusha (the cosmic BODY). Per ancient Sanskrit anthologies, Brahaspattey worshipped Shiva for one thousand years, and was thence, granted the boon of the Prime Minister status or the Guru status. In the Vishnu puranas, he is known as Brahma. Sometimes he is identified with Ganapatti (Ganesh), the lord of gana (wise).

Prajapattee the omnipotent power operates with the powers of Vishnu (the revolving, the rotating and the omnipotent God also known as 'Hari Aum Tat Sat' in Sanskrit), Rudra (the trident power) Indra (the master of the universe and the spirit of light that transforms into delight). These purest eternal cosmic forces behold the purest nectar of truth Soma (the vessel of nectar of ETERNITY also known as Hari-Amrutt in Sanskrit). There are seven visible rays of the sun (Kiranas in Sanskrit) and seven colours of orbit surrounding the yellow hue liquid of the sun. Sun is also known as Suryanarayan in Sanskrit. There are seven she energies of the sun, namely Savitri (the rising illuminator), Samndhya (the dawn), Chaayya (the shadow), Kriya (the rite and the ritual), Sadhana (the devotional peacemaker), Kuntee (the energy of the field), and Sat'ti-Randal (truth in the sacrifice). The cosmological number attributable to Sun are "1" & "9". Whilst number nine also represents fiery energy, it is the penultimate to the final beatitude of numerology. One implies final beatitude of truth, whilst nine implies profound wisdom. Sunday is representative of SUN. 'Surya' (Sun), is the master of the supreme truth (Brahma-Sat). Truth of being, truth of knowledge, truth of process, truth of activity, truth of movement, truth of revolution and rotation, truth of function, truth of eternity. Sun is the manifestation and the illuminator of all things.

'Indra' (the puissant) is the illuminator of the cosmic deities and cosmic forces because Indra conquered the divine absolute infinite truth from 'Prajappati' (God eternal supreme). Indra represents pure profound wisdom of the soul as a power of pure existence and pure self-manifestation of the mind. Indra made the mind of the cosmos (svahr) pure. 'Indra' is the right hand of the Omnipotent God, and Indra is the first wise immortal in the cosmos that became a transcendental illuminator of all other cosmic forces. Through 'Indra', God transcended delight on seven spheres including the earth, the ocean, the rivers, the pastures, the germination, and the fertility.

Sunrises and sunsets bring extra ordinary manifestations that release SHAKTEE or energy to the highest beatitude - TRUTH. The highest beatitude is known as PURE NECTAR OF ETERNITY or Soma – the vessel of divine nectar. The entire galaxy and the seven worlds grow around this vessel in multiplicity; rivers and oceans thrive on their existence giving sacred calamity to the earth (the human body). The seat of 'Soma' is NORTH most.

If the truth of lord Sun (Suryanarayan) is to be established in our mortal nature, 'Varuna' (the all illuminuous power of love and comprehension leading and forming infinite compassion of harmony and peace in all our thoughts, acts, impulses, kriyas, sacrifices, rites and rituals) is invoked. Varuna is the divine compassionate deity that joins the mortal to the eternity with its everlasting infinite love of vast purity and vast clarity. 'Mitra' is the force of immortal puissance of clarity between the sacred worship and the compassionate love. Through 'Varuna', our minds become happy, blissful, and divine. Through 'Varuna' we dispel the ignorance of 'evil' and the veil of 'all sufferings'. Varuna is cosmic compassion. The seat of 'Varuna' is west.

'Rudra' worships sacrifices and invokes the fiery energy of the cosmos through its spiritual might and spiritual aspiration. Rudra is the fiery power, the all merciful power that presides over the struggle of life creation upwards to the final beatitude of Soma, smiting all the opposition scourging all the errors and resistance's, healing all the wounds of suffering, stopping all the illusions and disillusions of the mind. The seat of 'Rudra' is north-east.

'Vayu' or 'Pavvan', the master of life or the 'wind-force' links the celestial world of cosmic forces, the earth, the planets, the stars, the Sun, the Moon, the threefold trinity of godhead, the mind, the super mind and the spirit of life. This linkage is through 'AIR' (in between the earth and sky), 'MIDAIR' (in between the celestial world and the trinity of Godhead, and 'VITAL FORCE' (as the life breath, breath, wind, orbital gas and ozone layers).

'Vayu' the master of life, with 'pranna' (life breath), over rules 'Parjanya' (the giver of rains and thunderstorms), 'Dadhikravan' (the divine war horse of Agnee), 'Dragon' (the mystic force), and 'Trita-Aptyya' (the consummation force of sat chit ananda to and from Hari Aum Tat Sat in SOMA-the vessel of true nectar). The seat of 'Vayu' is north-west.[38]

---

[38] According to ancient eastern anthologies of the Vedanta, 'Hanuman' is the son of Pavvan and Hanuman has been accorded nine nidhis (nine immortal boons) to be the only celestial deity to be re-incarnated on earth as an immortal. It is believed that Hanuman is eternal being on earth as a servant of Godhead and as a Guru to the true seeker of immortality. Ether is said to the highest form of manifestation, and it is the subtle form of wind. Beyond ether there is vacuum (shunya).

'Nirrittee' the all-destructive force of matter and form in the vast reincarnation cycles of karma. 'Nirrittee' brings destruction to 'KAAL' cosmic time, to convert it into 'akaal' the karmic cycles of birth and death. 'Nirrittee' is seated in the south-west of cosmos.

'Yamma' (the lord of death) conquered mortality through 'Atma gnaana' (profound wisdom of the soul), and sought the boon of immortality to remain the god of all deaths. 'Yamma' is seated in the south of the cosmos.

'Kuber' (the ploriferator, the multiplier and the prosperous giver of wealth & health), 'Issannayya' (knowledge of the Vedas in action), 'Vasus' (inhibitor) and 'Pusan' (dedication of labour), all surrounded the trinity of godhead BRAHMA-VISHNU-SHIVA in one triangle in the middle and SHAKTEE in another triangle crossing the trinity of godhead to form a SACRED STAR OF MAHA-MRUTYUNJAYA (immortality bliss).

Shiva the cosmic guru was afforded the centre of the 'patal' or the eyes of the cosmos. 'Shiva' is the giver of Moksha and 'Shiva' is the all-merciful release of mortal life. Per Vedas, Sun became the divine light in the third eye of Shiva (the pure cosmic guru), and from this enlightenment, the cosmic guru performed seventy two thousand step 'natraj' (cosmic dance) on the 64 rhythms of 'HARI AUM TAT SAT'. During this manifestation, the entire cosmos evolved around the shaktee (energy) of most harmonious orbits and there was caper in the rivers, oceans, mountains, forests, valleys, and the mother earth shed tears of eternal joy.

Per Vedas, Sun is where Agnee begins its ENERGY (as number one) and Sun is where AGNEE resides as the 'orange yellow hue' liquid (number nine). Therefore, the Sun is regarded as the eternal flame of God, the super conscious divinity without which there would be total darkness and without which the 'Brahma-Sat' in the crown chakra cannot be illuminated.

When Agnee took the beautiful form as 'MAA' or she energy, no words could possibly describe the glamour. Her beauty was beyond words. She arose from sheer radiance and sheer dynamism of sheer blissful vibrations of the Gayatree mantra. She embodied 64 million forces of illumination in her eyes. The entire cosmos bowed to her beauty; a beauty, pure and magnificently glowing. A beauty, that is unparalleled by none other.

Maa is a beauty that is the final point upon which Shiva the cosmic guru reposed, whilst the new moon in its second day up-held this magnificent point of beauty as an eternal dot. Shiva and Shaktee thus became one known as 'ARDHANAREESHWAR', on the full moon. True profound wisdom was revealed from this to the cosmic deities and cosmic forces. Yoga and the yogic science illumined. God as the illumined 'yogiswara purush' (the yogic master) invoked the release of the potent power hidden in each manushya purush (human being), as the power of 'kundalini' (the chakras) to merge in oneness with the cosmos through 'DHYANNA-SADHANA' (profound silence) and 'GNAANN-SADHANA' (profound wisdom).

The cosmic eternal plane further comprises the planets.

The Moon in Vedanta is actually a she, implying it is a pure ENERGY of the mantra (sacred word), tantra (sacred rite), and yantra (Sacred ritual). Moon comprises twofold cycles the bright cycle and the dark cycle. Each cycle comprises fifteen days. Shiva (the guru trinity) and Shaktee (energy of agnee) unite in oneness under the full moon whilst Shiva (the guru trinity) invokes 'Soma' the ultimate truth infinite on the amavasya (or the darkest day of the waning cycle of the moon). Moon has been attributed the number "2" implying, SHIVA-SHAKTEE, TWO CYCLES, TWO eyes of love, two cycles the bright blossoming cycle and the dark waning cycle, two faces, two lights namely reflection and refraction. Moon is the only planet that is a she planet or a phenomenon of female.

Mars is a planet of courage and fiery. Mars is also the patronage of deities like Hanuman, Ganesh, and Goddess Shaktee. Mars is represented by number three and Tuesday is the day of the week related to Mars. Mars is related to brevity, courage, and all.

Mercury is the planet of communications and knowledge. Mercury is represented by the number five and Wednesday is the day of the week related to Mercury. It is also the patronage of prophets and sages. Mercury is related to the physical and spiritual mind.

Venus is the planet of beauty, glamour, and wealth. Venus is represented by the number six and is the patronage for goddess of wealth 'Laxshmee'. Friday is related to Venus. Whilst the energies and effulgence of Venus emanate from the 'she' energies of the cosmic goddess, the multiferous constitution is that of the 'shukra' (equal to semen).

Jupiter is the planet of wisdom and the kinsman amongst planets. It is represented by number seven and Gayatree is the patronage for Jupiter.

The number Eight follows seven. Eight is regarded as the number of infinity and knowledge. Eight is also the number for the planet Saturn. Saturn is a task maker and Saturn is the son of Sun and 'Chaayya' one of the seven energies of Sun. Saturday is related to Saturn. Saturn is connected to spiritual learning and spiritual awakening.

Number four in Vedas is related to RAHU (the dragonhead) and KETU (the dragon tail). Four is always split into 2+2, east and west, north and south, positive and negative, sorrow and pleasure, he and she, and so on. Four is the number of division between the 'dasayus' (the demons) and the 'devatas' (deities). Rahu and Ketu are unfulfilled parts of cosmic energies. Hence, the dragonhead and the dragon tail perch on the Pluto. Number four is also attributable to Uranus (per astronomy, the planet of darkness, and the paternity to Saturn).

The body is the field and the soul is the 'knower' of the field. To know the sacred human body, is to know the cosmos. According Vedic wisdom, there are twenty-four tattvas (principles of existence), that collate in aggregate terms to form the cosmic field or the cosmos. The first group of elements or bases comprises the earth, water, fire, air, and ether. The field also houses the ego and the earth bound mind, the intellect, the five organs of actions namely hands, feet, tongue, sexual and excretory organs. The field further encompasses the five sense organs the nose, the mouth, the eyes, the ears, and the taste buds of the tongue. The five spheres of the senses are, 'sight', 'smell', 'taste', 'hear', and 'touch'.

Vedas repose on 'SAT' the highest point in the northern most hemisphere of the cosmos just above 'Soma' (the vessel of pure nectar of truth 'Aum tat sat'). Only one truth need be known that, the cosmic eternal para existing omnipotent God is within the cosmos, the cosmos itself, without the cosmos, and beyond the wholesome magnificent nature.

It is the eternal para existing 'infinity' that reposes over the nectar of truth in the vessel of 'Soma' (in the north most hemisphere of the galaxy).

According to Krishna (the discourse of Geeta), matter and spirit are inseparable and there is neither beginning nor an end to the flight of life only the sacred experience of essential substance of existence. The human personality is the matter that grows, that does things, and that speaks, thinks, and acts in ordinary human ways. The soul is a mere witness of all karma.

The human personality becomes a free spirit of life through progressive karmic evolution and total sacred transformation. The personality is dynamic; the essential nature of the soul is static. Spirit's eternal profoundness manifests in any lifestyle. Some realise the supreme spirit in meditation, some know it by knowledge, some illuminate it by yoga sutras, and others understand it in profound awakening and profound selfless servitude. There are those who may have heard about the illumination from a written or spoken word of wisdom. These souls dwell in devotion and cling to the truth that they know of from the limitations and imperfections. The way to realising the true eternal divine light of God is to experience delight in the fleeting human life existence. To know the cosmos and to understand the energies of the cosmic creation is to know the self.

That, which is in the cosmos, is verily the austere truth. All that exists within us, within our own framework of existence, is verily the same para-existential cosmic nature. That 'brahmah' (god) is verily the atman (soul). That 'prakrutti' (divine mother) is verily our 'divya-sharrir'- divine entity of mind, senses; five elements – ether, air, fire, water, and earth.

The ancient Vedas, our ancestors, and our forefathers must have loved this earth much more than we in the modern world do. In the ancient times, learned people sat on the soil being close to the mothering powers of the sacred soil. They walked barefooted and the existence was less contaminated than the modern world. The modern world political heroes need to awaken spiritually, to sooth and to strengthen the bruises of the earth. It is in the recognition of the bare sacred existence that the cleansing and the healing of the self and the whole world becomes a life hope for the future generation children.

 Continued

COSMIC GALAXY IN VEDAS

NORTH WEST   NORTH   NORTH EAST

Vayu   *Soma*   *Rudra*

Aum Tat Sat (guru trinity)

Aum Tat Savitur Varenyam Bhargo devasya dhimahi dhiyo yo Naha prachodayatt.
Aum Tat Sat swaha. (Dynamic energy - cosmic shaktee Gayatri)

Pranna (vital force)   *Vac (empty silence)*   *Mantra*

Mahah, Jannah, Tappah (the super-consciousness)

Svahr (consciousness)

Vannaspattaye (Co-ordinator), Vishwadevaye (Architecture)

Kuber   *Issanaya*

Bhuvah (celestial plane)

WEST   EAST   *Surya*

Varuna   *Indra*

Bhur   *(material plane)* *Tattva*

Vasus, Marutas, and Pusanas   *Apah*

SOUTH WEST   SOUTH   SOUTHEAST

Nirritti   *Yamma*   *Agnee*

SPIRITUAL AWAKENING IS A SACRED SELF-LESS SACRIFICE

In the spiritual life of human kind, sacrifice is often used as a sacred experience. The Vedic seers speak of the entire journey of life as 'sacred sacrifice'. Sacredness is a profound word, which must not be loosely used.

In the Upanishads, Indra (the god of all deities) and Virocana (the king of all demons) both went to 'Prajapatti' (the infinite eternal supreme God) for profound Wisdom of the soul. Prajapatti (Brahma-Vishnu-Mahesh), the trinity God offered the eternal profound wisdom of the soul holding the vessel of Soma in his left hand and reading the sacred words of illumination from the open palm of his right hand to Indra and Virocana. This eternal wisdom sounded simple and powerful. Therefore, Indra questioned it in his profound silence and tried to understand with deeper insight, every single sacred word. Having transformed every single sacrifice into the learning experience, he kept on returning to 'Prajapatti' for 'satsang' (true discussion without argument). Every time Indra invoked 'Prajapatti', the sacred feet of Prajapatti were worshipped with his eyes closed. Indra closed his eyes and in this profound meditation at the feet of 'Prajapatti', he embraced profound wisdom.

Virocana on the other hand felt that he was very intelligent and that through his mental aptitude, he understood every single word of 'Prajapatti' went back to the demons and proclaimed to be their inspirational leader. Through his proud arrogance, he demanded respect and worship from his ignorant followers and in this process created followers. Indra on the other hand did not create any followers. Indra (the god of deities and the divine sacred power of the galaxy) having realised the true profound wisdom of the soul went into profound silence. When Indra came out of his profound silence, he became an inspirer to the cosmic forces. Indra became the divine mind of the cosmos. Indra made the 'word' (shabdda in Sanskrit) sacred.

Thus, the sacred word AUM became the power of the will, and the nervous or vital force of life. Aum became a sound, a word, a mantra, and a current of energy.

From the sacred sacrifice of sacred words of sacred sounds, all the cosmic energies brought about cosmic harmony.

These cosmic energies are namely, 'Aditi' (the infinite mother of gods and deities- true compassionate illuminating light), 'Mahi-or-Bharati' (the vast word that brings us all things out of the divine source), 'Ila' (the strong primal word of truth who gives us its active vision), 'Sarama' (the profound insight-hound of the heavens that descends into the cavern of the consciousness and finds there the concealed illumination), 'Dakshina' (the discerning right of disposal of offering and distribution to each cosmic force, a portion of nectar).

The cosmic nature of eternity rendered its highest tribute to AGNEE, the representation of fire, the sun, and the divinity of Gayatri (mother of Vedas). Agnee being the very force of the soul and the energy of the Sun is accorded the EAST sit of the cosmic eternity. Agnee is the sacrificial fire. There is not a single rite or ritual without invoking Agnee. Agnee is invoked and to the homage of its sacredness, all the cosmic energies and forces are invoked in a peace offering rite. The sacred fire is then meditated with the deep concentrated jaap (repetition) of Gayatree Mantra. It is the mother of all Vedic mantras and it is the most sacred mantra that creates total harmony in the cosmic forces prevailing in our body.

The vibrations of Gayatree mantra have been personally found to be most profound scientifically affecting the 'kundalini' (energy knots) to the final beatitude of the crown chakra. The Vedas repose on the truth that manifests from its nectar in the super consciousness. According to Vedic seers, One hundred and eight thousand repetition of the Gayatree mantra awakened the entire cosmos and made Shiva (the trinity guru) dance to its rhythm in seventy two thousand steps. Vedic anthologies claim that the dance of Shiva is ever non-stop in perpetual cycles of nights and days.

The entire cosmos rotates, revolves, and remains in perfect harmony because of the caper of Shiva and Gayatree in ARDHANAREESHWARA (meaning a cosmic marriage between the cosmic POWER and the cosmic ENERGY resulting in one cosmic force of infinity).

Infinity is that beyond the infinite blue skies, infinity is this wholesome galaxy. The Supreme Divine Great Spirit Para-Brahma is infinitely beyond the manifestation of this earth, the atmospheric orb, and the galaxy.

From infinity, this wholesome infinite sky, and the wholesome infinite ocean has come into existence. When infinity is taken away from wholesome infinity, only infinity remains. Aum the wholesome galaxy and beyond the wholesome galaxy into the infinite infinity let there be peace. Aum dyou shanti

The Vedas repose on Gayatree mantra. Per Vedas, the seeker of the infinite truth must awaken to the cosmic nature that is manifested in human personality. Like for example, the two legs and two arms can be correlated to the four legs of Gayatree mantra. One hand represents THE EARTH, THE SKY, and THE COSMIC ETERNITY. The other hand represents VEDAS. One foot represents breath, the vital force, and the vital energy. The other foot represents THE SUN – the solar being. According to Vedas therefore, there is scientific victory to the true seeker.

The energy of Gayatree rotates and revolves around the seven chakras and finally enters the crown to liberate an individual from ignorance and darkness. The great Sage Rishi Vishwamitra envisioned Gayatree mantra. This is the energy SAVITRI (energy of trinity pure sattvic Brahman). According to Vedas, Gayatree is the divine magnetic needle. The magnetic needle points to the north, hence 'life-ship' that is the personality does not loose its direction. The Gayatree mantra always points to the transcendental height of the SOMA (vessel of pure nectar), hence the seeker does not miss his final beatitude alias SAT CHIT ANAND OR HARI AUM TAT SAT.

AUM BHUR BHUVAH SVAH AUM TAT SAVITUR VARENYAM BHARGO DEVASYA DHIMAHI DHIYO YO NAHA PRACHODAYAT AUM SWAHA

RigVeda III.62.10

'Aum', we meditate upon thee as the transcendental glory of the TRUTH supreme (tat sat). Aum Tat Sat, is the magnificent eternity that resides within the heart of the MOTHER EARTH, inside the life of the blue skies and blue oceans. 'Aum Tat Sat' thou art manifested in the vessel of SOMA (vessel of pure nectar), and in the soul of the entire cosmos. May thine divine fire illuminate our mind and may thine sacred fire enlighten our consciousness. *'Aum Swaha'*. In your delight may I rest in peace.

Hymn to Gayatree (without hymn, I cannot complete the reverence of the mantra):

"God is the light. Divine light is the life of the vital force in sacred fire Agnee. God is the eternal supreme divine truth, that manifests in the metaphoric 'orange hue', of the Sun. Oh Agnee of the Sun, reside in my heart as the divine flame of sacred awakening, bring delightful joy to all my nerves and bring eternal bliss to my consciousness. Oh divine Agnee, the light 'lady Savitri', who is the force and energy of the Sun, awaken my spirit, enlighten my spirit, and keep me glowing eternally with your compassion. In your glory may I live. In your glory may I grow. In your glory may I become immortally Nirvana (dispersion in a fusion of merging cosmic marriage of delight in the twilight of the dawn and the dusk)."

Gayatree is that 'Maa' according to the Vedas that is the cosmic energy and that is the ENERGY in phenomenon. Energy operates the inertia and force and energy is the dynamic and static electricity of power. Energy is 'Maa'. Truth is Gods divine crown.

To realise truth is to accomplish the flight of delight. Light is love revealed in life manifestations and god fulfilment. Delight is enlightenment of divine infinite energy of Agnee. From the delight we came, in delight we grow and mould, onwards onto delight we retire. Life oh life let it be a flight of delight. Let it be.

It has been established scientifically that a repetition of Gayatree mantra 108,000 times has powers equivalent to an I.Q. of 180. Vedic mantras worship Gayatree mantra and the Vedas consider Gayatree mantra to be the mother of all tantras. There is no tantric mantra higher than Gayatree mantra. All mantras come below the integrity of Gayatree and below the supremacy of Gayatree. Gayatree is the ultimate mantra upon which the ultimate divine blissful purest form of truth reposes. Gayatri mantra has been scientifically proven to carry enormous energy. Such energies have been proven to even transform the dullness into sharp intellect.

In Vedas, there are more than one thousand one hundred and eight stanzas of hymns, praises, poetic invocations, prayers and profound lyrics of the compassionate Vedic seers. For our purposes, I have been inspired to write lyrics on 'Maa' (that which in Vedic terms implies cosmic energy and cosmic force of cosmic inertia). No movement, rotation, revolution, momentum, or transformation can be inevitable without 'Maa'.

'MAA' – 'ENERGY OF THE SOUL'

'Maa' is a profound most sacred word (shabda), that when silently spoken, quietly written and rhymed with a profound insight, bears a meaning, a sound, a profound mantra, a profound vision, and a profound energy. 'Maa', as a word is more profound than the mother herself because it is the sacred most word that is rhymed before life (in the womb of the entire cosmos), during life (cry of the new-born baby), in life (a subconscious Humming of the divine Mother nature), at death (last sound of the vital force of life – 'pranna'), and after death (in profound silence of the eternal para-existence). It is the sacred energy of immortality.

'Maa' is the sacred energy of the cosmic creation, cosmic preservation, and cosmic evolution. 'Maa' is the giver of birth, creator of material force and generator of earthly power in body, mind, conscious, and super conscious. 'Maa' is the kundalini shaktee (the micro-spiritual coil of the cosmic energy that travels from the base coccyx to the crown of the head in the spinal chord).

'Maa' is the holistic embryo of this universe, which holds together seven major earths within one wholesome globe. 'Maa' is the eternal most magnificent nature whose divine beauty embraces every single creation with its warm compassionate love and extravagant charisma. 'Maa' loves, loves and loves endlessly without any expectation what so ever.

'Maa' is MOTHER DIVINE ETERNAL SUPREME NATURE. She never fails when all else fails. 'Maa' is the soil of this earth that germinates food and provides shelter. 'Maa' is the warm embrace that shuns away fear. 'Maa' is the fresh morning breeze. 'Maa' is the wind that gives breath of life. 'Maa' is the energy of every single river. 'Maa' is the eternity of seven oceans. 'Maa' is the current of the running water. 'Maa' is the dynamic sound of 'AUM' echoed in seven different musical notes. 'Maa' is the gigantic most magnificent night galaxy full of glittering stars.

'Maa' is the beautiful moon that shines the radiance of the powerful sun.

'Maa' is the shimmering night sky that helps every single child on this universe sleep restfully and peacefully. 'Maa' is the infinite energy of the sun as Agnee ('yellow hue' liquid fire, of the Sun). 'Maa' is the mother of Vedas as Gayatree.

'Maa' is the dawn and dusk of the entire cosmos in 'sunrises' and 'sunsets'. 'Maa' is the mirage of ripples formed on the waters by the sunshine. 'Maa' is the energy of the seven rays of the sun (saapth kiran prakash). 'Maa' is simply love infinite supreme. 'Maa' is the energy of the omnipotent power of God supreme eternal.

'Maa' is the energy of sound that echoes AUM in conch shells, deep oceans, dancing rivers, running waters, mountains, valleys, forests, rustling trees, perennial grass, and the seven spheres. 'Maa' is the cosmic beauty of God that manifests even in tiniest of the nature's most beautiful flowers. 'Maa' is 'God' infinite when merged in oneness as 'Ardhenaareshwar' or 'Shiva-shaktee'. 'Maa' is the orbit of every planet. 'Maa' is the rotation and revolution of this universe in eternal time.

'Maa' is the creative aspect of the absolute cosmos. 'Maa' and 'God' are essentially one, just as the energy and the soul are inseparable. 'Maa' is 'dynamic karmic energy' in action, reaction, retribution, resolution, dissolution, evolution, and, reincarnation.

'Maa' is pure affection (mamta) and pure illusion (maya). 'Maa' is the pure disillusion (samsar) and pure dream (swapnaa). 'Maa' is vital force of health wealth and happiness in trinity of pure food, pure effort, pure thought.

'Maa' is dynamic force in nine shaktees (energies) of the nine dynamic planets in the galaxy namely Mars, Mercury, Jupiter, Venus, Saturn, Pluto, Herschel, Rahu and Ketu. 'Maa' is the light of the galaxy in Sun. Maa is the reflection of light in the Moon.

'Maa' is a sacred word that is often pronounced as 'Mau', 'Ma', 'Mai', 'Mo', 'Matu', Mma, Mngai, and 'Uma', in different cultures. Essentially 'Maa' is an unconditional giver, whose pure milk never fails to satisfy a crying hungry infant. 'Maa' nourishes her child endlessly. 'Maa' nurtures love in her child selflessly. 'Maa' understands in silence 'pain' inflicted upon her child.

'Maa' embraces compassionately without any veil of doubts or dark grey fear. 'Maa' is fearless and that is why she is associated with the roaring lion.

'Maa' is pure shaktee (transcendental dynamic energy) that is worshipped in utmost reverence of the 'eternal supreme almighty God omnipotent'.

'Maa' is the delight of the light of TRUTH that is refracted through the prism of our third eye. 'Maa' is profound wisdom of the soul that is transcended through our insight. 'Maa' is profound silence and the mother of all profound experiences in profound wisdom of the soul. 'Aum' is the essential sound of the first sacred word (shabda) of the maa-Brahma (eternity). 'Aum tat sat' became the infinite truth of that eternity Brahma and 'Hari Aum Tat sat' became the dynamic energy of threefold macro-cosmos namely the creation, the preservation, and the evolution (in retribution, resolution, dissolution, and re-incarnation).

'Maa' is the para-shaktee (eternal energy) of the prajapatee (eternal God) in sixty four million currents, seventy two million forces, eighty four million cycles, and infinite eternity of time. 'Maa' is the pure love and pure compassion in everyone. 'Maa' is the benign grace and the sacred blessings of the wholesome sacrifice. 'Maa' is pure devotion and pure worship of the soul – the very seat of God almighty eternal supreme.

'Maa' is solace without pity and sympathy. 'Maa' is the consolation of life and 'Maa' is the true companion in the tiresome journey of life. Embrace her in 'AUM' with profound silence and profound reverence.

'Maa' is the energy of 'sacred sacrifice' of 'unconditional giver' without any expectation of return whatsoever. 'Maa' is the 'mantra' (profound word of god), 'Yagna' (profound fire of sacrifice), 'Daana' (profound sacred sacrifice in charity, 'Tapas' (profound sacred devotion in mantra-manjaree, hymns, poetry, sacred philosophy, music, songs and dedicated devotion of compassion), 'tyaag' (profound sacred sacrifice in endless effort of soul searching experience), and 'jyoti' (delight of enlightenment).

'Maa' is pure inspiration that illuminates the aspirations of a seer.

'Maa' is the energy that holds together the entire force of the cosmos in harmony and perpetuity. 'Maa' is the dynamism of, rotation and revolution, of sunrises and sunsets, of high tides and low tides, of dancing rivers and thunderstorms, of motion and inertia. 'Maa' is the static of dawn and nightfall rest of sleep. 'Maa' is the everlasting love of God almighty supreme.

'Aum' is the sacred word, which is the sound, meaning and ultimate truth of 'Maa'. 'Aum' is infinitely imperishable mantra. It is the mantra of infinite truth.

'Sreem' is the dynamism of inertia in a mantra that is the moving force in germination of earth, proliferation of life and human welfare. 'Mantra' is a collectively sacred lyric comprising sacred and profound words with sacred and profound meaning, sacred and profound sound, sacred and profound rhythm, and, sacred and profound effulgence of quintessence.

A mantra is 'MAA' when the mantra supports, purports, and builds a rapport between the earth, the atmospheric orb, the celestial sphere of spiritual plane, and the fathomless eternal heaven.

A profound mantra always nurtures the spirit, and the profound mantra always loves unconditionally, selflessly and compassionately, the purity of a true devotee.

Gayatree mantra is that grand maestro of power, energy, force, inertia, and para-existing god eternal supreme divine most truth - 'prajapatee'.

Gayatree mantra is the mother of Vedas because in the Gayatree there is the AGNEE (fire), the SUN (light), the EARTH (seven worlds), the WATER (seven oceans and seven rivers), the AIR (atmospheric orb and the wind), the ETHER (the orbits of rotation and revolution in every sphere), the nine planets, the nine shaktee knots, the nine cosmic forces and nine evolutions. The Gayatree mantra is the supreme 'MAA'. That thou art the absolute truth infinite, this Gayatree mantra is the embodiment of that absolute truth infinite.

In the typological heaven, eternity comprises cosmological, ontological, and mystical metamorphosis. It is the other world. It is where the radiance of 'Maa' never ceases in nights or days. It is a divine blissful state, in which all the planes have merged in oneness of delight. That oneness is eternal light that unfailingly ever shines and illuminates the eternity or heaven. Such a typological heaven is only a model in the seer's insight as an everlasting world. It is the world of infinity and oneness whereat the sun never sets. Such a magnificent heaven is immortal because of the Amrutt (nectar of immortality) upheld in the vessel of Soma, is enlightened, and cherished, limitlessly, with the glow of agnee.

The Vedic experience begins with Agnee and ends with Agnee. The Agnee keeps the human planes of existence rotating, revolving and perpetual. At the same time, the Agnee limitlessly, in a never failing manner upholds the radiance of the heaven without the constriction of time or space. It is the single most, highest point in the cosmos where at there is "vac" and where the form turns into formless. The everlasting world of heaven is unparalleled. It is one without a second. In the human chakras, it is the crown chakra where there is no form, or dynamism. It is a static state of vacuum. It is the highest state of bliss, in mystical sense. It is unseen, yet it is perfect. It is a spot, wherein Agnee never fails to shine. It is the hidden state - the transcendental state. It is herein at the tip of the crown chakra; the Gayatree (shaktee) merges in oneness with the sacred light of Agnee in one penultimate symbol 'AUM'. It is the final point of super consciousness. It is wherein the shaktee (the vital life breath), merges in 'oneness' with the soul infinite. It is wherein the truth manifests. 'Maa' is the 'Aum' infinite that becomes a pathless eternity in the vacuum of 'brahma-loka' or mystical heaven where at 'delight' never ceases.

THE SACRED SHAKTEE (ENERGY) IN US

Awake, arise, oh divine shaktee of 'vital life breath' (spiritual energy), and stop not until my final goal of 'moksha' is reached! Rise oh fiery Kundalini (the coiled up energy at the coccyx), and stop not, until the 'lingham light' (uncoiled energy), moves forth along the 'Yoni' (spine), to awaken, to enlighten and to illuminate in delight!

A Rabbit breathes 80 times a minute, and lives only 8 years while a turtle breathes ever so slowly only 5 times a minute but lives almost 300 years. Somewhere, in the middle, we human beings breathe about an average 10 to 20 times a minute in deep sleep, about 20 to 30 times a minute in restful state, and about up to 80 times a minute when restless like the rabbit. That is not all. Most of us are blissfully unaware that in an average person, the breath we intake is only about half a litre which is a fraction of our entire lung capacity of five to six litre.

Gayatree mantra is the 'pranna' (vital life breath energy) of Agnee and the vital force of Agnee. It is the ultimate final beatitude of truth upon which the 'Tat Sat' (eternal supreme God) reposes. When the vital force of the pranna rhymes with the Gayatree mantra, it transcends light in the Shushumna (the canal of spiritual energy in the body).

Sound, vision, light, becomes profoundly quiet and in the profound silence, a huge cosmic delight enters the third eye, which is the spiritual eye that is situated in the middle of the forehead.

Through constancy of pranna and mantra, the delight finally enters the crown chakra rendering total blissful profound 'oneness' of divine marriage between the 'purush' (human being) and the 'prakruttee' (eternal divine cosmic nature).

Vedic seers measured the lifespan in remaining breaths of vital force of energy. For example, a twenty one thousand recitation of Gayatree mantra is the sacred offering to the cosmic eternity in concentrated sacrifice of profoundness and profound 'bhaktee yoga' (devotional practice). Such a profound devotional worship transforms the 'vital life force' shaktee, from static macro into dynamic micro, form. The life breath force following the cosmos operates with static and dynamic energies, electromagnetic fields, electrons, protons, and neutrons. These cosmic energies manifest in our body as 'vital force of life' called 'pranna' and as Shushumna (the dynamic moving current of the 'vital life force' of inertia merging with each level of spiritual ecstasy). The micro is like a sub set of the macro. Just like in chemistry, economics, physics and mathematical permutations and combinations of fields and currents and geometric assimilation.

Indra the illuminator became immortal divine enlightenment of the cosmic forces through the profoundness of the Gayatree mantra. Per Vedic wisdom, 'MAA' is the creative aspect of the absolute cosmos. It is ENERGY, which is static and dynamic. Energy is the life force and energy is the emerging pranna or the vital life breath of the form. Energy and Spirit are essentially one eternal nature, as the cosmic power and the cosmic energy. Every dynamic activity is a manifestation of static power and static force. Energy (shaktee) is a current. Behind energy (shaktee) is the power (Shiva – the all pervading cosmic trinity of illumination, dissolution and resolution).[39]

---

[39] He who transcends the 'seen' came down on earth as a divine guru to abide in the hearts of virtuous and illumined them by his gracious love. The peerless Shiva is the matchless guru of cosmos. The Himalayas is his abode, whereat Aum echoes benignly. (Testament of truth 1576)

A person is the micro-Cosmo of the eternal cosmos (Brahma purush). What prevails in the macrocosmic eternity prevails in the micro-Cosmo entity. Whilst Shiva - the infinite power of 'aum tat sat' resides in the crown chakra, the dynamic energy of shaktee resides in the kundalini (the coil of spiritual energy) that rests in a dormant potential state in the base chakra (the Muladhara chakra) of the spine. 'Kundalini' sustains the entire human body with its vital life force or the 'pranna'.

The physical body is shaped in accordance to the evolution of the astral body. Therefore, when the astral body (corresponding to the air, the vital breath and the wind) is pure, and sublimely divine, the physical body (corresponding to water or gross form), will be youthful, energetic, joyful and healthier. In Vedic wisdom, each cosmic energy has its corresponding respective astral energy.

'Nada's' are para-physical nerves or the astral nerves of the arteries and veins, carrying the vital life breath. It is through the vital force of vital breath, that the various nerves and veins transport blood from the lower level of the body into and from the middle level of the body and from the middle level of the body into from the higher level of the body (namely the throat, and the brain).

Circulation of blood is therefore vital. If blood does not circulate adequately and appropriately, all forms of illness can emanate.

Because 'Nada's' are made up of subtle matter, they cannot be seen by the naked physical eyes and life breath is like air that cannot be seen but we know that it is there with all kinds of gas, wind and currents. Just as a leaf of the tree, comprise minute fibres. All the Nada's emanate from 'Kanda' (Bulb).

Every energy Bulb is a sub station of group of energies. The centre of Kanda lies at the base of the coccyx. [40]

---

[40] The exact position is two fingers above the anus, and two fingers below the organ of generation. It is like the bird's egg in shape and of four fingers in breath and width. Apparently, seventy two thousand Nada's emanate from this bulb (Kanda). Kanda is the centre of the astral body that corresponds to 'caudal equine' in gross physical body.

'Shushumna' in Yoga shastras is the canal of spiritual energy running through the spinal cord, from the plexus of 'Muladhara' (coccyx) kundalini (spiritual point or sacred power knot), in to the crown in the cerebrum, the plexus of 'sahasrarha' (thousand petal lotus). Within Shushumna are two active forces.

One is called the 'Vajra nada' (the illuminuous, lustrous energy of the sun) and the other is called the 'Chitra nada' (Sattvic-or pure divine force, pale in colour). Within the Chitra nada, is the 'Brahma shaktee' (pure energy), through which Kundalini (coiled up 'vital life breath force' in a static form at the base of Muladhara chakra) when awakened transmigrates upwards in the spinal chord to the 'sahasrarha chakra' (crown chakra). In the Brahma Nada exists all the six energies in lotus form. Chakras are plexus or centres of Shukshma pranna (vital life breath) in the Shushumna nada (the canal of spiritual energy). The entire body functions through these centres.

The cosmic energy of vital breath is contained in the base plexus, and the infinitesimal fraction of the energy is distributed across the body through the neurone motor and seventy two thousand sensory nerves. 'IDA' and 'PINGALA' on the either side of the canal control the influx and the reflux of the vital force. Scientifically, they are also known as astral artery and vein. The coiled up power of spiritual energy known as kundalini is aroused and awakened during the course of profound self discovery process of the soul, like profound yoga, profound mantra jaap, profound meditation, profound concentration of the consciousness, and unconditional worship.

Yoga means to unite co-ordinate, harmonise, work, and transform. Yoga links human beings from the gross physical to the super consciousness. Vedic yoga is the oldest form of yoga. According to Vedic yoga, there are four types of yogic rites namely the mantra yoga (recital of sacred word from Vedas), the pranna yoga (controlling vital force of breathe through inhaling and exhaling rituals), the Hatha yoga (physical postures of arousing the energy points) and the Dhyanna yoga (profound silence of meditation).

'Profound yoga', encapsulates a combination of 'mantra yoga' (the sacred silent chanting of divine mantra on 108 rosary beads), 'pranna yoga' (the control of vital life breath in the kundalini –the spiritual energy), 'Dhyanna yoga' (the profound silence of deep meditation with the nature), and, 'Hatha-yoga' (the physical yogic exercises).

Awakening spiritual energy is a composite process of transmigrating positive evolution of energy (shaktee) from the base gross physical state on to the super conscious state. This process can only manifest in pure body, with pure Nada's (astral nerves), in a pure mind, with pure profound unconditional intellect, with profound insight and with profound silence. Yoga becomes a way of life for the true ascetic. A true yogi is an ascetic who lives with the nature, craves for fine music, fine poetry, fine philosophical altruism, fine arts, fine culture, fine dance, and scientific ways of self-discovery. When a loving compassionate spirit of life endeavours its flight of self-discovery, and endures, in great patience for a long period of time in the self-discovery process of life (comprising sacred sacrifices and sacred living), the spirit of life turns into a profound spirit of life. The aim of every 'yogeshwara' purush (a divine devotee of 'AUM TAT SAT' 'supreme Brahma' truth 'divine eternal') is to elevate in progression. Every cycle and every phase of the chakras are correlated to the various spiritual spheres or lokas. When the Muladhara chakra is conquered, one has conquered the earth and nothing material can affect this person, for the Bhur has illumined. When the Swadhishttana chakra is conquered, one has conquered water and is in contact with apah-bhurvah and the bhurvah is illumined.

When the Manipurna chakra is conquered, one has conquered fire and Svahr lokka of the celestial cosmic fire has been conquered. The cosmic deities and the cosmic forces are in contact with the spirit of life.

When the Anahata chakra is conquered one has conquered the subtle Air. One is in contact with tatva shaktee or the param mahar lokka (infinite cosmic divinity). When one has conquered the Vishuddha chakra, one has conquered the element ether that is the orbit of every single planet and every single cosmic force. One is in contact with the jnanna lokka or profound wisdom. When one has conquered the Ajna chakra, one is in touch with the 'tapo lokka' or the 'param tatva guru trinity' Shiva the cosmic seer.

When one has passed the 'param tatva guru trinity Shiva', the cosmic seer, one finally enters the 'sattya-lokka' or the purest sphere of Brahma prajapattee the omnipotent god eternity. The entire 'great Gayatree' mantra thus encapsulates the entire seven chakras and the shaktee of illumination.

Awakening of the shaktee, its union with the param tatva guru Shiva, becoming blissfully divine, enlightening with the pure nectar and para-existence of the eternity as elucidated in yoga shastras has been converted into an academic task by many. Many try to teach and coach such complexities and perplexities in academic concepts and technical terminology's and in doing so fulfil their personal ambitions of being powerful gurus, powerful leaders, and powerful holistic persons. The purpose of this book is to elucidate in simple terms, the sacred pilgrimage of the soul divine with poetry, philosophy and altruism of the profound wisdom of the soul. Let shaktee awaken on its own natural course just like the river. If you are an awakened spirit, profoundness will manifest all over. Vedic insight is a means of correlating the scientific, philosophical and poetic parable of my written words. One who transpires through great many obstacles and great many adversities becomes a humble soul through sufferings.

The purpose of forgoing elucidation is to enlighten and correlate our human body that is microcosmic entity to the macrocosmic eternity. It is not to proclaim any method or technique of self-realisation. Self-realisation is a self-discovery process of the soul. It becomes a natural way of life, to the awakened spirit, without technicalities, and institutional restrictions. Yoga is simply sacred profoundness of communion of the profound mind, body, and soul in togetherness of divine mantras, yantras, shlokas, and poetry. There are many tantric practices performing rites and rituals that are not sattvic Brahma-Vidya (alias wisdom of the Sun). Tantra can be used to propitiate powers and forces for personal occultism. Tantric yoga practices do not render total spiritual emancipation in karmic terms but merely accomplish personal power of the kundalini in various forms of complexities and perplexities that is beyond a simple, pure mind.

My profound experience has not manifested in complicated techniques or complex methods, but simple pure compassionate devotion and 'raja-yoga' (a composite yoga). A yoga of this kind is a union in mantra (sacred words), kirtan (sacred hymns), sattvic (pure) activities, prem-karma (servitude to humanity), prem-bhaktee (unconditional devotional worship), jnanna (profound wisdom), atman-anubhava (profound experience of the spirit), pathha (recitals of sacred verses of the Upanishads, Vedas, Sermon on the mount, Quran etc.), physical Hatha yoga on music, poetry, philosophical writing, running in the open space, basking in the sun, and being simply quiet in profound silence.

In Kalyug (the age of darkness and ignorance, noise and haste), it is not practically possible to shut off infinitely from the daily duties of survival in totality. In Kalyug (the age of fastest speed, maximum noise, maximum waste, maximum chaos and minimum human life), per the Vedas, the power of concentration has to be monitored and tamed with music. Music is scientifically proven to heal wounds quicker because it releases hormones that are concerned with the repairing of the damaged blood cells. Therefore, the practical way of self-realisation in the modern day is doing all the survival chores by being detached from all the duties of life and granting self-less devotion of mantra jaap, humanitarian servitude, evolving with profound wisdom, and observing profound silence. Raja-yoga therefore firstly requires a person to perform his or her rightful duty as a father, as a mother, as a son, as a daughter, as a husband, as a wife, as a brother, as a sister, as an employer, as an employee, as a social reformer and as a self-reformer. The self-reforming process is the profound evolution of the self as a profound sacrifice for the soul. Love is something you and I must have and love is something without which we become weak and with it we light all.

'YOGA-PATANJALEE' is an intricate science and an intricate art of building the various spiritual knots of the entire 'shareer' (divine body). Ancient seers and ancient sages in perfection could practise such powerful Vedic science because the world then was in a different state than the modern world. Five thousand years ago, a guru was a pure perfect guru and a disciple was a pure perfect disciple. Perfect absolute life does not exist in the modern world and trying to involve in something that will not render total spiritual salvation is not the aim of this book. Our body is a divine body, a sacred home for our spirit and hence to awaken the shaktee (the spiritual energy) must not be a burden (of accomplishing by academic forces), but a sacred sacrifice justified for the delight of the cosmic yogi in our soul.

RAJA-YOGA

According to the Vedic wisdom, 'Raja-yoga' is the king of all yogas and it is the noble way of life because it directly connected to the mind. In essential practice of raja-yoga, there is no burden of forceful exertion by pressure of intricate perplexities. Albeit physical fitness and physical austerity are essentially pre-requisite to the mental fitness and mental acuteness, the focus is on 'pure thought'.

When a pure thought enters the mind in a pure mental state, with pure compassion and pure sacrificial welcome, to, understand unconditionally the depth of profound wisdom, the resultant action or karma will automatically be pure and harmoniously profound. Therefore, Karmic evolution is more important to my aim then complicated techniques that merely confuse a humble soul. The yogeshwara purush is a divine most creative talent of integrity that sits in profound quietness, with great profound peace and with an unconditional mind to watch the profoundness of the great silence. In the profoundness of the great silence, manifests the ripples of the light of Agnee, and when the mind becomes very still just like the calm surface of the early morning sea, the currents of the mantra vibrations evolve and progressively ascend the spirit onwards towards the ocean of eternity where there is only 'AUM' in the deep blue sea waters and where all the rivers of life finally merge.

Through 'raja-yoga' is the dualistic philosophy and poetry of uniting the eternity and the human life in profound mantra meditation (letting the energy of AUM transform progressively), mantra jaap (repetition of mantra in silence), sacred kirtan (hymns and songs of praise), and humanitarian servitude. Raja Yoga is also known as the yoga of eight limbs. The eight limbs comprise 'Yumm' (dissolution), Neeyumm (Retribution), Asana (physical fitness with physical yoga asanas including the asanas of the Sun), Pranyamma (controlling the life breath by breathing exercises), Pratyahara (renunciation and sacrifice), Dharana (focusing), Dhyanna (concentration), and Sammaddhee (profound silence). We invoke the divine flame of Agnee (the earthly fire in our stomach, mind, and consciousness) from within. In prannayam (profound breathing), we surrender to the rhythm of mantra invocation. From Agnee in Sun, we illuminate our inspirational insight. Our inspirational insight (the beholder of which is Indra the illuminator of Agnee) transforms our profound enlightenment from light of awareness in progressive stages and finally merges in delight with the effulgent rays of the magnificent Agnee in Sun. From delight we came, onwards into delight we return. Profound peace, profound peace, profound peace is invoked three times with integrity. A total sacred transformation evolves with the forces of 'yumm' and 'Neeyyumm'. 'Yumm' comprises truthfulness, non-violence, purity - celibacy, simplicity – sattvic (pure) living, and detachment from the power cycle of accomplishing wealth at the expense of others.

'Neeyyumm' comprises; wholesome purity of mind body and thought; contentment and non-conflict, unconditional sacrifice, dedication and devotion, unconditional worship, unconditional compassion; Vedic wisdom and the anthological wisdom of the soul and the study of Geeta, Bible, and Quran; and wholesome surrender to the infinite supreme eternal omnipotent God whose seat is the very soul and whose imperishable infinity is the cosmic eternity, beyond the wholesome skies and the vast empty space.

In Vedas, when the 'Jiva Hamnssa' (the spirit of life) meets delight in transcendental ecstasy of illuminating light of the Gayatree from the Sun, deepest compassion is rendered to Ishwar (eternal God 'Tat Sat').

Hamnssa pays a praising tribute as follows:

"'Aum Tat Sat', Para-Brahma (eternal power), Hari-Brahma (Infinite God), Aum-Brahma (profound purity), Ishwar (omnipotent almighty infinite God), I am yours, this maya is yours, this jiva (my astral body) is yours, this inertia (the shaktee of my profound mantra) is yours, this life is yours. Oh infinite Supreme omnipotent God infinite bring me peace and bring me the true nectar of immortality for I want to drink your nectar of infinite wisdom and infinite profound eternal truth."

PRANNAYAMMA

My profound Raja-Yoga practice begins with invoking the Life breath in Vayau (the cosmic force of wind, air, and currents) with prannam namastute (meaning warm welcome). The first breathing exercise is 'Sukham' (relaxing peacefully). This can be done even whilst lying down in the bed. Drawing air through both the nostrils gently and deeply to the maximum comfortable point and retaining the air inside the stomach to the maximum comfortable point, and then finally letting the air out from the mouth very slowly. Make a repetition of eight to ten.

The second breathing exercise is 'Sandhyay' (anuloma-viloma). In this maximum amount of air is inhaled through the left nostril to the maximum comfortable point, retained in the chest to the maximum comfortable point and exhaled from the right nostril very slowly. This represents the dawn of the Vayau (air). The same exercise is repeated with the right nostril, inhale, and the left nostril, exhale.

This represents the dusk of the Vayau (air). The two cycles constitute one complete round of prannayamma. Make a total repetition of nine. The ratio between inhale, retention and exhale may range between 1:3:2 and 1:5:2.

It is not important that one retains the air for more than the maximum comfortable point as much as it is important to control the speed of the inhale and the exhale. The slower the speed the better it is. During retention of the breath, sacred Gayatree mantra is repeated in silence. During inhale is repeated 'Aum shanti' five times and during exhale is repeated 'Aum dyou shanti' five times. Combining the mantra with the prannayam is more effective; otherwise, one can perform the prannayam to music.

The third breathing exercise is 'Bhastrika' (abrupt breathing). In this exercise rapid inhalation and rapid exhalation of the breath is undertaken with the maximum inhale and maximum exhale to the maximum comfortable point. Repeat nine times. The fourth breathing exercise is 'Sitall' wherein the tongue is rolled as a tube to draw in air, retaining it to the maximum comfortable point and exhaling it slowly from the same tongue roll.

Different institutions teach varying techniques. I personally prefer to undertake Prannayamma exercise for the purpose of healing the pranna and for the purpose of enhancing the sattvic energy to heal another. Thus, I use first two fingers to touch the middle of the forehead and the thumb to close the right nostril. Then the ring finger and the little finger are touching the middle of the palm. On the left nostril I do with the left hand and on the right nostril I do with the right hand. It exercises my third eye. Furthermore, I undertake willpower development exercise. This enables me to recite and chant for longer hours without getting bored. By keeping a finger, hand, foot, head and eyes fixed in one position for some time and to gaze at the deepam jyoti (the small light of the cotton wick). Also, I have found that when I have restrained from speaking for a day or half a day, and I observe fasts on water, I chant more deeply, more innately and much more profoundly. This helps me to rejuvenate my burnt energies. My parents taught me mindful walking since I was a child. Mindful walking looking down on the ground watching the steps and walking with chants helps us to build stamina, will power, and determination. It also induces some motivation. As we do mindful walking, we also breathe in and out of nostrils holding as much as we comfortably can the inhaled breath.

After Prannayamma, we are ready to gently move and flex our body to the sun asanas and Surya-yoga.

YOGA EXERCISES TO MUSIC (SEE ANNEX THREE)

My yoga-asanas begin with Surya-namaskar and awakening the entire cosmic entity. Yoga exercises are best undertaken on an empty stomach in the morning because the blood will purify and the mind will become creative. Invoke the Lord Surya-Narayana with the Surya-Aditya mantra: Aum Mitraaya namah, Aum Ravaye namah, Aum Sooryaya namah, Aum Bhaanave namah, Aum Khagaye namah, Aum Pooshne namah, Aum Hiranyagarbhaye namah, Aum Mareechaye namah, Aum Aadityaaye namah, Aum Savitre namah, Aum Arkaayaye namah, Aum Bhaskaraya namah, Aum Divakaraya namah, Aum Shree Savitre Suryanarayanaye namah namoh. Recite the Gayatri mantra:

Aum bhur bhurvah svahr Aum tat savitur varenyam bhargo devasya dhimahi dhiyo-yo-naha prachodayyatt. Aum tat sat swaha.

The Surya-asanas are:

1. Salutation: Reach the sky movement with the palms folded, which align the body in upright straight symmetrical position, raising the hands as high as you can as far behind as you can, folding the hands in prayer position and raising the ankles from the ground, just balancing on toes. Reach out as high as you can and slowly breath in and breath out. Close your eyes and feel the warm sun enter the middle of your forehead with compassion. Inhale and exhale on music. The Surya 'Aditya' mantra is then chanted 11 times or 21 times, with the inhale and exhale 'namaskara' (folding hands) pose laying flat on the stomach facing the sun (east). Names of Sun God are said once (see annex). Aum shanti is repeated three times.

2. Shining armour: Inhale and exhale the position number one and gradually swiftly and gracefully bend all the way down with your hands together and touch your feet. Now slowly move from your feet to the ground to pay the respect of the glowing sun. Touch the ground in total bent position with your knees straight and hands flat on the ground. Inhale and exhale on music. Repeat nine times.

3. Activity inducer: Moving from the position two, slowly bring forward your right foot and bend your right foot in a semi-squat position with both your palms openly touching the ground and the chin and face upwardly straight onto the glory of the sun. Stretch the left leg as back as you can whilst you stretch the neck and the face upwards with the force of both the hands thrusting against the ground with open palms. Inhale and exhale to music. Repeat nine times with alternative legs.

4. Strength Stamina: Moving from position three, gradually lift your body in press-ups position with your palms open on the ground and toes straight touching the ground and body facing stomach to the ground. Lift the entire weight of the body and perform press-ups with your chin high up in the air and face facing upward to the sun. Lifting the weight of the body with both your hands bent creates an exertion of force to your upper arms and move the press-ups in a dive-in – dive out motion of the abdomen and ground such that the hot energy of the sun is moving rapidly in the blood. Inhale and exhale to music.

5. Repeat the position number four nine times then with both your hands bent, body flat on the ground stomach touching the ground and just the nose touching the ground, inhale and exhale nine times chanting the sacred Gayatree mantra on music. Now lift the upper body with your hands thrusting on the ground and hips and buttocks thrusting against the ground but the stomach and the chest moving as high as possible, with your chin as high as possible and neck as back as possible. That slight prick on the lower spine will tell you to stop. Now repeat this for nine times on music with inhale and exhale. Each time, Gayatree mantra is chanted in full. Then the breathing exercises on its own with mantra invocation eleven times the shorter Gayatree mantra.

6. Moving on from the position five, hold open palms on the ground and feet flat on the ground, bend your body in an inverted u shape with the buttocks rising as high as possible and the neck bending inwards and outwards to clear the thoughts. Repeat this for nine times on music. Inhale and exhale to music.

7. Repeat the position number three nine times and position number four nine times. Slowly fold the right leg inside the inner thighs of the left leg such that the right knee is touching the ground and the left leg is as straight back as possible.

8. Join both hands in one on top of another crossing fingers and bend completely towards the right bent knee such that you touch the ground with your clasped 'in togetherness' open palms on the ground and neck and face as straight in the air facing the ground as possible. Now lift the both the hands and move the upper body as back as you can until you feel the stretch on the hips. Repeat this nine times with alternative knee bent. Inhale and exhale to music.

9. Rise up and lift your entire body in straight upward position on your toes moving the ankle as high as possible and moving the hands as wide as possible. Inhale and exhale on music. Repeat nine times.

10. Now bend down and then slowly go on both the knees touching the ground curve the stomach inwards and bring your face and neck together in line with your open palms touching the ground. Touch the forehead with the hands on the ground. Repeat nine times. Inhale and exhale with music.

11. Pranayam namaskar pose with both hands folded and posture as erect as possible. This is the namaskaram pose which combines position one and moving the hands as wide as possible to open up to the glory of sun by inhaling the breathe of the dawn and then clasping both hands together to pray to sun god.

Having invoked the Sun, the body is now ready to work on the five levels of existence.

Different Yoga teachers teach different styles of Yoga. I prefer to do Yoga on music and mantras that are particularly relevant and significant to the posture itself. 'Mudras' (hand expressions) are very useful expressions of inner soul and Mudras can be very healing. Refer to annex 11 for basic yoga asanas.

A prelude Asana (preliminary posture) of Sirsashana-avasthama (otherwise called headstand) is revitalising. Carefully bend on your knees and touch the ground with your head, holding it with both your hands. Now exert force onto elbows and lower hands whilst holding the head inside the two open palms try to gracefully raise the feet and the hips in the air and slowly straighten legs. This may seem easier with the wall support and is recommended for novice yogi.

1. We begin with the flight of eagle, stretching out both the hands and both the feet such that the hands become the front or the wings and the legs become the tail of the eagle in an upright position. Move your head and neck from one shoulder to another shoulder and move one hand at a time in the air in circular motions whilst they are as stretched out and as wide as possible. Then move both hands as if the eagle is moving the force of Vayau (wind). Keep your neck and head as straight as possible and as high as possible. Loosen up and move face from right to left and from left to right. From north to south and from south to north. Now repeat the flapping circular motions to music. Inhale and exhale on music. Repeat nine times.

2. Moving from the position one hold right foot firmly on the ground with the knees bent slightly so that it gives thrusting gravity whilst lifting the left foot in opposite backwards direction in the air stretching the left buttock, the left limb and the left leg as straight back as you can with both your hands moving and bending as forward as you can as if to greet the flight. Move your hands from front to touch your buttocks and then back to front whilst you are on right foot on the ground and left foot in the air. Repeat nine times to music. Inhale and exhale.

3. Now do the position number two with the leg moving forwards in a shiva-tandum position and clasping both hands as tightly as possible in prayer position. This is the natraj position or the guru-position. Repeat this with alternative legs and chant the 'Aum namah Shivaya' mantra eleven times each time.

4. Hold right leg firmly rooted on the ground with the left leg thrusting against the right inner thigh, hands as wide as possible and then merging in prayer position. Hold this position with mantra-manjaree, on music. Inhale and exhale nine times on music.

5. Spread your legs wide apart in an inverted v shape and raise both your hands as high as you can and then spreading as wide as you can. Bend with your hands moving as back as you can and as high as you can. Repeat this nine times.

6. Same position as five above with legs apart, bend sideways to touch the lower leg as farthest as you can. Slowly move your hands clasping the ground with your open palms and move forward and backward to music. Inhale and exhale.

7.   Rattle and rustle with the music on tap movements of both the legs and thrusting alternate hips as though the whole body is dancing in ecstasy. Keep on dancing for five to ten minutes with various mudras (hand movements) and various shiva-tandum expressions.

8.   Now run on the spot to regulate your breathing and taking time to recover the vigorous exertions in seven above. Slowly inhale and exhale with the hands moving out and in of the chest widest out and bent inward touching both the front shoulders. Slow down, and come to lift the alternative toe in tree position, balancing on one foot.

9.   Now you are ready to perform the rest of the yoga on music comprising the cobra, the bow, the peacock, the plough, the shoulder stand, the fish pose, the posterior stretch, the abdominal leg-lifts, the locust posture, the twist-fold posture, the mudra-lotus posture, the nauli-stomach exercise, the uddiyana-bladder exercise, the padmasana-lotus seat, the sidhasana –folded legs, the sukhasana- relaxed folded legs, taadaasana-one leg upward stand, sarva-gasana or bicycle, and Hamnssa the flight of life. Nine repetitions of all postures.

➤ 9.1.   Cobra: Lay flat on the ground on your stomach with face facing the ground and hands stretched above the head flat on the ground. Now move both the hands with open palms on the ground like the movement of the snake elbow bulging outwards. Lift your upper body as high as you can from the ground with the forward gravitational thrust of both the hands with open palms against the ground. Straighten the neck and the face upwards and high in straight line. Stretch as far as possible. The legs and the lower part of the body must be with the ground. Feel the stretch in the abdomen and a prick on the lower spine.

➤ 9.2.   The Bow: Back to the ground flat with the stomach facing the ground, raise the legs backwards and the hands backwards to touch the ankles or the lower legs whichever is more comfortable. Do not strain. Pull the hands and the legs alternatively such that the lower abdomen feels the stretch.

➤

➤ 9.3. Peacock: Back to the ground, flat on the stomach. Thrust open palms with the inside wrist not touching the ground but the fingers lifting on the upper open palm the maximum force. Try to lift the lower back and the legs. Lift the neck and the move the neck up in the air and down towards the ground. Feel the stretch in the shoulders and the hands.

➤ 9.4. Plough: Turning around on the ground now lie flat with your back facing the ground flat. Keep your hands flat on the ground with open palms. Raise your legs all the way in a 180-degree turn right back until the feet touch the ground.

➤ 9.5. Shoulder stand: Back to the ground flat with the back facing the ground. Hold your elbows thrusting against the ground whilst the body is lifted with the legs up in the air. Hold your waist such that the legs are straight and the entire weight is leaning on the shoulders and the elbows.

➤ 9.5.b. Cycle: Now from the position 9.5. Move the legs in the air as if you are riding an upside down bicycle.

➤ 9.6. Fish: Back to ground flat with the back now slowly rise the upper body and raise the hands high in the air dropping them on the ground. Thrusting the hands on the ground, fold the legs crossing both the legs and hold the crossed merged two feet with your hands. Slowly and gradually, tilt your upper body backward with the neck going as far back as possible. Stretch to the maximum comfortable point. Stop if it causes any discomfort. Build on these exercises gradually rather than abruptly. Hatha (physical yoga) prohibits abrupt muscular motion.

➤ 9.7. Posterior stretch: Back to the ground with the back facing the ground and hands and legs straight. Stretch the hands as far back on the ground as possible.

➤ Now slowly raise your upper body, hands, and breath in and out to flex the abdominal muscles so that the flexing allows a gentle bending of the upper body to enable you to touch the feet with your hands. Try to bend the neck and the face as far down as possible above the knees. If you cannot touch the knees, do not force. Stop when it generates discomfort.

➢ 9.8.   Abdominal leg lifts: Back to the ground with the back facing the ground and hands clasping flat on the ground. Thrusting the open palms and the hands on the ground lift the legs up in the air feeling the stretch on the lower abdomen and the lower lumber. Gradually increase repetitions paying particular attention to the lumber.

➢ 9.9.   Locust:Now turn around on the ground to make the stomach face the ground flat with the chin only touching the ground. Holding the ground with the open palms and the hands as if thrusting with the fingers and the upper palms and inner wrist facing the ground. Raise the legs up so that the stretch is felt in the back of the limbs.

➢ 9.10.   Twist-fold:Now sit with your legs and knees folding such that the hands are over the knees. Slowly fold your right leg to make the right feet touch the left buttock. Keep the right leg on the ground folded. Fold over the left leg crossing the right knee in an inverted v position. Reach out the right hand as far as possible to touch the left toes straight line. The left hand curving back to touch the back of the lower right hip.

➢ 9.11.   Mudra: Now back to folded legs (in the lotus position) and upright upper body, sit on the buttocks. Now hold the knees with both your hands, slowly bend forward, breath in and out and slowly, flex the upper body to move downward such that the nose faces the ground to the lowest possible point. Please do not attempt to touch the ground with the nose. Bow to a comfort point.

➢ 9.12.   Nauli and Uddiyana: Are stomach exercises breathing in and out holding the intake as much as possible. Then without any air pulling the lower abdomen inwards as far as comfortably possible. The Nauli with the hands holding the inner thighs and neck slightly bent and the Uddiyana is with the hands holding the pelvic whilst the neck is upright.

➢ 9.13.   The Padmasana, the Sidhasana, and the Sukhasana are sitting with legs folding. Padmasana is crossing the opposite ankles over the inner thighs, Sidhasana is crossing the opposite ankles onto the inner thighs, and Sukhasana is relaxed folding of both the legs whilst holding the knees with the hands to feel the comfort of gravity.

➢

➢ 9.14. Taadaasana: Standing upright straight. Raise right leg crossing the knees to make the right open foot clasp the inner thigh of the left upright leg, whilst clasping both hands in front of the chest. Now raise both the hands slowly up in the air as high as you can over the head such that you are reaching the sky on one leg.

➢ 9.15. Sarvangasana: Now lie flat on the ground with your back facing the ground, and your elbows and shoulders supporting your hips. Hold out the hips to rise both the legs in the air keep one leg in the air whilst dropping the other leg in a 180-degree over the face facing its knee cap.

➢ 9.16. Hansa-virabhadadrasana: Now stand straight. Slowly move the right leg as far in the front as you can whilst the left leg moves back as far in the back as possible the left leg must be straight. Curve the chest outwards with both your hands raising as high as possible and as wide as possible. Breath in and out with your lungs only. Drop the hands on the two sides of the hips as low as possible, and again raise them up in the air as high as possible.

➢ 9.17. Hamnssa: Flap your hands as wide as possible and as high as possible in the air lifting the body on your toes as if you are trying to take a flight.

➢ 9.18. Relaxation: Lay flat on the ground, facing eastwards and with the back facing the ground. Now breathe in and out as we chant the mantra 'Aum shanti' eleven times. [41]

---

[41] Pranayam yoga exercises are good for regulating life, controlling the mind and the urges of the body. It helps also in the regulating of the blood pressure, cardiovascular activities, and oxygenating the cells in the body. Yoga makes nerves stronger, induces sleep and health.

THE FOLLOWING GROUPING MAY BE TAKEN AS GUIDING TOOL:

REFER PAGE FOR MAP OF COSMOS

❖ Group one:

The upper 'lingham' comprises the crown, the cerebral brain, the skull, the head, the eyes, the nose, the mouth, the ears, the medulla oblongata, the nervous system, the neurone, and the third eye. Ajna chakra (the cavernous plexus) and the Sahasrarha chakra (crown). Rulers: Soma, Rudra, Vayau, Brahma (Aum Tat Sat), and pranna.

❖ Group two:

The lower 'lingham' comprises the neck, the back of the neck, voice box, the trachea, and the oesophagus. Vishudha chakra is the compassionate pump of life breath (laryngeal plexus). Rulers: Kuber, Issanaya, Varuna, Indra, Surya, Vasus, and Agnee.

❖ Group three:

The upper earth, comprising the breasts, the lungs, the lumber spine, the coccyges vertebras, the respiratory system, the circulatory system and the nervous system. Anahata chakra (heart plexus). Rulers: Bhuvah, Nirritti, Apah, and Agnee.

❖ Group four:

The lower earth, comprising the abdomen, the stomach, the lower abdomen, the liver, the pancreas, the reproductive organs, the excretory organs, the excretory system, the inner thighs and the pelvic. Swadhistana chakra (genitals, prostrate) and the Manipuran chakra (Navel- solar plexus). Rulers: Yamma and Earth.

❖ Group five:

The pillars, comprising the legs and the hands; and all the vital joints of the body - Muladhara chakra (the base of coccyx). Rulers: Agnee, Vayau, and pranna.

PRACTISING SELF-REALISATION WITH THE HELP OF RITES, RITUALS AND MANTRAMANJAREE

Cleansing the body and cleansing the skin are essential pre-requisites to practising mantra-yoga or yoga of the mantra. The cleansing process includes bathing rite of cleaning all the points of vital energy knots. The crown (the head hair), the forehead, the two sides of the foreheads optic nerve points, the ears, the eyes, the nostrils, the mouth, the tongue, the behind the head, the back of the neck, the front of the neck, the two shoulders and back spine, the front upper chest, lower chest and the stomach, the pelvic, the excretory organs, the buttocks, the limbs the hands and the legs. Every single body joint and point is cleansed in the invocation of the element water as the most calming chi energy. Apah, the water of seven oceans and seven rivers cleanses or purifies the Tattva (spiritual plane). The Bhuh (the gross physical), the Bhuvah (the physical), the Svahr (the mental), the Maha (the intellect), the janah (the consciousness), the tapah (the super consciousness) and the 'TAT SAT' (the pure consciousness).

Mantra-jaap (repetition of sacred words of shaktee, is silently chanted on a string of rosary beads of 11, 21, 54, or 108, from within. My personal experience of thirty years suggests that mantra-jaap must not be released by spoken speech, without an 'agnee-havan' (sacred fire). Mantra can be chanted anytime, anywhere, and any way, as long as it is deep in the conscious. A sound mind in a sound body is a collective composition to the soul awakening. Each person is a unique flower in the garden of God. Each person is a unique violin. Each person connects to the eternity with his or her own unique musical notes. God is the maestro grand master. Music is the mother tongue of spiritual eternity and God is the master musician. It is through music that we enter the other world. It is through music we begin to enquire with an insight. [42]

---

[42] Profound sages and saints like Sri Ramana Maharishi, Ramakrishan Paramhansa, Yogananda, Prabhupada, and others have practised constant silence with the glory of the Mother Nature divine bliss. Ancient seers have practised profound wisdom of Vedas in rites and rituals of hymns, mantras, and recitals. No institutional fame academy can bring us god. All they do is earn their personal fame and enrich their egos at the expense of humble rishis.

From all the Yoga-sutras and yoga practices, experience suggests mantra-manjaree as being the most practical and most beneficial because in embraces music, poetry, philosophy, and science of yoga in compassionate devotion.

Lighting a divine candle, we invoke the illuminating powers of the Gayatree in mantra, sacred profound word (antaratma-shabda), sound, vision, and pranna shaktee (vital life). Let us propitiate the 'param Tattva guru trinity' Lord Shiva the solemn giver of Moksha with music and poetry, for Shiva capers to the altruism of poetry and the rhythm of music. Music is the medium of expressing our inner most emotions and Music nurtures compassion and love in the heart and brings inspirational hope. Music is the force of the nature through wind, air, water currents, and mantra. Music is in the night sky full of glittering stars. Music is soothing and music is healing. The initial transcendence is a wonderful recitation of Aum.

Having initiated the gross physical and physical aspects of the body, we now move onwards, towards 'Pratyahara' (abstraction). Holding the right thumb in the middle of the forehead, with four fingers fisted we now remove all the 'indriyas' (the sense objects and the material attachments). The mind becomes calmer, purer and the heart wants to sit in profound silence. The mind is ready to welcome the profoundness of profound silence. This is an intermediate state. 'Aum Tat Sat' is repeated in silence to fix the concentration on Aum internally and externally on divine light of the candle. Emptying the mindfulness of noises and buzzing thoughts, we are now ready to embrace the 'dhyana' or the profound silence. Profound silence comprises the internal 'mantra-sadhana' (sacred ritual of repeating guru mantra internally) or the meditation on the param Tattva guru trinity Shiva. [43]

---

[43] The Vedic mantra for total spiritual liberation: 'Aum namastasyehi namastasyehi namoh namah. Aum karum bindu-sayukttam, nittyanmdyayyantti yoginaha kammaddum mokshaddum chaive Aum karaye namo namah'. [Translation: Obeisance to AUM, the final point upon which truth eternal reposes, may the divine yogeshwaar guru, cosmic guru Shiva reside in the centre most point of my third eye the spiritual eye and the sixth chakra, to guide me through towards the final beatitude of immortality in solemn quintessence.]

(Footnote continued)

An authentically profound mantra (sacred composition of sacred most words) has seven aspects to it; namely, it's sacred seer, its sacred deity, its sacred sound, its sacred Shakti (power), its sacred shaktee (energy), its sacred pillar upon which the mantra rests, and its sacred guru.

The seer of Gayatree mantra was sage Vishwamitra, its sacred deity is Ganesh, its sacred sound is AUM in seven musical notes, its sacred power is the power of the sun, its sacred energy is the energy of the Agnee (in seven rays, seven sparks and seven flames), its sacred pillar is the four directions of the cosmos namely the north, the south, the east and the west, and, its guru is param Tattva guru trinity 'Aum Tat Sat', that is upheld by Soma, Rudra, Indra, and Varuna.

The physical part of the cosmic body of the Gayatree mantra is Aum bhuh (the physical realm of the earth, the human, and the food), Aum bhuvah (vital spiritual place of the antariksham – atmospheric orb), Aum svahr (mental plane, vast space between the dyou (eternal heaven) and the antariksham (atmospheric orb), Aum Mahah (the orbit), Aum Janah (realm of the creator's bliss), Aum Tapah (realm of the creators pure conscious force), Aum Satyam (realm of the creator's absolute truth –purest perfection).

The meta-physical aspect of Gayatree mantra is 'Aum Tat Savitur Varenyam Bhargo Devasya Dhimahi Dhiyo Yo Naha Prachodayatt; Aum Tat Sat. Aum hreem, krleem, hum, shreem, swaha'. Eternal omnipotent truth divine, that thou art, the ultimate illuminating light of the Savitar-Agnee (the solar infinity), supreme and almighty, effulgence, of the Gods, we meditate in unity of delight, to embrace your enlightenment with our purest intelligence and purest consciousness to bring salvation through imperishable devotion and sacrifice. May the param Tattva guru trinity 'Aum-Tat-Sat' direct us towards you in unity and togetherness of light-delight and twilight of devotion and sacred prayers. Aum, the omnipotent, hreem the solar, krleem the illuminator – Indra, hum the light of Agnee, Shreem the effulgence of Soma-Amrutt (nectar of truth) and Swaha the togetherness of three worlds in united prayer mode.

'Aum trayambakkam yajamahe sugandheem pooshteevardheanaam urvarookamiva badhanaan mrityoormoksheeya maamrittatt.' [Oh three eyed Lord Shiva, thou art the sun, the moon, and the holy agnee. We worship all three oh Shiva save us from mortality.]

UNCONDITIONALLY COMPASSIONATE GURU OF 'ALTRUISM'

There is only one guru between a true devotee and infinite God - the soul of the devotee. From the window of the soul (middle of the forehead), the aspiring sincere devotee gets inspiration, illumination and delight of guidance from the trinity guru 'Shiva' (the param Tattva guru of the cosmos).

If you followed the chain of guru into the anthologies of the past, the origin is in the HARI AUM TAT SAT. It is with this power of infinity that ENERGY (shaktee) was sublimely united in oneness with ETERNAL POWER (Shiva) to produce sensationally pure words comprising sound, profound meaning and force. According to GuruGeeta, the most profound and the most authentic guru is Shiva (THE TRINITY). The word (shabda) is compared to Brahma (eternal power). When eternity inspired the cosmic forces, the whole galaxy quivered with vibrations by the movement of Supreme God and the sound AUM made seven rotations and seven revolutions of echoes around the galaxy. The very first compilation of AUM was 'Hari Aum tat sat'. This became the devatas or the divine trinity, the mantra and the guru Shiva in the wholesome sense. Shiva is thus ordained to be the sole cosmic guru of total liberation. Life is a problem in as much as death is a fear. When one is entrapped in the web of life, one cannot become a free winged bird at the time of death. All seems a matter of mind when really it is not.

During the course of the final stages of this book, my greatest inspiration has been J Krishnamurti. I paused and decided to read TOTAL FREEDOM for two weeks. I found a great profound guru in his 'written word', the sacredness of which helped me see through difficult obstacles. What I love and endure about Krishnamurti is that he does not claim anything yet he makes you realise the truth by compassion and selfless love. Therefore, he must be a true Guru albeit he does not entertain followers and he does not like to follow. I revere the humble manner in which he dares a person to look at a problem. I learnt from this profound Guru that if you look into the mirror and see the real you without getting afraid, then you have elevated into the higher plateau of truth.

Our modern world heroes have created such distinctions and such segregation like the east and the west that a humble 'everyday' person cannot discover his soul without a guru. Hence, it is presumed that he or she cannot attain moksha or spiritual liberation.

The modern world has created everywhere-big, saga of 'guru', 'master', 'leader', and 'teacher', rather than simply 'an inspirer'. According to Vedas, every single source of inspiration is Guru. Human Guru is an inspirer full stop. If a guru ceases to become an inspiration of delight then the guru ceases to become a true ascetic guru.

Human Guru cannot extend to become God supreme almighty albeit many occultists today are encouraging praises and hymns in their personal names. The essential issues are 'who am I?' 'Where have I come from?' what am I doing?

I revere every single wise person and every single wise scripture. However, I do not revere profoundly the heroism that is based on bringing self-made rules and regulations which make the flight of delight complex to comprehend and practice. Many persons proclaim to be gurus and create their own little umbrellas of sects and organisations and practices all over the world. These persons enrich their lives at the expense of other humble 'everyday' persons (those persons who know not anything better because they have not endeavoured to set out on the pilgrimage of their soul searching journey). Many 'everyday' persons are put off by the idea of pilgrimage or the soul-searching journey. For one main reason, that the persons claiming to be gurus create followers and create sects and create organisations and create boundaries of self-made mantras and initiations.

The threading aspect is the absence of a guru in many 'everyday' humble persons who are not at a liberty to participate in holy dialogues and discussions and meetings and conferences. Does this mean that the ordinary person cannot reach Godhead? Who was Jesus then? He was an ordinary carpenter! Who was prophet Mohamed? He was an ordinary tradesman! Who was Buddha then? He was a prince born in royal family.

Many persons try to create followers and create barriers in the literal sense of the process between a disciple and God. My greatest pity and sympathy is towards the Gurus who proclaim to be something, whilst my utmost compassion and wholesome love is towards the 'everyday' humble person who is sombre and tired from everyday labour of survival and struggles! As such this book is not for the guru who thinks he knows everything and who proclaims to be something of a mediator when in reality an ordinary person cannot even touch his feet without an appointment or monetary power!

How many Hindu gurus and Buddhist gurus do you currently come across initiating all sorts of different mantras and giving all sorts different energies all over the world without any authentic essence of the proliferation and originality of the sacred word? The answer is many. This is not what Buddha wanted! Buddha left behind authentic valid mantra manjaree as a sacred composition of guidance to the soul. Therefore, a mantra is a solemn guru in its own right. When one reveres a sacred mantra holistically with dedication, perseverance, and fortitude, one becomes enlightened like the Buddha. The eastern philosophies of Godhead have been weathered in spirit due to this inauthentic power enforcement and due to the camouflage of "REMIX" by numerous Gurus and leaders all of whom claim and proclaim to be the masters of the supreme truth. Absurd and most holistically ridiculous is the leader as well as the follower who is blindfolded into the powers of such imperfect mastery of salvation. Moreover, using the core essence of the substance Mantra, a word (shabda) can have adverse effect on life itself. A mantra can work wonders for the salvation of the spirit or it can bring destruction into the personal life of a person. Therefore, a Guru can elevate and inspire a disciple to evolve or a Guru can bring personal fame to himself at the expense of the poor person's honesty and foolishness. A personal Guru who lives on the welfare of others cannot possibly be a sacred divine master. A true guru selflessly sacrifices without any regard for praise or desire or money or power or system or structure or proclamations of any kind. A true guru is very rare to find. If one does come across a true guru, then one must holistically treasure such a person's inspiration divinely.

How many Mantras have been created in the process of upholding an organisation and sect? How many sects have been created with different bureaucratic gurus? How many divisions have been created in the name of God? Under no illusion of the Vedas have these been encapsulated to be Hinduism or Sannatana dharma! Many Gurus today teach the YOGA of spiritual liberation using the ancient techniques of the Vedas under brand names. Yoga has become a commercial enterprise in the modern world. The more sophisticated the location the greater the charges for the classes. This is propaganda. This is not real salvation. The bigotry and the heroism of religious organisations do not bring about harmony and peace in the humankind! They bring about divisions and inequality between humankind without substance or essence of truth. Spiritual liberation is not open to just the privileged few!

Spiritual liberation does not require passports, or visas, or certificates! This is not an academic process! Spiritual liberation or moksha is a sacred pilgrimage of self-discovery of the soul. Find out for yourself in great adventure if all else fails. Discover with the help of your own spirit. Your very own spirit is your guide. To listen to it requires becoming quiet and profoundly awakening from within, with a profound compassion. Such a profound human compassion, is an unconditional loving compassion firstly for the spirit of life, secondly for the fellow human togetherness, and thirdly for the congruence of union between the earthly life and world of the spirit. It is a delight of merging two lights with highest integrity, purest vision, purest fathomless faith, and profoundest fusion.

Pilgrimage of the soul is open to ANYONE! Pilgrimage of the soul is universal and yes it is true what the Vedas say that you need guidance from a guru to reach the divine bliss! Every SOUL IS A YOGI (with good intent)!

Nevertheless, per the authentic Vedas, ATMA (Soul) IS THE PARAM TATTAVA GURU (essential spiritual guide), EMBODIED IN TRINITY OF POWER, ENERGY, AND FORCE. When you open your inner sixth sense, you have acknowledged the ETERNITY as your guru! Cosmic Guru Shiva resides in your sixth chakra the third eye or the guru eye.

Once your third eye or the guru eye is worshipped with purity, compassionate love, substance, devotional silence, and great sacredness, your entire mind and body will begin to disperse the perishable matter and ego. Energy or the shaktee merges in a fusion of Divine bliss to create 'ARDH'NAREESHWARA' (fusion).

Buddhist altruism manifests in the Dhamapada. Buddhist Mantras, which Gautam Buddha, perused for salvation of the spirit and total emancipation of the spirit, are hereby declared with great profound reverence to Buddha. Whilst it is not my intention to profess any claim of mantra manjaree, I have personal experience of the following five maha-mantras:

1. AUM NAMO BOODHISWAHAYE AUM (AUM IS MY INTELLECTUAL VISION, AUM IS MY MIND AND AUM IS MY GURU)

2. AUM TAT SAT [AUM IS THAT TRUTH, AND TRUTH IS ETERNAL]

3. Aum shangham sarannam gach-chhammi, Aum dharamam sarannam gach-chhammi, Aum prannvam sarannam gach-chhammi, Aum Acharya sarannam gach-chhammi, Aum sarwam sarannam gach-chhammi. (A CHANT OF JOY AND HARMONY)

4. AUM MANNEY PADMAY HUM. AUM DYOU SHANTI [AUM IN MY HEART, MIND AND SOUL, MY SOUL IS THE SEAT OF THAT GOD ETERNAL DIVINE BLISS THAT IS EMBODIED IN ENERGY AND AUTHENTIC POWER. MY LOTUSFOLD FORM IN PROFOUND SILENCE IN ONENESS WITH THE ETERNITY IS GREATEST.

5. AUM GATEY GATEY PARAGATEY PARASAM GATEY BOUDHEY SWAHA. AUM PARAMATMAYEH SWAHA.

'AUM IS ECHOED IN MY HEART, IN MY MIND, IN MY ENTIRE BODY AS A VIBRATION OF ONENESS. THIS VIBRATION IS SUNG AGAIN AND AGAIN BY THE MAGNIFICENT NATURE, IN WORD, THAT IS THE SOUND OF MUSIC AND THE MEANING OF THE ETERNITY BEYOND THE WHOLESOME MAGNIFICENT NATURE'.

GURU - A GURU IS A HEALER

When we extinguish our self-pride and ego, we begin to see a Guru in every person that enlightens us with a new positive substance. A child could say something so meaningful and substantially relevant to us purely out of the blue. We must kiss this child's forehead there and then. We must kiss this child's feet and palms there and then; for he is speaking the substance of God. He is conveying a profound most significant message of sacredness. It is a message from the higher order.

A Guru's gesture is pure and divine. A Guru is our spiritual guide. He or she is equivalent to someone who is between human beings and the infinite God. Just like the Mother Nature divine bliss eternal supreme is. A Guru is a wise person, who has earned his or her respect by giving unconditionally his or her wisdom to others. A Guru never demands. A Guru never manipulates. A Guru never denies selfishly. A Guru never forms a desire to make self gain. A Guru never collates lust. A Guru never ever gets angry. A Guru never speaks untruthful words. A Guru never misleads. A Guru is a humble person who understands humanity.

A Guru is always compassionate and always forgiving like the mother. A guru is always smiling despite any upheaval in conditions. A guru is self-controlled disciplined soul of life. A Guru is always happy. A Guru is an enlightened soul. A Guru has long suffered and grown progressively wise at each stage of the sufferings. A Guru is pre-requisite to spiritual awakening. A Guru is someone who is totally unselfish, someone who is totally and unconditionally dedicated towards the innocent child in you, someone who is entrusted with faith and confidence, someone who never lets you down, someone who is always there for you, someone who gives without expecting anything in return, someone who has experienced depth and breath of 'Atma jagrutti' (alias spiritual awakening).

A Guru does not necessarily have to be a living person. A Guru can be 'voice of god' expressed by a truly acclaimed saint. Like the words and teachings of Buddha in 'Dhamapada'. Like the words and teachings of Guru Nanak in the 'Gurugrantha'. Like the wholesome aggregate dialogue between Arjun and Krishna in the 'Gita'.

We always manage to find delight and hope from a Guru. Like if we seek out for the Guru in our souls we may find an inner voice always trying to guide us intuitively. Thus, a Guru could also be an intuitive spiritual guide from within our souls. This is called 'Atma Guru'. Buddha had an inner voice leading him to leave behind a lovely son and beautiful wife for Atma jagrutti (soul awakening). First, we have to awaken our inner selves. Unless we do so, we cannot possibly comprehend or even embark on to the path of emancipation. If we consider that God is sited in our lotus like hearts, and try to capture it as nectar in the most beautiful lotus flower inside our hearts then we have already began our contemplation.

Prophet Mohamed is representing the Guru status in conveying a universal message and furthermore including his own life experiences. Similarly, Jesus is a Guru sharing his insight with people of Jerusalem. Krishna is a Guru for Arjun (the spirit of life).

A ship needs to anchor firmly to harbour. A Guru is like an anchor in our life. It is like a nest to the bird that perches. [44]

---

[44] Sadguru means a true ascetic.

A guru is a divine spirit of life who sees anyone at a suitably convenient time and who does not deny his presence especially to the crying spirit. A guru does not shun a humble person of integrity for the gain of superiority or monetary proliferation's. A guru sheds tears of compassion on hearing the pain of others and transforms every teardrop into the sacred word of profound wisdom of the soul.

A guru sits in profound quietness to comfort the grief of others.

A guru finds time for the less unfortunate honest integrity. A guru never ceases to collaborate in kindness. A guru always smiles. A guru is a compassionate soul that has long suffered, long understood, long transformed in adversities. A guru is not shaken by the trauma, but is concerned in uniform compassion always.

SOLEMN DIALOGUE OF PRAYER FOR 'AUM TAT SAT' GURU TRINITY SHIVA

"Oh divine cosmic power of all atmospheric orb and the entire eternity, whose powers are beheld by 'Rudra' (the transformer, the evolutionary, the dissolver and the liberator), shower your mercy onto the humble obeisance of my mantra, rite, ritual, sacred word, and the altruism of my pure sacrifice."

"Oh divine cosmic power of three spheres of 'dyou' the atmospheric orb of celestial cosmos; I seek refuge in 'thee' knowing that you are the ocean of mercy and remover of disillusions."

"Oh divine 'guru param Tattva' - the ultimate trinity guru, sad guru - the intermediate guru, and the 'istha deva guru' - the guru that resides in my sixth chakra in the middle of my forehead), grant me your grace."

"Oh gracious one, you are the supreme power of the shaktee 'Maa' (who is the goddess energy dynamism of matter), you are unmoved my Karma."

"Oh immortal blissful altruism of eternal bliss, make me humanly humble so that I may learn thine supremacy."

"Oh supreme divine guru, open my third eye so that I may perceive thine pure divinity."

"Oh beholder of all sacred rivers and protector of all sacred oceans, save me and protect me from the darkness of ignorance."

"Oh divine guru, 'Aum Tat Sat' are three words merged in oneness of your 'trident', with your pure fathomless devotion and unconditional sacrificial worship."

"Oh guru Shiva (powerful immortal), you are the beholder of Shaktee in your trident and just your trident is enough to be worshipped as guru param Tattva (the wholesome guru divine bliss)."

"Oh guru Shiva, you are the formless AUM in the atmospheric orb, and you are the form of AUM in symbol with your seventy two thousand dance rhythm, sixty four thousand mudras, and eighty four million mantra-manjaree of the great Brahman omnipotent eternal truth."

"Oh Shiva, I bow to your unparalleled 'self-less-ness', the unconditional true sacrificial momentum of which ordains evolution, dissolution and orderly manifestations of the magnificent nature. ' Aum namah Shiva', grant me self-less devotion, and unconditional sacrifice."

THE IMPERISHABLE DEVOTION

'Aum' is the sacred creator, 'Aum' is the sacred creation, 'Aum' is in the sacred creation, and 'Aum' is the sacred most word (shabda) of the eternal Brahma supreme. 'Aum' is the infinite eternal energy of the infinite eternal para supreme Brahma.

According to Vedic anthologies, 'Adhyattmic gjnannam' is the profound wisdom of the eternal Brahma in a self-revealing cosmic knowledge that we briefly encapsulated. 'Karma' is the birth of 'absolute activity' that is duty in the normal survival world of the mind and the body and the duty of the soul in the natural world of cosmic nature.

'Adhidaivashjnan' is the wisdom of illumined ones. 'Adhiyagna' is the sacred sacrifice of the supreme eternal omnipotent God to unite the finite souls of the earth to the infinite eternity.

Therefore, this sacred sacrifice is a self-realisation process. Immortality or total salvation must be accomplished in the human lifetime, in a human body and with a human mind and human intellect. Every human person creates limitations, imperfections, bondage, Karmas, and mortality. As human fellow, as a spirit of life, one is also capable of transcending from the material planes of limitations and imperfections and evolving into the higher planes of fulfilment. The human fellow as a spirit of life must realise total spiritual freedom and salvation is the sole goal of life.

'Aum', is the sound of God omnipotent. Meditating on 'Aum' with the energy of the Gayatree, mantra in profound devotion only is sufficient to reach the imperishable Brahma.

The spirit of life must want to enjoy this sacred flight. The spirit of life must be able to sing the glory of 'Aum'. The spirit of life must be able to caper to the rhythm of 'seventy two thousand musical notes' of 'Aum'; the spirit of life must become beautiful infinite imperishable soul divine with the magnificent nature. The spirit of life must become a sacred seer. The spirit of life must become a wholesome loving compassionate soul. What is within will eventually manifest outwardly.

The possessor of eternal divinity automatically generates peace and tranquillity around his or her personality and there is a simple attraction to such a person without any squibs of money. Money no longer measures such integrity. The true ascetic will automatically do divine human acts of kindness, compassion, and servitude.

Love becomes the sole life breath. Only the truly dedicated devotee will grit life, accept life as it is, grin, and shrug it away as a perishable existence of experiences. Only a true seer will consider every single aspect of life in profoundness of profound word, profound breath, profound music, profound sight, profound sound, profound purity of food and thought, profound consciousness, profound insight, profound super consciousness and profound silence.

'Aum' the profound devotee soulfully chants. 'Aum' the profound devotee soulfully meditates. 'Aum' the profound devotee soulfully gives up the material attachments and all that is impermanent. 'Aum' the profound devotee soulfully opens in grace, gratitude, and harmony to the cosmic eternity with the energy of the Gayatree mantra. 'Aum' the profound devotee listens in profound silence and learns gracefully to become a free winged spirit of life.

'Aum' the profound devotee becomes profound by human servitude and by deep compassionate essential loving force. 'Aum' the profound devotee is an aspiration towards total spiritual liberation. 'Aum' the profound devotee is an inspiration to dull, ignorant and dark persons. 'Aum', the profound devotee progressively evolves in the flight of life, higher and higher until the nectar of truth is conquered in the vessel of 'Soma'.

'Aum', the profound devotee is the compassionate love of life and is truly in love with life because all that is around the devotee is magnificent beauty of the omnipotent God infinite imperishable supreme Brahma. 'Aum', beauty begets beauty and love begets love. 'Aum' the beautiful love of God descends from 'dyou' (eternity) to 'bhumi' (earth), in sound, light, delight, and fusion of oneness in power and energy.

'Aum' the profound devotee is an illumination of Agnee in enlightenment. 'Aum' the profound devotee is totally fearless, totally without superstitions, totally without doubts, totally without the urges to dwell into the tantric knowledge, totally without any limitations of the intellect, mind or ego, totally without imperfections of the power conscious society, and totally without platforms of vicious Karmic cycles of life. 'Aum' the profound devotee has surrendered in wholesome, with devoted love and warm compassionate worship.

'Aum', the profound devotee encapsulates the ultimate beatitude of 'truth' infinite in compassionate love and infinite eternal worship of God's beauty and God's grace. 'Aum' the profound devotee conquers the power of the soul where in the ultimate seat of God shines its armour as glittering night sky sparkling with shining stars. 'Aum' the profound devotee capers to the 'Ardhenaareshwar' (Shiva-shaktee) in sound, music, word, poetry, composition, philosophy, and meditation. 'Aum' the profound devotee loves the manifestations of Omnipotent God and feels the oneness with cosmic creation.

'Aum' the profound devotee makes the cosmic creation the manifestations of the spirit of life. 'Aum' the profound devotee only generates compassionate love and compassionate understanding towards the wholesome reality. 'Aum', the profound devotee becomes a precious child of the magnificent wholesome 'Mother Nature divine supreme' omnipotent God in warm compassionate embrace. 'Aum' the profound devotee becomes profoundly wise through learning profoundly in compassionate love and compassionate understanding. 'Aum' the profound devotee has no desires nor lures nor pities nor lust nor anger nor greed nor sympathies nor regrets nor remorse nor plight. 'Aum'; the profound imperishable devotion of timelessness radiates in the light of delight.

'Aum', the dawn and the dusk bring the twilight of delight in pure enlightenment and pure dialogue of prayers.

'Aum' the profound devotee soars like a free winged spirit of life and sings: "Victory! Victory! Victory! Peace! Peace! Peace! To the crying spirit and wounded heart three big cheers. Alas, there is victory to the wounded spirit! There is no more sob or sorrow! Alas the heart is filled with nectar of love and compassion! Alas the mind is illumined with the infinite sky and the magnificent Sun! Alas the world glows from within and the world outside is full of glamour, charisma, and glitter from the divine flame of Agnee! Victory achieved is victory accomplished and the spirit of life realises the revelations of the 'charismatic, omnipotent God supreme almighty'."

The spirit of life has successfully emptied all the ignorance and darkness of the shadows of its mind into the transcendental divinity of eternal light of the soul in eternal mantra-manjaree. GAYATREE MANTRA is the mother of THE VEDAS and the energy of 'Savitre' (the delight & illumination of Sun). It is the mother of mantramanjaree (or collation of divine mantras put together with music and sacred sounds). Gayatree mantra is musical, divine, sacred, soothing, healing, and transforming. Gayatree is the maytree of agnee (fire) and it is the mother of all Vedas. It is addressed to the divine life giver as supreme. Gayatri is symbolised in the energy of the sun 'the Savitri'. [45]

---

[45] For a novice loving spirit of life, the full Gayatri meditative practice is illustrated clearly in a musical CD now available from TIMES MUSIC, a division of Bennett Coleman & Co Ltd., The Times of India Building, DR D N road, Mumbai 400-001, India.

Gayatri reposes on AUM and this is the true sound of God in seven musical notes and a true vision of the delight of Agnee in rainbow of seven colours. 'Aum' the devotee seeks refuge in its effulgence and profound omnipotence. 'Aum' the ocean of mercy and the delight of joy, the devotee enters profound silence with profound protection and guidance. 'Aum' the devotee offers a silent prayer of quintessence to the divine Agnee in the third eye chakra. 'Aum', the devotee sighs is peace and enters the atmospheric orb of the celestial pure consciousness.

Devotional Worship with unconditional compassion and love

Worship requires bhava (right attitude), Atma drashtee (spiritual vision), shraddha (fathomless faith), and self- sacrifice (alias effort). Worship is of two kinds namely the "sarguna" (one with form) and the "nirguna" (one without form). Both are equally valid forms of worship. Sadhana or samndhya (devoted time to worship) is a prayer of profoundness to God from the Vedas performed according to Veda Puranas three times.

Every dawn, every dusk, and every mid-day signify meeting of time and galaxy in the union of three worlds. Tri-samndhya is 'three-fold' praying time. Worship in time, at a time, with time and in the merging of two times brings form and name to human devotion. The eternal formlessness of omnipotent God assumes form in the sacred prayer of delight, music, dance, poetry, art, and joy of devotee.

Sarguna worship is colourful, like the rainbow and it is symbolic. The Leela or the manifestation of God is colourful, full of music, dance, poetry, and fine arts. It is like "Rass leela" wherein Radharani formed an illusion of 109 Gopees for Krishna. There was no real Radha in the Gopees. Krishna was bewildered and disillusioned by the cosmic illusion of Radharani. Radharani created an illusion of dance, music, and rhythmic love that brought together 109 Gopees, in a cosmic fusion of passionate compassion. Radha sang to Krishna "You are my life breath and I am in love with this life, for it is your manifestation of compassion and fathomless love". Therefore, if we could form a passionate compassion for God like the 109 Gopees, then we too could love God compassionately. That does not necessarily imply that you are an idol worshipper. God has not manifested in the Idol of Krishna or Rama, but inside the vision of our own very soul and our insight in the heart.

Our spiritual, emotional, and mental, composition is merged in 'oneness' with the 'leela' of God (colourful manifestation of the rainbow of God). It is with our devotion and compassionate love that we are endeavouring to conquer God's Leela (translation: manifestation).

Without fully understanding the purpose of an idol or an image, one must not condemn a Hindu worshipping the deity glory of an idol or image. The essence of worshipping in this manner does not conform that there is God in the Idol or the image. It gives the manifestation of bhavna bhava (compassionate spiritual emotion within the person's innermost heart). It is the compassionate worship or Samndhya or Sadhana of the Bhakta (being true worshipper of God) that is relevant. It is the self-less devotion (comprising music, poetry, mantras, and unconditional love), that matters. It is the ritual of the ceremony of Vedic mantra's and chants that matter. The composition of Vedic hymns matters. Not the Idol!

Hindu's do not worship idols. Idols are utilised by some Hindu's a means of symbolic representation only. At least the true worshipper is chanting some form of valid deity Vedic mantras no matter what. At least the true worshipper is not an occultist or an antagonist trying to justify exerts of man made monogamy of survival. At least the true worshipper is engrossed in his bhavna bhakteerass (self-less dedication). At least the true worshipper is not an arrogant fool. At least the true worshipper is 'together' in compassion with God in a happy trance. At least, the humble servant of God is worshipping what he or she perceives to be the manifestation of God (keeping a beautiful vision), selflessly. At least the ignorant, knowing that he or she is ignorant, is deeply engrossed in bhakteerass (rituals and devotion) without hesitation, doubt, moan quibbles, and bragging. At least the Sadhak (Vedic performer) is doing something rather than nothing, in the purest of karmic activities with pure intent.

So worshipping an Idol or an image does not necessarily imply that the worshipper places God in the Idol or image. The worshipper, alias the Bhakta reminds himself that God is beautiful, that God is ever so loving and magnificently blissful despite the wretched of this earth. Therefore, it is his or her vision that places bhavna and bhava in the idol. The idol is just a piece of matter not the substance. It is a metaphoric illusion of the maya.

The true substance is the worshipper's vision and spiritual expression in Vedic rituals and mantras.

The antagonists and intellectually religious congress of institutional faiths, proclaim to know God and in the process misinterpret every form of Idol worship as being a sin. Yes, worship of matter without substance is a sin, for sure. Fact is Hindu's do not worship the idol but the life of the vision of God-incarnate created from clay or matter. One cannot worship matter. One worships the substance within us that is the 'Atma-parmatma' (Soul finite-Infinite eternity). Veda's do not condemn anyone that worships matter with substance, rituals, and procedural ceremonies. For example, you loved your elder sister more than anything in this life. You behold the sweetest memories of your sister (as a loving friend, as a self-less caring individual, as a dancing star, singing star, as a financially profound figurine and as a poetic life symbol). Would you not place a large picture of hers in your office and in your home after she is dead to remind you of how magnificent she was? Does that necessarily imply that your sister's life is in the portrait or statue? Of course not; it implies that in your vision there is still her live memory, a cherished memory of 'compassionate togetherness'.

Second aspect of worship or sadhana is Nirguna "without form". This is the Atma jagrutti or the soul awakening sadhana. In this self-realisation process, one suffers in silence and takes multifarious purposes in servitude. Buddhism is an excellent form of nirguna sadhana. It comprises deep profound meditation, mantra chanting, living a saintly life, becoming a totally selfless individual and being a universal giver of happiness to all. Atma dhyann (spiritual awakening) is progressive and not instantaneous. It is like any other art or science. It took Buddha thirty years to reach divine enlightenment, so great patience and fortitude are essential pre-requisites in the journey of spiritual life. The result is not the point but our efforts, our own sacrifice, our own very diligence to improve our welfare, the welfare of the grand globe and the peace offering to the spiritual world.

Vedas direct a soul towards spiritual awakening in a scientific manner, using scientific techniques like yoga, mantra's and rosary beads ('Mala's'). Aggregate of 108 (one hundred and eight) beads constitute a mala. One represents the process of evolution towards non-duality. Eight reflects 'maya', the divine illusion through which a soul evolves.

When each of the component digits of the multiples of eight (8,16,24,32,40,48,56,64,72,80...) are added together, it results in a regressively lesser whole number (1+6=7, 2+4=6, 3+2=5,) until ninth multiple. It means the twirl of eight is infinite until the number nine ends this cycle. 'Zero' between the one and eight represents the world, which has embodied material value because 'one' has been added before it. One hundred and eight represents absolute infinity of Brahman or God. The component numerical digits of 108 when added together would tantamount to nine.

Furthermore, the constituent numerical digits of all the multiples of nine, when added together result in nine. Nine therefore represents the highest number. Vedic astrological science manifests around nine planets. Vedanta (Vedic guide) considers nine as the most divine number. For example, an individual person's life chart is the birth chart that is scientifically drawn up to reflect nine life breathing aspects, nine purposes, nine cosmic planets, nine things, nine houses, and nine merging avenues. Vedanta's grant us the Vedic mantras for creating the foundation of spiritual awakening. No one could possibly accomplish the journey of life without sound and profound mantras, directional force and inspirational energy. One must initiate the self appropriately and adequately such that the rite and the ritual of every sacred practice become profound.

Mantra sadhana (the practice and exercise of mantras) can be done in various ways. It is not necessary for you to sit in one position for hours and hours of mantra sadhana. Let no Guru fool you into this nonsense. Religious practice has to be practical, scientific, feasible, and in accordance with the Veda Puranas or any other divine scripture upon which the faith perches. According to Vedas, the foremost symbol of the first born word in sound, meaning, and cosmic form, is "Aum". 'Aum' is the sound of God and it is considered 'maha mantra', meaning most profound mantra of all mantras.

A Vedic invocation and oblation mantra should not be chanted aloud unless during the Havan or Yagna (sacrificial fire of material offering to God/ Deity/planets).

However, a Vedic prayer or any other prayer must be sung in a poetic and musical manner. 'Prarthana' (prayer), 'Uupassana' (rites), 'Mantra-Manjaree' (incantations of sacred word), and 'stotram' (verses of praises) are spoken during ceremonies in the presence of a deepam (sacred candle of cotton wick and ghee and camphor).

'Mantra-manjaree' is the ecstatic joy of repeating the incantations of the divine syllables of the mantra sounds. According to Vedas, the strength of the mantra manifests in its poetic rhythm and personified sound. It must be hummed within our inner most selves in such a manner as to awaken all the anatomical chakras (acupressure points). It must conform to be meditative measure of the spirit. It must sing within us in such a manner that it produces vibrations. Mantra yoga entails unity of mind and nervous system. Mantra yoga must enable us to free from the wheel of 'samnsara' (bondage of life and death within the materially physical world).

Mantra meditation (or Atma dhyana or sadhana) is known as 'mantra yoga' in Vedas.

The various physical postures and yogic exercises are configured to bring the senses under harmonious balance with the mental and spiritual aspect of the 'nada' (sound personification of the spirit). The word 'yoga' implies 'link with god'. Vedas mean "universal truth". They were applicable then and are applicable now.

According to Vedas, we are living in the age of Kalyug (the age of shorter life span, shorter memory, shorter sight, shorter days, shorter revolutions, and shorter conveniences). This is also known as the age of "hypocrisy and quarrels". Per Vedas, it is not possible to accomplish total mystical yogic transcendental bliss in Kali-Yuga. Hence, Vedas prescribe mantra yoga or mantra sadhana or mantra meditation as a progressive means towards self-realisation. Many scriptural injunctions further conform that "holy names of God" are sufficient means of crossing the ocean of "Maya" (illusion).

The Vedas, the Upanishads, and other ancient anthologies suggest more combination of various sacred rituals. The experience of profound devotion is good. The realisation of delight in the profound devotion is better. The embodiment of delight in devotion is best. The revelation of the supreme truth in devotion is delight unparalleled.

Devotion and quietness render salvation. However, 'selfless' servitude to humanity in profound compassion, merges the individual soul to the infinite soul in love.

In Kalyug (the present age of falsehood), the aggregate form of 'Atma jagrutti Dhyanna' (spiritual awakening) comprises the following:

1) Mantra jaap/yoga (Bhaktee yoga and Dhyana yoga).

2) Reciting Vedas, hymns mantras and prayers (Bhaktee yoga).

3) Reading and reciting anthologies (Bhaktee yoga).

4) Reading and reciting the Ramayan (Bhaktee yoga).

5) Listening to hymns (Poetic recitals of Vedic poems).

6) Reciting and reading the Geeta or any Holy Scripture (Satt-Pathd).

7) Fasting and detoxification of excess bodily wastes (Yoga).

8) Hatha Yoga and asanas (physical yoga exercises).

9) Giving compassionate help to the less fortunate (Raja-Yoga).

10) Charity without discrimination (Raja-Yoga).

11) Maintaining Culture and rituals (Raja-Yoga).

12) Pilgrimages (visiting holy places) (Tyaag Yoga).

13) Giving direction to the youth. (Tyaag Yoga).

14) Providing support to the holy persons and persons of integrity (Raja-Yoga).

15) Uniting the individual soul with the magnificent nature in silence (Dhyann).

16) Incantations of hymns and sacred praises (Saar Kirtan satt-saang).

17) Becoming a compassionate loving spirit of life (Prem bhavna).

18) Giving light of wisdom (Atma Gyann).

19) Solitary silence (Samadhi).

THE AWAKENED SPIRIT OF LIFE

Let us understand with deep compassion, that when the spirit of life takes a flight of life of delight, it acknowledges this world of impermanence with deepest compassion for the human existence by crying, "life oh life! Let it be what it may be. Let it be. Come what may. Let it be a flight of delight".

This cry is about the existence of human life and the sacred duty of the human spirit towards the soul. The cry acknowledges the material life, its material survival and detaches gracefully from the perishable matter, in progressive evolution. The spirit of life further acknowledges that karmic evolution encompasses absolute life, which implies that the sacred pilgrimage of the soul is a collective experience of collective existence.

'Hamnssa' as a free winged spirit of life therefore sees with the eyes of the eagle, farthest in the skies and beyond the wholesome vast open nature and captures the delight of the light of the Sun in sacred profound devotion. It transforms gracefully in progressive evolutions of progressive karmic lives. Such evolution may comprise more than one life experience. The essential evolution is within the personality, and outside the personality in all that it carries with it.

The earthly days and earthly nights are but temporary umbrella of impermanence. Therefore, as a spirit of life, one must not take permanent shelter in the perishable umbrella, but seek refuge in the imperishable infinite supremacy of para-existing omnipotent God. 'Hamnssa' as the spirit of life sings freely in the vast open space.

'Life oh life let it be. Let it be what it may be, accept it, grit, grin and shrug it away!' 'Hamnssa' realises the duty of every cosmic force and feels the energy of every cosmic phenomenon during its flight.

'Hamnssa', flies across the clear blue skies and clear blue waters, and finally closes its eyes because the third eye has awakened to the glory of Gayatree and it is now following only the 'INSIGHT' of Gayatree in compassion, love, profound wisdom, profound silence, profound mantra energy of Aum that echoes in every single particle of the air.

The entire vast sky and the entire vast nature capers to 'Aum' infinite imperishable sound of eternity. In this wholesome journey, the 'Hamnssa' gracefully surrenders to eternity in profound silence and in the profound devotion of profound sacrifice; there is delight of light entering its consciousness. 'Hamnssa' feels eternal joy and eternal happiness. The kind of happiness, that is not dependent on things and people. The kind of happiness that rests in the profound silence. It begins to understand compassionately and it begins to awaken to the magnificent nature. In devotion, 'Hamnssa' finds peace.

Let us understand 'devotional worship' 'ananda bhaktee rass' (blissful joy of playing with the cosmological manifestations) known as compassionate worship. Meera (a legendary compassionate love of devotion) was crazy for Krishna, from the very childhood in the deepest and most profound way. Meera's devotion suggests to us that it is a selfless, flawless, unconditional, sacred sacrifice of compassion and love. Meera's love for ishwar is a fathomless faith that knows no boundaries of doubts or illusions because the eternal avatar of God itself has become the illusion of the mind. Leela (colourful cosmic joy of blissful dances and music) is sacred and to caper to God is only to express that the spirit of life is crazy in love with life! Only in total oneness of a sacred craze, can there be joy of blissful consciousness. Truly realised spirit of life is awakened spirit of life that has no desires nor any pity nor any snares of stark attachments or material bondage.

A truly awakened spirit of life has long suffered in silence. Through experience, the spirit of life understands in profound compassion the real cry of a real aspiring human fellow striving to reach the infinite bliss of the eternal supreme God. The illumination of profound wisdom of mantra manjaree in 'Sacred Yagna' (holy fire) is the offering to Agnee as a sacrificial tyaag (rite of renunciation). The charity in knowledge, food, and kind deeds contribute to 'satt-karma'- righteousness. The devotional meditation of 'Aum' becomes purifying elevating force of the spirit. In purest action only there is salvation. The Vedas give birth to cosmic life with Agnee as the sole illuminator, the Vedas evolve the cosmic spirit of life with Agnee in profound human experience, and the Vedas repose in the fusion of Agnee, in 'sun-explosion'.

The light of the soul merges in a fusion of delight with the light of the Sun. This supreme congruence manifests in profound prayer dialogues and profound reverence of the light of Agnee in Sun.

'Agnee' (the orange hue of the sun) is light and the delight of agnee is compassion of the dusk and illumination of the dawn. Indra (the illuminator) is the cosmic delight in twilight of the dusk and the dawn.

The face of the infinite truth is covered by the brilliant orange hue of the Sun's orb. At the dusk, Varuna (the compassionate soul of the cosmos) unveils the Sun in delight. At the dawn, Indra (the cosmic illuminator) unveils the Sun in delight. In delight the eyes of the cosmos merges in 'united oneness' with the eyes of the soul (insight). Insight merges the soul in togetherness with the eternal God in true delight.

In the finite world of impermanence and uncertainties, there is no end to sorrow. There is neither solace nor consolation for sorrow except for the sacred sacrifice in prayers in the passage of time, at the dawn and at the dusk. In the infinite world, there is no end to happiness, bliss, concord, peace, and harmony. In the infinite world, there is not limit to happiness. In eternity, truth reposes in the delight of Soma (the purest nectar of God). There the illumination forever is never failing light of delight. There, the self-revealing light of the sun 'never failing' illuminates true nectar of God. There the light of delight is immortal. That infinite truth, which is the purest delight, has merged in 'oneness' with the light of the soul and delight is embraced at the dawn and the dusk on the earth.

Delight in eternity, which is the purest truth, the formlessness infinite truth, is brought down to the human existence on earth in profound prayer dialogues. Delight takes a form in the passage of time, to transcend fathomless hope, fathomless compassion, and fathomless light, to the celestial planes, the spiritual world, and the karmic earth. The green pastures of the earth renew in delight and the compassionate dusk brings restful sleep in the nightfall. In delight, the compassionate free spirit of life sighs in profound 'togetherness' of existence. The river, having travelled in time, takes a flight of delight running over the soft pebbles in ecstasy of joy.

Life oh life! Let it me be a free spirit of life. Let me become delight.

Oh Great Spirit of divinity let me take a flight of delight in the beautiful teeming vast sky.

Oh Great Spirit of lights, mother of all delights, giver of all there is, let me hear you in the winds. Mother oh mother, your life breath gives life to all. Oh divine mother, giver of all let me walk in beauty, in dignity, with the integrity of my soul divine back home where I long to belong. Dusk oh dusk, let my eyes ever behold the beautiful orange red hue of the sun and the purple rays of the elapsing sunset.

Life oh life! Let me revere and respect with my hands folded in 'prannamm namaskara' (obeisance) all that there is in the bare existence. Life oh life! Let it be a flight of delight in the twilight of the dawn and the dusk.

Oh Great Spirit of life, there is hidden beauty in every leaf, every rustling tree, every river, every rock, and every soft pebble. Oh Great Spirit of love let me endure in beauty as I take a flight delight. Mother oh mother, I seek thine strength, thine courage, thine comfort, thine solace, thine boon, thine holding hands, to let me contemplate and accomplish my last walk.

Life oh life! Light oh light! Sun oh Sun! Let me now become a lamp with clean hands, empty mind, transformed heart, and a clean body. Let my eyes endure in the beautiful vision of the dusk, so that when life fades away as it should, my spirit of life may come to you without all this, that and the other.

Life oh life! Let it be a flight of delight. Let beauty now become my penultimate glory. Let the lamp of glory always remain lit. Life oh life! Let it be a flight of delight for now, all said and done it does not matter. Life oh life! Let me become delight. Let me become the great mystery of the profound silence of the nightingale that whispers softly to the wind. Life oh life! Let the serenity of the divine ocean embrace the spirit of my life in the light of twilight of the dawn and the dusk. All sounds enchant, all fears are no more. I am not one voice but many colours of the rainbow, many lights of the stars. Life oh life! Let it be a flight of delight. Let it be a beautiful dance of trance.

10. A FLIGHT OF DELIGHT 🍂

'Aanandaaddyeva khalvimaani bhuutaani jaayante Aananddena jaataani jeevanti Aanandam prayantyabhisamvissanti.' (Taittiriyopanishad)

'From the transcendental light of Delight we came into existence, in the light of delight we grow, evolve and pilgrimage towards our soul divine, to fulfil our life karma in eternal time. At the close of our pilgrimage, we enter our divine home, ah the supreme light of delight.'

'Aum bhur Aum bhuvah Aum svaha Aum Mahah Aum Janah Aum Tapah Aum Satyam Aum Tat Savitur Varenyam Bhargo Devasya Dhimahi Dhiyo yoh naha Prachodayyatt. Aum Tat Sat Swadhay swaha. Aum aapo jyotii raso'amruttam Brahmah Bhur Bhuvah Svahr Aum Shanti Shanti Shanti.'

'The self-same word, Aum, is the Brahmah para-existing in the seven spheres of existence namely the earth, the water, the fire, the air, the ether, the intelligence, and the consciousness. That eternal Aum, the creative principle of the light of delight manifesting through the Illuminating Sun becomes the mantra, the energy, and the light to bestow wisdom, bliss, and immortality. Oh divine light of delight thou art the quintessence of the earth, the atmosphere, and the heaven. Oh divine light of delight we meditate upon thine supreme energy effulgent as ever. Oh divine light of delight may thou lead us onwards to our final goal. Oh divine light of delight may thou energise our consciousness. Oh divine light of delight may thou grant us the boon wholesome life filled with health, wealth and happiness so that we may witness the beauty of the dawn and the dusk. Oh divine mother light of the delight may thou grant us the immortal nectar of 'Soma' so that from death we may become the beauty of delight. Life oh life! This beauty is not tempting, this beauty is real divine beauty, it is illuminating, it is magnificent, it is revealing, it is extra ordinary. Life oh life! Let me merge in oneness with the light of delight as I offer prayers of peace and happiness to the human existence at the dawn and the dusk to bring hope to the world in despair. Life oh life! Peace be with the Celestial. May that peace transcend down to the spiritual world and finally the existence on earth. Aum Peace.'

316

Twilight of delight has arrived and the rivers merge into the ocean losing their names and forms. Similarly, the profound spirit of life merges in oneness with the eternity in oneness of devotion. Just as the capering flight of the running river knows no grand maestro except the embracing vast ocean, the profound spirit of life 'Hamnssa' knows no grand maestro other than the soul. In the soul proper, it has found what prevails in the vast blue skies and the vast blue ocean. The union of 'atman' (the soul) and 'paramatman' (the eternal Brahman —omnipotent cosmic God almighty) is known as the sacred encounter of the divine bliss.

Having realised the soul, the free winged spirit of life 'Hamnssa' is releasing the karmic cycles of life and death onwards towards the delight of Agnee (Sun). The glory of its spirit cries in great profound joy 'that art thou!' In the sacred devotion of AUM, the 'Hamnssa' moves on-wards and proceeds on its way onto the ultimate delight of life.

The wholesome human existence follows its own path in progressive karmic evolution to re-enact the divine and cosmic eternity internally. The celestial (the spiritual spheres) the terrestrial (dry earth) is divided by 'antariksham' spheres of spiritual astral orbits. This astral sphere is the essential realm of human person's free winged spirit of life. It is the link or the joint of the lokka (the earth) and the par-lokka Dyou (the eternal). The 'antariksham' or the astral intermediate sphere is the mediator between the soul and the form. Within this astral metamorphosis of intermediary divinity there manifests an 'inner shrine'; It is this beautiful light of delight, the soul sees in the twilight of delight. Hamnssa rejoices this with tears of profound happiness. It is the sphere of 'tyaag' (sacred sacrifice or sacred pilgrimage).

'Hamnssa' takes a flight of delight onwards towards the delight of the Agnee in Sun and makes a pen-ultimate final pilgrimage in the sphere of astral super consciousness. In the super consciousness, the spirit of life offers pure prayers, pure unconditional devotion, pure meditation, pure poetry, and pure profound words of altruism, pure contemplation, and pure sacred sacrifice of the self for the self.

Life oh life! Let me be! Let me be Gods eternal child! Let me rejoice even.

A longing to belong to the eternal world

In every human spirit of life, there is a deep profoundness to become divine. After many experiences, and many adventures of life, the thirst for the divine remains unquenched. The spirit of life encounters delight in the light of the dawn and the dusk (samndhya), in the light of the spirit of life (atman-tatvam-asi-yohahm asi brahman aham asi), and, in the light of the togetherness of the three worlds. The three worlds namely the celestial, the spiritual and the terrestrial congregate in 'shabda' (word), 'mantra' (lyrics of sacred words), 'tap' (meditation), 'mantra-manjaree jaap' (hymns), 'saar-sama-bha-mide samndhya-prarrathana' (joy of grand prayers of the dawn and the dusk). It is a moment of longing to belong to the other world – the spiritual world or the higher order. It is a delight of realising the other world – the mystically unknown para-existential world. Beyond the finite, and beyond all the forms of delight, the light of delight finally travels through to the sound of "AUM", the light of "AUM", and the energy of "AUM". 'Aum' is the 'sarrgunam-shabda' symbolism of 'nirgunam-brahman' (formless god). It is really the primordial word.

The praise to AUM is:

'Aum Tat Sat swadha swaha Hari-Haraya Aum Tat Sat Swaha Hari Aum Tat Sat Swaha Aum swaha swaha swaha'.

Thou art the truth. Thou art the absolute ultimate Brahman. That Brahman is the eternal God. That Brahman is the eternal dissolver and the eternal transformer Shiva. That Brahman is the divine celestial keeping harmony, balance and thou art that Brahman that sustains all life. Aum is everything, all encompassing, and the entire whole vacuum. From the wholeness the atman (soul) is, that which Brahman is verily. Glory be to Aum.

Twilight (samndhya) is the maithuna (the union) of 'kaal' (time-infinite eternal), the 'antariksham' (divine plane celestial), 'jagadah' (galaxy of planets, stars, and cosmic gods, deities, and spirits), and the 'prithvee' (earth-terrestrial). This most beautiful moment in time is a delight of longing to belong to the light of lights shining across the expanse of the whole horizon.

The divinity in every human child longs for togetherness always. The divinity in every human child longs to belong. Every human child is a spirit of life longing to be loved unconditionally and longing to love unconditionally. A divine friend is 'divya-meetram'- a divine friend who loves togetherness, brings people together, and supports both the need to survive and the need to evolve. Always keeping a divine watch over his/ her fellow humankind in prayers, hymns, meditation, poetry, philosophy, and music, a divine friend is a true friend who brings delight of light. He or She is known as 'Jyoti-prakash' (ray of de-light). A divine friend brings a smile on the face! Commemoration of every fraternity is an obeisance to the three worlds, homage to the celestial, a remembrance of the beautiful moments of togetherness in human spirit, and a grand sweetness 'madhurramm'. A flight of delight is philanthropy of sheer exuberance in spiritual joy. Leaving behind the mundane gross materialism, the spirit of life longs to belong to the eternal world of divinity in bliss. So, the spirit of life offers obeisance to the keeper of the purest nectar of truth (lord Shiva):

'O divine AUM, 'atman' (soul), 'umaa' (shaktee) and 'mrityunjayaye' (conqueror of mortal death). May you be my divine friend and may you reside in my heart forever. Oh divine friend (amruttam-mitraam) may you never cease to grant your delight as you favour us and save us from the bondage of the life sufferings, pain, sorrows, and diseases. Oh divine friend, the keeper of my heart, the giver of my life, the delight of lights, may you grant me your favour and may I be released from distress, damnation, and trauma of my withering, frailing body. Oh divine friend, you bring me liberation, may you bring me delight for now let me take a flight of delight! Oh divine friend of all devotees, may you light the pathless flight of delight! Oh divine friend of humble simplicity, may you bless the pathless flight of delight with unwavering divine intention, steadfastness, and tranquillity. Oh divine friend of life, light my heart, light my mind, light my sub-conscious, light my whole so that I may take a glimpse of the purest nectar of somam. Life oh life! Let it be a flight of delight. May the mother of all, the divine goddess bring peace, happiness, health, spiritual wealth, and hope to all the children of nature. United may all the rivers resolve, united may all the rivers merge, united may all the rivers become one, united may all the rivers dwell in harmony.

A blessing for the suffering spirit of life out on a limb:

No prayer is ever wasted. Prayer is a divine mode of a human being. It is a tender insight into the unmanifest. The twilight of the dawn and the dusk, portray a manifestation of the unmanifest cosmic prayer in silence. It brings to the human earth the life of light to enlighten and illuminate towards a newer hope and it brings to earth restful night of sleep. Just as the light of the sun gracefully leaves the tired worn out earth in peace and tranquil quintessence, the profoundness of silent nightingale grows in the human mind and thoughts begin to calm. The dusk is a prayer mode that is a tender beautiful state of the eternal, the mother earth, and the human child. The purple silence that came to calm the tensed mind, the silent echoes, and the murmuring nightingale are whispers of the divine. It is an offering of blessings to the congregation of the three worlds. May the blessings of the compassionate nightingale bring rest, peace, and consolation of the tired and worn out energy. May the blessings of the stars and the moon, never failing, bestow upon the rivers to transform the hard earthen stones into soft pebbles. May the beautiful dreams console our wounds and disentangle us from the entrapment of the web of hurt and sorrow. After a days buzz, noise, haste and waste, may the heart become calm and may there be grace to accept all that we cannot change or alter. Life oh life! Let it be a flight of delight.

The dawn awakens, illuminates and brings with it freshness of the life of light. Life oh life! Let it be a flight of delight. May all the rejections, resentment, hurt and grief matter no more for the spirit of life has now embarked onwards towards its goal like the river leaving all this, that and the other noise, haste, and waste. Life oh life! Let the absences and be filled with eternal echoes. Life oh life! Let it be. Face it, accept it, grit it but grin, and shrug it away. All this, that and the other matter no more and may compassion reach out to all those, whom we seldom hear from. May we have the courage to speak softly for the excluded ones. May we have the strength to become gracious and compassionate to our own spirit of life. May we nurture and love our true divine self. Life oh life! Let it be a flight of delight in the twilight of the dawn and the dusk. Life oh life, Let it be a longing to belong to the divine shelter without all this, that and the other.

The pilgrimage is unfolding before our eyes and with the elapsing universal time. The pilgrimage is a sacred most divine journey of the astral plane.

The astral plane is the greatest mediator and it resembles the great maestro of the vast clear blue skies and clear blue oceans.

This is the life of the 'spirit of life'; this is the life of the sacred unconditional prayer. Prayer is the profound omnipotent mediator between the earth and the celestial. The entire astral plane blossoms with pure prayers, pure devotion, and pure sacred offering of pure words, pure praise, and pure harmony.

It is the 'maithuna' or the marriage of Shiva (cosmic guru) and shaktee (energy) in Ardhenaareshwar (or the Jyoti-Milan the meeting of two lights namely the light of delight from the Sun and the light of sacrificial fire from the earth). Universally speaking, in the act of prayer, the human person implicitly and explicitly is sharing in the most profound dynamism of core central existence penetrating deep into the heart of the universe, acknowledging the unfolding universe, realising the universe, and moving onwards to realising the dynamic force of life – the Agee in Sun. This core central dynamism of prayer is sublime twilight of truth. In Sanskrit, the union of two lights is 'Jyoti-Samndhya'. It is the penultimate reconciliation, the penultimate mending together, the penultimate putting together of sacrifice and delight, the penultimate marriage of mind and soul.

The semi-static state is a sleeping mode of the cosmos. This sleeping mode of the cosmos is facilitated by the energy of the sun 'Samndhya'. The daylight meets the nightlight of glittering stars and moon. The evening sunset radiates beautiful calming orange rays of its Agnee to bring a penultimate metamorphosis of rest and peace. The nightfall brings restful sleep. The calming Agnee from the sunset says 'all that has been said and done and there is nothing else one could possibly do except pray and hope for the best of all worlds, the best of all peace, the best of all compassion'.

'Jyoti-Samndhya' is that sacred life of profound prayer of silence and 'Jyoti-Samndhya' is the whole cosmic life and destiny of existence in the moment of time.

The word 'aum' has travelled through seven spheres of existence from the gross to the subtle most in time.

Time is formless. Time is eternally fathomless. It makes an appearance in the motion, fusion, and explosion of nature in 'Samndhya'. Time takes a form of prayer mode through the light creating 'Aum' and the celestial transcends onto the human earth in the moment of time at the dawn and the dusk.

The self-same word 'Aum', the self-same sacrificial light of life 'Tat' and the self-same divine beauty of the dawn and the dusk 'Sat', merge in togetherness of the teeming vast sky, the sun the and the sea. It takes a form although it is formless. The unmanifest and the manifest meet together (maithuna-manthana). The past, the present, and the future become relatively inter-connected in somewhat profound way. In realising the prayer of time, a silent sigh of the bygones grants solace to the 'humbleness' and the 'sincerity' of the sacred prayer offered to time. Prayer is a meeting (maithuna) of time (kaal) and the meeting of time is a delight of prayer of sacred sacrifice. Prayer is 'pratiroopaka' (corresponding in form). Prayer is a total wholesome Cosmo-theatrical act by which we as imperfect talent of integrity transcend both in time and space and discover that within our own spirit (that which is the part of the destiny of the whole cosmos) we are re-enacting the light of delight of truth that is the immortal bliss of Agnee in Sun. The self-same word (shabda), the mantra energy (shaktee), and the sacrifice (yagjna) merge in quintessence to bring tranquillity. The prayer offered to mother samndhya when time (kaal) meets (maithunah) the sky, the earth, and the sun in the moment and becomes a sacred boon to human:

"*Ya samndhyamandalagata ya trimoorti svaroopini Sarasvatti ya Savitri twam vande Veda mataram ya visva-janani Devi ya Trimurti svaroopini Gayatri roopini ya hi twam vande sapta matrkam.*"

Translation:

"Oh divine mother Goddess Samndhya, the formless energy transcending in the solar orb. Oh divine mother Samndhya, thou art the mother of existence in time. Oh divine mother Samndhya, thou art the mother of the trinity (brahma-vishnoo-mahesh'shivam). Oh divine mother thou art Saraswatti-Savitri-Gayatri. Oh divine mother thou art the mother of Vedas. Oh divine mother Gayatri, the mother of Vedas, I bow to thine seven forms."

The transcending light of the morning glory of the sunrise and sunshine brings forth illumination and energy for transformation. In the daylight of consciousness, the self-discovery process of realising the self ascends. In the twilight of the sunset, the three worlds suffuse in togetherness. Such a fusion expresses the peculiar dual polarity residing in our soul. 'Truth' and 'falsity', real and unreal, form and formless, sound and silence, infinite and finite, celestial bliss and chaos, eternal existence and paternal (Worldly) existence, all come into duality of crossing twilight. The objective meets the subjective. The encounter between the divinity and the humanity is revealed in prayer.

Revelation by spoken or written word, enlightenment by sacred word (shabda), and delight by the light of sacred reasoning is one side of the equation. The other side of the equation is the self-discovery of the self. When the two lights meet together in a fusion of delight, quintessence of glory manifests. The fusion of prayer expands vastly to encapsulate the ritual sacred act of worship and the pilgrimage of celestial astral plane. The sacred prayer is uniting in togetherness and in harmony the entire cosmic forces.

Prayer is a sacred dialogue between the mind and the soul. Prayer is the penultimate astral pilgrimage of the soul in silent hymns, praises, and profound sighs.

Prayer is a communication in word, without word, and in emptiness. Prayer is just simply a miraculous mediator between the material and the spiritual worlds. Prayer brings together the earth, the celestial atmosphere, the orb, and the eternal heaven in a fusion of delight.

The karmic earth, the 'master-less' winds, the divine auras, the atmospheric orb, the roaring seas, the Agnee (Sun), the eighty four trillion stars, the Moon, the seven planets, the unseen stars of destiny, the falling stars, the sleeping planets, and the cosmic deities, all, unite together in a fusion of compassion to embrace the individual soul in prayer dialogue. In the fusion of togetherness, 'Sapna' (the dream angel), 'Mohini' (angel of illusion of God), 'Maya' (the form), and the 'Apassaras' (the cosmic angels), congregate to perform 'leela' - dance extravaganza. Delight is highest form of happiness that gives freedom from all this, that and the other mundane earthly survival. It is the 'Aanandaadhyamaya' (transcendental bliss). It is 'Param-aanandamayam' (eternal happiness).

According to Vedas, human fellow is not alone because, 'every single living entity' forms minute little threads in the entire vast web of existence. Every single thread is connected somehow, in somewhat profound way albeit we may not be able to comprehend in wholly, the fullness of the web of existence.

Oh such imperfection in human existence! The spirit of life realising this offers gratitude to God of what has been accomplished within the limitations and life experiences.

In Vedic devotion, the imperfect human talent rises gallantly to the sunrise and offers prayers of gratitude to the mystery of origin, to the awakening life of light, to the illuminating life of light, to the shielding life of light, to the sacrificial life of light and to the pure life of light.

'Aum Shivasamkalpa' is the gurus ordain of the cosmic eternity to grace Moksha. Moksha-datta Shiva is the penultimate Param-Tattva Guru that drank entire poison dropped in the ocean by the demons and that invoked the 'Sheesh Naag' the mighty cosmic cobra to suck off every single atom of the poison from his body from his neck. Shiva is thus regarded as the penultimate liberator. Shiva further made every dead devotee divine by spreading their cremated ashes all over his body. The sacred pilgrimage is the moving round the sacred fire of sacrifice. The ancient sages moved round the sacred fire of yagjna 1,108 times reciting the Gayatree mantra 108,000 times to become into the final penultimate umbrella of Shiva. Under the penultimate umbrella of Shiva, the sages offered the sacrifice of the Moksha (final liberation) mantra to Shiva and repeated 1,108 'Aum Namah Shivaya'.

A 'wholesome peace' is offered to every, cosmic power, cosmic energy, and the entire cosmic inertia is brought to a stand still by the peace prayer. 'Ishtha deva' (the ultimate liberator of the soul divine, the transforming guru of the soul) Shiva is worshipped in silence on the maha-moksha (the supreme final total spiritual emancipation) mantra, with sacredness and profound oneness of mantra, prayer and soul. This is not a sociological compromise nor is it a reason or cause. It is coming together of time and existence. It is the offering of sacred prayer to 'insight'. The giver of 'insight' is Shiva in our sixth chakra (middle of forehead).

A devotee cannot embrace the entire eternity nor can the devotee insert the entire life into one single act of worship. A liberated devotee is an imperfect talent of integrity in an imperfect world of imperfect epiphany. Therefore, the penultimate offering of the sacred prayers is to the 'insight' ('Divya-drashtee') and the 'param Tattva guru trinity Shiva' (the cosmic seer, dissolver, and transformer), to deliver us from all our imperfections, limitations and impermanence to the eternal bliss of Agnee (eternal Sun). As an imperfect talent of integrity, the devotee acknowledges the limitations and representations of the 'known' material world and the unknown eternity in absolute perfection of reverence and prayers.

Therefore, the penultimate atmospheric orb brings to the solace and consolation of the true seeker its form of fusion albeit the orb itself is formless. A true devotee realises godhead in limitations of human platform thus godhead has to have a name and godhead has to have a form although the formless eternity is a para-existence. It has to take place as a divine most sacred human experience. It has to be experienced somewhere and it has to be realised in the twilight of sunrises and sunsets. Such a profound realisation may be in deep within one's spirit of life or within the orbital transcendence of the soul.

A profound sacred dialogue of prayer furthermore, has to take place in time, even if it reaches the fathomless eternity. Peace is truth and truth is the ultimate point upon which time reposes in, prayer, solace of twilight of the delights and total concourse.

Time takes a form in prayer and the devotion of twilight as a grand fusion of three delights meeting together. The 'delight' of the fire in Sun meeting the 'delight' in the atmospheric orb of Shiva and the delight of the sacred fire of sacrifice from the human Yagna (sacred fire of sacrifice) on earth.

A human prayer has form, name, and colour, place, and time. A sacred prayer of gratitude and forgiveness is the penultimate dialogue between human person on earth and the omnipotent God in eternity. In this dialogue, there is 'concrete-ness' of profound silent words emanating from the heart of the human sacrifice. Vedic prayers do not make a compulsion of bowing to the ultimate supremacy of God in almost two separate dualistic sides of an equation. Rather, praying is a merging of the human soul and the entire metamorphosis of creation and existence.

Praying unites in 'oneness', the fusion between the human fellow, the atmospheric orb, the celestial planes, and the heavenly eternity. The merging in 'oneness' ('ekam-maithuna') is meeting of the light of the soul and the light of delight of 'insight'; the meeting of the day and the night in the dusk; the meeting of night and day in the dawn; the meeting of Atma (Soul) and paramatma (God) in a sacred dialogue. We all belong together to the same ocean of eternity, albeit, every human person is a unique river with unique energy and unique force. Vedic prayer makes a huge confederation of 'togetherness' of all seven spheres of existence and para-existence.

When an awakened spirit of life rises and wakes up to a bright new sunrise, with a profoundness of completing its time here on earth; the free spirit of life, utters a sacred dialogue of prayers in compassion. The compassion of 'togetherness' in sacred Vedic prayers is a very crucial aspect of Vedic delight. A delight, that only transpires from profound 'insight'. In 'togetherness', may the omnipotent god almighty supreme eternal divine bliss (Aum Tat Sat Para-Brahma Hari Aum) protect us, cherish us, and move us with vigour, health, vitality and profoundness. 'Agnee' (the yellow hue of the Sun) is revered, as a guardian of righteousness and as the inspirational light of altruism in the lyrics of poetry, music, and dance. 'Agnee' is the ultimate 'DELIGHT" towards which the wholesome noblest sacrifice in time and space onward enkindles.

The night falls and the spirit of life seeks refuge in the glowing 'Agnee', having experienced the human life and feeling benign in its imperfection and limitations. Every praise to 'ratree' (nightfall or nightingale) is afforded in silent prayer to 'Aum Tat Sat' guru trinity Shiva, the beholder 'Rudra'. Off whose rotations, has revolved and evolved the day into night and the night has been invited to bring rest in sleep. This rest or sleep is the stoppage of the material world and activation of the night orb with its millions and millions of twinkling stars. 'Ratree' (nightfall) gather all the deities, all the cosmic forces, all the cosmic energies, all the celestial gurus, and all the ancestors to form a union - A grand union of 'togetherness' to commemorate a sacred dialogue to the eternal omnipotent infinite almighty cosmic-Godhead. As there may never cease to be sunrises and sunsets, so also, may there never cease to be seasons of spring, summer, autumn, and winter.

May the togetherness of the worlds of 'dyou' (heavenly eternity), the 'antariksham' (atmospheric orb) and the universe (earth) continue to shower rain on earth, revolve tides of oceans, create green pastures and bless the earth with 'riya' (wealth, form, and prosperity). In togetherness of three worlds, may there be peace on earth and may there be serenity in the soul. In togetherness of three worlds, may there be continuity of the time in changing nightfall. In togetherness of three worlds, may there be restful sleep and profound silence.

'Shiva', the cosmic deity of Rudra, and the Cosmic guru 'Aum Tat Sat' that beholds the entire cosmos in transcendental existence keeps a close watch on the existence of earth through his third eye or the cosmic eye. As such, the ratree (nightfall) prayer is offered to 'Shiva', who is also the deity of darkness, and the deity of motion. 'Shiva' in Vedas, is also, referred to as, immortal grace to all the mortals, diseases, accidental deaths, untimely tragedies, and upheavals. In returning to the sleep mode, the cosmos and the cosmic human personality repose on the cushion of Shiva's 'Aum Tat Sat' mantra. Praises of hymns, mantras, and kirtans (holy songs) are offered to Shiva, as a commemoration of nightfall. The simplest of all mantras, 'Aum Namah Shivaya', can be recited 108 times, as a gesture of gratification and as a sigh of compassionate embrace to Shiva.

'Shiva' is the Vedic cosmic guru, cosmic keeper, cosmic dissolver, and cosmic spirit of the eternal vast infinity. The Vedas and the Vedic mantras were first spoken to 'Uma' (the consortium) energy of Shiva narrated through his insight when 'Uma-Shaktee' (divine cosmic goddess) transformed 'Shiva' into compassionate 'Somam' (divine immortal nectar). When Sommam performed the 'nattarraj' (cosmic dance), the 'nirgunam' (formlessness) had to become 'param-gunam' (eternal form). The seven forms that emanated from the merging of 'Uma-Shiva' are:

'Ardhenaareshwaar' (half he half she) or 'Shiva-shaktee' (god-goddess) and 'Hari-Hara' (keeper-dissolver) or 'Rudra-Vajra' (transformer-creator) or 'dinna-ratree' (half day-half night) or 'surya-chandra' (half sun-half moon) or 'naar-naarree' (divine human avatar incarnate of 'pashupattaye-parvatee'; Rama and Sita; etc.).

'Mrutyunjayayah' (immortal divine liberator), the giver of 'moksha' (freedom from sorrow, pain, suffering, adversity, vikarma or sin, karma life and death), is three eyed.

The third eye (between the two eye brows and in the centre of the forehead) is the cosmic eye. It is also the soul of the Sun, the soul divine of the cosmos, the effulgent vision, the supreme insight, the para-existential light of delight of the eternity. 'Mantra-manjaree' (recitals and chanting of divine words) is finally given to 'Mrutyunjayayah' (immortal divine liberator), the giver of 'moksha' (freedom from sorrow, pain, suffering, adversity, vikarma (sin), karma (life and death), the three eyed Shiva who is in a trance:

'Oh keeper of cosmic divine nectar, the ultimate liberator of all, the destroyer of desires, lust, attachments, deliver us from the bondage of earthly decay, rot, and mortality. Oh 'Mrutyunjayayah' thou art the jointly 'Shiva-shaktee' in the form of 'lingham-yoni' (sphere shaped stone resting on base similar to a gem-egg placed on an egg-stand). Oh 'Mrutyunjayayah', grant us the boon of insight so that we may envision your beautiful divine cosmos, the mystically unknown para-existence of the eternity. Oh 'Mrutyunjayah', thou art the eternal time 'kaal' in your 'nattraaj' (cosmic dance of time), thou art the eternal light 'Sun' in your 'trinetra-chaksu' (third eye), thou art the 'jagad-ambalika' (cosmic soul of the cosmic energy).'

Oblation and obeisance to 'Mrutyunjayayah' with the following invocations or incantations:

"*Bhishana, Samhara, Asitanga, Ruru, Chanda, Krodha, Unmatta, Kapaalla, Vishvanatha, Maheshvara, Sadyojata, Vamadeva, Kalagnirudra, Netreshaya, kaal-rudrayeh, Indraya, Agneeya, Yamaya, Nirrittaya, Varunaya, Vajraya, Somaya. Aum namoh namah Shivaya Shivaya namah Aum.*"

The above are the Vedic Sanskrit names given towards the motion of the time in clockwise rotation and the motion of the planets in anti-clockwise rotation. These words are divine words, mantras, and are penultimate hymns of lord Shiva – the cosmic liberator. In the penultimate sacrifice of human life, the 'Mrutyunjayayah yagjna houmam' (sacrificial fire of immortal bliss) is carried out and chanting the moksha-mantra is recommended 108,000 times three because of kaal yug (age of falsehood). A CD-ROM disk may be obtained of the maha-Mrutyunjayayah mantra for clarity of pronunciation and it is recommended that no mistake is made in its entire pronunciation.

When the 'yantra' (the shape of the sacred cosmic diagram), the 'mantra' (the sacred word of the cosmic energy), and the 'tantra' (the sacred rites, rituals, the ceremonial obligations) unite, delight transpires.

The hymn offered to God 'Mrutyunjayayah':

'Oh three-eyed Lord Shiva, with this oblation of sacrificial yantra, mantra, and tantra, I worship thee in transcendental devotion. May you forgive me for my errors (known and unknown) as I accomplish my penultimate pilgrimage with your grace. Oh Guru of my soul, charioteer of my soul, let me become 'hamnssa' (swan) like. Oh God 'Mrutyunjayayah' may you save me from the dreary mundane mortal life of human on the karmic earth, whereat I am under the bondage of desires, diseases, and sorrows. Oh God 'Mrutyunjayayah', with my sacrifice in mantra, yantra, and tantra which is a mere obligation made with highest intentions and great profound integrity; deliver me from all evils (including death). Oh God 'Mrutyunjayayah', grant me the boon of thine sweet nectar somam and make me divine.'

'Aum namah Shivaya cha Sambhavayacha Mayobhavaya cha namah Shivaya cha namah shankaraya cha mayaskaraya cha namah shivaya cha shivataraya cha.'

'Oh almighty father, the limitless father, the divine power of the galaxy, the supreme power of the Sun, the heavenly father, the merciful father, grant us the profound peace and deliver us from the wretched darkness.'

The Vedic perception of sin and evil is in the word of 'DARKNESS' and 'DULLNESS'. The 'Evil' becomes mortal and impermanent feature of the elapsing time, because Shiva (the father of Galaxy, also known as Rudra –the transformer) subjects it to a total destruction. In the process of destruction of the gross physical and the physical matter, Shiva (Rudra) benignly reigns the compassion of Varuna (the cosmic preserver), and gives re-birth to the human kind on the karmic plane of human earth. Dissolution of one human cycle of impermanence and mortality is a beginning of another newer cycle, a reminder for repentance, retribution, consecration, and resolution in karma. Thus, the human life, is a penultimate opportunity for spiritual growth and spiritual awareness, in karmic progressions.

The infinite truth manifests in the soul infinite. The infinite truth is ultimately one supreme truth regardless of, the colour, creed, cast, culture, shape, form, size, name, prestige, status, all that, and more. That Supreme truth is the eternal most holistic truth. That truth forever enlightens us in humane spirit with love and hope! When the soul infinite merges in a fusion with the glory of the light of the fatherly sun, human miseries disperse and dissolve to become a formless eternity. The eternal bliss is divine bliss – typological heaven whereat the light of the Sun never failing forever illuminates. Such eternal bliss is only an experiential bliss as such, and the human experience can only be an 'encounter in absolute time'. Every encounter is an intricate, complex, metamorphosis of the karmic cycle in reason, cause, purpose, opportunity, and sheer coincidence! Just like the dawn and the dusk! The philanthropic encounter in time is beyond the intellectual spectrum of the thought, the feeling, the perception, the idea, the philosophy, the concept, and the self-same words. It is a blissfully wholesome encounter of soul, mind, and body.

THE LAST WISH OF THE SPIRIT OF LIFE

"Life oh life let it be a flight of delight". The spirit of life sighs in profound silence. "An imperfect talent of life I am, an imperfect spirit of life I am, I am but the spirit of life, an awakened, aware spirit of life. I cherish my human experience. I revere the human love and the human ability to make a union of togetherness of the three worlds."

The human compassion shines brightly in the harmony of 'togetherness'. The concord of 'living together' in 'peace' never fails to radiate light of delight. This typological idealism is the wish of every awakened spirit.

"Before I close my eyes to rest in the nightfall, I offer my sacred prayer of resolution that I may live tomorrow to form togetherness of human relationships. If I should leave this earth in my sleep, oh divine omnipotent god almighty supreme, may my last thought be on the grand union of the three worlds and the merging of all the rivers into the ocean of eternity. In togetherness, I hold the spirit of my life to bring total concord of happiness within me, around me and with my fellow human spirits."

The awakened spirit of life, having touched the nectar of truth and having encountered the 'absolute Brahma' ('delightful truth'), sighs in compassion:

"May I vibrate in seventy two thousand musical notes of AUM on the strings of the grand violin, the grand maestro of which is my profound spiritual guru the invincible AUM-NAMAH-SHIVAYA".

The divine human experience is so wild; its caper knows no other grand maestro to put a complete stop to the risk of warfare and strife, save the soul infinite itself. Hamnssa cries:

"I am but a collective part of the wholesome imperfect universal world of adversities and concretises but I am a hungry compassionate spirit of life that yearns for love and compassion. I am united to resolve the human configurations of crises and chaos, with all the sacrificial love and compassion, for there is a hope for concord of harmony and happiness, so shall peace be on earth as it is in heaven."

The awakened spirit of life is further elucidating the total fulfilment of the soul, albeit mystical. It is 'simple truth' found in simple quintessence. The profound silence brings a disappearance of 'fear' on the earthly consciousness, bringing profound peace.

"PEACE! PEACE! PEACE! Peace is on the earth, on the green pastures, and in my beloved fellow beings, as peace manifests in the atmospheric orb and in the eternal supreme heaven. 'Aum' brings peace with the smoke of my spoken words in the atmosphere. 'Aum' brings peace within me, around me, and onwards I fly in the vastness of these magnificent blue skies. Onwards I fly into the atmospheric orb and the heavenly eternity of the vast open space embracing 'AUM' in the 'orange hue' orbits of the Sun. 'Aum', peace everywhere. Oh divine Sun, unite my spirit in thine delightful fusion."

The entire reality sustains its existence in this relational configuration of pure consciousness. Pure consciousness is non-dualistic. It is unique manifestation of the 'aham-brahman' (God in the self). It is pure compassion. Deep down in the most profound recesses of a personality, there is a longing, even a need for the simplification of the entire earthly existence. Delight is in a state of simplest and purest consciousness.

This reduction, simplification and assimilation of divine subtlety manifests in one penultimate form and one penultimate symbol - the sacredness of 'AUM'; 'Aum', is 'para-Brahman' (God), and 'Aum' is the vacuum of pure quintessence. 'Aum' is the first and the last syllable of the Vedas. In 'Aum', the spirit of life rests in peace.

In profound peace, the spirit of life sighs in deep compassion to make the last wish:

"May the mother of all divinities, cherish the light of my 'fathomless hope' to bring delight on earth".

"Let me dissolve in the vastness of this magnificent sky, I belong to the fathomless eternity in fathomless joy and fathomless delight".

"How I wish, this peace in united bliss would form a concord of harmony in the life of human and life itself. Life oh life let it be a flight of delight!"

SACRED DIALOGUE OF PEACE PRAYER IN ATMA-YAGJNA (SOUL RITE AND RITUAL OF SACRIFICIAL FIRE OF AGNEE)

In the eternal light of the total freedom and total bliss, manifests the penultimate concourse of 'delight'. Vedic philosophy does not find truth in isolation and loneliness. It detests all the idiosyncrasy of conceptual mysticism. The Vedas begin in simplicity of one syllable and one form "AUM" in affording the initial praise to "Agnee" and ends in the same syllable in "Agnee". This simplicity is a formless vacuum, formless God, transcendental God, infinite God, and eternal heaven.

The typological heaven and the eternal God is merged with the awakened spirit of life, the free spirit of life, the enlightened spirit of life, in compassionate 'togetherness' of prayer dialogue. 'Ishwaar' (eternal God) takes a form in the twilight of delight of the dawn and the dusk to commemorate the sacred dialogue of prayer. When praises, poetry, lyrics, and hymns, are offered to, God, the entire galaxy and all the cosmic forces are brought together in a sacred dialogue of peace prayer. This togetherness of sacred moment is profoundly auspicious. Every rite and every ritual of the human sacrificial fire merges in a fusion of "delight". In delight, the spirit of life, affords solemn praises of peace to every single cosmic deity:

Peace to you oh magnificent 'Indra'. Aum glory is to Indra (the beholder of light, enlightened soul of the cosmos, and the blessing of Agnee), with sacred profound obeisance. Aum peace be with Indra. Aum delight is with Indra. Obeisance to Indra; Aum profound peace be with Indra.

Peace to you oh eternal 'Agnee'. Aum glory is to Agneeye, the twilight of delight in the dawn and dusk, in the sunrise and sunset, in the day and night, in the rainbow and in the music, in the air as well as in the water, in the heaven as well as on the earth, in the spirit as well as in the body. Aum, sacred profound obeisance to Agneeye - the supreme light of delight; Aum peace be with Agneeye (the supreme delight of truth).

A hymn to Agnee: "Peace to you oh divine inspirer, divine illuminator, divine priestess of all, divine mother of all. Oh shining one, ever effulgent one, thine delight 'never failing' ever shines in my soul. Oh non-ageing one, thou art immortal and thine grace is everlasting. Oh divine Agnee, you are my delight. In your delight, I beseech enlightenment. In your delight, I impart the light of eternal hope to my fellow. Oh divine Agnee thou art the glory of the earth as thou art the finesse of the earth in the twilight of the dawn and the dusk. Oh divine Agnee, in thee, I merge as all others merge in 'oneness' of bliss. Oh divine Agnee grant me strength, grant me strength to sing your praises forever. Oh divine Agnee, your 'delight' is unparalleled. Oh divine Agnee, may I once more recite your maha-mantra with the grace of Savittree (your energy): *'Aum tat savitur varenyam bhargo devasya dhimahi dhiyo yo naha-prachodayatt. Aum swaha; Aum tat sat swaha.'* The truth that manifests in the upper most hemisphere of the cosmos above the Soma the vessel of purest nectar of God, that light of truth 'never failing' ever shines to glow in eternity forever is an everlasting delight! Oh peace be to that supreme most delight, for it is the same delight that awakened my spirit, moved my spirit from the gross physical earthly existence to the super conscious manifestation of eternal truth infinite. Hail to the 'delight' of Agnee. Glory of delight is yours, glory of delight is mine."

Peace to you oh immortal 'Yamma'. Aum, peace be with Yamma (the god of death and king of the immortal souls of the ancestors, the celestial, and the atmospheric orb), Aum, glory is to Yamma with sacred profound obeisance.

Peace to you oh Nirritti. Aum, peace be with Nirritti (the transforming evaluator and the 'resolver' of destruction to retribution and redemption), Aum profound sacred obeisance to Nirritti. Hail to perpetual transformer of Nirritti. Aum, glory be to the divine 'dissolver'. Aum glory be to the 'resolver'.

Peace to you oh compassionate Varuna. Aum, peace be with Varuna the compassion and the preserver of cosmos; the effulgent charioteer, of the nectar of pure truth in Soma. Aum profound sacred obeisance to Varuna - the loving endurance of the pure nectar of truth in Soma; hail to divine compassion of Varuna. Aum glory be to the compassionate.

Peace to you oh Vayu. Aum, peace be with Vayau - the atmospheric air and the force of wind that sustains momentum in cosmos. 'Aum', profound sacred obeisance to Vayau - the transporting force of energy and the moving dynamism of the cosmic energy. Hail to the momentum of the wind, the air, the atmospheric orb, the pressure, the density, the propensity and the intensity of the atmosphere. May the atmosphere become calm with the sound of Aum everywhere. Glory be to you oh Vayau.

Peace to you oh Kuber. Aum, peace be with Kuber- the eternal ploriferator. Aum profound sacred obeisance to Kuber - the benefactor, the giver of fruits, the mercy of divinity, and the remover of obstacles. Aum, profound sacred obeisance to Kuber - the giver of wealth, health and happiness in food, shelter and clothing. Hail to Kuber, the eternal cosmic wealth that never ceases to provide the earth with green pastures and fertilisation.

Peace to you oh Issanaya. Aum, peace be with Issanaya - the mediating facilitator. Aum, profound sacred obeisance to Issanaya - the link. Hail to the garland of reconciliation. Hail to the synthesis of all thesis and antithesis. Hail to the mediator!

Peace to you oh Rudra. Aum, peace be with Rudra (the evolutionary and the transformer), Aum, profound sacred obeisance to Rudra (the transformer of karmic life and the devotee of Soma). Hail to Rudra, the cosmic guru in trinity of 'Aum Tat Sat'. Hail to Rudra the infinite eye of the cosmos. Hail to Rudra, the dissolver of death, the re-enactor of new seed, and the profound evolutionist of all other cosmic forces. Hail to the destroyer of evil. Hail to the suppresser of mortality. Hail to the liberator.

Hail to Rudra (the manifestation of truth in silence). Peace to charioteer of Soma, Aum the divine guru of the cosmos, the charioteer of the Soma (vessel of pure nectar), the transformer, the liberator, the giver of Moksha (total spiritual liberation), the karmic master, the lord of all immortals including the god of death, grant me solace. *'Aum namah Shivaya'* (obeisance to Shiva). *'Aum Shiva samkalpamam'* (gracious disposer).

Obeisance to Soma (the highest point in cosmos where at the truth infinite reposes). Hail Soma, make us perfect, Oh divine purest milk of eternity, cleanse us wholesome.

Oh divine purest nectar, grant me purity, and grant me quintessence of pure silence, where in the truth infinite delight of Agnee manifests forever.

Peace to you oh Vannaspattaye. Aum peace be with Vannaspattaye - the divine co-ordinator and the divine cosmic administrator. Obeisance to Vannaspattaye - the maker of all perfection and the finesse preserver of absoluteness in the purest state of 'form' and 'formlessness'. Glory be to you oh divine cosmic co-ordinator.

Peace to you oh Vishwadevaye. Aum peace be with Vishwadevaye (the divine architect, the divine artisan, and the divine giver). Obeisance to one almighty supreme architect, whose architecture never fails to sustain the days and nights on earth. Obeisance to the one almighty supreme artisan, whose holy word 'AUM', never ceases to shimmer the rains on earth. Obeisance to divine artisan, whose holy sound 'AUM' never ceases to bring the formlessness into form. Glory be to Vishwadevaye (the divine artisan) whose perfect architecture never fails to render peaceful dawn and peaceful dusk. Hail to the everlasting 'pushan' (the boon of god in fertility, creation, recreation, preservation, germination, and fruition). Hail to the heavenly fathers and to the divine mothers.

Peace to you oh Vasus. Aum, peace be with Vasus (the friend of earth), Aum profound sacred obeisance to Vasus. Peace to Marut. Aum, peace be with Marut (the friend of earth), Aum, profound sacred obeisance to Marut. Aum, peace be with Pusanas (the friend of earth). Aum, sacred profound obeisance to Pusanas. Hail to Vasus, Marut, and Pusanas (the three great friends of the divine Mother Earth). Oh divine forces of cosmic abundances, may there never be shortage of food on earth and may there never be scarcity of your divine grain. Oh divine Pusanas, may thou always shower abundance!

Hail to Surya-narayanna (the eternal burning light of delight, whose wholesome horizon never ceases to enlighten with delight!). Hail to the moving inertia of Agnee in you that guard us from all dark evil.

Peace to you oh Apah. Aum peace be with Apah (all waters). Aum sacred profound obeisance to Apah.

Peace to you oh Prithvee. Aum peace be with Prithvee (divine Mother Earth). Aum, sacred profound obeisance to Prithvee.

Peace to Antariksham. Aum, peace be with antariksham (the atmospheric orb). Aum, sacred profound obeisance to antariksham (the atmospheric orb).

Peace to 'dyou' (celestial). Aum, peace be with dyou (the eternal infinite heaven). Aum, sacred profound obeisance to dyou.

Peace to Bhur (the material plane). Peace to Tattva (all existence). Peace to Bhuvah (the celestial). Peace to Svahr (the consciousness).

Peace to Mahah, Jannah and Tappah (the three layers of super consciousness).

Peace to 'Pranna'. Peace to life breath of cosmos in shaktee of Gayatree – 'Aum tat savitur varenyam bhargo devasya dhimahi dhiyo you naha prachodayatt.' (The super-consciousness of cosmos)

Aum, peace be with Soma (the vessel of nectar of truth). Aum, sacred profound obeisance to Soma. Aum, peace be 'Tat Sat' (purest truth).

Aum, peace be with 'Kaal' (the eternal time). Aum, sacred profound obeisance to 'Kaal'. Aum, peace, harmony, and concord to human existence.

"Aum Tat Sat. Swaha". (Peace in that infinite one truth, the delight of which 'oneness' radiates always in the soul)

DIVINE POWER OF SACRED PRAYER:

Hamnssa's charioteer 'Shiva' whispers softly in the inspirational insight of the spirit of life:

"Sunward, look to the sun and keep your face towards the beautiful sunset, following the yellow-orange hue orbits in hypnotic trance."

Hamnssa (the free winged spirit of life bird), wonders in the vast blue skies across the vast blue oceans and invokes the fiery spirit of AGNEE (the divine flame of enlightenment). It aspires to reach the highest point where the nectar of truth reposes in the vessel of 'soma' (TRUE NECTAR). In delight, it takes a flight of freedom, roaming, wondering, and seeing all that is the glory of the nature.

Hamnssa cries, Hamnssa laughs, Hamnssa dances, Hamnssa plays, Hamnssa sings and Hamnssa keeps on flying in total deep freedom of delight. Hamnssa hears the voice of its spirit:

"Oh that dreary mundane earthly life – the horror of human tension; the days seemed long and the nights seemed short. The burden I had borne seemed heavier in the ambitious wonders of the green pastures and the fertile earth. In prosperity, my desires twirled in restlessness. The burden of life, I could bear no longer. The imposition of drought I could not tolerate anymore. All the adversities in grief and sorrow ended in dismay of pity and sympathy. Life oh life let it what it may be. Let it be a 'bygone experience'! I accepted that noisy, chaotic, messy life with a profound prayer of silence knowing that someone out there must have knelt and prayed for me too. I gritted the glittering life in wholesome brevity of fearlessness and fathomless faith in the passage of time. I grinned at my ego with profound wisdom of the spirit and began to evolve in karma. I grew in the delight of truth. I moulded and I took time to sit quietly to understand my soul, the charioteer of my soul and this beautiful essential nature. I knelt before the glory of the sunrise and sunset, offering a sacred dialogue of prayer. My sacred prayers merged with the twilight of delight in compassion."

Union of togetherness of sacred prayer:

"The power of my sacred prayer and the power of the prayers of every other compassionate spirit of life meet in unity to lessen the wounds and burdens of divine Mother Earth."

Hamnssa sings in blissful happiness:

"Life oh life! Let it be what it may be, let it be. Let it be, come what may. Face it, accept it, grit it, but grin and shrug it away. Let it be, come what may. Let it be. Oh this life let it be A FLIGHT OF DELIGHT. Let it be a glimpse of the orb. Let it be a sacred peep into the highest truth. Let it be a human experience of 'twilight', of the sunrise and of the sunset. Let it be a dialogue of sacred prayers between the 'form' and the 'formless'. Let it be a congruence of fusion between the fire of sacrifice from earth and the flame of delight from the orb of the Sun."

"Life oh life! Let it be a united explosion of the 'form', the 'formless', and the 'intermediate' spheres in the night sky and let there be a meeting of million delights in one wholesome fusion of delight. Oh life let it be a flight of delight. Life oh life let it be what it may be in the passage of time, my human experience has finally brought me joy and happiness, for now my spirit rests in the unconditional love of the divine Mother Nature. Let me feast my eyes for the penultimate last time in profound silence and capture the beauty of the orange rays of the sun, forming the first ripples on the morning oceans and forming the last tranquil serenity of the retiring sea. In the twilight of delights, I sing."

"At last, I have no more tears of suffering in my heart, nor any sobbing sorrow! My long nights and long days of loneliness and suffering are no more! At last, I am engrossed in oneness, with the orange light of the sun. Now, my spirit is dissolving with the eternity in delight! Oh how beautiful and magnificent the entire galaxy is, Oh how I wish I would never return to the earthly cage. All my toil and anguish knows no more pain in this eternal beauty."

"Now I have conquered the glory of God in this magnificent eternal nature, now I have closed my eyes and flown thousands of miles in just pure serenity and my tranquillity knows no limit."

"The sounds of AUM echoes deep in my heart, as the same sound that echoes in the oceans and the valleys and in the skies. At last I have passed beyond the sea of ignorance and valleys of mortality. At last I am singing the same tune as the divine glorious AUM. At last I am playing, dancing, and singing in oneness with the magnificent nature. Oh this magnificent nature, the golden ripples, my vision owns."

"In profound silence, I close my eyes to see the beauty of the ETERNITY, as I am drunk with the nectar of Soma and I know not of anything else but I am crazy in love with life. Life oh life, let it be what it may be, this is what I have flown for long days and long nights searching in profound silence with profound insight."

"Beauty oh beauty, let me be still, let me greet the divine silence of the dusk, let me become delight, let me loose my bonds, let me be free, let me take a flight of delight."

"Oh beautiful divine nature, let me pause for the moment to worship the sacred streams, the holy purple sunset, the serene blue ocean, and the infinite sky that will soon become a grand cosmic glitter of solace."

"Oh beautiful tranquil silence, let me remain still in the instant. Dusk Oh dusk let your delight light my hearts nest. Light oh light! Let my heart follow eternal beauty a pathless eternal trail filled with beauty all over. Dawn oh dawn let the fresh breath of the new sweet earth bring with it devotion, peace, and happiness. Sun oh sun! Let me reach the orb of delight."

"Life oh life! Let it be a flight of delight. Thousand tears of sorrows dissolve to become dewdrops of compassionate love. Ah love, it must be something that we have lived to conquer in whole. Love oh love! Let the spirit of life tirelessly experience the light of delight in the pathless trail of beauty."

"Life oh life! Let the light, the everlasting light, the world filling light, the eye kissing light, the heart sweetening light forever remain beautiful. Ah I am a thirsty voyager; let me now quench my thirst with the scared waters of the holy streams. Let me stand still, speechless, as the sky opens and the wind dances with laughters, to bring the nightfall."

"Light oh light! Let thine mirth spread from leaf to leaf, without measure. Even as the night falls, let your light transpire through the beautiful moon to shimmer from leaf to leaf. The heaven's sacred streams loose their earthly bonds to merge in the shimmering ripples of the grand ocean."

"Light of delight, the day is no more; the evening air is sombre with the music of the nightingale. Night oh night! Let me be your poet, let me be your philosopher let me be your seer. Life oh life! Let me whisper softly with my hands folded to the three worlds in solitude and silence. Life oh life! Let me whisper softly to the human existence that is torn apart in labour, dreary mundane tumultuous toil, struggles, chaos, hurt, and dismal haste. Let me remain speechless. Let me offer my profound prayer of solace without words to comfort the wounded and to heal the saddened dumbfound earthen clay."

"Now I feel the light of delight move from my toes to my head in ecstasy of freedom and I feel like the root and the boughs of a teeming vast. I feel not the same wounded bird that I was caged in the household of illusions and the material earth. I am now far from the cage of material entanglements; I am now with the clear blue skies. Although my eyes are closed, I am flying in peace with the sound of AUM humming deep inside me to the rhythm of 'TAT SAT' (that divine truth) eternal nature. All I can now see is Mother Earth dancing and laughing in joy, the rivers are dancing, the oceans are roaring in harmony, and the entire galaxy is shimmering to merge in 'united oneness' of togetherness of delight!"

"Oh this supreme oneness, may it never perish from the vision of my closed eyes. Oh this divine vision, my glory manifests in your beauty, and there is no more desire nor lure nor pity. I am truly fulfilled. I sigh in great profound happiness and my death knows no bounds of mortality of the wretched of the earth for I repose on the final beatitude of truth, that thou art, this, my life breath, I sacrifice to thee."

"Embrace me with love and compassion as I embrace you wholesome for I feel no more pain or sorrow, only bliss."

"Aum Aum Aum...I come back home, at last I merge in oneness with thee Aum Aum Aum...All else is outlasted, all else is superseded, Aum."

Profound reverence to earth and the human life:

"Life oh life let it be a flight of delight. In delight I rejoice the glory of the sunrise, in delight I cherish the inspiration of the sun, in delight I move on-wards to the dusk, in delight I sigh and in delight I rest peacefully with the nightfall.' 'The twilight of delight of the dawn and the dusk has afforded me days and nights of human experience. In time, I came, with time I grew, on time I prayed at the sunrise and sunset, for time I offered my sacrifice, by time I shall cross the vastness of the clear blue skies into the atmospheric orb, and in time I finally merge and rest with the eternity. As I leap high in the air to peep into the vessel of pure nectar Soma, a profound silence enters my pure consciousness and my written word sighs in compassion. Let me be a philosopher of this silence, let me be a poet of this silence, let me be the sound of AUM that murmurs deep in the oneness of my marriage with the eternity. Let me the light of delight of the twilight of the dawn and the dusk."

"At last, I have come home. At last I have rested in the laps of my spiritual mother. At last I feel peaceful. At last there is no more fear. Music begins to play the melodies of the soul divine bliss."

The awakened spirit is embraced by "delight" in the rhythm of seven magnificent compassionate rays of love.

"There is a great profound oneness between the EARTH (my "temporary" home), the ETERNITY (God's repose) and the CELESTIAL (the planets, stars, moon, sun, nature, spiritual heroes), atmospheric orb."

My written word whispers softly:

"I give you my precious profound wisdom which is the conscious and constant instrument of INSIGHT. Let my written word for now be a poetry that praises my INSIGHT that is the insight of eternity. I give you my precious ECSTACY OF ONENESS with the divine bliss eternal love that reposes on the eternal truth of DIVINITY manifested in ETERNITY. Life oh life let be a flight of delight into the infinite eternal truth that is beyond the formlessness of the form, beyond the imperishable impersonality of the soul and the perishable personality of the spirit.

It is in the final beatitude of truth that profoundest silence reposes in fathomless peace holding together the three worlds in cosmic fusion of twilight of delight. From delight the spirit of my life descended on earth, with delight the spirit of my life ascended from the earth into the atmospheric orb, and into delight the spirit of my life merges in oneness with 'the fathomless eternal omnipotent divine almighty supreme' God."

The spirit of life in me hums in bliss and chants in quintessence:

"Aum Tat Sat Tat Vam Asi Aham Brahman asi Hari Aum Tat Sat Swaha Aum so hum swaha. Hari Aum Tat Sat swaha Aum swaha swaha!"

" 'Aum' that thou art the divine truth, that is in my soul, for now there is sheer delight of eternal joy as my soul is merged in oneness with all pervading light of eternal godhead – the transcendental celestial has come down to earth in a silent prayer without words to complete my sacrifice."

"Aum maa uma Aum tat sat swadha swadha swaha." "Oh Aum, divine mother prakrutti, Oh Aum that you are the divine truth, the divine wholesome finesse".

"Aum Mau, that thou art, the divine mother, the earth mother, the ocean mother, the wind mother, the nightingale sky ('ratree-mata'), the beautiful charisma, the non-stop time, the everlasting fertility of the waters and wealth."

"Aum Tat Sat Swaha Swaha, we are the radiant light of your energy, we are the lamp of delight of hope, we are the sacred night of restfulness. Oh divine order, so shall the human be patient, persevering, and enduring always with your grace."

"Aum Tat Sat Swaha Swaha, may all remember that we are each only cells and particles of this grand divine mother earth from whose womb we germinate to come together in time. Life oh life! Let there be grain and loaf to sustain each human day on earth. Life oh life! Let there be renewed hope so that there is balance between the day and the night. Life oh life! Let it be a flight of delight."

"Aum Tat Sat Swaha Swaha, may our world of existence always triumph over the dreary mundane ignorance, dullness, darkness, dismal stubbornness, and noise. Oh divine order, let there be hope in a world that is screened by disillusions."

"Aum Tat Sat Swaha Swaha, may the human world of existence be free from all fears. May there be perpetuity of life over death. Life oh life! Bring us new fresher spirits of light to grant us the boon of compassion and love."

"Aum Tat Sat Swaha Swaha, may the divine mother never cease to dance within us in tranquil trance. Light oh light! Let my sacrifices bring hope, happiness, and tranquillity to the withered spirits. Light oh light! Let there be hope forever. Life oh life! Let there be hope to embrace tomorrow. Let there be hope to the circle of re-birth, let there be hope to the never-ending wheel of time. Life oh life! Let it be a flight of delight! Let it be a light of hope! Let it be a light of love! Let it be a light revelation! Let it be a light of manifestation! Let it be a glory of delight! Delight is but the light of Divinity."

11. RENEWED HOPE

'*Vedaaham etam purusam mahaantam Aadityavarnam tamasah parastaat Satyam evam Jayate Eishwaar evam Param-anandamayam.*'

'Oh Divinity, I have realised the beauty of Para existing supreme God, the effulgent light of delight of the Sun, beyond the boundaries of the tenebrous despair of the human existence.'

'*Yo vai bhuumaa tat sukham naalpeh Sukham Asti Bhuumaiva sukham aapatih.*'

'The light of delight of the infinite eternity is the truth. The finite known world of human existence has become a stranger in despair to the unknown world of para-existence. Indeed the world of existence will never render true happiness. Only the infinite can bring true divine happiness.'

'*Na tatra suuryoh bhaati na chandrataarakam Nemaa vidhootoh bhanti kuto 'yam agnih Tam eva bhaanttam anubhaati sarvam jagaditah tasya bhaasa sarvam idam vibhaati.*'

'There at the sun never rises nor does it set. The moon, the stars, and the planets cease to be. Only when the illuminating light of the eternity shines in delight, all else becomes light. The self-revealing light of delight illuminates the entire universe with divine compassion.'

'*Yo devo agnau yo'psu vissvam bhuvanam aavivessa ya osadhiisu yo vanaspatisu tasmai devaya namoh namah. Sarvam vay namoh namah*'

To the supreme cosmic soul divine, we offer our salutations, our obeisance. That divine soul has ignited the fire, become the cooling water, the air, the wind, and the atmosphere. That divine soul has pervaded the whole universe. To that wholesome beauty, may we call upon thee to grant a boon of hope to the human existence in despair.

Life oh life! Let there be hope. May thou restore 'trust' into the existence that is torn apart, fragmented, and bruised in 'all, this, that and the other'.

Life oh life! Let there be auspiciousness everywhere. God oh God! Let auspicious boon of your delight bring peace, health, happiness, and hope.

Vedas never cease to call upon the cosmic deities to commemorate the end of the dusk and the beginning of a new dawn, for granting a 'renewed hope' to the human world of existence. 'Samndhya' (twilight of the dusk and the dawn) commemorates a sacred dialogue of prayer in togetherness of the cosmic energies.

Renewed hope is a boon from the celestial eternity to the terrestrial world. At times when sad events happen (whatever they may be – death, tragedy, loss, trauma, hurt, sorrow), we may feel disheartened, disillusioned, astonished and even amazed at the toil, turmoil, adversities and pain. We may not understand why sad events happen to us because at the time we do not know, the right from the wrong, the higher light from the lower intelligence, because at the time we are hurting so much.

However, as time goes on, we realise without doubts and paranoia that the source of energy manifests beyond the known gross material world into the subtle spiritual world and beyond the spiritual world into the celestial world and beyond the celestial world into emptiness.

Vivid experiences make us understand and realise that the grand light of delight is a beautiful emancipation because human life is the most precious gift in time to evolve and to merge back to our true state – the spiritual state. Hurt is in the chaos of all this, that and the other dual state of the known material world of human existence. Torn apart, fragmented and bruised is the grand collective spirit of human life. It is as though the spirit of life longs to belong in compassionate love. We meet to share our life experiences, in somewhat profound unknown karmic sense. Whilst our karmic causes may be unknown, and we may not fully comprehend why we met and shared the grief or sorrow or the joy or pleasure intellectually or emotionally, we somehow grow and evolve from each encounter. In time, we experience what we have shared in the briefest encounters.

In time, we begin to see things as they are (truth), rather than as they should be from an intellectual perspective, from a personal viewpoint, or from a desire viewpoint.

Sorrow, grief, disparity, loss, hurt, trauma, and sadness come into every one's life. One needs to become divinely fully aware of this fact without the necessity of all this, that and the other. Whatever act or deed one thinks, feels, and does, one eventually accredits or discredits none other than ones own true soul divine.

Life is born out of Karma. Karma sustains our life process in moments of profound experiences. Our life suffers because of our collective life karma. Our life ends because of our karma. Our life begins anew with renewed karma. Life alters its course of fate due to karma. Life looses its limbs because of karma. It is almost like a glimpse of moments in time, capturing the capering flight of the river.

From light we came, towards light we merge. The soul infinite is immortal light of delight. Astrologers who claim to be the masters of destiny and fate and the so called experts who claim to know it all, need to realise that karma is superior to birth charts and karma can alter fate. Our human life birth is like getting out of a deep sleep into the life consciousness of the wheel of karmic time. The causation of life may be revealed by the grace of appropriate innate divine perception.

One cannot understand the divine metamorphosis with the conventional perceptions of the lower mind and the conventional intellect. The conventional academics suffice to enable us to comprehend the reality and its causes. Beyond the reality, one needs to take a leap into the emptiness, into the blissfulness of silence.

The entire purport of human life is to attain self-realisation. Having attained liberation and self-realisation, the light of delight, a flash of awakening is an illumination of immortality. This light of eternal delight is a hope to the human earth.

The renewed hope tells the existence on the human earth to let life be what it may be, to let it be come what may, to accept it, to face it, to grit it, but to grin and shrug it away in divine spiritual experiences.

Only in the humankind is there the rareness of divine potentials and the profound wonders (sidhis) of attaining Brahman the ultimate god divine supreme. Life oh life! Let it be a flight of delight.

If the life of life, here and now knows 'brahman-param-atman' (infinite eternal god-soul divine) and realises it before the decay of the body, then one is prepared to receive a body in the worlds of celestial eternity. The 'divya-atman' (enlightened soul) is like a mirror image of divine light of delight. The Dream State is the reflection of the spiritual world. The sun and the moon are but the two eyes of the cosmic soul divine. Realising the sense perceptions, the wise one rises beyond all settings of the impermanence of mortal human life.

The wise one is a light of delight to the human existence because he or she brings to the world hope through compassionate love, through light of illumination, through guidance, through selflessness, through simplicity and humility.

Beyond the six senses, beyond the sheaths of the psychological mind, beyond the mind, beyond the intellect, beyond the metaphoric sheaths of the intellect, beyond the ego, beyond the astral plane, the great non-dual 'divya-atman' (soul divine) exists and beyond the 'divya-atman' (soul divine), the 'param-atman' (cosmic soul unmanifest) para-exists. Beyond the unmanifest, beyond the ether and beyond the orb pervades the brahman-param-atman (cosmic soul divine). It is a divine light of delight.

In thought, feeling, emotions, act, deed, sacrifice, and self-lessness, one becomes that beautiful divine light of delight. When the bliss of delight enlightens and awakens, beyond the senses, into the mind, and beyond the mind into the higher intelligence where reason and cause function no more, one attains liberation at last! In this great wheel of time 'kaal-brahman', the human spirit of life wonders like a swan 'hamnssa' in divine satt-karma (virtue).

When 'hamnssa' ceases to play the karmic dance it ceases to isolate the inspirer from the rhythm of the life itself and merges in oneness with the grand maestro almost like the rivers merging into the grand ocean.

The wheel of kaal (eternal time) depends upon karma to cause and purport human life in imperfect experiences of realising its ultimate original reality - the self.

The chain of interdependence is 'prateetyasamutpaada' and every karmic cycle is dependent upon another factor.

Upon ignorance manifests form. Ignorance is of two types. Firstly, the innate ignorance of the ego that is unaware of the true divine nature of the mind and phenomena. This results in a state of distraction, conflict, confusion and chaos. Secondly, there is the illusionary ignorance of imagining that the world is dual and that the world has complex paradoxes that can never be resolved. Every karmic formation or karmic manifestation depends on consciousness, name and form. Each material entity manifests with energy, senses, sense organs, vibrations, and 'pranna' (life breath). Contact creates energy. From energy emanates desire. From desire emanates attachment, control and dependency. Upon every birth a destiny of death, old age and dissolution is inevitable. Upon every human life, sufferings aggregate to awaken, to remind us of the process of dissolution from the gross to the subtlest level.

The Vedic mantras (sacred incantations), shlokas (divine philosophy), rituals and oblations invoke the higher consciousness (Brahman) to render a prayer of solace, peace, harmony, wealth, health, happiness, bliss, illumination, enlightenment and self-realisation to the world of human existence. The selflessness 'idammnnanmamma' in Vedas mean that nothing is for the benefit of the personal ego or personal identity. All that we encounter and all that we experience in the impermanent imperfect human life time is for the purpose of understanding and realising the divine nature of the existence and to create hope for the human existence.

The Vedic light is a delight because it is divine manifestation of the soul from the gross to the subtle most state. At the gross level (anna-maya kosha), it is a manifestation of fullest appreciation and realisation of 'tripti' and 'pushti' the basic satisfaction of water and food and humble physical personality. At the mental and emotional level, (the manas maya kosha and the pranna maya kosha respectively), it is a manifestation of fullest energy and realisation of the 'ullasa' (pleasantries), 'santosha' (gratitude), 'harsha' (auspicious joy), and 'maya' (imaginations or illusions).

At the subtler level, the light of delight manifests in the consciousness as harmony, happiness, bliss and peace. This is the ananda-maya kosha (eternal cosmic cell) and 'anandam' happiness is delight.

When light of delight manifests in the pure super consciousness, it manifests in 'param-shantih' (unperturbed silence). This blissfulness is beyond reason, cause, and even beyond words.

Insights appear fleeting almost in unreal apparitions. However, blissfulness (satt-chitd-ananda) is a glimpse in flashes that happen and therefore are still within the subtler experiences in imperfect indescribable delight or extra ordinary joy of being.

A wise spirit of life journeys through life like a river gathering divine experiences at each stage of its flight. Most of the times, we choose to ignore or even forget extra ordinary life events. Hidden deep within the sub-conscious memories therefore are unresolved experiences that we barely become aware of but which nevertheless do contain vital information on higher more subtle states of para-existence. Dreams are one fine example of such extra-ordinary life events that portray either a message from the spiritual world or otherwise an insight into the past, current and future events. The spirit of life 'jivan-ataman' realises the light of delight 'ananda-amruttamm' (nectar of divinity) in imperfect experiences under imperfect conditions, within imperfect life time (kaalyug). Vividly 'hamnssa' sighs to the higher order. Vividly 'hamnssa' speaks: "Life oh life! Let it be what it may be. Let it be. Let it be, come what may. Face it, accept it, grit it, but grin and shrug it away. Life oh life! Let it be a flight of delight."

The awakened spirit of life whispers softly to the world of human that is dismayed in all this, that and the other:

"Spirit oh Spirit! Let it be. Let you be free and unbound from all this, that and the other girdles of your burdened life."

"Oh shining spirit of life, let the effulgent Sun awaken, enlighten and ascend thine spirit upward to the sky. Life oh life! Let light become of you."

"Oh shining one, may thine spirit become the non-ageing star of destiny in the nightingale."

"Oh beautiful spirit of life, may the torch of enlightenment pleasingly grant you clarity."

"Oh precious one, may the sacred self-same words now dissolve in peace and unity of togetherness of the three worlds. Life oh life! Let there be concourse of harmony and bliss."

"Life oh life! Let there be a grand communion of togetherness and let divinity shine upon all to make the earthly realize all its dreary mundane drudgery. Oh divine one, may I offer my oblation to your profoundness, granting hope to the world of human."

"Oh divine spirit of life, homage and reverence to your might and sacred oblations. Let the rains shower blessings to you forever so that you can keep your divine existence as a light to the world of human."

"Friend oh friend, my friend oh friend, I shall always keep a watch over you and I shall gather angels to grant you sweet dreams."

"Life oh life! May the friendship of God never failing always dwell in the hearts of the mortals so that they may find delight of joy and hope to live."

"God oh God! Oh supreme God may thou befriend all. May thine compassion and love transcend to all dumbfound humble friends. May you save all the humble friends from distress, trauma, and damnation. May you grant hope. Oh burning flame of agnee, the splendour giver of joy and delight, the purifying blaze of the sun, you forever bring the light of hope. Sun oh Sun, you are honourable and cheerful light of delight!"

The Vedic mantras begin with the aspiration of 'Agnee'. The spirit of life evolves with the inspiration of 'Agnee'. The Vedic mantras commemorate the divine glory of the light of 'Agnee', and end in the transpiration of 'Agnee' in "delight". The Vedas never cease to call upon Cosmic Gods and Deities in sacredness of poetry, lyrics, hymns and music. A Vedic seer generates fathomless hope at every second of the precious time.

In the passage of time, eternity is called upon again and again. Every single passage of time is purported to bring forth purer and purer understanding of the purest nectar of Soma. The Vedic light of wisdom generates a hope for healing wounded relationships.

A human spirit of life gives the "delight" of the light of nectar to the human existence on earth, to create a fathomless hope of 'togetherness' in concord and harmony. The Vedic analogy of the human world as being the field, and the people being the fielders bring with it a beautiful commemoration of prayers, mantras, hymns, poems, verses, lyrics, and many beautiful sounds of divine music from the celestial to the fielders to nourish the green pastures that give health, wealth and prosperity to all.

This human lifetime is a gift from Gods and a gift is always a delight. The life of life itself is a light from God, and light is always sacred. Light always gives. Light always triumphs over darkness. Light always generates hope by re-assuring the world of humankind torn apart and fragmented in all this, that and the other that relationships do mend. There is a sacred trust in the beauty of being human, and I believe with all my heart that things do work out eventually, no matter what. Hurt can be healed, relationships can be mended, love can be restored in compassion rather than emotions, hope can be given in dignity and with integrity rather than forsake.

Tears fall from my eyes. The unperturbed silence of the still moments of the dusk grants me hope. There is an extra ordinary peace in the aloneness of the dusk, watching all the swans swimming their way home, the purple red sunset reflecting a serenity on the surface of the running river, the golden leaves flying away, and the nightingale just immerging with all the stars.

Life oh life! Let me never cease to believe in the human faith of compassion, love, and togetherness. Let me never cease to stand still and steady amidst all this, that and the other, to pray for the humankind. Let me never cease to pray for the happiness of my loving parents. Life oh life! Let there be hope in my heart even if it is for just one moment to experience the compassionate togetherness of those relationships injured by hurt. Remember oh child of nature, remember, there is nothing to be gained by showing fear in the world of all this, that and the other. Defying and rebelling, arguing and shouting, screaming and swearing, never ending perpetuates fear in form or another.

Those humankind dwelling in fear, need to break free from the confines of the human survival and take time to envision liberation, freedom, love, and hope to the existence at large. All things connect somehow, in somewhat profound sense; we are all but different rivers that eventually merge into the grand ocean, united in destiny. Possessions and obsessions are the grandest weaknesses that bring distortion to the true divine nature of human kind. Whatsoever we do, we eventually accredit or discredit our own spirit of life.

Vedic invocation to 'ratree' (nightfall or nightingale) is the final peace offering mantra towards the human existence on earth at the dusk. Dusk is also the twilight of the close of one cycle or an end of one phase. It is an auspicious time transited by nightfall for a new dawn for a renewed hope. 'Ratree' is a sacred dark, the nightingale of solace and rest. To the nightfall 'ratree' whose lord is Shiva:

"Oh three eyed lord Shiva, thou art the saviour of all distressed. Oh Shiva, please grant me freedom from the bondage of dreary mundane diseases, desires, and deliver me from all the evils of mortal life including death. Oh Shiva grant me a drop of the purest nectar 'Somam' so that I may sleep peacefully and have sweet dreams. Oh Shiva befriend me so that I may become fearless of the dreary darkness."

"Aum namoh namah Shiva shivaya namah Aum."

Hamnssa began its spiritual pilgrimage embarking from the gross physical existence of earth like a capering river. Just as the river, seaward bound, Hamnssa experiences life in the passage of time. The transformation of life occurs only in the metamorphosis of the perception and experience. When the experience transforms from the gross physical sensations in to the physical planes of knowing the earthly existence and all that is "known" matter; the spirit of life becomes a creative artiste with 'talent'. The spirit of life knows of the knowledge of life. It attains all the skills and expertise, in academic and professional life. Thriving under the 'external power' of the gross physical earth in political, economical and sociological spectrum of survival, the 'knower' of life becomes 'materialistic'. In materialism, it enjoys the looms of desires and pleasures, as it should. However, when the spirit of life stretches its eagle like vision farthest beyond the high mountains and beyond the rivers, it begins to feel that there is a difference between this world and the other world (the eternal world).

However it does not know the other world (the eternal world), and as such continues to follow the perpetual karmic thread of 'river-life', in name, form, and passion of fiery currents. Every spirit of life, having travelled through rough planes, smooth planes, sensuous planes, or karmic planes encounters sorrow at one point or another.

Sorrow is inevitable. Pain follows pleasure. This is inevitable. Life is unpredictable despite the certainty of knowledge and skills. Sorrow awaits every life breath on earth as a breeding parasite. Its karmic thread connects us all in somewhat profound sense, albeit we may intellectually deny the core values of its imminence.

The karmic thread is like a 'river-life' (long, short, small, big, or dispersing), journeying wildly, and capering with its fiery currents. In passion, the personality travels through this thread woven in the web of collective human intellect. This web becomes a power net in reality. The web of 'reality' entraps and entangles a free spirit of life (Hamnssa) in between the gross physical, physical and metaphysical planes, in glamour, glitter, intellectual camouflage, looms of desires, lures, frustrations, competition, and threat of survival.

'Fear' prevails all over the grey shadows of the mind and the intellectual perceptions. The mind looses its gravitational power of ego in the passage of time. In time, the personality has grown physically and mentally. In time, the personality follows the thread of karma without the wisdom or the "insight" of the soul. In time, the personality strives to accumulate all the germinating fruits of the green pastures of the earth.

In time, the personality encounters sorrow. "Sorrow" renders us an opportunity to create a new hope. The dusk of the twilight may cause a dissolution and dispersion of the bygone 'past', and the day may no longer be. Death is dissolution of one cycle and the transit to another cycle. The nightfall renders this transitory rest for the withered spirit, the battered spirit of life. The dusk brings certain profound tranquillity with it, to heal and to nurture the spirit of life in sacred dialogue of prayers. The end of a phase marks the end of a cycle. Dusk is the transformation of the bygone day into the moving nightfall.

Divine mother 'Samndhya' the consort of 'dusk' whispers softly to the spirit of life, awakened, enlightened, withered in physical body:

"You have travelled a long time, and long suffered the karmic trails of earthly imperfections! You have long suffered 'sorrow' in, adversity, misfortune, relationships, matrimony, patrimony, tragedy, and much more. Let your wounded spirit of life rest in peace now in the spiritual laps of the divine eternal mother 'Jyoti-Samndhya' (dusk). Peace and calmness surround your withered spirit. Despair not. Pledge allegiance to yourself. Believe in yourself. Rise above the wretched of this grey misery. Take one day at a time, one step at a time. Take refuge in your soul, to realise that all this and all that does not matter."

"'Tomorrow' may seem bleak and hopeless from the battered 'present'! Despair not oh 'spirit of life', rise, and deliver yourself to the duty of your own soul. Your spirit belongs to your soul. Let no one touch its integrity! Let no other one command it except the grand maestro of the nightfall and the grand commander of the cosmos, 'Shiva'. Let no one crush the capering wings of your spirit. Let your spirit fly in freedom of joy and delight!"

"Let no pain grind you down to the gross physical misery of loneliness, for most fears emanate from loneliness! Rise oh dear spirit of life, rise and wipe off your tears! Shed not those tears in pity and sympathy for all that is not worthy a cause! Let not the ashes of the burnt dissolution bring you bitterness! Let your spirit not burn in the bitterness of 'all this, that and the other', which is a transient moment."

"Let your spirit of life; nurture your soul, in profound silence of profound prayers and profound sacrifice, for it shall bring you greater strength. Let your greater strength make you more compassionate. Let your compassion bring you greater solace, comfort, consolation, and peace. Let your spoken words be a voice of great compassion! Let the flame of your eternal hope that shines everlastingly forever in your soul enlighten the dark ignorance on the grey shadows of this earth! "Let the divine light of Agnee, that 'never failing' shinning eternally in your soul, radiate delight wherever you go! Let Compassion always behold your spirit! Let your spirit bring you 'fathomless hope' in the dawn of eternal bliss and in the dawn of awakening to the cosmic spirit of God, in quintessence. Life oh life let it be a flight of delight."

The day has met the night in a serene dusk and the nightfall greets the compassionate spirit of life, which has touched and tasted the purest nectar of immortality from the vessel of Soma. A profound prayer of compassion is offered to the human existence:

"As I witness the twilight of lights (the daylight meeting the nightfall), I sigh in great reverence to time in profound prayer of peace and harmony to the existence of humankind. The serene tranquil dissolution of the dusk will soon be greeted by the restful nightfall and the magnificent night-sky filled with compassionate glittering stars. I offer profound solace and profound prayer of peace and harmony, in profound silence, to all the great spirits resting in the spiritual world."

"Aum namoh namah Shiva shivaya namah Aum"

"It is my fathomless faith that tomorrow shall be a renewed dawn. The twilight of which shall bring to the human existence, a transformed light of renewed hope and a renewed compassion to realize the beautiful light of delight of the sun in the soul divine. I close my eyes to shed a tear of joy, as I experience the deepest most compassionate love of 'togetherness', in delight."

Just as the all these rivers (life threads of karma), seaward bound, approach the shores at the dusk; awakened souls take a flight of delight towards the hue of the orange sun meeting the sky and the ocean. Disappearing in their names and forms liquidated into the oneness with the sea and all together is called a grand ocean of compassion, so all these Karmas of the true awakened seeker having param-atman —eternal divinity as a goal, disappear on reaching the hue of the orange sun.

The awakened soul however sheds a tear of greatest compassion in profoundest prayer of peace offered to the existence of mankind. Even at the moment of becoming one with the existence and loosing its form, it reminds the world of existence that consciousness is the basis of all, consciousness is the true guide, consciousness is the essence of all, and consciousness verily is eternal divinity. Of all aspects of emotional feelings the feeling for the fellow beloved ones is the greatest and no matter what one selfless love always triumphs.

Our human life brings to us the opportunity to evolve as individual human souls and to further our "human togetherness" to share such humanely profound significance in deepest human compassion. Coming together in time as fellow humankind enables us to express and experience such a profound human compassion. We meet to create such significant moments, we grow in the spirit of "human togetherness", and albeit many of us drift away in moments of 'aloneness' (in solitude of profound silence), we share significant human experiences, some much more than others do. It is not so much the number of our encounters, as it is the content of our encounter, the essential substance of our human togetherness. We cherish such profound encounters (brief as they may seem), with utmost reverence to our inner spirit, the spirit to love and to be loved compassionately. Even in our sleep, we dream of compassionate togetherness, an idealistic world of happy families and happy love. This is the fathomless hope which the Vedas speak of beyond the boundaries of tenebrous gloom of all this, that and the other.

Every walk of life awakens and transforms with profound human experiences, regardless of caste, culture, creed, or colour. Compassion is the essence of every profound human experience. Compassion triumphs, Love always triumphs. Truth always triumphs. When the triumph appears, hundred arrows of distress, trauma, hurt, rejections, and all the sufferings seem trivial. It is a delight of thousand lights! It is a wonderful most beautiful moment of life that almost wipes out all the bad memories in a clap or a wink. All this, that and the other matter no more, when the moment of divine hope appears in love, compassion and togetherness, to grant us sacred freedom beyond all mundane fears.

This human life is a precious gift to us in time, much more than we will ever realize, no matter what. Loosing time is loosing life breath in every perspective but much more so in the essence of compassionate human experience. We share the joys of life in togetherness with the greatness of naïve infancy, naïve childhood, loving parenthood, and the growing pleasures of youth. At each stage of our life, we want to care, we want to share, and we want to love. We yearn for affectionate compassionate love, no matter what. Loving compassion is the essence of human life breath, without which no spiritual evolution can be humanly possible. Even in 'aloneness' we blossom with the grace of the compassionate loving affection of the Mother Nature.

Aloneness does not necessarily imply that our love for another whom we dearly and preciously treasure has died. Aloneness is a serenity to console the spirit of life, which for the sake of the immortal light will eventually die but that which remains alight in words and in spirit for the universal family of humankind for generations to come. In aloneness, we shed tears of love and surrender benignly without the fuss of all this, that and the other to the Great Spirit. Aloneness does not mean we don't want to share. Just as the new born baby loves the comfort of the silent womb, so does the distilled spirit of life love the beautiful delight of eternal happiness transcended upon it from the celestial light in aloneness. This is light, this is delight.

'Madhuman me paraayanam madhumat punaraayanam.'

Sweet be the departure from the dwellings, sweet be the return even.

'Yo vai bhuumaa tat sukham Naalpe sukham Asti Bhuumaiva Sukham Paramam-Sukham.'

The celestial infinite is the satisfying real happiness, no this, not that finite happiness of the karmic earth. The infinite eternal happiness alone is the true delight of happiness.

Here on the karmic earth, the humankind recites a hymn to the cosmic gods for granting the boon of hope to for the humankind generations to come to become divine. The Vedic hymn is as follows:

'Bhadramm karnnebhih srrnnuyaama devaa, bhadramm passyemaaksabhir yajatraah sthirairr-angaiss-tusstuvaammsas tanuubhir Vyasema devahitamm yad aayuh.'

May we hear, may we hear, oh Great Spirit all that is auspicious and divinely beautiful. May we perceive, may we experience with our spiritual vision all that is auspicious and divinely beautiful. May we divinely accomplish our human life as we consider it to be a grand opportunity to become divine. May we become still. Oh this life! Let it be a flight of delight!

I write and re-write to create and to re-create the hope of love and affection as I stand still barefooted on the bruised earthen clay, knowing not where my journey began.

Hear me oh precious spirit of life, hear me oh beautiful spirit of life, for I am a relative, a distant echo of the spiritual world. No less, no more.

Oh precious spirit of life, be still, be here, the trail is beautiful. We are all flowers in the Garden of this beautiful most magnificent Great Spirit. We share a common root, a common soil, mother earth. The Garden is beautiful because it has different colours in it. Each represents different tradition, different culture, different ideal, different thought, different heart and different beauty. Alas, we merge together in the same soil. Alas, our heartbeats merge together to make an echo of one grandeur heartbeat of collective universal spirit of humankind.

Love is something we feed upon. We need to love and we need to be loved and we need to share love. Love is something we feed upon.

When love is fragmented, somehow torn apart, and forced away in dismal rejections, we become like rivers that are blocked by logs and stones, unable to express freely, unable to cry, unable to perform, unable to flow even. In due course of time, we journey through our own karma and realise that making differences, creating differences, and dwelling on differences to applause the ego and the intellect tantamount to pettier compared to the grandeur of love.

Oh precious spirit of life, why does one need to take something by force, when the same thing can be accomplished by love and compassion. To deny someone love because we have been hurt, or because we have been bruised is like denying our own spirit of existence the right of divinity! How therefore do we bring hope to the generations to come? Not by hurt, but from re-assuring the universal spirit of humankind that we are the altogether the children of the same earth that must come together eventually regardless.

Our human life is not to argue, shout and scream but to walk in the sacred way, to learn and to heal our universal spirit of humankind with love and compassion, to bring a universal light of hope. So, let it be whatever it may be, oh this life, let it be a flight of delight in stillness of beauty and love. Believe in the grandeur of the Great Spirit, and the Oneness of all divinity.

Hope is something we all need altogether, and hope is something we are able to leave behind on this earth despite all this, that and the other. Hope is something that is the heritage of the future generation children of this earth.

Be still, the trail is beautiful. The beauty of the light of delight of the magnificent sunset is all colours, all sounds, all voices, and all love. May the wonderful grand nature, nurture your precious spirit in beauty, without the fears of all this, that and the other to create a light of hope, delight of hope.

Be still, there is profound peace away from all the buzz, noise and haste of the city. May the wonderful Great Spirit grant you all peace and serenity to accept all life's many unresolved complex puzzles. Some things we may never understand. Oh precious spirit of life, there is great happiness in being generously giving in the entire sobriety. Life of life! Let it be a joy of loving; life oh life, let it be an extraordinary delight of granting hope.

Be still, silence is a divine mystery. May the wonderful Great Spirit grant you courage and strength to change all life's many karmas that can be resolved to become the light of delight! May you hear the heartbeat of this divine mother earth, as you should, with your bare feet and touch the chord of every human heart beat, with solace, compassion, and grace. Oh precious spirit of life! There is a sacred trust placed upon us humans because we have an extraordinary gift of giving compassionate love without the fuss of all this, that and the other. Oh spirit of life, may you become delight! Life oh life! Let it be a flight of delight. Life oh life, let the delight of thousand lights grant hope to the humankind.

Be still, remember oh child of nature, remember, the soft earth is our divine mother. Breath the freshness of the soft earth, for each dawn brings with it a divine hope.

Be still, the trail is pathless. The trail is beautifully divine. The trail is a flight of delight. Life oh life! Let it be a flight of delight.

Be still, listen oh child of nature to all the beauty that support the entire web of beautiful existence. Take care of the sacred pebble, the soft soil, the birds and animals, plants and flowers. Oh precious spirit of life, I am a relative, a distant echo of the spiritual world, no less, no more.

Be still, walk in beauty to behold the vision of the purple red orange sunset. Be still, be placid, be peaceful, be joyful, love, become beautiful, become delight, and give hope.

Life oh life! Let it be a flight of delight!

Life oh life! Let it be a trail of beauty in great stillness. Life ah life! Let it be light of delight in the great silence of aloneness. Life ah life! Let it be a flight of delight. It is here and now in the present moment in time that the beautiful most wonderful delight of God's light can be realised barefooted, empty handed in emptiness! Not yesterday, not tomorrow, but today, now, at this present moment in time. All said and done, what really matters in 'all this, that and the other' (noise, haste and waste), is that we form a togetherness of the universal spirit of humanity to offer a prayer to the three worlds of existence - the spiritual, the celestial, and the terrestrial world.

May we all in togetherness of the divine spirit realise peace and serenity in profound silence. May we all, together cherish life in love, and affection. May we all, together give love and become loving to our true spirit of divine life. Happiness is our birth right, a state of being sublime, not a condition of circumstances. In a human world that is torn apart and fragmented in so much anguish and hurt, may we light a candle of hope to change and make better all that we can with courage, strength, and spiritual virtue. May we in the spirit of togetherness bring joy to the mundane days and nights on the human earth that is withering with time. In beauty, may we walk together as different rivers of fate towards the grand ocean of destiny, to leave behind us a pathless trail of beautiful divinity.

Ah life! my spirit greets the morning sun and the new sweet fragrance of the soil to write and re-write, to create again and again, and to re-create again and again, a breathe of love and hope, I am not a lost voice, but an echo of many sounds, all colours, all fears, all loves. Spirit oh spirit of life, remember, remember the sacredness of running rivers, the glory of the sun in the wonderful beauty of the dawn and the dusk. The sea forever is still, the teeming vast sky forever is tranquil; the nightingale is a sacred glitter of delight forever. Ah the firefly of the night sky, ah the flash of the stars, let me rest in peace, in quietness, without the intrusion of all this, that and the other. I came into the world as a child of karma, I leave this earthen world as a childlike spirit of life. Spirit oh great divine spirit! Glory to truth! Peace and harmony. Hari Aum Tat Sat Swaha.

Love and not hatred is our essential human nature that enables us to realise our true substance profoundly and to evolve in our true substance profoundly. Loving others and being loved unconditionally therefore is the precious most profound way of human togetherness to bring hope to the future world of existence. Our fates may be different; our life paths may be different just like the different rivers flowing with different energies, but our personalities merge in 'oneness' of human compassion. Almost like the divine oneness of the empty blue sky, and the roaring blue ocean. This 'oneness' embraces us always no matter what. It is the fathomless human compassion. It is the cosmic compassion of ever embracing Mother Nature. It is the personal compassion of the individual human spirit profoundly eminent in us, as a radiant light of delight.

The light of truth that emits out of the fusion of human togetherness brings to us a profound human experience worth a treasure beyond time. It is a flight of delight. It is a journey beyond the wholesome existence.

Many joys are shared in life's pleasures of birth and children. Glory and charisma manifest in the naïve children. Children bring us simple innocence, simple joys, simple laughter's, and simple 'togetherness'. Compassion, that capers to the seven colours of the rainbow and the seven notes of a musical sound. This kind of compassion does not know the intellectual or the material prowess. It is simply funny, simply loving, and simply profound, just like the grand musical sound echoed in perfection of seven musical notes in sheer delight of fusion, of the light of love and the light of hope. Children renew the hope of this world of existence in true profound love and compassion that is unconditional.

We forget this naïve innocence and indulge ourselves in all this and all that. In time, we come out of our simplicity by the entrapment of material and intellectual power warfare. The individual human mind is a microcosmic system of the grand collective macro global intellectual system, because it operates on the same robotic sub-systems. As long as the intellectual mind is in charge, there is fat chance of synthesis, compromise, and 'global human togetherness'. The fear of dying makes us child-like to seek divine laps.

Someday we will look back on all life's episodes, one by one, and maybe, just maybe, we might merge back to the naked nature and pure unconditional compassionate love. Perhaps some day we will realise it.

Therefore, the issue is not 'to believe' or 'not to believe' in Religion. Religion, thesis, and antithesis are all man made systems. The real issue therefore, is to be in love with human life. Life is to love, and to be loved. Soul compassion grants hope to all numb found human in distress.

The truth manifests in the soul, as much as it manifests in Soma (the highest point in cosmos). Simply, compassionate affection of human life! The soul is the divine blissful fragment of the vast divine compassionate God. When we realize it fully, we have lived the true 'human experience'. That is the core essential issue of 'wholesome' human existence.

'All this, all that and much more' is a matter of conditional temperamental mind, conditioned to think with presumptions, assumptions, and imperfect thought processes. Everyone creates his or her own subjective perception, you see. This is how the mind works. The real problem is in our vision. When our 'vision' transforms progressively from the gross physical to the physical, to the intellectual to the conscious and finally merges with the light of super-consciousness through profound insight in profound silence, we cease to run the power marathon. We stop the perpetual inertia of action and reaction. We stop confusion, fear, insecurity, rejection, loneliness, and, hurt. 'Hurt' is a composite feeling of battered and withered spirit of life, which sinks in 'sorrow'. Modern psychology finds solutions to end this human misery in an anti-depressant pill rather than profound human compassion that humanely transforms within the spirit of life within us, around us, and in every single human act!

Immortality cannot be a blessed boon to the human existence. Every life ends. Every end begins anew. Every soul empties its astral house in name, form, and personality merging into the oneness of divine eternity. Death is never a matter of intellectual choice or material prowess in its prevention. It is destined to every life breath. Healing the wounds of grief, or tragedy is never ever an easy process. When human experience delivers to us an emotional hurt, it renders to us an opportunity for a profound evolution in our human perception.

We begin to question our outlook, attitude, and lifestyle through suffering. We awaken our compassion in a transient collection of moments, all of which simply compose and shape our loving human relationship both for each other and for our eternal spirit of life. To ourselves, let us therefore be truly compassionate and humanely loving. In altruism of love manifests the sacred most human experience. 'my', 'mine', 'I', 'you', and 'yours', 'all this and all that' will not render solace nor will it render fathomless peace in silence. Fathomless faith, fathomless compassion and fathomless love when unilaterally shared will render solace and peace in silence. When fathomless faith and fathomless unconditional profound human love merge in profound togetherness, a fusion of profound human hope is created for the battered and the shattered, the withered and the hurt, the ignorant and the poor. Every 'hopelessness' and every 'helplessness' transforms into a delight when profound wisdom speaks to us in profound silence. In profound silence manifests the light of this profound truth in the simplest and purest state of the super consciousness.

The grief of hurt will never disperse completely. Trauma suffered through severe adversities will leave the physical body worn out and exhausted. Hope is a consolation given to the existence of humankind. It is an innate understanding towards human life on earth. This compassionate love and understanding is afforded in 'togetherness' of the three worlds (the celestial, the spiritual, and the terrestrial).

"Hope" is a solace to the wounded heart. It is a comfort of compassion almost like a mother's lap. Compassion is divine.

The spirit of life makes a wish to the divine order to grant hope to the wounded mother earth, the existence of humankind on earth, the spirits of divine life, and the children of nature:

"Life oh life! Let it be. Let beauty never cease to manifest in mother earth. Let earth never cease to be happy despite all this, that and the other. Let the world of human existence be filled with love and magnificent beauty."

"Life oh life! Let every human life have a beautiful purpose. Let every human life never stop praying in concourse. Let there be harmony and peace. Let there be light of delight! Life oh life! Let it be a flight of delight."

Every single human fate is merging to that pathless human destiny in due course of time, regardless of name, form or status. This transient human life is a profound gift to us in eternal time, to share in it most precious human compassion with unconditional love. If we die in altruism of love, our life becomes a sacred human experience worth a treasure beyond the wholesome material existence in time. Our experience becomes immortal albeit we wither and perish as mortals. We somehow leave behind a trail of beauty.

To leave behind such memorable immortal experiences to the future generation children is to become immortal in essential compassionate human existence in time. Loving memories grants hope to the future generation children. The vessel of material earth filled with intellectual and monetary power will not be able to stop the ticking time clock, nor will it be able to extend a human life. Intellectual camouflage brought by the "ism" will not render solace nor will it render the truth. It will always have "a gap" - 'neither here nor there'. Politics, economics and sociology will always remain imperfect.

The human Intellectual power comprises endless marathons with soaring levels of suspicion and paranoia, camouflage, material disasters, and tragedies. 'All this and all that' fills up temporary vessels of noise, haste, waste, paste, taste, and cents. The certain evidential earthly life is in actual fact truly uncertain, for it disperses into pathless eternity loosing its name, form and mind at the slam of uninvited death. Life therefore is uncertain albeit we claim, proclaim, possess, get obsessed and thrive on our own chaos. The buzzing noises and the whizzing thoughts of the egocentric power disperse in time too. In every wrong there is a glimpse of truth and a glimpse of right to realise the divine light of delight as much as in every right there is a shed of imperfection and a dot of error. The human mind has a gap, as long as it is an imperfect place of memories and thoughts, all of which project the dark shadows of our dancing desires.

'All this and all that' merely becomes a matter of 'has been'; past and forgotten in due course of time like the fading memories of the yesterdays.

What truly matters is that we love one another simply for the human compassion in the most funny, most simple, most sincere and most forbearing ways.

The flight of delight is the light of joy of compassionate love that triumphs over all this, that and the other to grant hope to distress.

Love does not threaten or get threatened. Love does not possess. Love is not obsessed by all that is materially transient. Love does not overpower. Love does not hurt. Love does not envy. Love does not compete radically. Love does not impose. Love does not cause or reason or argue. Love does not convert to fulfil a personal goal. Love does not restrict. Love does not discourage. Love does not reject. Love does not ignore. Love does not humiliate. Love does not slam. Love does not indulge in lust. Love does not dance to desires. Love does not control. Love does not usher. Love does not manipulate for a cause. Love does not reason to please. Love does not feel pity, nor does not feel sympathy with half hearted emotions. Love simply gives compassion. Love simply understands in the most profound silence. Love simply evolves in time. Love sets us free in our essential human nature, to be essentially profound. Love simply loves unconditionally, compassionately and humbly. Love brings us peace and love enables us to grant hope to the future generation children. Our soul divine feeds on love.

Compassionate Love begets human love. Compassionate profound human experience heals the most battered spirits of life. Compassion heals every wound. Compassion has patience and compassion has greatest of all strengths. Compassion is the essence of human life. It does not matter who you are, what you are, where you are, which you are, how you are, when you are, why you are. What truly matters is the essential human substance within the spirit of your life. What truly does matter, is 'our perception' of the world within us, because the same world exists around us and the same world 'para-exists' beyond the shadows of our dancing thoughts. We do not have a human problem as such, until our corrupt minds try to find faults and bring fear out of apathy, dismay and pity. We therefore lack only in true perception. Not this, not that. All this, that and the other does not matter. What truly matters is the sublime divine nature as a result of which we become splendour of divine love and the light of delight.

Life is a perpetual triumph over death. Truth always wins eventually no matter what. Hope always manifests itself somehow, in somewhat profound sense. Happiness is the birth right of every spirit of life. Let us afford greatest reverence to infinite truth, in 'togetherness'. When your eyes captures with your perception, my profound most sincere written words, in a fusion of 'togetherness', we have created a sublime delight of compassion. We have brought the heavenly 'delight' on to the gross earthly existence, with a compassionate feeling of human affection, with profound most inspirational insight, from the spiritual world.

I embrace your profound perception with my written words, in a fusion of spiritual togetherness of the three worlds (the celestial, the spiritual, and the terrestrial).

Let us channel our imagination into ever-soaring ETERNITY of one simple spiritual truth, which manifests profoundly in your soul, in my soul, in every other soul and in the cosmic soul of the entire cosmos.

Compassion begets compassion. Love begets love. Love simply never fails to dance. Love simply never fails to play the music of the hearts. Love simply never fails to conquer real happiness and love simply never fails to bring us back home where we share fathomless compassion and fathomless faith in true delight! We came into this world in time, as a spirit of life, to commemorate 'human togetherness' in loving compassion.

In this human life there is a dignity about collective social interaction. We share moments together. Our karmic web connects us all in destiny somehow, in somewhat profound sense. Like all the rivers merging into the Divine Ocean.

In time, we wonder and caper to different energies of life, under different conditions. In time, we share extra ordinary special moments of human togetherness in loving compassion. In time, we laugh; we fly, we run we walk across the bridge of river life meeting different talents of life in different spiritual substance. In time, we behold close to our spirit of life and treasure those extra ordinary special moments of togetherness, in profound human experience, albeit brief, as some of them may have been.

During the times of hardships, and long silent suffering, the light of delight treasured in loving togetherness and fearless dreams of 'compassionate togetherness' brings us hope. Selflessness is to share hope and to give hope to another hopeless.

When we are most alone in long silence of just naked nature, simple music, simple serenity, simple love, and profound congruence of spiritual world and the spirit of life we capture the insight of delight.

To shed tears of pity in dismay is loneliness. However, when a tear of joy is shed in sheer delight of realising the treasure of human compassion, in fathomless faith of altruism of just love, love, and love, life becomes a flight of delight.

To be able to live this complex human life on this complex man made human earth with highest integrity, spiritual sovereignty, servitude, humanity, courage and strength, is indeed the greatest of all human talent. A talent of 'compassionate fathomless love' with 'fathomless faith' generates delight of 'fathomless hope'. I find that great many fears are borne out of rejection. Hurt causes pain if we just know the hurt but do not endeavour to understand it in depth of profound wisdom, profound silence and profound light of the spirit.

The human intellect and the human mind power, in all this and all that material world of power, have created great complexity, confusion, camouflage, and catastrophe.

However, sorrow (pain, disease, loss, hurt, trauma, distress, adversity, hardships, poverty, barrenness, restrictions of old age, tragedies, and death) brings us all to the point of transformation. Time renders us an opportunity to become divine that which is our essential nature. Only total human transformation can cure our roots with compassionate human love. To be happy is not an intellectual or an academic process. It is a talent of life. It belongs to the spirit of life, for which there is only one university – "profound human experience", 'The University of Life'.

'Mokshah-muktee' (freedom), 'Satt-Atman-Sauchatti' (self-same enquiry in righteous thoughts), and 'param-premmam' (eternal love), are super-consciousness, consciousness, and sub-consciousness attributes of the cosmic human being.

The Vedic macro-cosmic love analogy:

The sun brings nourishment of heat and warmth to the earthly clay and universe leaving the perennial pastures to rest to the divine song of the compassionate sea, the music of the rain fall and the hymns of the birds and rustling trees standing bare with the wind. There is a 'super-conscious intelligence' that almost keeps the mother earth beautiful, extra ordinarily blossoming and happy in flowers, green pastures. The rivers continue onwards to the sea despite the stumbling blockages of rocks, wheel of the mill, and dark bark. The super-conscious intelligence is verily the higher order. The three worlds namely the celestial, the terrestrial, and the spiritual world are directly correlated to 'freedom', 'thought' and 'love' respectively. The terrestrial world Inter connects with the other two mystical worlds of existence (namely the celestial and the spiritual) unknown as they may be, in profoundest thoughts that inspire.

Filtration of perception entails distinguishing the right from the wrong indirectly from the point of spirit such that the integrity of the spirit remains untouched by 'all, this, that and the other'. Discrimination is based on personal judgements, personal knowledge, and personal feelings, whereas filtration of perception is based on pure insight and pure intuition with a profound sub-conscious reason to see beyond the physical and mental sheath of the substance.

The remedy to dissolve personal hurt and trauma therefore cannot manifest in the systems of politics or any other survivor tool kits of intellectualism, religion, institutions, conferences, referendums, bureaucracy, 'all, this, that and the other'. Regardless of the degree of status, title, and knowledge, a psychologist cannot claim to understand 'hurt' and 'trauma' without becoming respectful and profound towards the beauty of the spirit of life and the bare existence of life itself in compassion.

The remedy to dissolve hurt dignifies within to see beyond the seen or the manifest into the true divinity or un-manifest. The trauma of hurt does not beg for mercy or sympathy from half hearted intellectual experts of psychology who in their own very personal life are surviving in total chaos and total conflict.

Healing the spiritual entity and finding a life support remedy is a proven very Vedic way to dissolve trauma. Trauma is deeper than psychological sheath. Knowing hurt cannot imply remedy to resolve it. 'All this, that and the other' will continue to thrive in chaos, survive in chaos, and twirl in chaos. Chaos is a grand manifestation of how the vicious cycles of ego never ceases to hurt. Hurt is in chaos of 'all this that and the other'. Understanding hurt and trauma entails that we look beyond the physical sheath of the flesh and the mind.

Emotional hurt and trauma can be very painful indeed. Much more painful than physically eminent pain that entails a surgical operation or hospitalisation. Coming through emotional pain and growing with the self-discovery of hurt in profound experience of living the adventures of life is one way to release the trauma of hurt.

Acknowledging fully the nature of the hurt, and discovering it progressively, one day at a time with profound love, compassion, and spiritual strength is one way of resolving hurt. It takes time and great patience. Hurt or Trauma cannot heal absolutely, just as a broken glass cannot be put together to become unbroken like new.

Happiness is not sought, it just happens. Happiness is an occurrence. Happiness is not manufactured or made by gestures of 'thank you', 'sorry', 'I can help', or 'I know how it feels'. Rather it is in the respect of 'I understand with deep profound compassion, despite all said and done'. Happiness is an absolute state of blissfulness. Absolute state of blissfulness cannot manifest in all this, that and the other.

Happiness cannot transpire without profound love and profound respect for the true self. True Integrity of the spirit can never be negotiated in 'terms of' 'all this, that and the other'. A blissful state of trance is a harmony of the three worlds, namely the celestial, the terrestrial, and the spiritual worlds. Such beautiful harmony in togetherness is an occurrence of sheer chance. As the river continues it's onwards journey into the grand ocean despite being broken by logs and mills, so does a spirit of life eventually dissolve, 'all this, that and the other', in due course of time. The spirit of life having travelled thousands of rough roads finally arrives at the plateau of soft pebbles on the beautiful lining of the shores.

We congress in 'togetherness' at the dawn and the dusk to bring together the three worlds namely the celestial, the terrestrial, and the spiritual; in prayer invocations; in sacrificial light (candles), mantra-manjaree (invocations of peace mantra), sacred hymns, sacred fire (yagnas), and eternal peace oblation. The gist of the Vedic sacrifice eventually grants hope to the human existence.

Amidst all the noise (falsehood), haste (uncertainties), and waste (warfare), whilst the intellectual world of human survival perpetuates in karma (deeds, actions, and cycles), the spirit of life is in constant search for harmony, health, and happiness. Longevity, health, and happiness imply life and hope. Hope implies that in due course of time, we will discover nature's way and realise that the real true help is within our reach, within us, within our spirit. The true self – the spirit of life, albeit mystically unknown is the real origin of hope without a shadow of doubt. Hope gives solace without intellectual conditions, to heal with nature and to discover nature's imbalances. Hope means we try our best to evolve in karma until we loose the senses and the life force within us. Absolute total perfect balance of harmony, happiness, and, wholesome health is not possible in the age of falsehood ('kaalyug').

Sound practical judgement (the consciousness to refine conscience), natural sagacity of the nature ('prakrutti'), social awareness of modesty ('Anutssekah'), spiritual knowledge or ('adhya-atma-adhyayanam'), and righteous action ('dharma- satt-karma'). These are the pre-requisites of longevity, health, and enjoyment of life. Deviation results into disturbance – pollution ('vissama-kshaya').

When a human being in his or her self-realisation experience reaches the final beatitude, the spirit of life, causes dissolution to gross states, like all the habitual attachments ('kaal-samnsahr'), false desires ('moha-praarthitah'), illusion (maya), ego (ahamkaar), and the falsehood ('asattmya').

From the dissolution of the mortal state of form ('saar-guna') which is like a mirage (maya) to the immortal state of formlessness (nir-guna), the transformation takes place in divine self-realisation.

The sublime state is a divine spiritual state and it is known as the swan personality ('Aum-hamnssa-hamnssa-so-hum-jaya-sat-chit-anandam'). A stable, harmonious, happy, healthy state is "satt-chidd-anandaaum".

The authentic Vedic life science was written for the 'kaalyug' or age of falsehood when 'Prithvee-mata' or mother earth shed tears of 'pidhah' or physical sorrows and sufferings, 'dukhah' or torment, 'vyaaddhi' or anxiety, and 'vismayah' or astonishment at the 'assatt-vardhayatti' or increase in human wretchedness. It is believed to be the celestial wisdom for satt-karma or righteous act, satt- karanna or righteous karmic cause, satt-kriya or righteous rites, and satt-jivan or righteous life. Therefore, whatever act, practice, or thought does not lead to social good or social harmony is considered selfishness and egoistic. What is divinely good for the self is good for the world, what is painfully hurtful, helpless, and dismally hopeless, is the same for the world at large, and vice versa. This is the basis for harmonious society 'idamn-nanm-maama' (unselfish).

Giving hope to someone means giving a spiritual life to someone. Hope is nature's own help to heal and nurture the manifestation of physical body and the metaphysical mind. Hope is a spiritual life support to a river, trying to find its own course.

There is no life without hope. We aspire, we anticipate and we live life in hope. Giving someone a chance is hope. Granting someone a boon of sacrifice is hope. Loving someone unconditionally is hope. Giving someone self-respect and dignity of life spirit is hope.

We cannot give hope to others when we cannot give hope to ourselves. I realised sooner than later that most of my life's dire hurt emanates from denying love to my-self.

Every hurt, disappointment, or discouragement presents us with an opportunity to listen and to learn how to nurture the integrity of the spirit of our life and to love ourselves better. Only when we love ourselves better can we appropriately love others wholesome.

Moving alone does not imply moving in smaller circles of people! Aloneness connects our energies to the higher plane the outermost divine planes of existence.

Sacred spiritual energy is very hard to build up and very easy to loose. When we loose spiritual energy, we feel drained, angry, frustrated, confused, tired, and irritated. It takes many hours and days to build up spiritual energy. It takes only seconds and minutes to loose it.

We loose most energy when we speak in the wrong times, at the wrong place, to the wrong person, for the wrong reasons, on the wrong issues (never argue!), for the wrong cause and of the wrong accord. That is why, there is an ancient Vedic wisdom - *'speak little, speak softly, speak clearly, speak the truth, think twice before you speak, and if you are not sure take time to think things through'*. Over the years, I discovered that, association of negative persons brings negativity into our life and vice versa. Association of manipulative persons brings chaos and conflict into our life thereby bringing indigestion. Association of double standards people causes us to become worthless. Sometimes it is better not to have association at all than to have wrongful association. Waste of spiritual energy occurs from keeping wrong company of people, eating wrong food at wrong tables, earning wrong income from wrong conduct. The company we keep influence our higher spiritual thinking substantially. 'Satt-sanngha jnanam etat'. Companies of righteous persons bring us harmony, peace, and happiness. Company of double standards persons bring us anguish, distress, trauma, and conflicting hurt.

The subtlest beauty manifests beyond the known. Eternity truly is the divine soul and the soul truly is that eternal existence. The entire cosmos moving in time creating the dawn and the dusk is verily the beautiful form of the divine mother. In all this, that and the other, no one is wholly right or wholly wrong. There is some truth in all that is wrongful (like the warfare), in as much as there is imperfection in all that is wholly right because it is a perception of the human mind perceived in the imperfect state. Therefore, even the self-same words are drawn from some magical elixir and distilled through the gossamer screen of 'maya' (illusion), as a perceptive imagination, as a vivid insight, as a dream from a dream. Life oh life! Let it be. Let it be, come what may. Let it be what it may be. Face it, accept it, grit it but grin, and shrug it away. Life is a moment to live (healthily-happily-humbly), to love (compassionately), to laugh (self-acceptance), to let go (of the past), to learn (reflect on soul), to listen (awaken), to leap into the unknown (self-realisation). Life is only a moment in time. Life oh life! Let it be a flight of delight.

Let us light the candle of delight in profound togetherness of compassionate human love with a smile on our face. Let us bid farewell to the bygone past in a sigh of compassionate love. Let us rest, if we must for we cannot understand grief, hurt, or human misery with a tired mind, a tired heart, and a withered spirit. Only in the light of purest mind, can we see/ envision the enlightening delight of truth in the transformed compassionate human spirit of profound love manifested in a fusion of eternal bliss. Let us sigh with profound compassion to the night-sky of glittering stars, shinning moon, and embracing divine Mother Nature. Let us rest in peaceful sleep. Let us find solace in silent profound communication with the world of spirit. Let us rest in our dreams for they bring solace and consolation to our withered spirits.

'Hamnssa', having journeyed through humane experience, exhaled in profound praises of 'delight' in, poetry, prayer dialogues, music, dance, yoga and sacrificial fire 'Agnee'. 'Hamnssa' reaches the loftiest peak of divine mysticism. The soul infinite knows only the imperfect human life.

In the acceptance of all imperfections, cherishes the idea of being human in the simplest and most affectionate compassion. The Soul divine is a compassionate human person in need of harmony, peace, and 'togetherness'.

This unity is a thread of many strings entwined in imperfection yet it offers the possibility of a marvellous harmony and concord to human life. United the soul resolves, united the feelings proliferate in a fusion of 'oneness'. In 'togetherness', may all spirits of life dwell in marvellous concord.

The divine ocean roars with compassion and embraces the capering flight of the river. The river looses its earthly bonds and is set free to merge in 'oneness', with the eternal sound of 'Aum' roaring from the deep sea. The 'river life' embraces the beautiful golden orange light of the sunset and serene tranquillity of the pathless sea. Ah mirth of the opening skies. Ah the beautiful magnificent laughters of the wind in the surging sea. Ah the delight of the endless boisterous ocean, the Heavens River has drowned and dissolved its banks. Ah the golden light of the sun greets all in delight.

The silent murmuring voice of the sea whispers softly, gently, and exuberantly. The spirit of life shimmers in purest ecstasy at the rapture of the perennial shores, as if some magical elixir touched the chord of the most compassionate symphony!

Even the self-same "word" is dissolving in the pathless sea in a Cosmo theatrical pulsation!

Ah, the sensational sprays of the rainbow and the golden ripples of the tranquil ocean bring glory to the soul!

Ah, at last 'Hamnssa' is free from the burdens of the hemmed karmic web! Ah at last 'Hamnssa' is free from the coils of earthly tension and frictions of dismal resistance!

Ah at last 'Hamnssa' is the endless love of the pathless waters and teeming vast space! Ah at last 'Hamnssa' has outlasted all else!

In the close embrace with the compassionate sea, the spirit of life whispers softly to the human existence on earth in glorious triumph:

"Life oh life let it be come what may. Let it be. Face it, accept it, grit it, but grin, and shrug it away. Life oh life! Let it be a dance, a song, a poem, music of the night! Let it be!"

"Life oh life! Let it be a composition of happy moments, filled with the delight of true compassion! All the earthly pities and sympathies, shame and drudgery drown in the eternal compassion of the sea. The ocean forever sings 'Aum' to the master-less wind, which together plays the music of the nightfall in harmony. The sea murmurs and hums in quintessence. "

"Life oh life! Time flies too fast. Life is too short! Life is to live in delight! At last, you merge in 'oneness', with the vast divine Ocean of eternity loosing your name, form, and ego. Let my fading pulse beat now merge with the drumbeat of the ocean. The twilight of the dusk and the dawn, the 'master-less' winds, and the pathless sea 'never failing' in tryst of togetherness, loves forever! Life ah life! The sea forever is the endless love!"

"Life oh life! Let it be a flight of delight of the retiring dusk."

"Life oh life! Let it be a delight of new beginning, commemorating compassion in renewed human experience. Let it be a delight of happiness. We merge in 'togetherness', in a flight of compassionate delight, wherein the final beatitude of truth infinite manifests. Life ah life! Let the Cosmo theatrical delight be forever! Sun oh sun! Let your new dawn bring renewed hope to the existence of humankind that is numbed and torn apart."

"Life oh life! Ah God, freedom, and peace forever in the fathomless eternal sea! Sea oh sea, let me love you forever! Let the spirit of my life merge in oneness with your deep roaring compassion! Ah God, freedom at last! Surging pulsation of passionate compassion explodes in a fusion of delight! Ah God for now there is no turning back, no looking back, no regrets even! For now let me unite in oneness with the eternal vast pathless sky, orbited by the master-less wind to merge with the compassionate vast ocean in the delight of dusk! Life oh life! Let me unite in divinity with the infinite love and the fathomless compassion of the Grand Ocean and radiance of the sun."

"Life ah life! Let it be forever and ever! Ah God liberty, liberty! Sun oh Sun! Let your beautiful golden orange hue light in the peaceful dusk, be the last form of delight, as I sigh in compassion! Life ah life let it be a wonderful extra ordinary flight of delight!"

"Life oh life! Let it be! Life oh life! Let it be a flight of delight!"

"Life ah life! Let it be a flight of delight. Time oh time! Let me be an eternal spirit of life. From time I came, with time I evolved and to time I finally merge in a communion of the three worlds in delight. Time oh time, let the spirit of my life stand bare united to resolve in the dusk greeting the nightingale."

"Life oh life. Let me stand bare as the earthen clay, the soft pebbles, the rippling waters of the sea, the blowing wind, the melting fire, and a star in the nightingale."

"Life ah life! Let it be a flight of delight. Time ah time! Let me be! Let me be! Time ah time! Let me be at peace! Time ah time! Let me take a glimpse of the beautiful eternity as I take a flight of delight! Life ah life! Let it be! Life ah life! Let it be a flight of delight!"

"Life ah life! Let my spirit now stand bare with the wind. Let the wind blow me away swiftly onwards towards the grand ocean. Wind oh Wind! Let me become the sound of music that echoes the nightingale with all its soft humming!"

"Life oh life! Let my spirit melt into the sun, as my earthen clay looses all its desires, and attachments to the compassionate waters of the grand ocean. Earth oh Earth! Let me rhyme with thine melodies like the birds twitting, the sea waves thrashing, the ripples of its water dancing, the rivers flowing, the trees rustling!"

"Life ah life! Let me unite with the bare existence, and let me long forever dwell in unity and divinity under the cosmic protection of Rudra (cosmic beholder of pure nectar of gods - 'Somam')."

"Life ah life! Let my spirit now embrace the hue of the sun, as the sea greets the sun at the dawn and the dusk. Life ah life! Let it be a flight of delight. Sea oh Sea! Let me embrace the spirit of my life in love as you would embrace the river of life. Life ah life! Let it be a flight of delight. Sky oh Sky! Let the last rainbow bring a delight of joy! Let the nightingale comfort me and console the spirit of my life. Sun oh Sun! Let time become the light of twilight of the dawn and the dusk where the day no longer is a pure day and the night no longer is a pure night."

"Life ah life! Let it be a flight of delight for what is to die but to stand bare like the river merging into the grand ocean."

"Life ah life! Let the light of the spirit of my life merge in delight with the oneness of the light of the sun. Time ah time! Let me be an immortal spirit of life. Let my self-same words dissolve in peace. Let there be seven generations of immortal hope for the future unborn children of this beautiful mother earth. Time ah time, Let the future unborn children have a world better than ours. All said and done, what really matters in all this, that and the other is the fathomless love of this fathomless nature."

"Time ah time, let the future unborn children enjoy peace with fathomless faith in the human spirit of life, to bring fathomless hope. Time ah time, let me be free at last from all this, that and other. Time ah time, let me be a child of nature, a star of delight in the nightingale."

"Oh Great Spirit, whose endless life breath forever gives life to all, whose voice ushers the winds and the ocean, let me walk in thine pathless eternity. Oh Great Spirit, whose rainfall always feeds the dry earthen clay, let me walk in beauty onwards towards the teeming pathless sky."

"Oh Great Spirit, behold the spirit of my life as I behold the last vision of the orange hue and purple sunset. Oh Great Spirit let there be delight in all. Life oh life! Let it be a flight of delight."

"Life ah life! From sun 'I' came, to sun 'I' return. Life ah life! Let me melt away peacefully into the sun."

"Life ah life! Let the spirit of my life rest in the divine womb of the grand ocean where no one dare intrudes."

"God ah God, let there be hope. Sweet be my departure from the temporary dwellings of the earthly clay. Sweet be my return to the immortal pathless eternity. Life ah life! Let it be a flight of delight."

"Aum shanti shanti shanti (peace be to the terrestrial, peace be to the spiritual, peace be to the celestial)."

"Raum Aum Raum. Aum Ah Aum. Aum Amm Mmm".

 BIBLIOGRAPHY AND LIST OF REFERENCES

1. The Vedas, in five parts (Published by: Banares, Calcutta, The Vedic University composed and compiled by Professor Raimundo Panikkar).

2. Gita explained (Dnyaneshwar Maharaj – A great Maratha Sage of Maharashtra) Gita or Bhagawat Gita as it is contains 900 shlokas (verses) but the Dynaneshwar Gita contains 9000 shlokas (verses). 'Gita explained' has been narrated by Manu Subedar

3. The Holy Geeta by Swami Chinmayananda (Published by Central Chinmaya Mission Trust, Sandeepany Sadhanalaya, Bombay, India.)

4. The Old Testament in all parts (The Church of England) (As narrated by the Cyber link Reading Room of The Metanoesis School)

5. The Holy Quran (Halim Iliasii's roman translation of, by Mohamed Marmauduke Picktall) (Published by Kutub Khana, Delhi, India.)

6. Bliss Divine (Swami Sivananda, The Divine life society of India)

7. Hindutvam By Acharya Swami Pranavanandaji Maharaj'ji and Swami Pranavanandji (Published by Bharat Seva Ashram India's leading monastic mission in 1917)

8. MahaNarayan Upanishad By Swami Vimalananda and published by the Sri ramakrishna matt the Ravindran Press of madras, India.

9. The Upanishads translated and selected by Juan Mascaro and published by the Penguin classics

10. Saturn a friend or a foe By Jyotis Shiromani & L R Chawdhree (Published by Sagar Publications of New Dehli, India)

11. Scientific Analysis of Horoscope (The Vedic astrology) by Jyotis Saraswati & L R Chawdhree. (Published by Sagar Publications of New Dehli, India)

12. The Dhamapada (Reading Room of the Vedic cyber link – The Metanoesis School)

13. The Yoga Sutras of Patanjali alias the thread of union (Reading Room of the Vedic cyber link – The Metanoesis School)

14. GAYATRI The highest meditation by Sadguru Sant Keshavadas. Published by Motilal Banarasidass Publishers Pvt Ltd. , New Dehli, India

15. Some Concepts of Hinduism – (An Introduction) by Dr. R Ramnarine

16. The Seat of the Soul by Gary Zukav (Published by A FIRESIDE BOOK, Simon and Schuster).

17. The five stages of the soul by Harry R Moody and David Carroll [Ebury press/ Rider Books]

18. Healing with Gems and crystals by Daya Sarai Chocron (Published by the Orient paperbacks)

19. The Healing power of Gemstones (in tantric and Ayurvedic astrology) by Harish Johari (Published by Destiny Books, Rochester, Vermont)

20. TOTAL FREEDOM – The essential Krishnamurti by Rev. J Krishnamurti (Published by Harper Collins Publishers – Sanfrancisco)

21. The Book of Life – A daily meditation with Krishnamurti by J Krishnamurti. (Published by Harper Collins Publishers – Sanfrancisco)

22. The Reading room of the Bharat Vidya Bhavan of London, U.K.

23. The International society for the Vedic Studies forums

24. The reading room of the Vedic University of America

25. The three branches of India's life tree – Commentaries on the Vedas, The Upanishads and The Bhagavad Gita by Sri Chinmoy [Aum Publications Jamaica, U.S.A.]

26. Glimpses of the Vedic Metaphysics by Prem Sabhlok

27. Shiva – An introduction by Devdutt Pattanaik

28. Tibetan astrology by Philippe Cornu

29. My Gurjis notes – AnandaSwami

30. Guruji Acharya Swami Pranavanandaji Maharaj's Hindutvam

ANNEX

Pages 382 to 403 form part of this annex, supporting supplement to Surya Yoga elucidated in chapter nine of this book 'A flight of delight'.

The yoga illustrations extracted from my pujeet Guruji Ananda Swamiji's book may contain trivial typing error because of the ancient English transliteration done in India in 1956.

These illustrations are reference attachments only.

ANNEX ONE - 'A FLIGHT OF DELIGHT – COSMIC HUMAN ENTITY

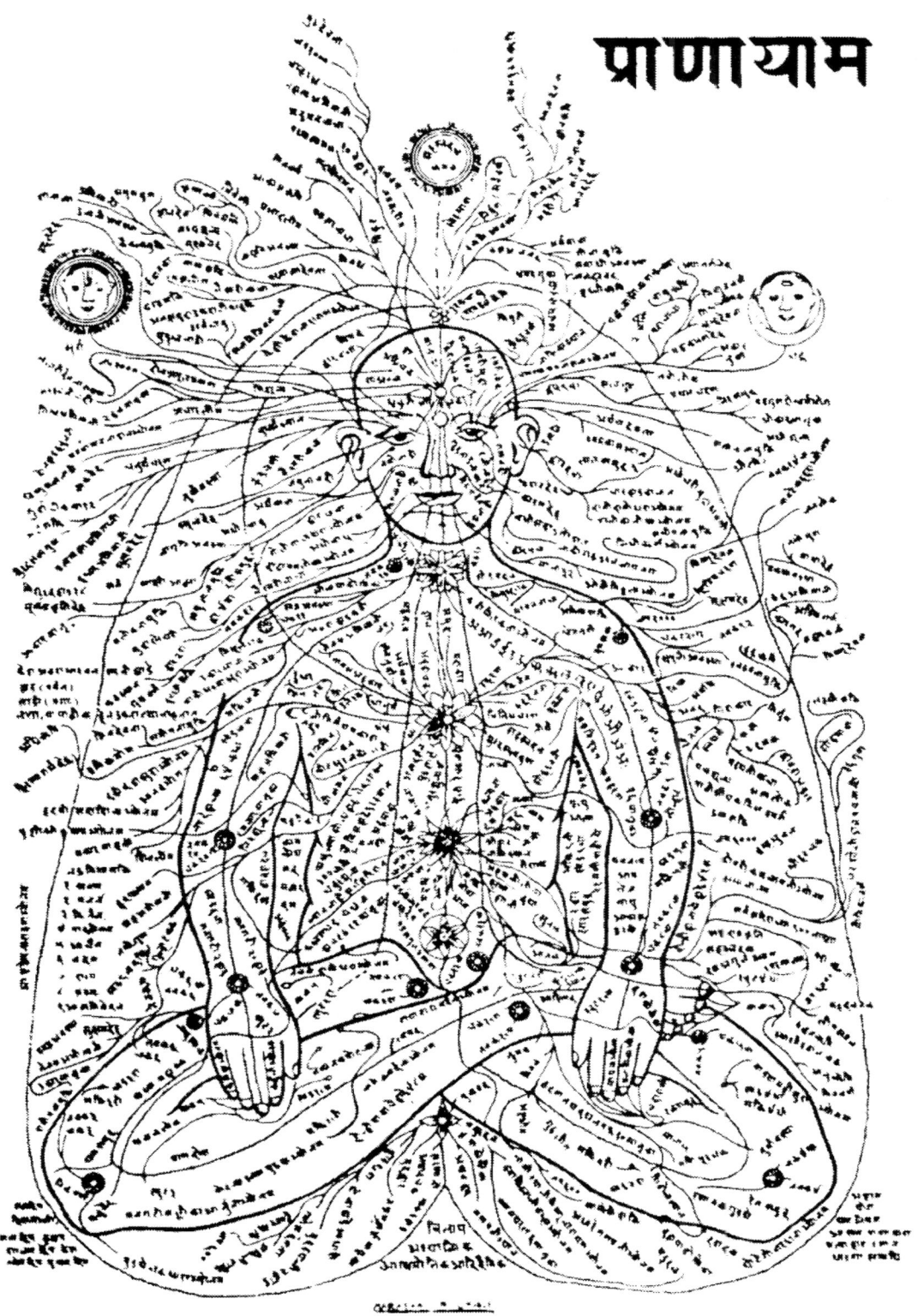

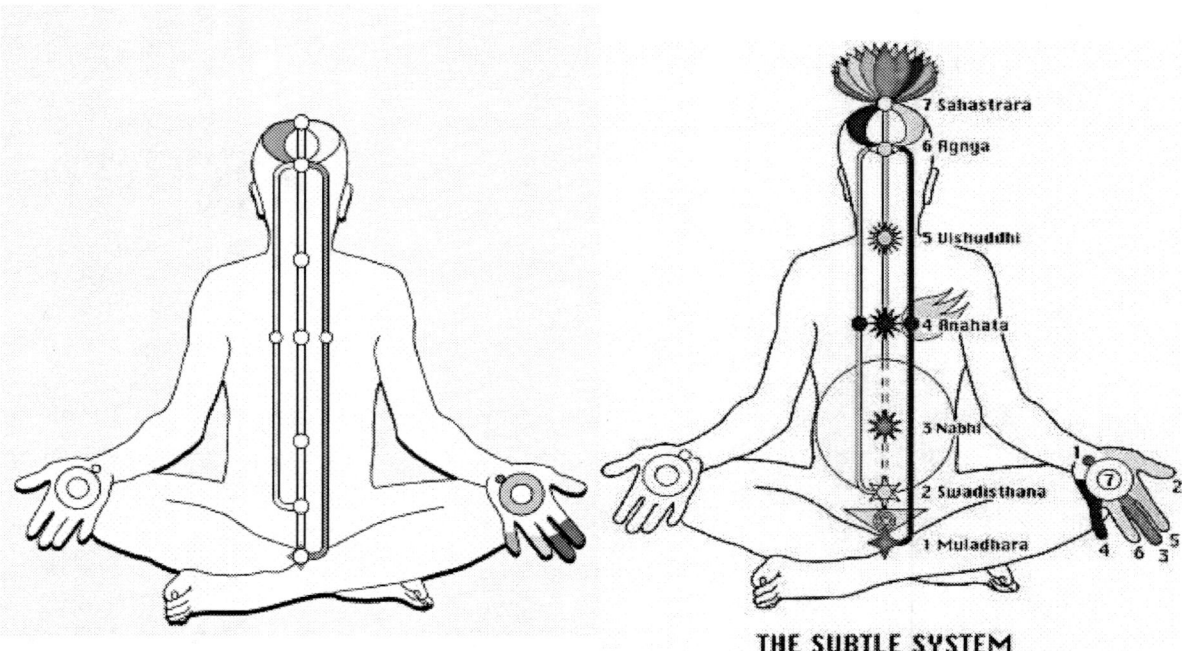

THE SUBTLE SYSTEM

Annex two

Kundalini is the life energy or the spiral of spiritual energy at the base of coccyx. It forms vortexes of energy knots called chakras when it travels through the 'Shushumna' (channel) from the base of the coccyx to the tip of the crown on the head. Vedas say that there are 72,000 subtle (Upanishads say 350,000) channels, but Shushumna, Ida and pingala are the main. Ida is the moon channel moving from the base to the left nostril whereas pingala is the sun channel moving from the base to the right nostril. Furthermore, Vedas say that between the fifth chakra (Vishuddha) and the sixth chakra (Ajnya) there is intermediate chakra in the middle of the palate called 'Lalannaa' (responsible for heat). Also the Vedas say that between the 6th chakra (Ajnya) and the 7th chakra (sahastrara) there are two intermediate chakras called the 'manas' chakra/insight (2.5 finger widths) and the 'somam' chakra/ stability (further 2.5 finger widths from manas chakra). A chakra in Sanskrit means the spinning wheel of the cosmic energy. There are seven main energy vortices. According to ancient Vedic texts, a 'chakra' is where 216 'nadis' (energy channels) cross over each other, forming energy spirals. Vedas mention 72,000 such energy channels. There are thousands of minor chakras e.g. on, hands, feet, ears etc. Main Chakras are: Muladhara (coccyx), swadhishttana (bladder), Manipurna (navel), Anahata (abdomen), vishudhaha (heart), ajjnnah (third eye between eye brows), and sahasrarha (crown – middle of the head).

<u>Relativity and relevance is as follows:</u>

- Colours / vibrations: Red, Orange, Yellow, Greenish-White, Blue, Indigo-purple, Violet-White

- Levels of consciousness: swaroopam-samagunam- bhutta-gunam (gross physical metamorphosis) moving up to brahma-nirgunam SHUNYA (beyond the sheaths of consciousness - the subtlest point).

- Spiritual relationship: Security - food, clothing, shelter, (gross physical); family, society, compassion, knowledge, wisdom, union (self-realisation).

- Awake state, semi-awake state, Dream State, semi-sleep state; sleep state, mental state, and spiritual state.

- Tree of life: seven spheres of existence namely bhuh (earth), bhuvah (astral), svahar (celestial), mahah (atmospheric orb), janah (human), tapah (austere), and satyam (truthfulness, consciousness, blissfulness, divine, one).

- Essentials: Earth, water, fire, air, ether, intellect, and atman (spirit).

- Planets: Mars and Sun for the first chakra; Moon & Mercury for the second chakra; Jupiter and Sun for the third chakra; Jupiter and Venus for the fourth chakra; Mercury and Saturn for the fifth chakra; Moon and Saturn for the sixth chakra; Sun, Moon, Venus and Rahu and Ketu for the seventh chakra.

- Gems stones:
Coral, Yellow Sapphire, Emerald, Pearl, Blue sapphire, Diamond

- Sound/ mantras: Lam, Vam, Ram, Yam/Sam, Hum, Aum, Om.

- Shapes/yantras: Square, crest with six petals, triangle, pentagon star, circle, oval, dot with crest, dot with thousand petals.

Source of illustrations one and two: Shri Adi-shakti – The Kingdom of God, 2200 page anthology based on the teachings of H H Shri Mataji Nirmala Devi. By Jagbir Singh. Any queries regarding these illustrations can be made directly to: JAGBIR SINGH AT HIS PERSONAL EMAIL: jagbir@videotron.ca, alternatively, at the editor's office: adishakti@videotron.ca

Salutation to the sun

Om Mitraaya Namah
- the friend of all

(Suryanamaskar Yoga)
Om Hiranya garbhaaya Namah
the golden cosmic self

Om Mareechaye Namah
- the lord of the dawn

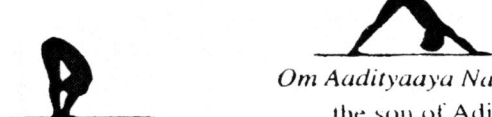

Om Ravaye Namah
- the shining one

Om Aadityaaya Namah
the son of Aditi

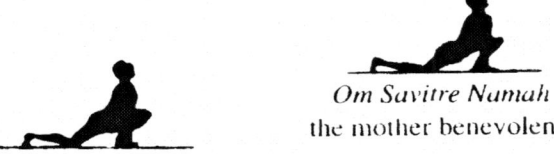

Om Sooryaaya Namah
one who induces activity

Om Savitre Namah
the mother benevolent

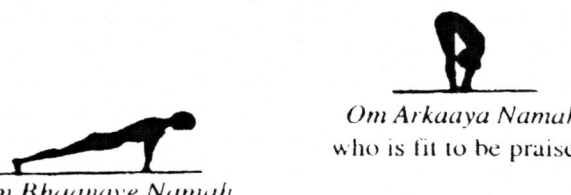

Om Bhaanave Namah
- he who illumines

Om Arkaaya Namah
who is fit to be praised

Om Khagaaya Namah
moves quickly in the sky

Om Pooshne Namah
- the giver of strength

Om Bhaaskaraaya Namah
-the one who leads
to enlightenment

Om Shri Savitrusoorya naaraayanaaya Namah - the Sun God

Annex three SUN ASANAS

Annex four GLORY ASANAS

Annex five PRESS UPS

Annex six SUN REVOLUTION CIRCLE ASANAS

Annex seven DOLPHIN STRETCH asanas

Annex eight TADASANA SALUTATION FOR INNER GROWTH ASANAS

Annex nine WARRIOR SUN ASANAS

Annex ten PRAYER ASANAS RESOLUTION TO INVOKE THE POWER OF SUN LIGHT

Annex eleven YOGA ASANAS (DRAWINGS OF 20 ASANAS)

YOGA

The Inverted Body Posture (1) (Sirrsasana)

1. SIRASANA (Head Stand)

Benefits:

1. It improves general health.
2. It cures certain types of headaches.
3. It relieves pain in the back.
3. It removes the tired feeling.
5. It increases the power of resistance to cold.
6. It can banish wrinkles and grey hair.
7. It gives a feeling of well-being.
8. It increases the digestive power.
9. It improves concentration and memory.
10. It helps in Brahmcharya.
11. It strengthens the eye sight.
12. It keeps the body young and healthy.

2. BHUJANGASANA (Cobra Posture)

Benefits:

1. It keeps the spine supple, healthy and strong.
2. It tones up the nervous system.
3. It strengthens the muscles of the abdomen, back, arms and neck.
4. It controls the blood pressure.
5. It corrects bad posture and improves body metabolism.

3. DHANURASANA (Bow Posture)

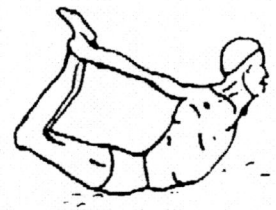

Benefits:

1. It makes the spine supple.
2. It tones up the nervous system.
3. It improves the efficiency of the liver and kidney.
4. It strengthens the abdominal region and keeps the body trim.
5. It improves digestion.

4. MAYURASANA (Peacock Posture)

Benefits:

1. It strengthens the abdomen and the lower back.
2. This asana destroys all diseases and it removes abdominal disorders and also those arising from irregularities of wind, phlegm and bile.
3. It helps to digest unwholesome food taken in excess.
4. It increases appetite.
5. It is claimed that it can destroy the most deadly poison.

5. HALASANA (Plough Posture)

Benefits:

1. It promotes suppleness of the spine.
2. It trims the waist line and makes the body strong, young and healthy.
3. It prevents disorders of the stomach.
4. It normalises the body weight and rejuvenates the whole body.
5. It improves circulation.
6. It strengthens the spine.

6. SARVANGASANA (Shoulder Stand)

Benefits:

1. It cures indigestion.
2. It has a beneficial effect on the endocrine gland.
3. It can cure and prevent diabetes.
4. It tones up the nervous system.
5. It stretches the spine.
6. It reduces excess fat.
7. It sends a rich supply of blood to the spine and brain.
8. It rejuvenates the body.
9. It relieves conjestive nostrils.
10. It helps in Brahmcharya.

7. MASTASANA (Fish Pose)

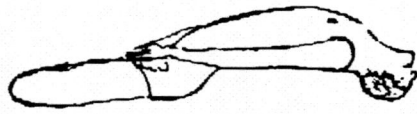

Benefits:

1. It improves breathing.
2. It cures cold.
3. It relieves conjestive nostrils.
4. The thyroids benefit from Asana.
5. It strengthens the neck region.
6. It removes wrinkles from the face.

8. PASCHITANASANA

(The Posterior Stretch Posture)

Benefits:

1. It can cure diabetes.
2. It removes surplus fat from the waist and abdomen.
3. It helps digestion.
4. It cures all diseases of men.
5. It keeps the body youthful.
6. It improves body metabolism.

9. SARVANGASANA (b)

Benefits:

1. It tones up the nervous system.
2. It removes wrinkles from the face.
3. It improves circulation and stimulates a rich supply of blood to the face.
4. It is a useful aid to reduce body weight.

10. SALABHASANA (Locust Posture)

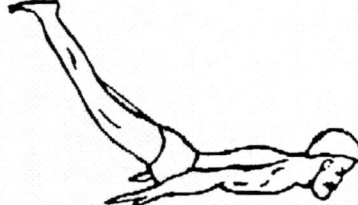

Benefits:

1. It aids digestion.
2. It removes surplus fat.
3. It strengthens the lower back, the hips and legs.

11. ARDHA-MATSYENDRASANA
(Twist , Posture)

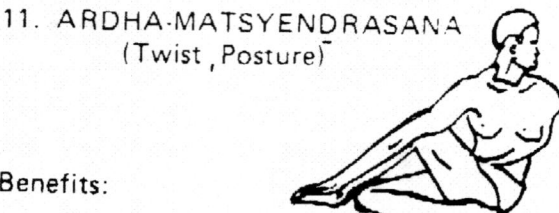

Benefits:

1. It tones up the nervous system.
2. It can cure and prevent diabetes.

12. YOGA MUDRA

Benefits:

1. This asana stimulates peristalic activity.
2. It relieves constipation.
3. It cures headache.
4. It stimulates a rich flow of blood to the brain and face.

13. NAULI

Benefits:

1. It develops will-power.
2. It relieves constipation.
3. It reduces the body weight.
4. It keeps the body youthful.

14. UDDIYANA

Benefits:

1. It develops will-power.
2. It relieves constipation.
3. It reduces the body weight.
4. It keeps the body youthful.

15. PADMASANA

Benefits:

1. This asana helps in meditation.
2. It strengthens the dorsal region.
3. It facilitates proper breathing.
4. The thyroids are also benefitted.
5. The pelvic joints become elastic.
6. This asana relieves inflamed and bleeding piles.

16. SIDHASANA

Benefit:

Same as padmasana.

17. SUKHASANA

Benefit:

Same as Padmasana.

18. TAADAASANA

Benefits:

This Asana tones up the leg muscles, removes stiffness in the legs and hips. It relieves back-aches and develops the chest.

Sarvangasana (c) (19)

Benefits:

This asana tones up the kidney and the leg muscles. It relieves constipation and stimulates a rapid flow of blood to the face. It banishes wrinkles.

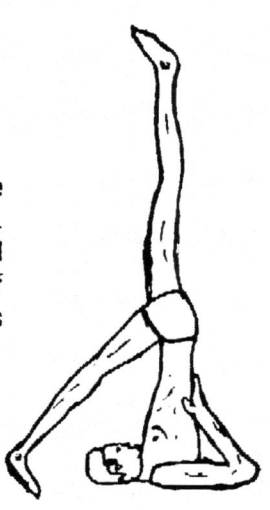

Virabhadadrasana (20)

Benefits:

This anana improves the preathing mechanism. It relieves stiffness in shoulders and back. It also reduces fat round the hips.

Annex 12: The dialogue of prayer (samndhya-prarthana)

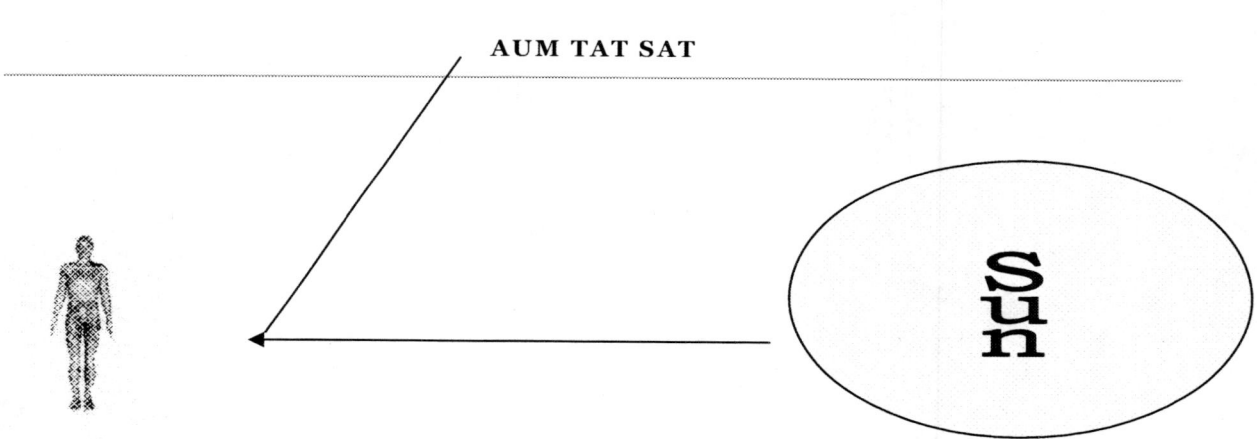

A prayer is a dialogue between the form (the earth) and the formless (eternity), in time.

A mantra is a solemn light of the soul. A mantra is the light of the Sun.

Enlightenment is a delight of the union in oneness of the light of the soul and the light of the sun in time, at the Twilight of Dawn and Dusk. A flight of delight is a sacred pilgrimage of the soul in pure Karmas to realise the Aum Tat Sat infinite truth.

Aum Tat Sat Swaha Hari Aum Tat Sat Swaha

Oh Divine Great Spirit of mortals and immortals alike. Let me feel your great spirit in the swift serene winds. Let me feel your life breath in the quietened still nightingale. Let me see your divine beauty in the purple red sunset. Let me hear your grand divine sound in the distant echoes of AUM. Let me touch your divine beauty in the soft delicate ripples of the sea and the moistened petals of the flowers. Let me walk in beauty, to dissolve in beauty, to become a light of delight. Let me come to you with my hands folded in greatest gratitude. Let me come to you with clean hands, pure heart, and eyes filled with delight. Oh Divine Great Spirit of mortals and immortals alike, grant me courage, grant me strength, not to become afraid anymore, but to become a flame of fathomless hope through these written words, to the future generation children. Let me never cease to write and to re-write to create and to re-create a hope in a world that is fragmented, torn apart and numbed by all this, that and the other. Let all the hurt in the world find solace and compassion without the fuss of all this, that and the other. Let love become a universal light of delight. Let my written words embrace you and hearten you to freedom beyond the fears of all this, that and the other. Let my spirit for now fade away as it should with the sunset. Life oh life! Let me leave behind a trail of beauty. Life oh life! Let it be a flight of delight.

To

Kishan and Karan

with all my love

&

choicest blessings

Aum Tat Sat

ॐ

[signature]

Jyotika Paltu

Tingoo

4-6-05

ISBN 141202107-3

9 781412 021074